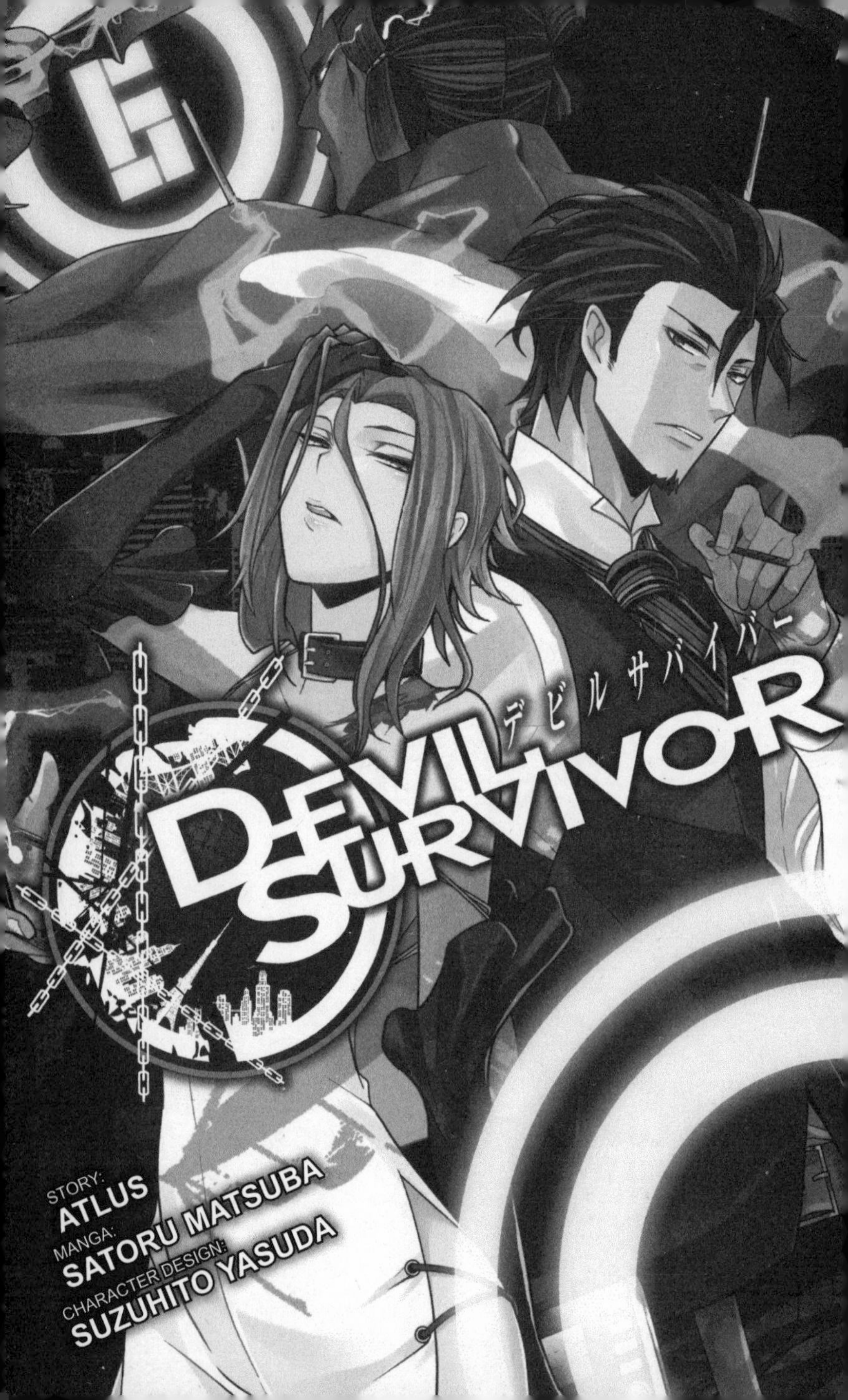
デビルサバイバー
DEVIL SURVIVOR
STORY:
ATLUS
MANGA:
SATORU MATSUBA
CHARACTER DESIGN:
SUZUHITO YASUDA

MAIN CHARACTER

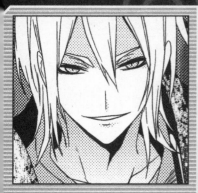

NAOYA
(NAOYA)

Kazuya's cousin. He lost his parents at a young age and lived with Kazuya's family until last year. He's known as a genius programmer with staggering insight.

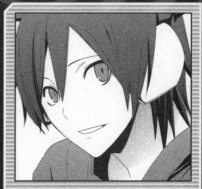

KAZUYA MINEGISHI
(KAZUYA)

Used a portable gaming device known as a COMP to make contracts with demons after gaining the power to command them. He defeated Beldr, a contender for the crown of the demon king, and absorbed his power.

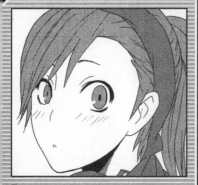

YUZU TANIKAWA
(YUZ)

Kazuya's childhood friend and high school classmate. Is currently working with Kazuya and Atsuro.

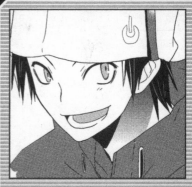

ATSURO KIHARA
(AT-LOW)

Kazuya's classmate and best friend. He's an aspiring programmer, and has been hanging with the big boys on the Internet since he was in grade school. Is currently working with Kazuya and Yuzu.

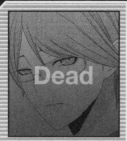

KEISUKE TAKAGI
(K-T)

A middle school classmate of Atsuro's. He had a righteous streak, which led him to save Atsuro from bullying, and hated all kinds of wrongdoing. He fought Kaido as a way to stay true to his convictions, and lost his life in the process.

Dead

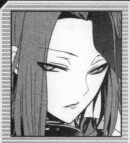

YOSHINO HARUSAWA
(HARU)

Current lead vocalist of the indie band D-Va. She worries about the band's former vocalist, Aya, who was a strong influence in her career. Her singing voice seems to have the power to summon demons, but…

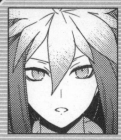

AMANE KUZURYU
(AMANE)

A priestess of the Shomonkai religious organization. She can create barriers to prevent demons from approaching.

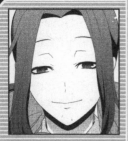

MARI MOCHIZUKI
(MARI)

A nurse at an elementary school. She once worked as Atsuro's tutor. A friend of Kaido and his brother since childhood, she has an ongoing hatred for the killer who took Kaido's brother from them in the Bloodless Murders.

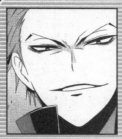

TADASHI "KAIDO" NIKAIDO
(NIKAIDO)

Leader of the Daemons, a gang based in the Shibuya area. He's searching for his brother's killer so he can settle the score. He harbors a secret fondness for his childhood friend Mari.

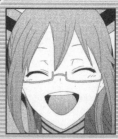

MIDORI KOMAKI
(DOLLY)

An Internet idol who enjoys tremendous popularity as the cosplayer Dolly. The influence of her late father, combined with her own desire to transform herself, gives her a strong yearning to be a defender of justice.

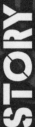

5TH DAY (REVELATIONS)

The latest Laplace Mail contains a shocking prophecy about the deaths of Mari and Keisuke. Trapped in a lockdown fraught with violence, and with limited time, Kazuya and his companions take desperate action to change the fates of their friends. Although they defeat the vampire Kudlak and rescue Mari, Keisuke clashes with Kaido and loses his life in his efforts to uphold his own brand of justice. In the midst of despair, Kazuya, Atsuro, and Yuzu go to learn the truth of the Tokyo Lockdown from the government officers guarding the Akasaka Tunnel.

Our story charges into the 6TH DAY (THE DECISIVE MOMENT)!

CONTENTS

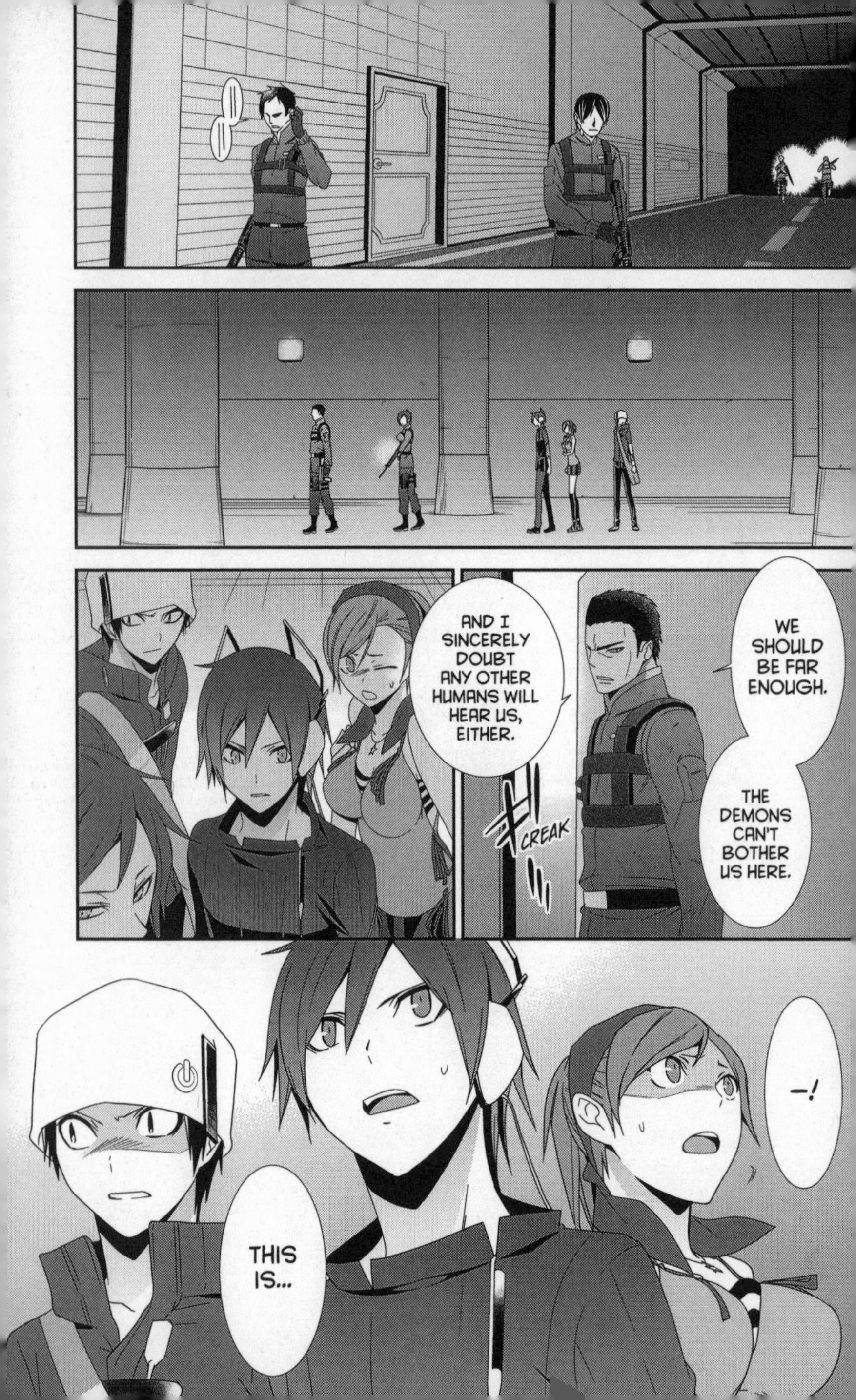
WE SHOULD BE FAR ENOUGH.
THE DEMONS CAN'T BOTHER US HERE.
CREAK
AND I SINCERELY DOUBT ANY OTHER HUMANS WILL HEAR US, EITHER.
—!
THIS IS...

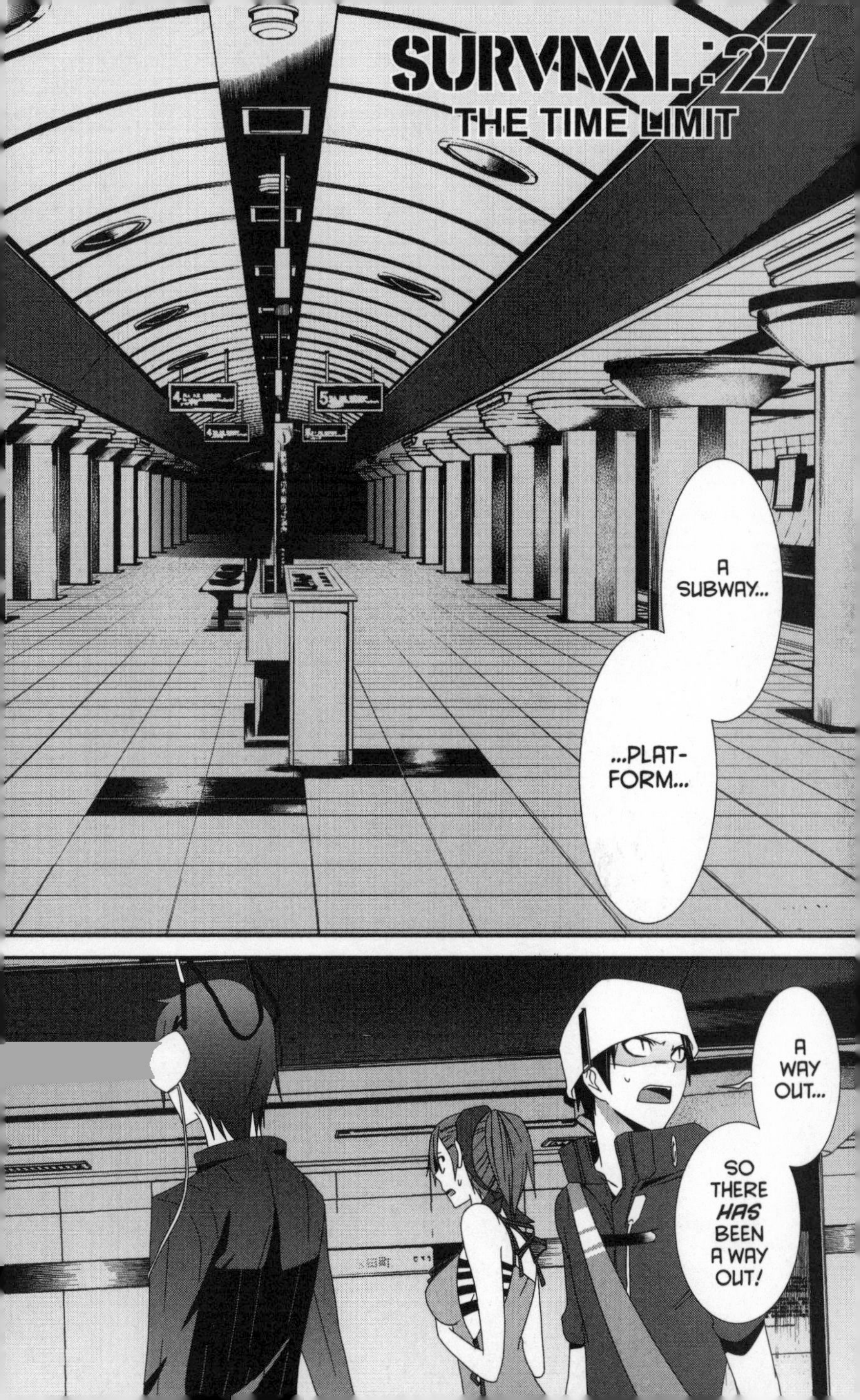
SURVIVAL: 27
THE TIME LIMIT
A SUBWAY...
...PLAT-FORM...
A WAY OUT...
SO THERE HAS BEEN A WAY OUT!

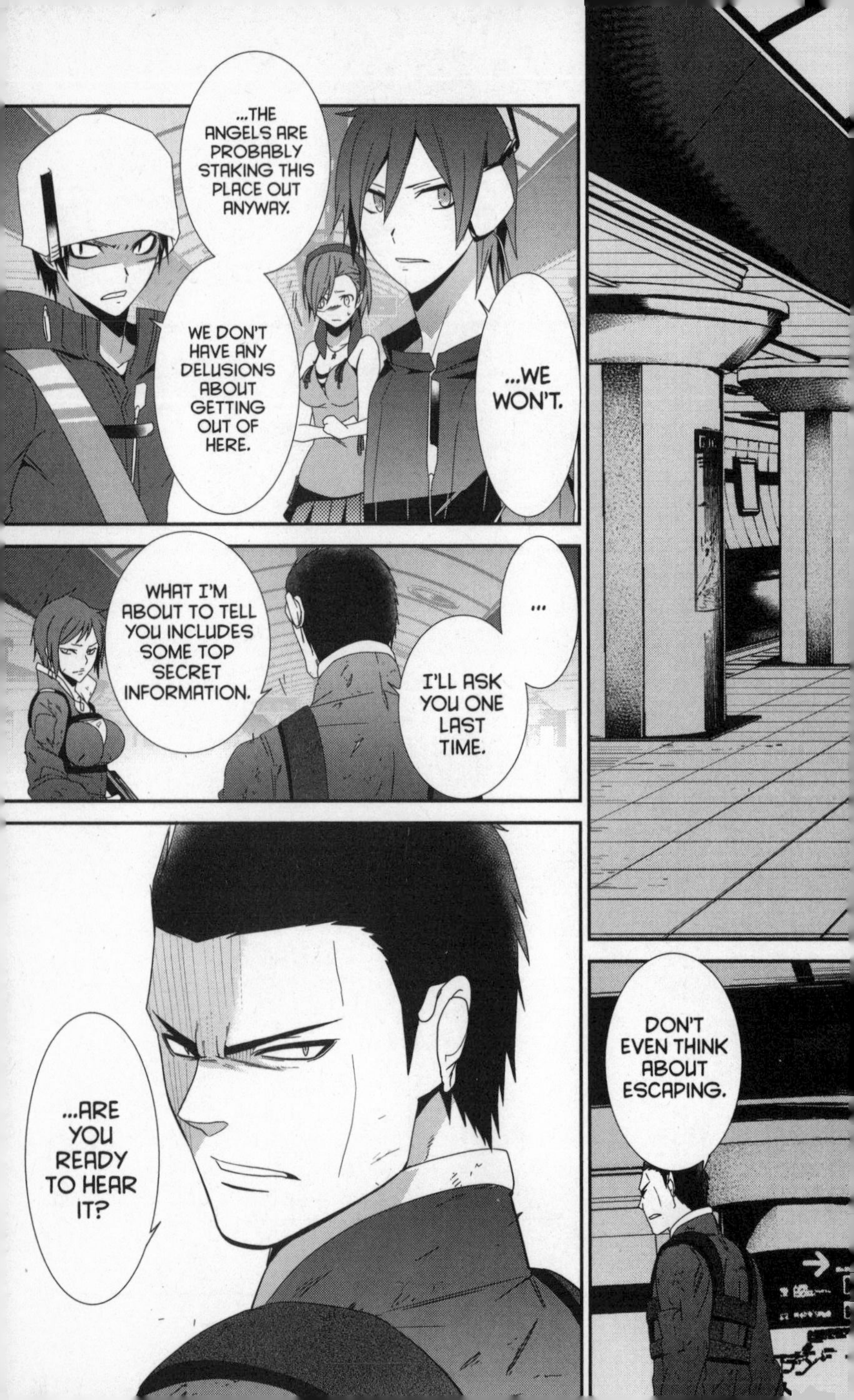
...THE ANGELS ARE PROBABLY STAKING THIS PLACE OUT ANYWAY.
WE DON'T HAVE ANY DELUSIONS ABOUT GETTING OUT OF HERE.
...WE WON'T.
...
I'LL ASK YOU ONE LAST TIME.
WHAT I'M ABOUT TO TELL YOU INCLUDES SOME TOP SECRET INFORMATION.
DON'T EVEN THINK ABOUT ESCAPING.
...ARE YOU READY TO HEAR IT?

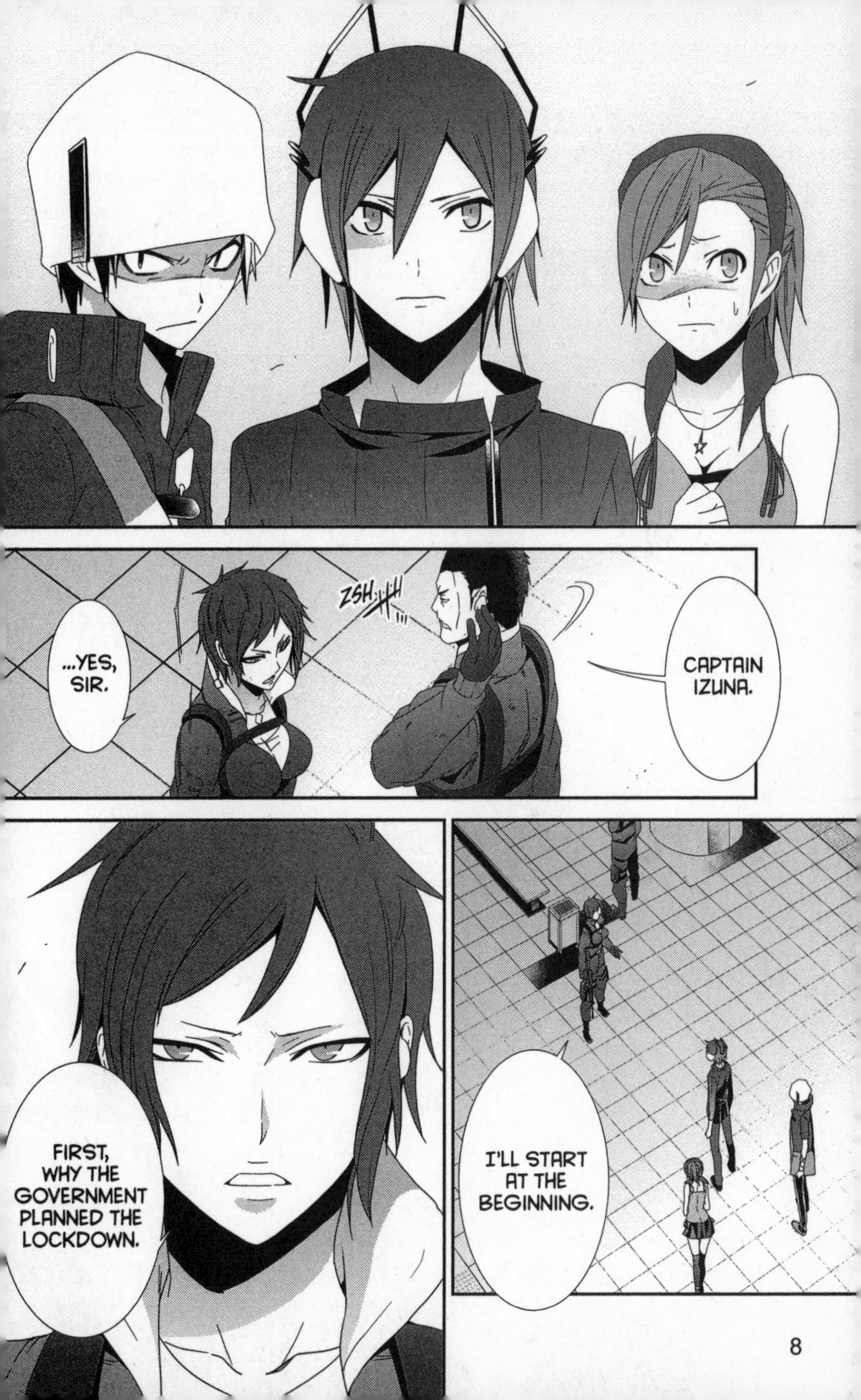
CAPTAIN IZUNA.
ZSH
...YES, SIR.
I'LL START AT THE BEGINNING.
FIRST, WHY THE GOVERNMENT PLANNED THE LOCKDOWN.

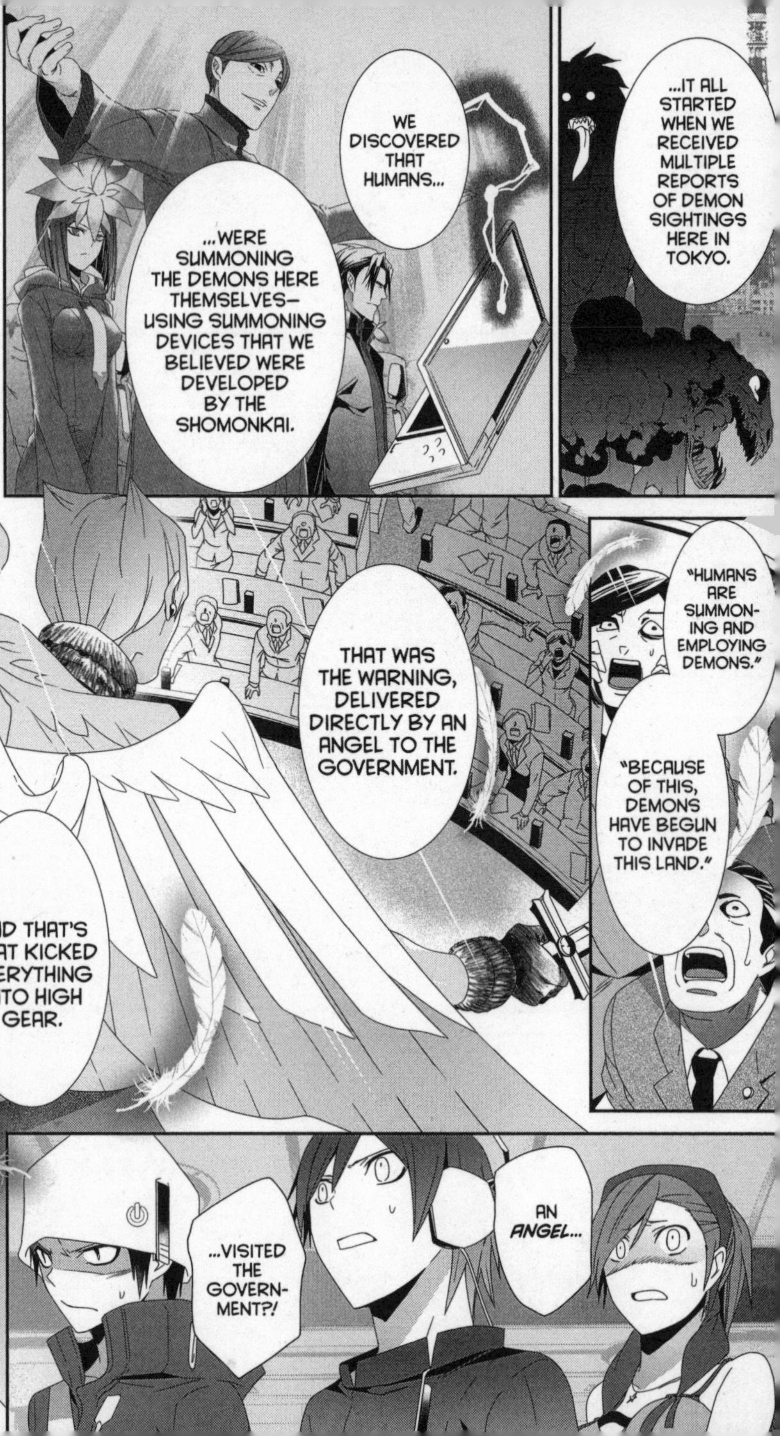
...IT ALL STARTED WHEN WE RECEIVED MULTIPLE REPORTS OF DEMON SIGHTINGS HERE IN TOKYO.
WE DISCOVERED THAT HUMANS...
...WERE SUMMONING THE DEMONS HERE THEMSELVES—USING SUMMONING DEVICES THAT WE BELIEVED WERE DEVELOPED BY THE SHOMONKAI.
"HUMANS ARE SUMMONING AND EMPLOYING DEMONS."
"BECAUSE OF THIS, DEMONS HAVE BEGUN TO INVADE THIS LAND."
THAT WAS THE WARNING, DELIVERED DIRECTLY BY AN ANGEL TO THE GOVERNMENT.
AND THAT'S WHAT KICKED EVERYTHING INTO HIGH GEAR.
AN *ANGEL*...
...VISITED THE GOVERNMENT?!

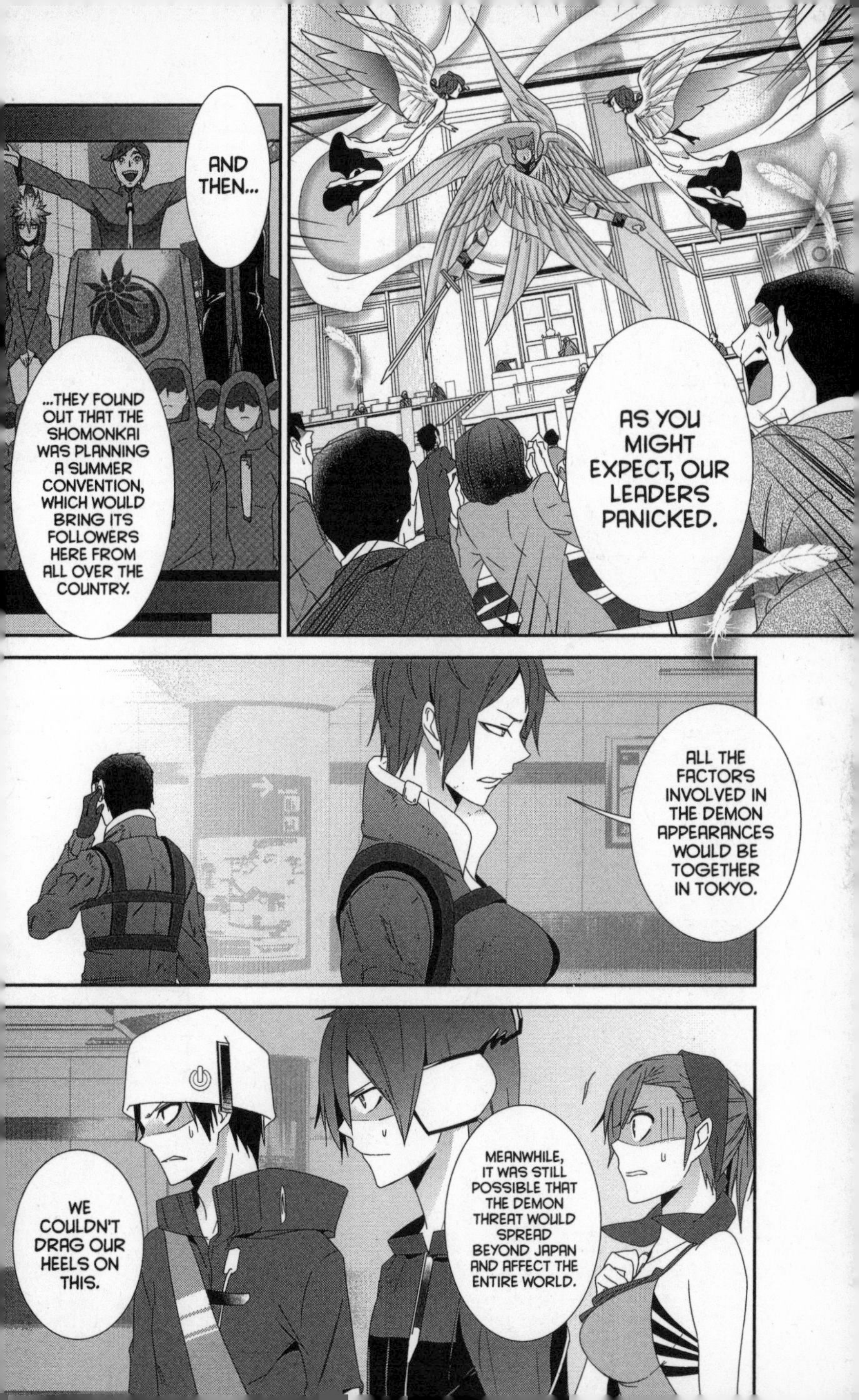
AS YOU MIGHT EXPECT, OUR LEADERS PANICKED.
AND THEN...
...THEY FOUND OUT THAT THE SHOMONKAI WAS PLANNING A SUMMER CONVENTION, WHICH WOULD BRING ITS FOLLOWERS HERE FROM ALL OVER THE COUNTRY.
ALL THE FACTORS INVOLVED IN THE DEMON APPEARANCES WOULD BE TOGETHER IN TOKYO.
MEANWHILE, IT WAS STILL POSSIBLE THAT THE DEMON THREAT WOULD SPREAD BEYOND JAPAN AND AFFECT THE ENTIRE WORLD.
WE COULDN'T DRAG OUR HEELS ON THIS.

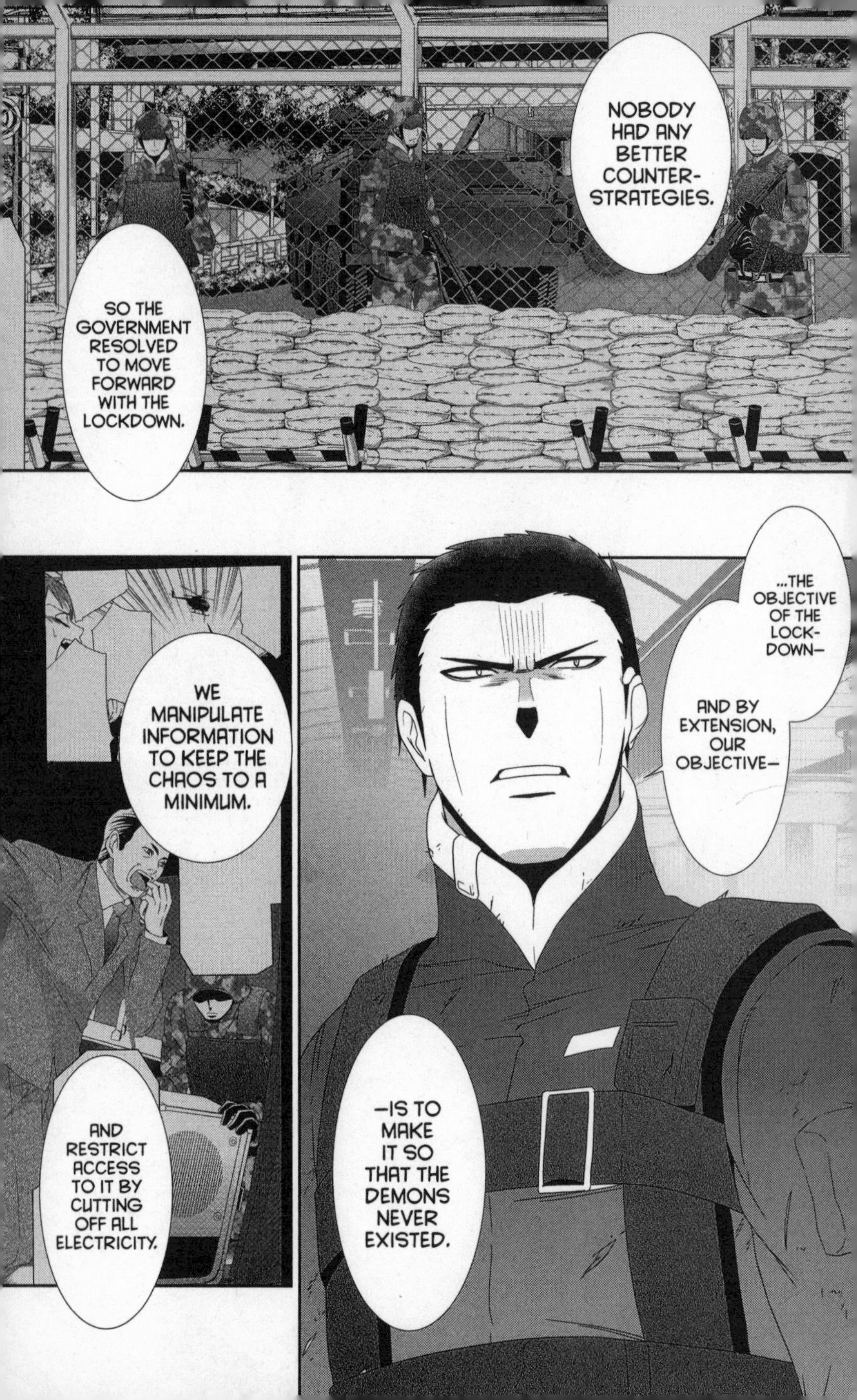
NOBODY HAD ANY BETTER COUNTER-STRATEGIES.
SO THE GOVERNMENT RESOLVED TO MOVE FORWARD WITH THE LOCKDOWN.
...THE OBJECTIVE OF THE LOCK-DOWN—
AND BY EXTENSION, OUR OBJECTIVE—
—IS TO MAKE IT SO THAT THE DEMONS NEVER EXISTED.
WE MANIPULATE INFORMATION TO KEEP THE CHAOS TO A MINIMUM.
AND RESTRICT ACCESS TO IT BY CUTTING OFF ALL ELECTRICITY.

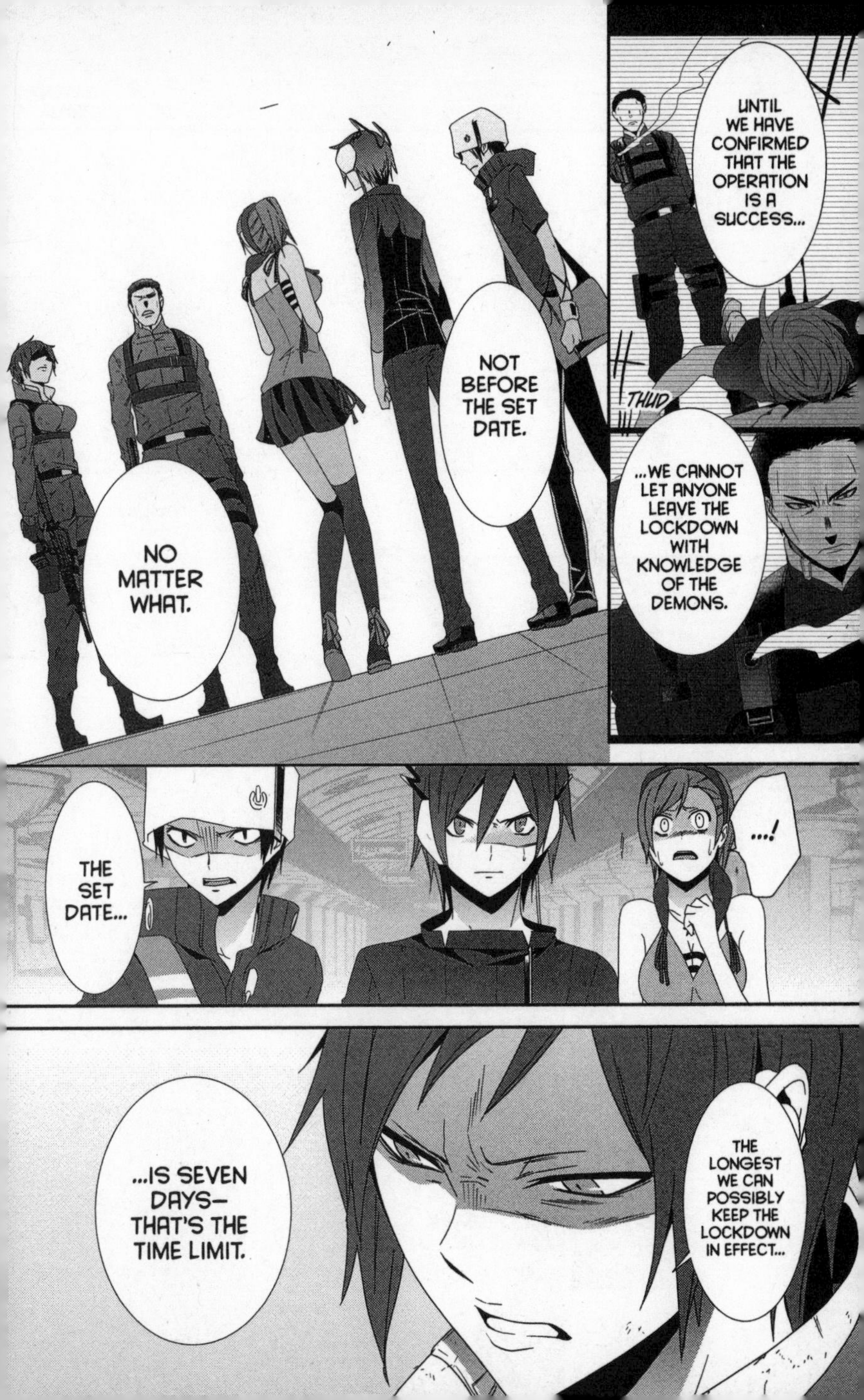
UNTIL WE HAVE CONFIRMED THAT THE OPERATION IS A SUCCESS...
THUD
...WE CANNOT LET ANYONE LEAVE THE LOCKDOWN WITH KNOWLEDGE OF THE DEMONS.
NOT BEFORE THE SET DATE.
NO MATTER WHAT.
...!
THE SET DATE...
THE LONGEST WE CAN POSSIBLY KEEP THE LOCKDOWN IN EFFECT...
...IS SEVEN DAYS— THAT'S THE TIME LIMIT.

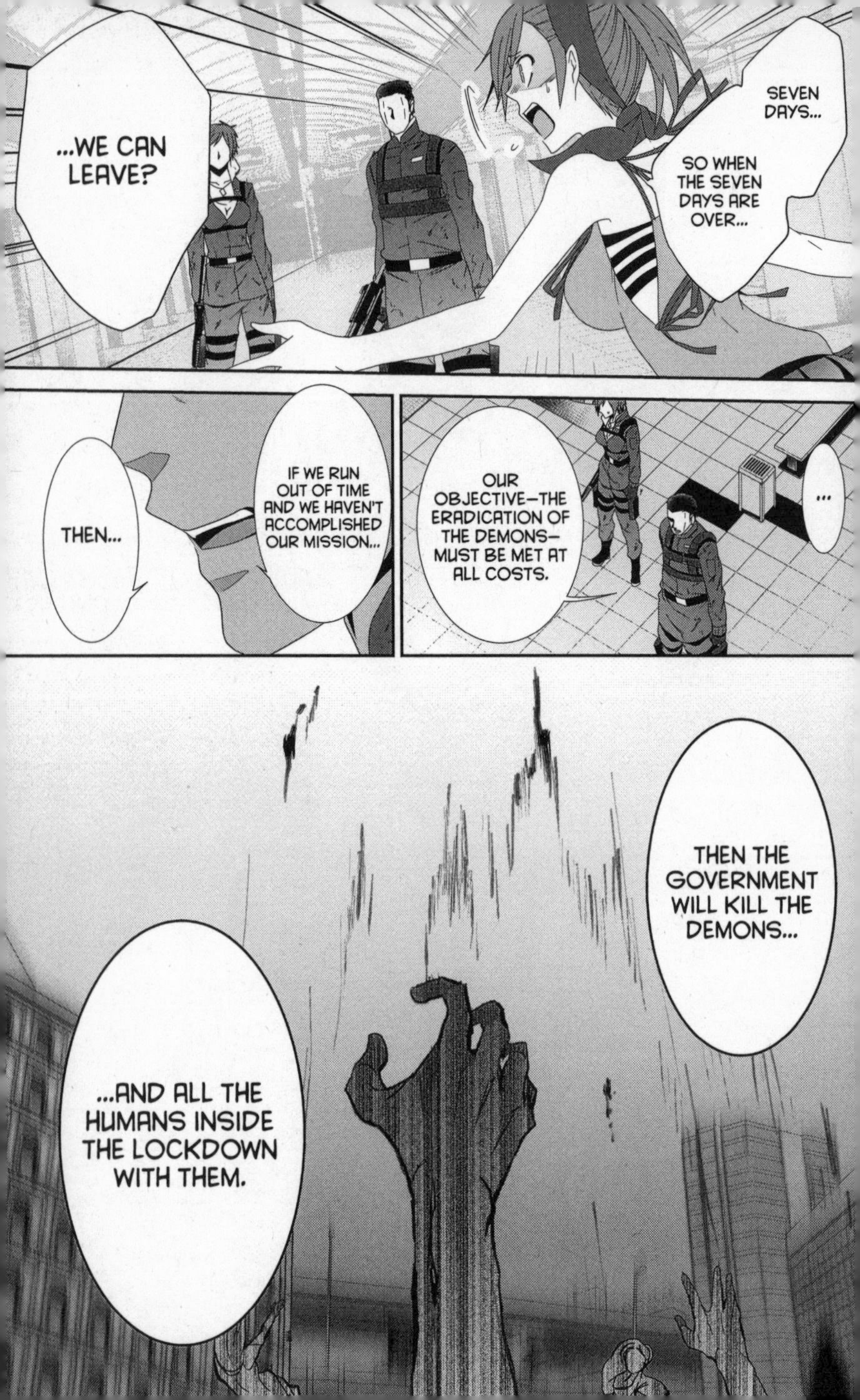
SEVEN DAYS...
SO WHEN THE SEVEN DAYS ARE OVER...
...WE CAN LEAVE?
...
OUR OBJECTIVE—THE ERADICATION OF THE DEMONS—MUST BE MET AT ALL COSTS.
IF WE RUN OUT OF TIME AND WE HAVEN'T ACCOMPLISHED OUR MISSION...
THEN...
THEN THE GOVERNMENT WILL KILL THE DEMONS...
...AND ALL THE HUMANS INSIDE THE LOCKDOWN WITH THEM.

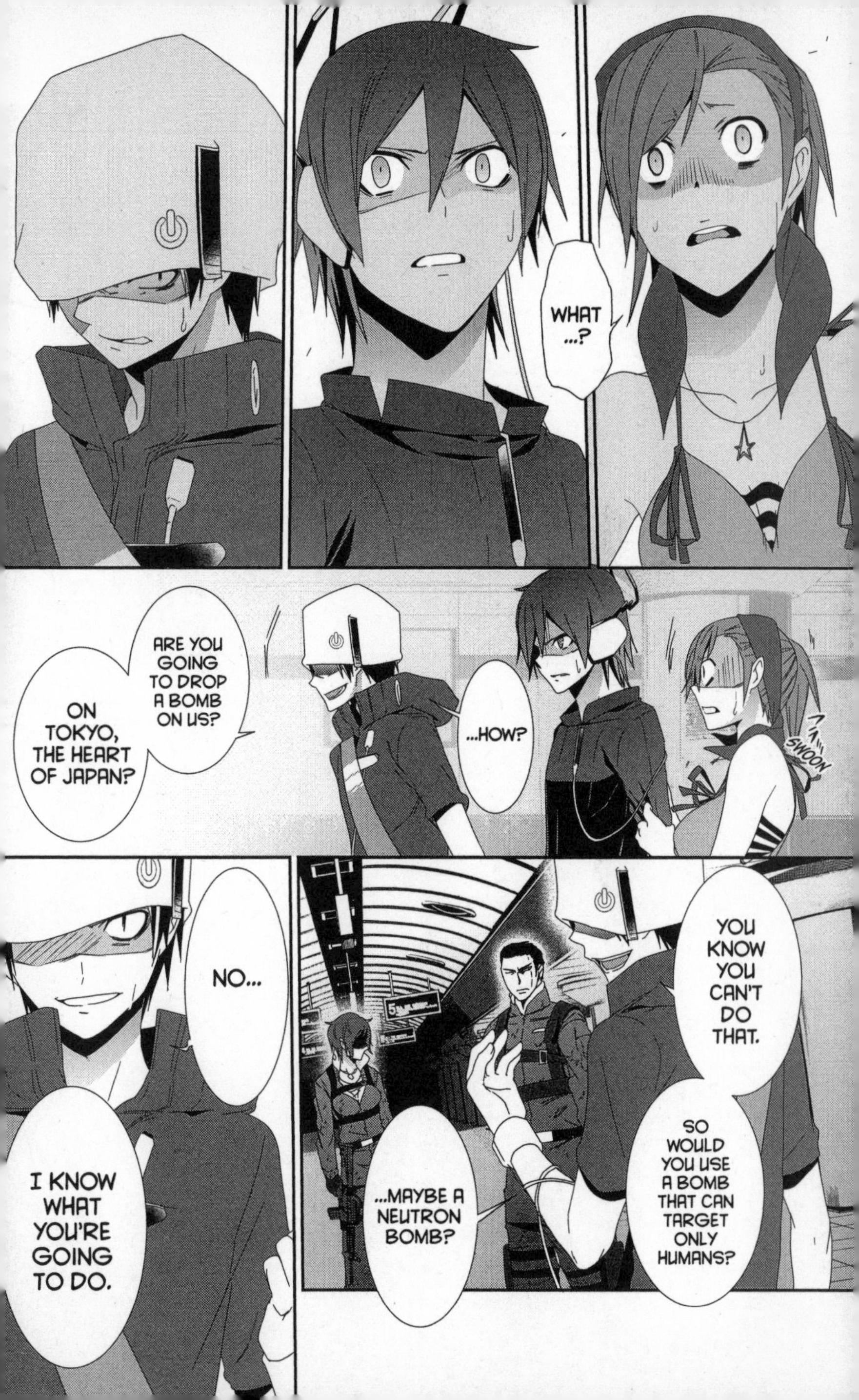
WHAT ...?
SWOON
...HOW?
ARE YOU GOING TO DROP A BOMB ON US?
ON TOKYO, THE HEART OF JAPAN?
YOU KNOW YOU CAN'T DO THAT.
SO WOULD YOU USE A BOMB THAT CAN TARGET ONLY HUMANS?
...MAYBE A NEUTRON BOMB?
NO...
I KNOW WHAT YOU'RE GOING TO DO.

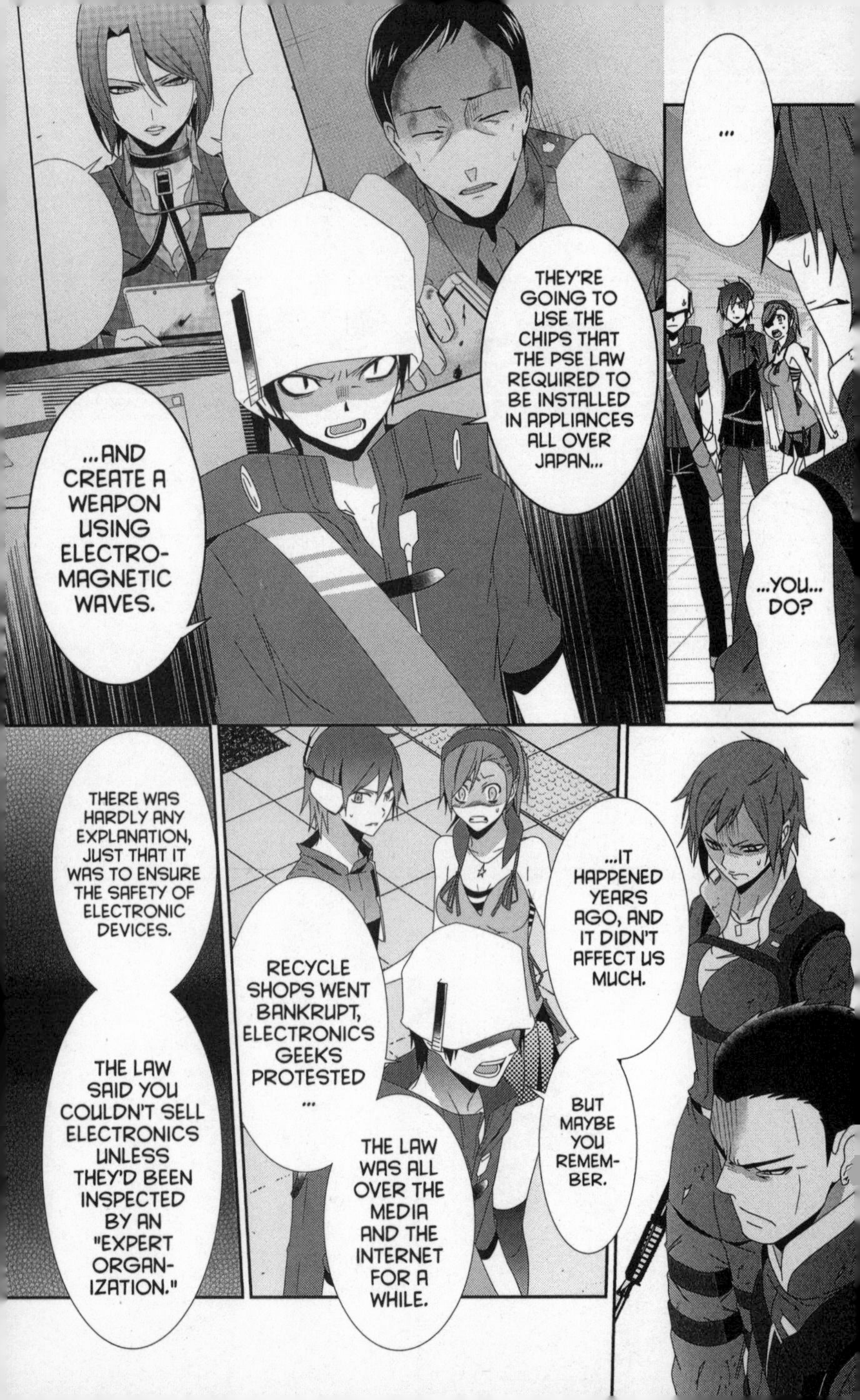
...
...YOU... DO?
THEY'RE GOING TO USE THE CHIPS THAT THE PSE LAW REQUIRED TO BE INSTALLED IN APPLIANCES ALL OVER JAPAN...
...AND CREATE A WEAPON USING ELECTRO-MAGNETIC WAVES.
...IT HAPPENED YEARS AGO, AND IT DIDN'T AFFECT US MUCH.
BUT MAYBE YOU REMEMBER.
RECYCLE SHOPS WENT BANKRUPT, ELECTRONICS GEEKS PROTESTED ...
THE LAW WAS ALL OVER THE MEDIA AND THE INTERNET FOR A WHILE.
THERE WAS HARDLY ANY EXPLANATION, JUST THAT IT WAS TO ENSURE THE SAFETY OF ELECTRONIC DEVICES.
THE LAW SAID YOU COULDN'T SELL ELECTRONICS UNLESS THEY'D BEEN INSPECTED BY AN "EXPERT ORGAN-IZATION."

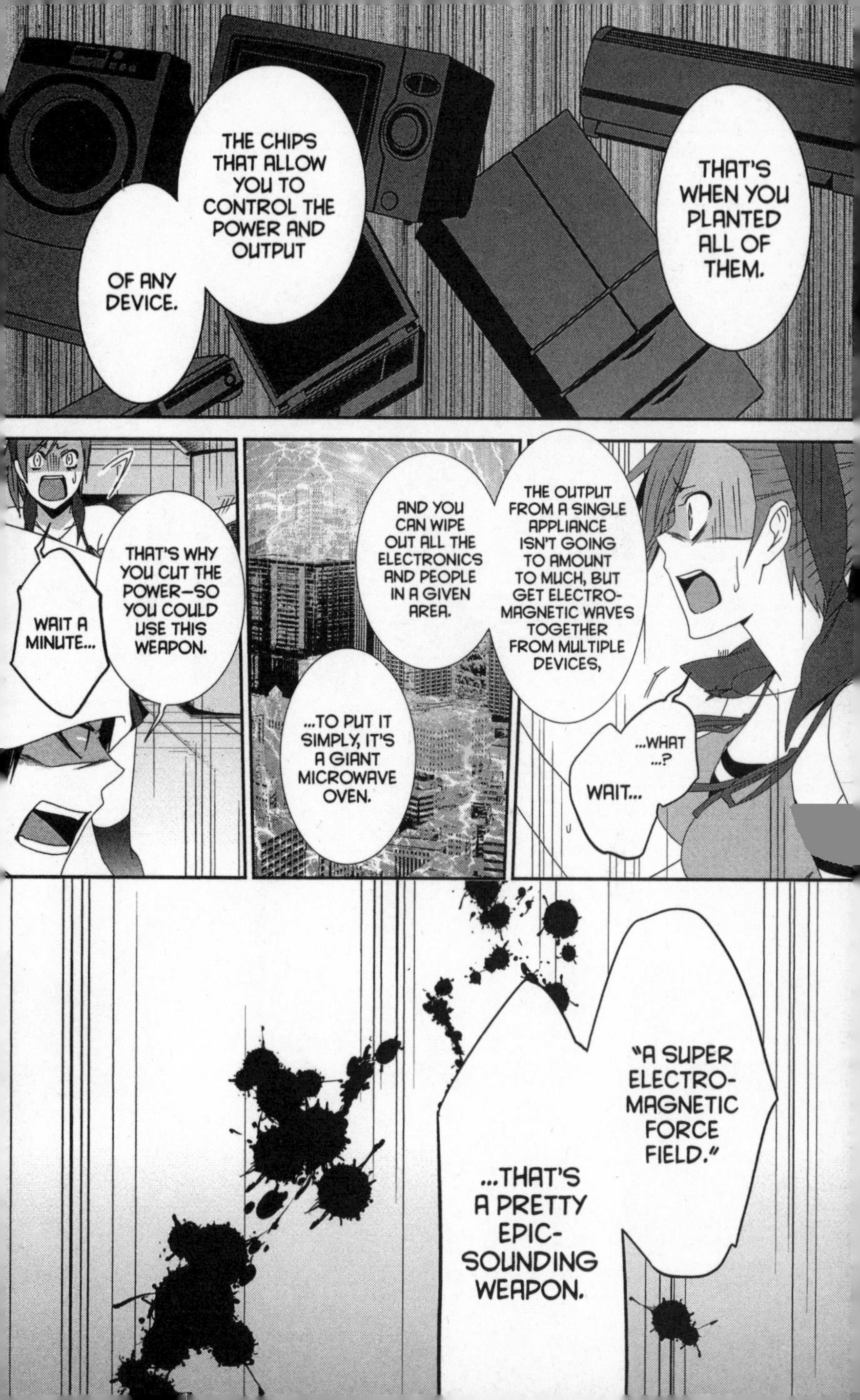
THAT'S WHEN YOU PLANTED ALL OF THEM.
THE CHIPS THAT ALLOW YOU TO CONTROL THE POWER AND OUTPUT
OF ANY DEVICE.
THE OUTPUT FROM A SINGLE APPLIANCE ISN'T GOING TO AMOUNT TO MUCH, BUT GET ELECTRO-MAGNETIC WAVES TOGETHER FROM MULTIPLE DEVICES,
AND YOU CAN WIPE OUT ALL THE ELECTRONICS AND PEOPLE IN A GIVEN AREA.
...TO PUT IT SIMPLY, IT'S A GIANT MICROWAVE OVEN.
...WHAT ...?
WAIT...
THAT'S WHY YOU CUT THE POWER—SO YOU COULD USE THIS WEAPON.
WAIT A MINUTE...
"A SUPER ELECTRO-MAGNETIC FORCE FIELD."
...THAT'S A PRETTY EPIC-SOUNDING WEAPON.

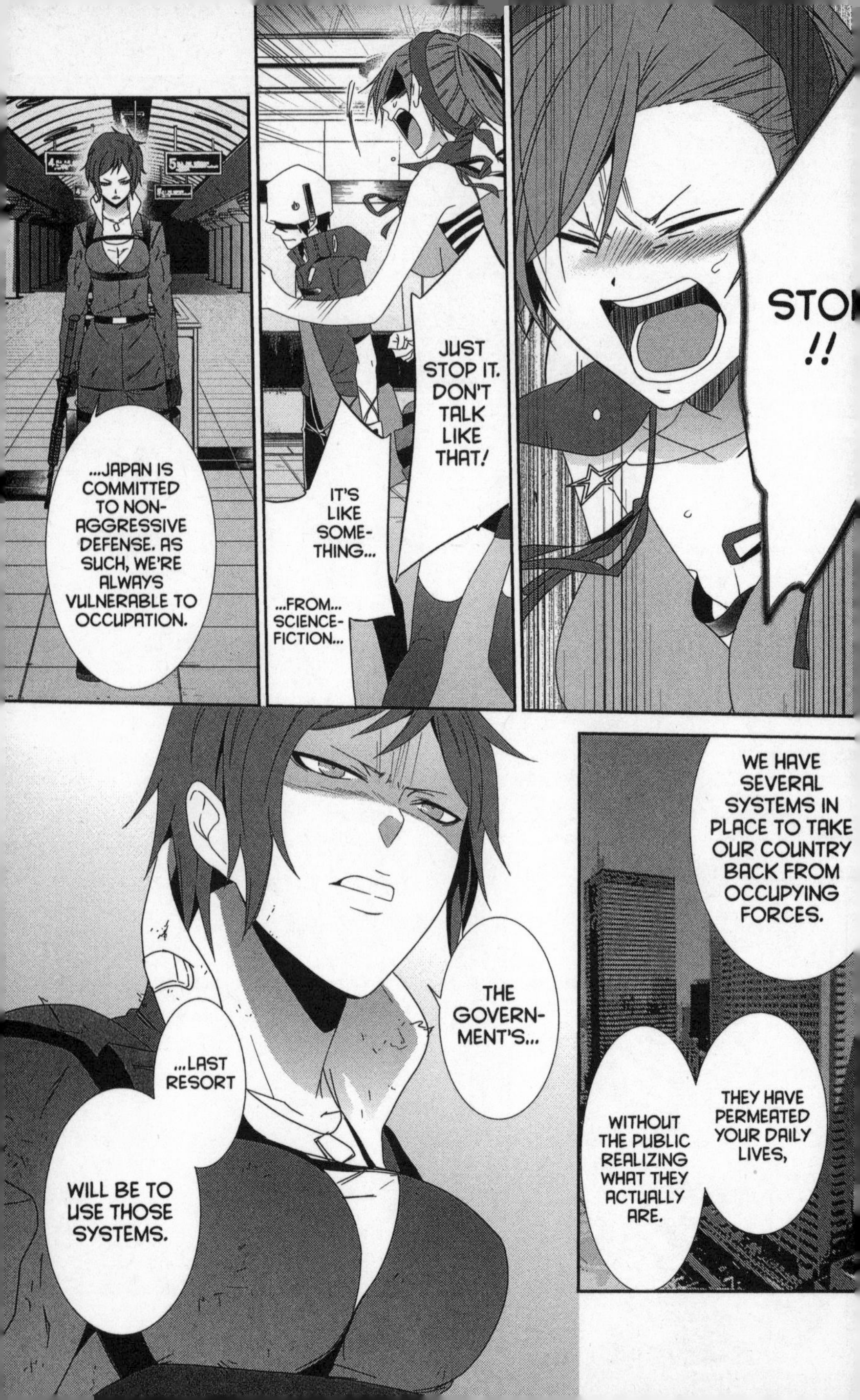
STO!!
JUST STOP IT. DON'T TALK LIKE THAT!
IT'S LIKE SOME-THING...
...FROM... SCIENCE-FICTION...
...JAPAN IS COMMITTED TO NON-AGGRESSIVE DEFENSE. AS SUCH, WE'RE ALWAYS VULNERABLE TO OCCUPATION.
WE HAVE SEVERAL SYSTEMS IN PLACE TO TAKE OUR COUNTRY BACK FROM OCCUPYING FORCES.
THEY HAVE PERMEATED YOUR DAILY LIVES,
WITHOUT THE PUBLIC REALIZING WHAT THEY ACTUALLY ARE.
THE GOVERN-MENT'S...
...LAST RESORT
WILL BE TO USE THOSE SYSTEMS.

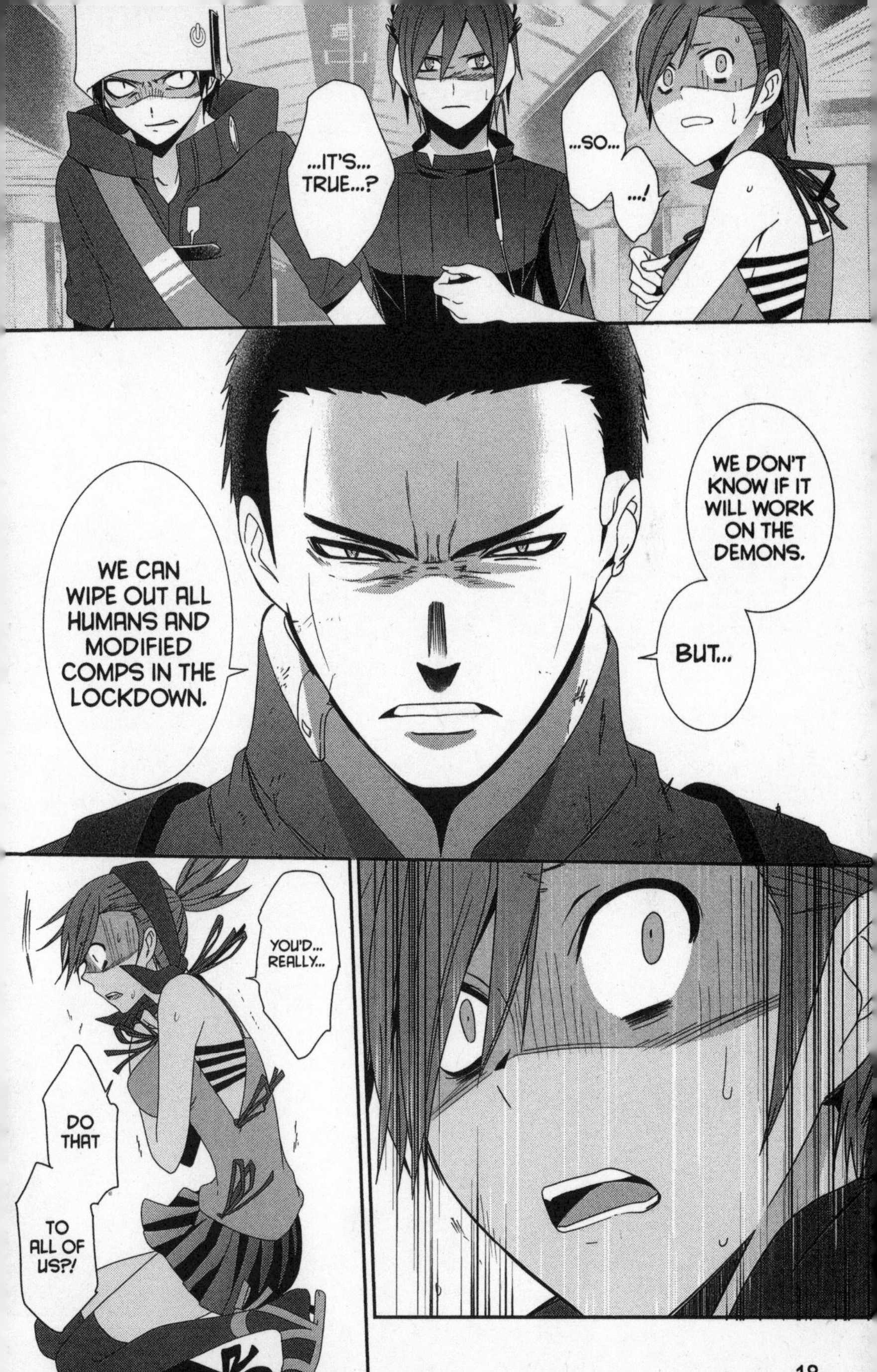
...SO...
...!
...IT'S... TRUE...?
WE DON'T KNOW IF IT WILL WORK ON THE DEMONS.
BUT...
WE CAN WIPE OUT ALL HUMANS AND MODIFIED COMPS IN THE LOCKDOWN.
YOU'D... REALLY...
DO THAT
TO ALL OF US?!

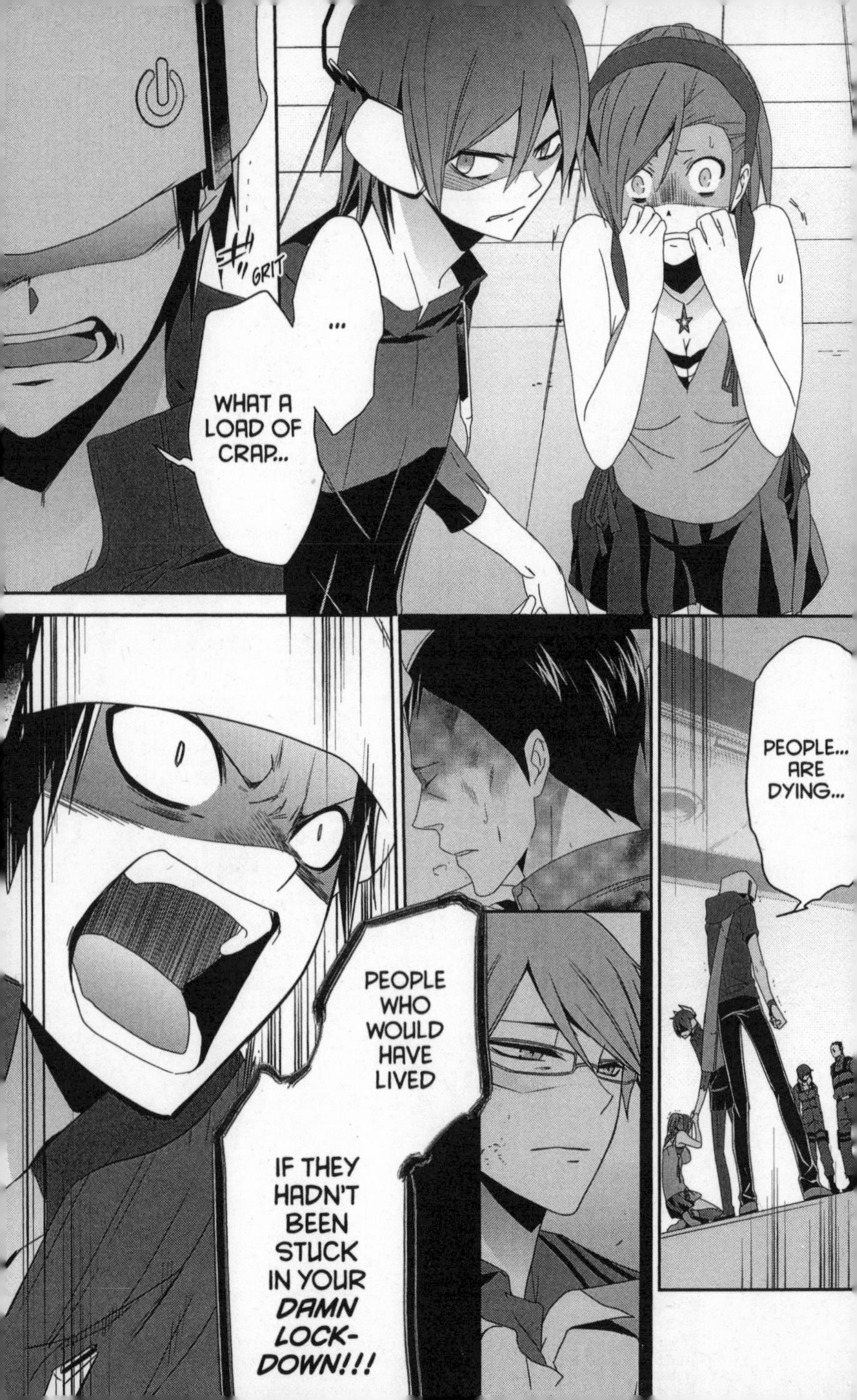
GRIT
...
WHAT A LOAD OF CRAP...
PEOPLE... ARE DYING...
PEOPLE WHO WOULD HAVE LIVED
IF THEY HADN'T BEEN STUCK IN YOUR DAMN LOCK-DOWN!!!

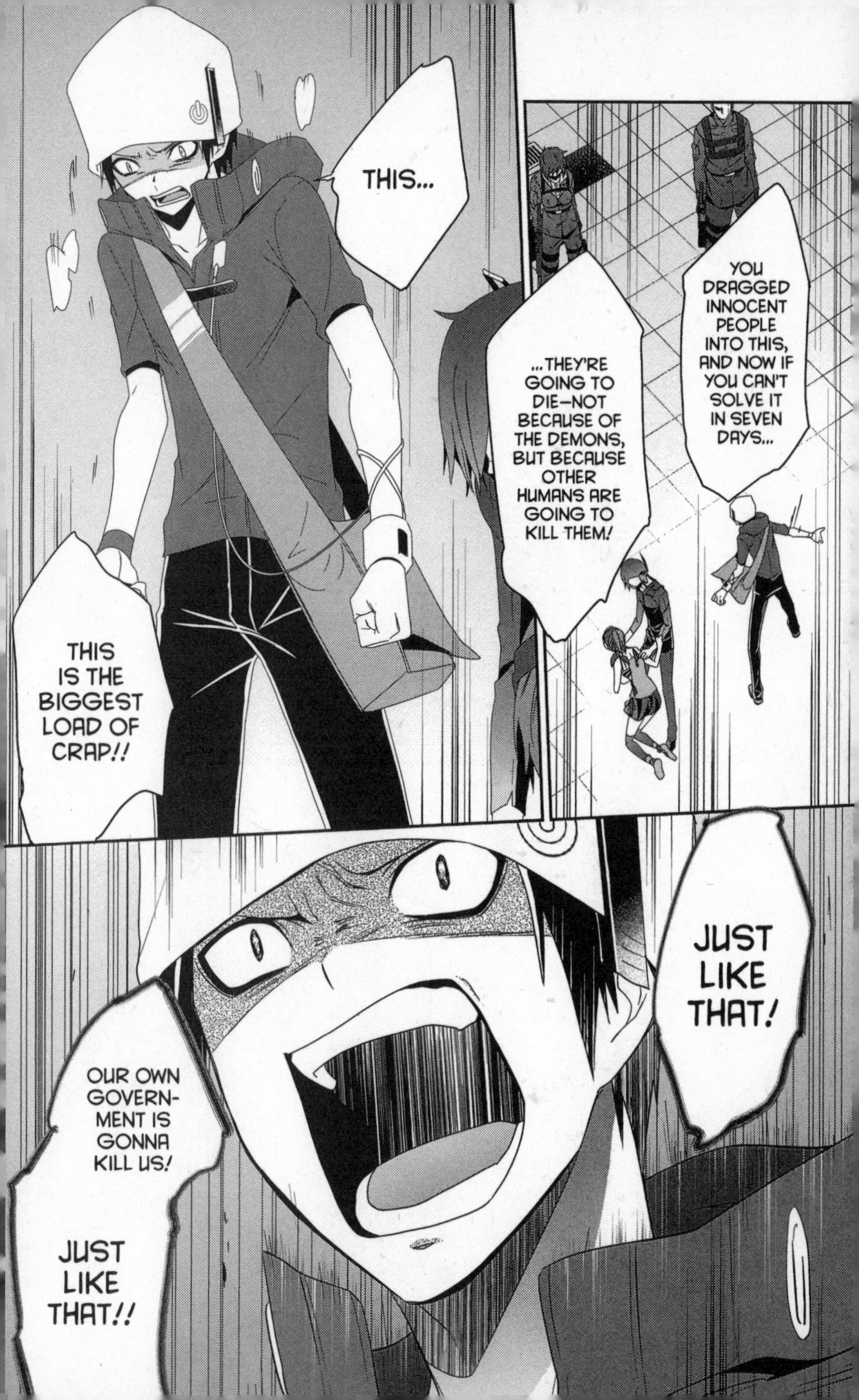

YOU DRAGGED INNOCENT PEOPLE INTO THIS, AND NOW IF YOU CAN'T SOLVE IT IN SEVEN DAYS...
...THEY'RE GOING TO DIE—NOT BECAUSE OF THE DEMONS, BUT BECAUSE OTHER HUMANS ARE GOING TO KILL THEM!
THIS...
THIS IS THE BIGGEST LOAD OF CRAP!!
JUST LIKE THAT!
OUR OWN GOVERN-MENT IS GONNA KILL US!
JUST LIKE THAT!!

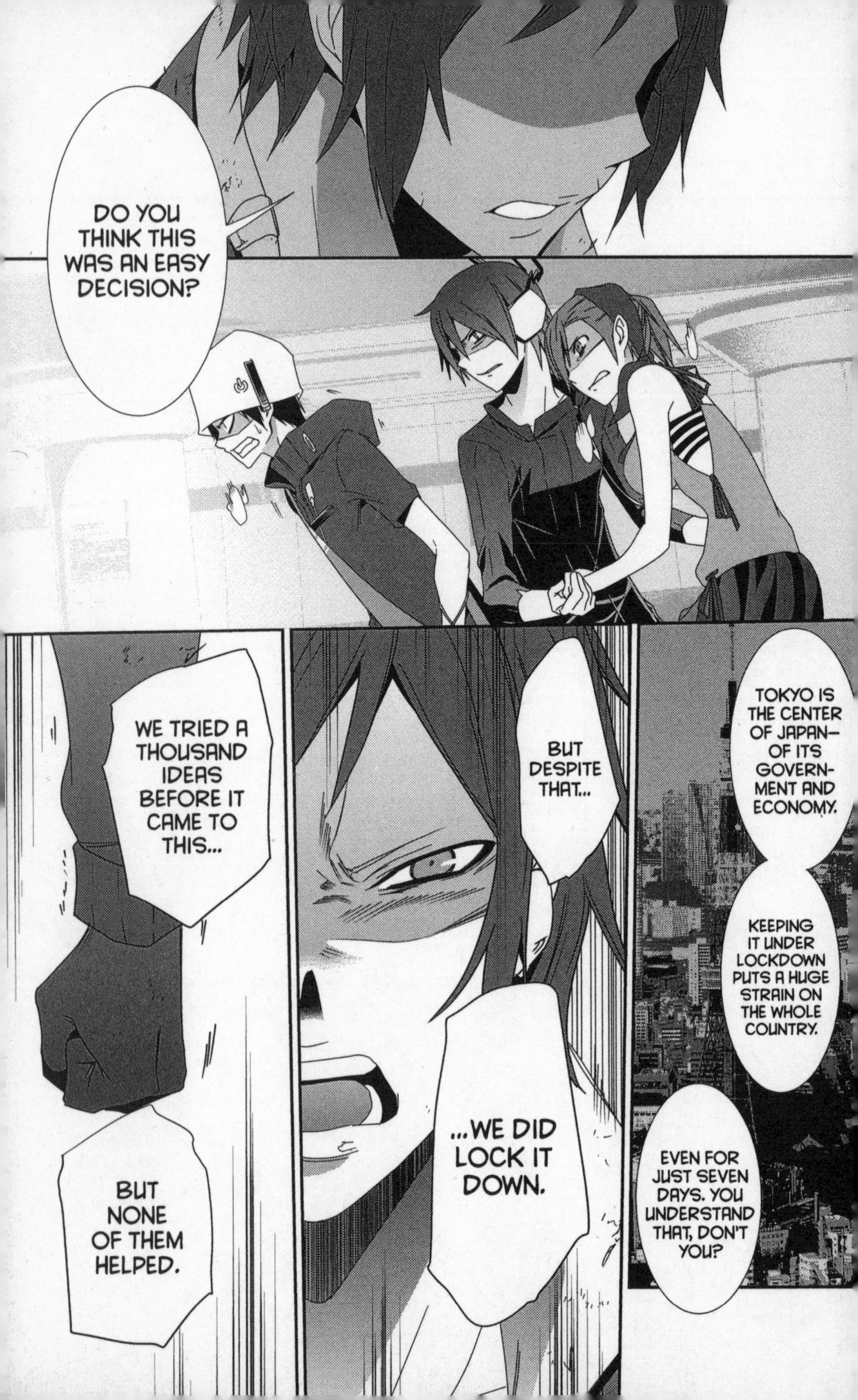
DO YOU THINK THIS WAS AN EASY DECISION?
TOKYO IS THE CENTER OF JAPAN—OF ITS GOVERNMENT AND ECONOMY.
KEEPING IT UNDER LOCKDOWN PUTS A HUGE STRAIN ON THE WHOLE COUNTRY.
EVEN FOR JUST SEVEN DAYS. YOU UNDERSTAND THAT, DON'T YOU?
BUT DESPITE THAT...
...WE DID LOCK IT DOWN.
WE TRIED A THOUSAND IDEAS BEFORE IT CAME TO THIS...
BUT NONE OF THEM HELPED.

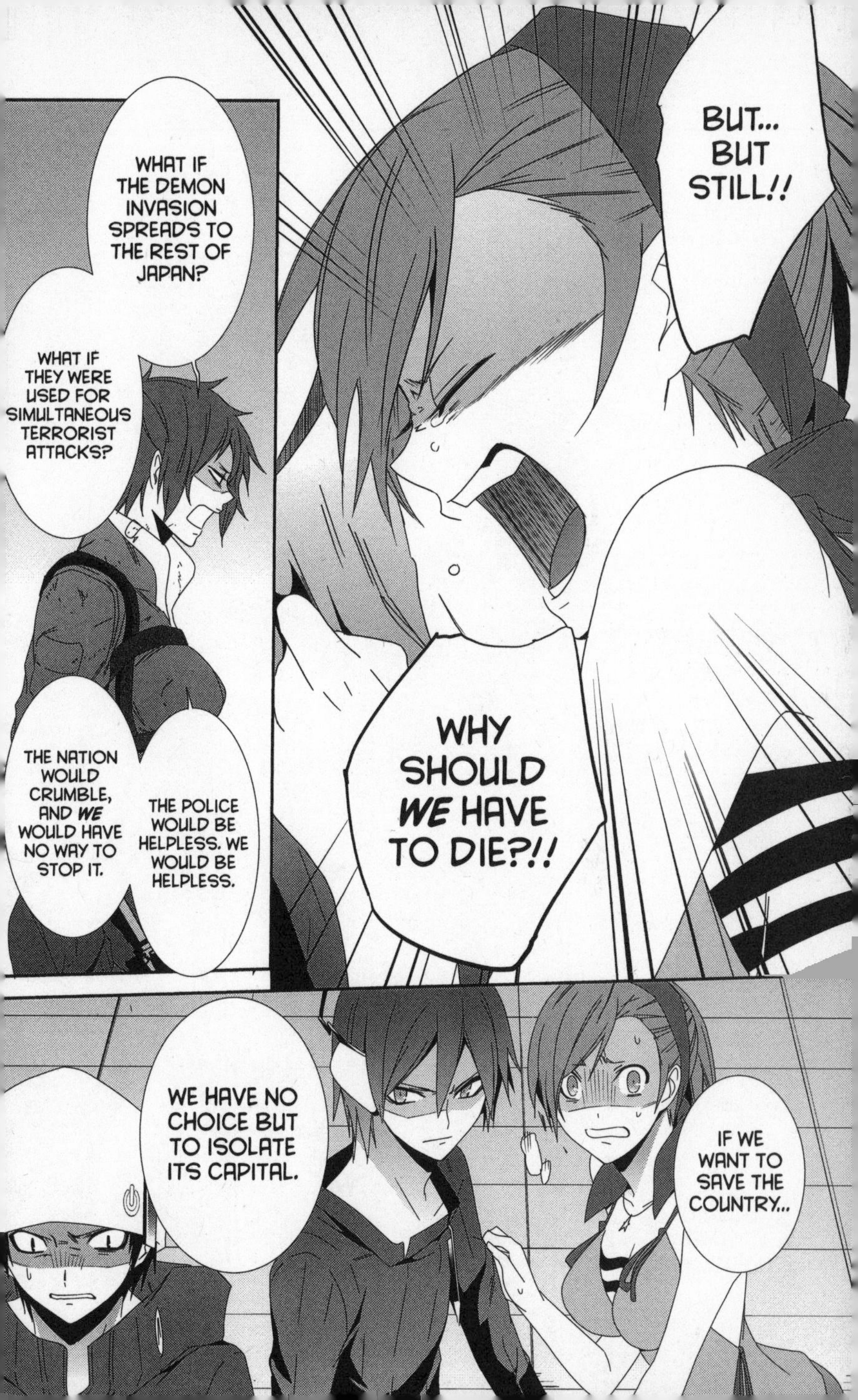
BUT... BUT STILL!!
WHY SHOULD *WE* HAVE TO DIE?!!
WHAT IF THE DEMON INVASION SPREADS TO THE REST OF JAPAN?
WHAT IF THEY WERE USED FOR SIMULTANEOUS TERRORIST ATTACKS?
THE POLICE WOULD BE HELPLESS. WE WOULD BE HELPLESS.
THE NATION WOULD CRUMBLE, AND *WE* WOULD HAVE NO WAY TO STOP IT.
IF WE WANT TO SAVE THE COUNTRY...
WE HAVE NO CHOICE BUT TO ISOLATE ITS CAPITAL.

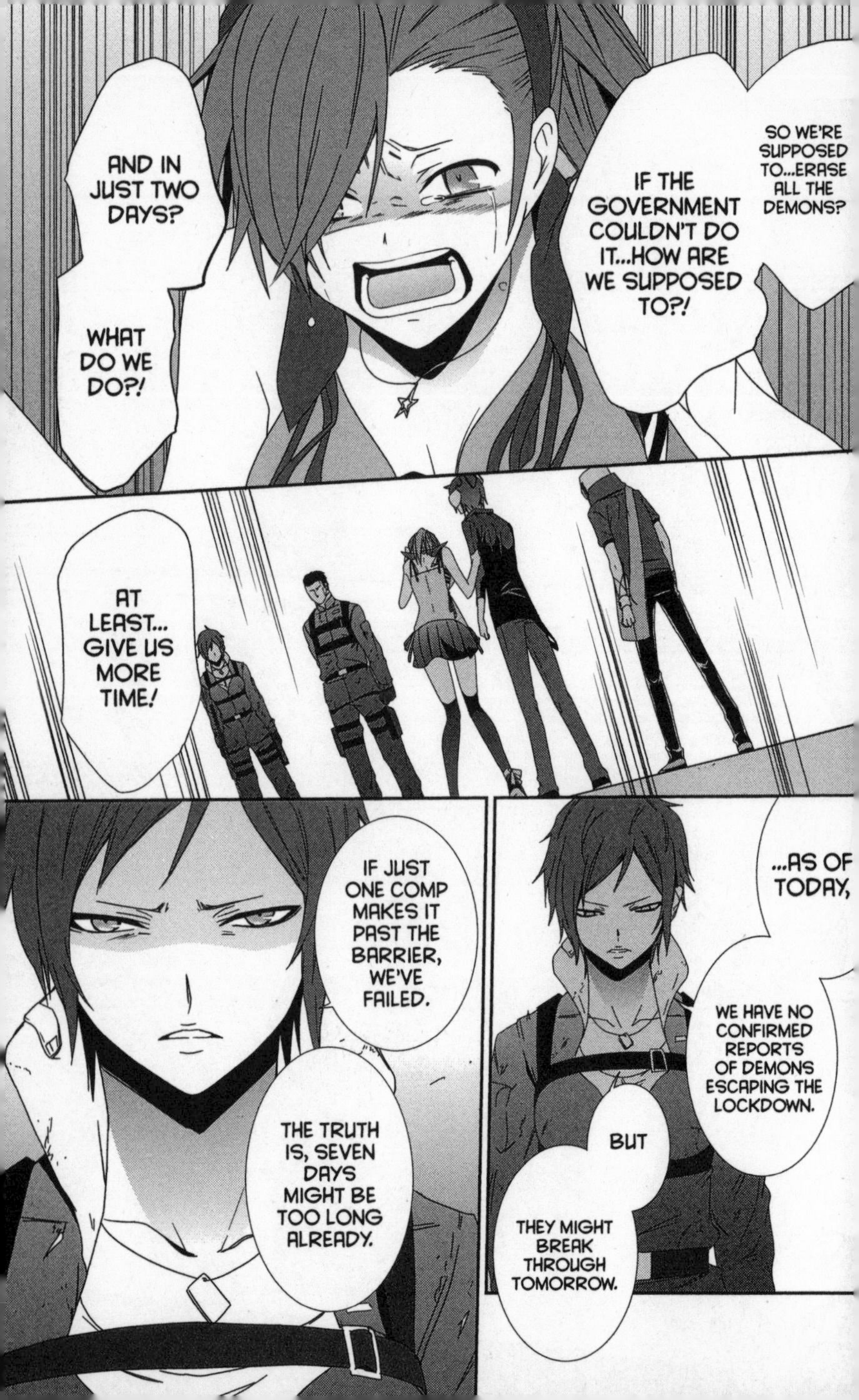
SO WE'RE SUPPOSED TO...ERASE ALL THE DEMONS?
IF THE GOVERNMENT COULDN'T DO IT...HOW ARE WE SUPPOSED TO?!
AND IN JUST TWO DAYS?
WHAT DO WE DO?!
AT LEAST... GIVE US MORE TIME!
...AS OF TODAY,
WE HAVE NO CONFIRMED REPORTS OF DEMONS ESCAPING THE LOCKDOWN.
BUT
THEY MIGHT BREAK THROUGH TOMORROW.
IF JUST ONE COMP MAKES IT PAST THE BARRIER, WE'VE FAILED.
THE TRUTH IS, SEVEN DAYS MIGHT BE TOO LONG ALREADY.

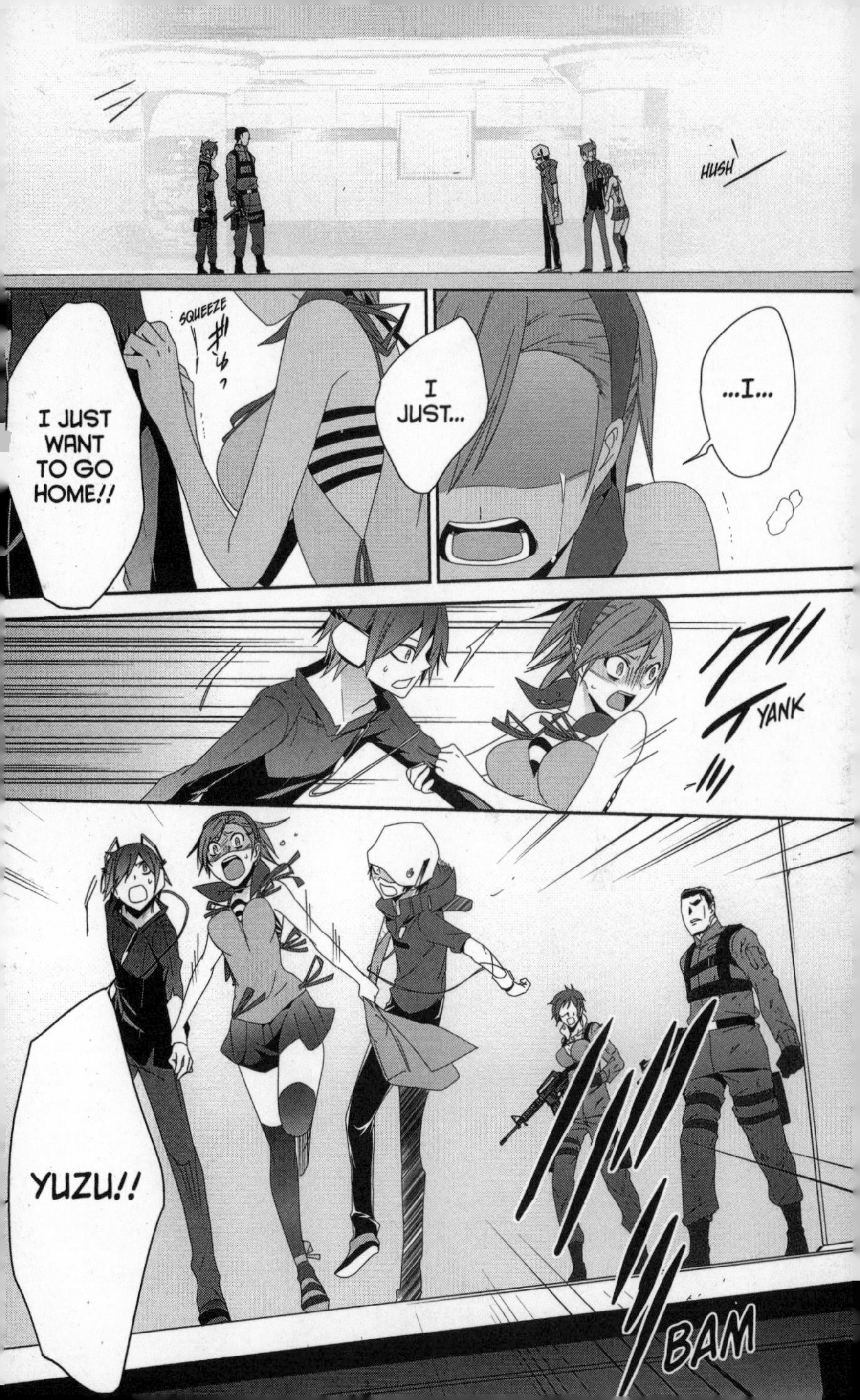
HUSH
...I...
I JUST...
SQUEEZE
ぎゅっ
I JUST WANT TO GO HOME!!
YANK
YUZU!!
BAM

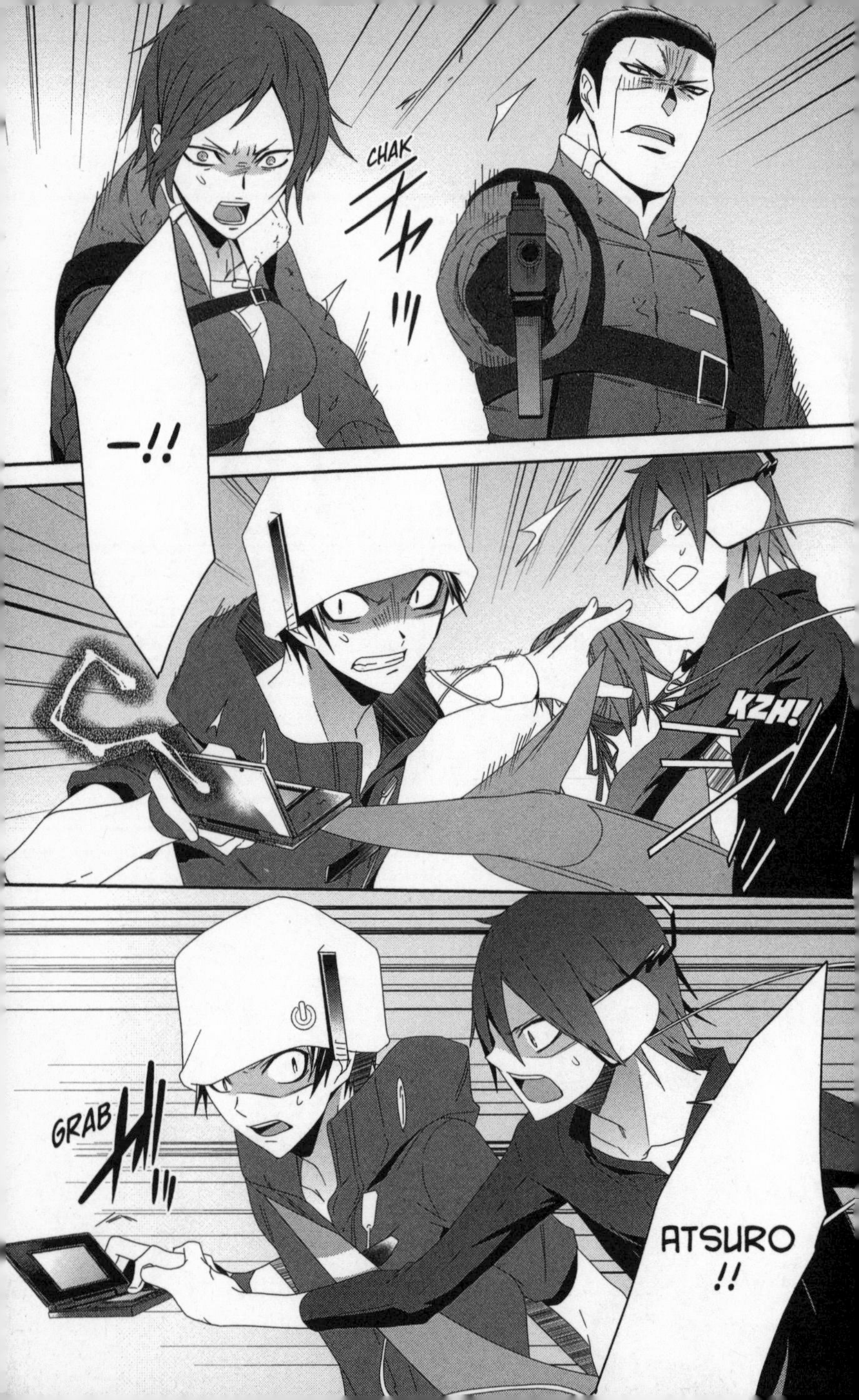
CHAK
—!!
KZH!
ATSURO !!
GRAB

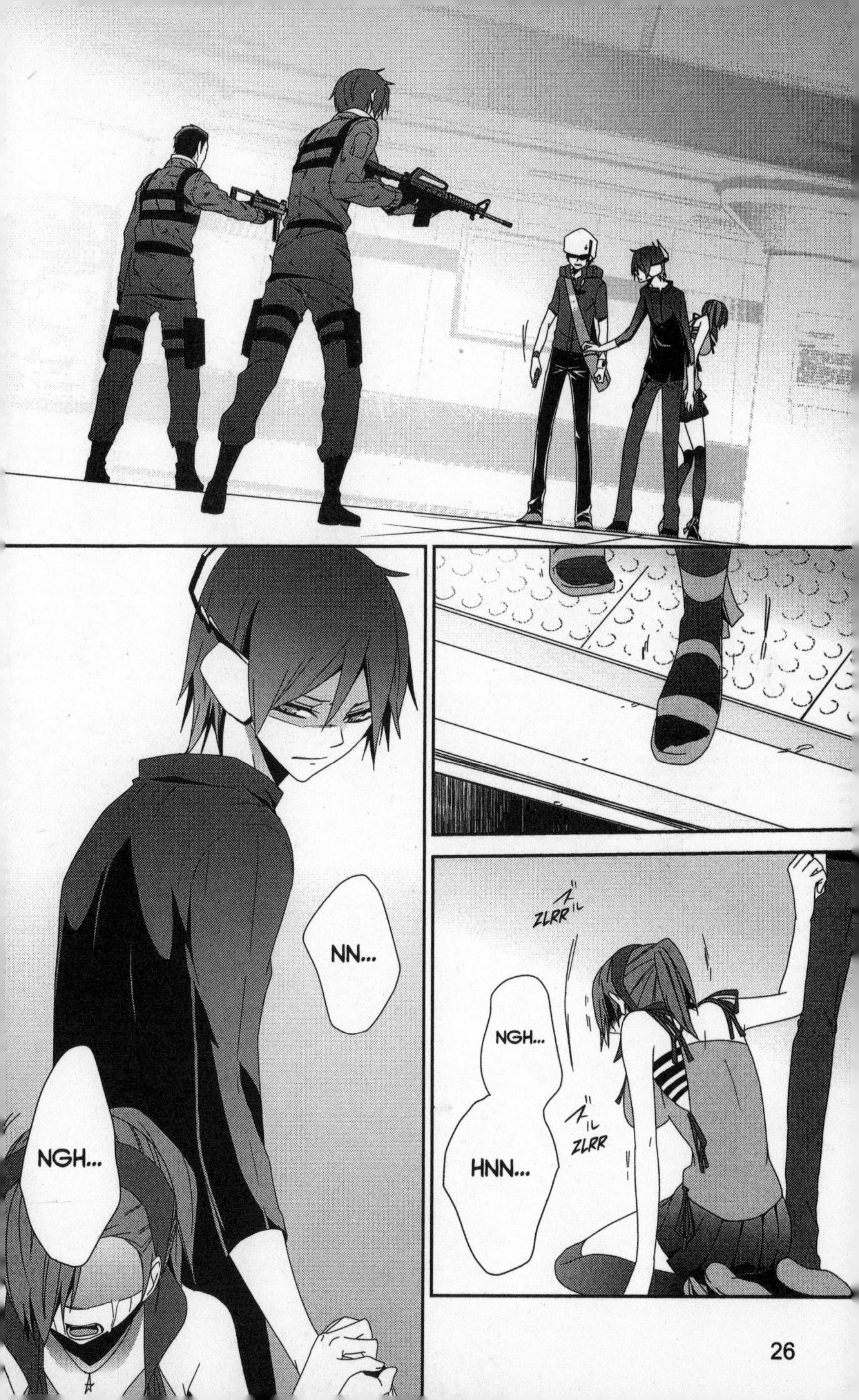
ズル
ZLRR
NGH...
ズル
ZLRR
HNN...
NN...
NGH...

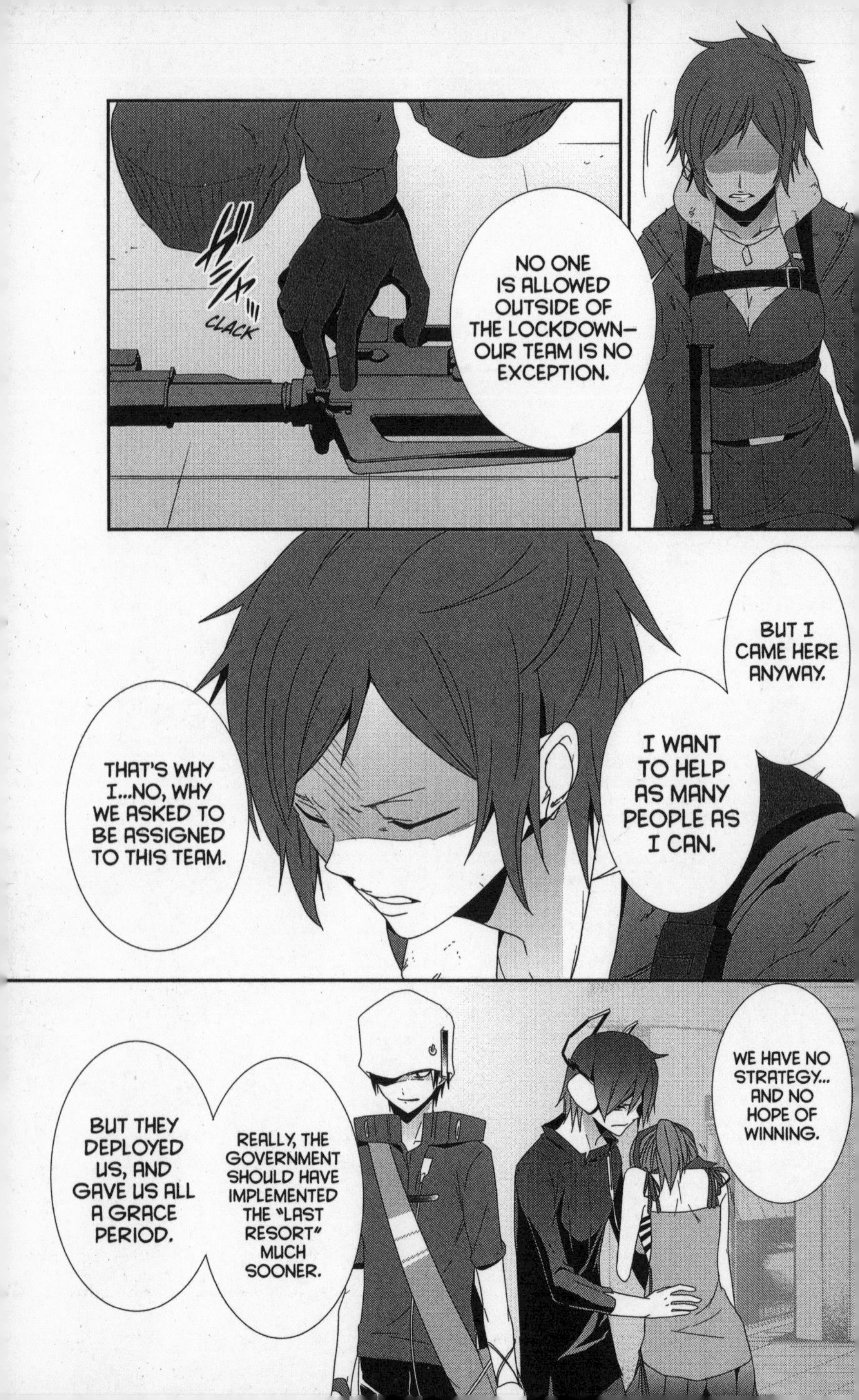
NO ONE IS ALLOWED OUTSIDE OF THE LOCKDOWN—OUR TEAM IS NO EXCEPTION.
CLACK
BUT I CAME HERE ANYWAY.
I WANT TO HELP AS MANY PEOPLE AS I CAN.
THAT'S WHY I...NO, WHY WE ASKED TO BE ASSIGNED TO THIS TEAM.
WE HAVE NO STRATEGY... AND NO HOPE OF WINNING.
REALLY, THE GOVERNMENT SHOULD HAVE IMPLEMENTED THE "LAST RESORT" MUCH SOONER.
BUT THEY DEPLOYED US, AND GAVE US ALL A GRACE PERIOD.

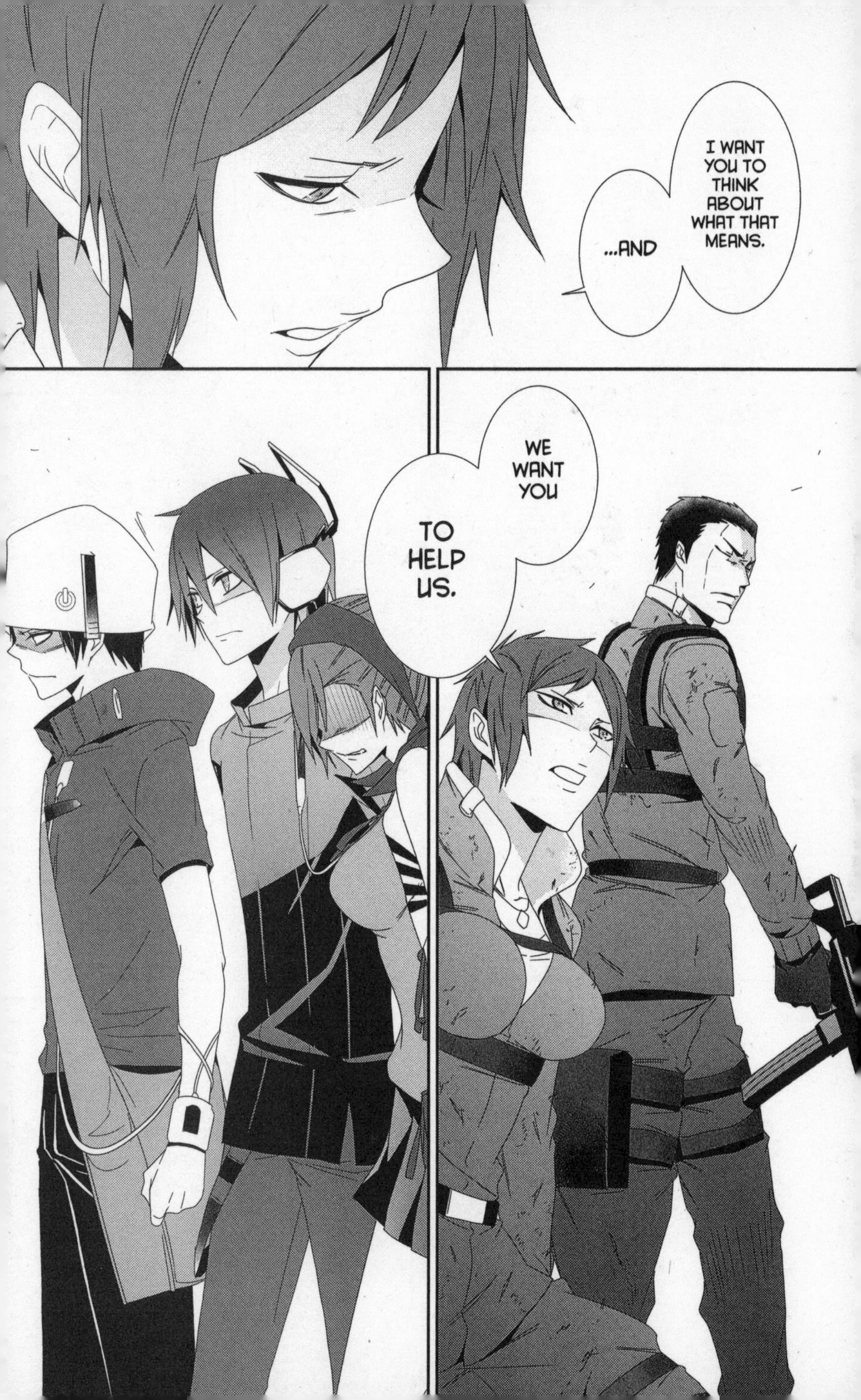
I WANT YOU TO THINK ABOUT WHAT THAT MEANS.
...AND
WE WANT YOU
TO HELP US.

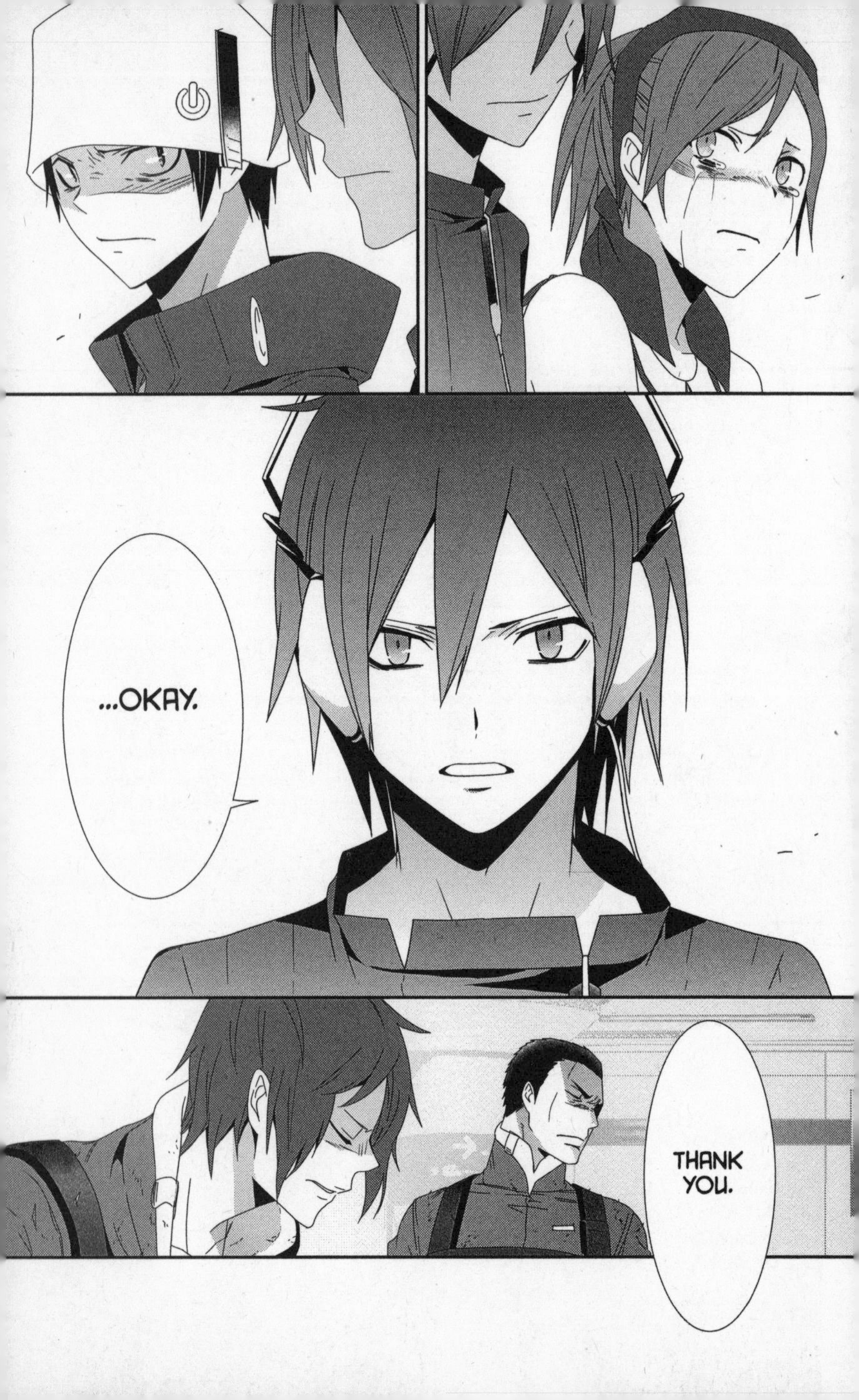
...OKAY.
THANK YOU.

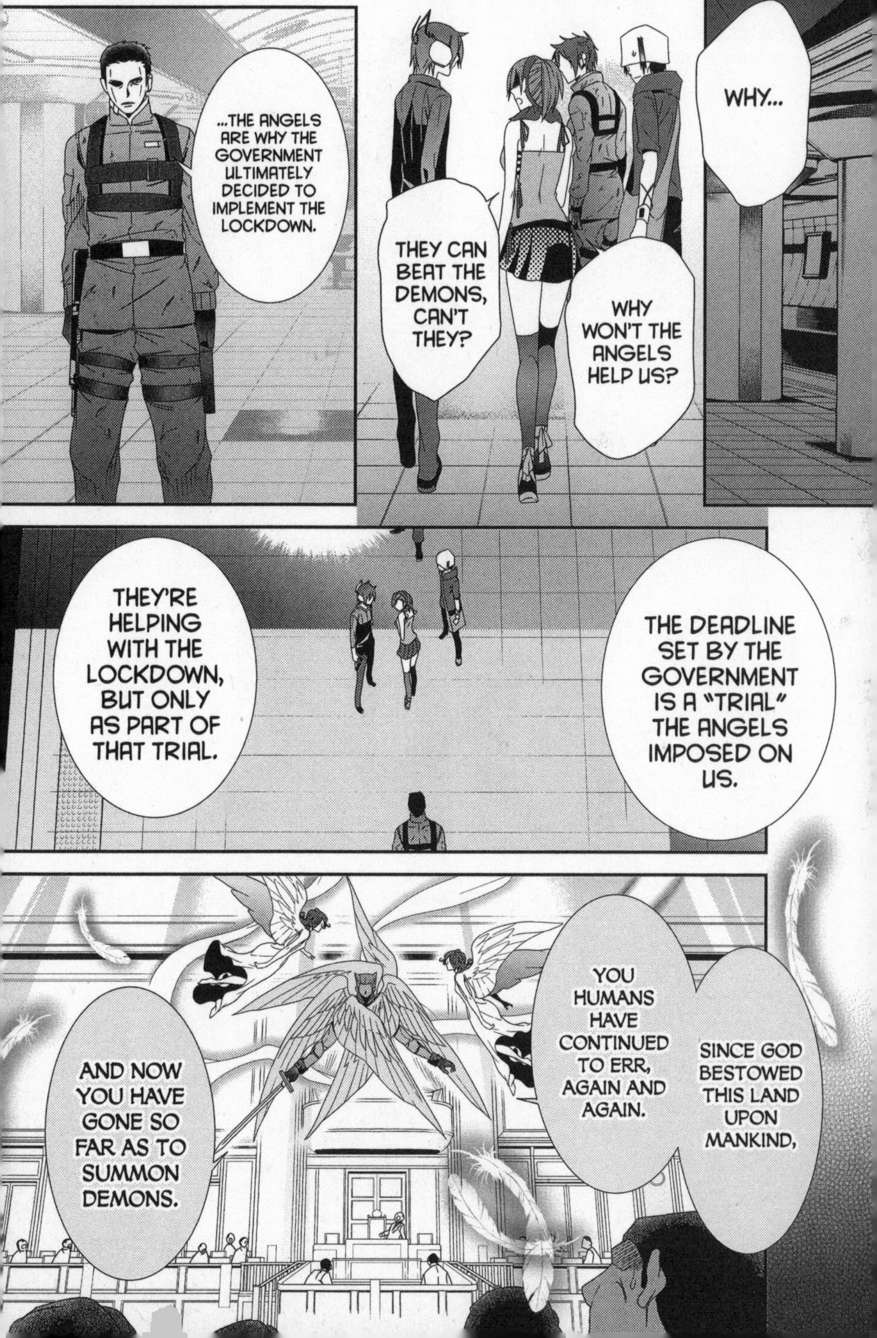
WHY...
WHY WON'T THE ANGELS HELP US?
THEY CAN BEAT THE DEMONS, CAN'T THEY?
...THE ANGELS ARE WHY THE GOVERNMENT ULTIMATELY DECIDED TO IMPLEMENT THE LOCKDOWN.
THE DEADLINE SET BY THE GOVERNMENT IS A "TRIAL" THE ANGELS IMPOSED ON US.
THEY'RE HELPING WITH THE LOCKDOWN, BUT ONLY AS PART OF THAT TRIAL.
SINCE GOD BESTOWED THIS LAND UPON MANKIND,
YOU HUMANS HAVE CONTINUED TO ERR, AGAIN AND AGAIN.
AND NOW YOU HAVE GONE SO FAR AS TO SUMMON DEMONS.

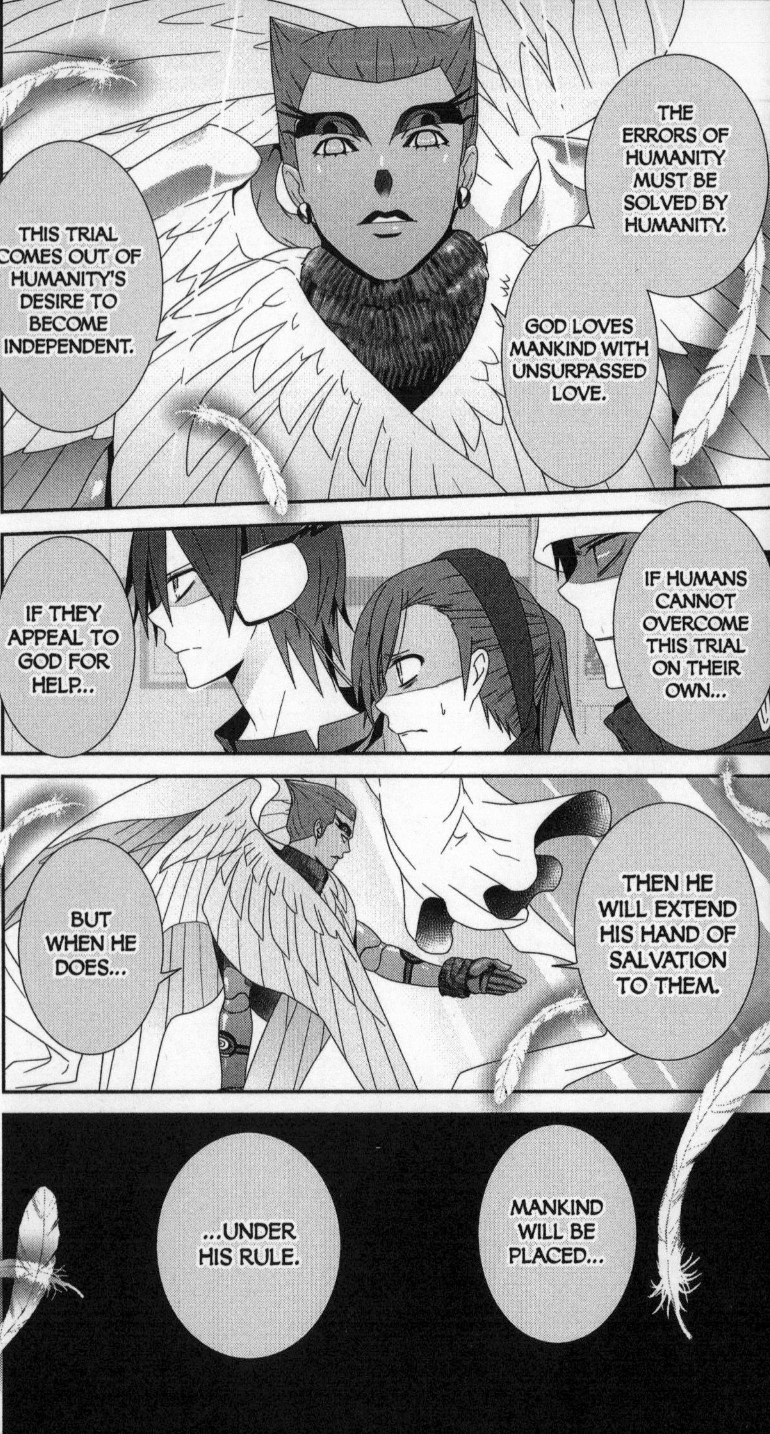
THE ERRORS OF HUMANITY MUST BE SOLVED BY HUMANITY.
GOD LOVES MANKIND WITH UNSURPASSED LOVE.
THIS TRIAL COMES OUT OF HUMANITY'S DESIRE TO BECOME INDEPENDENT.
IF HUMANS CANNOT OVERCOME THIS TRIAL ON THEIR OWN...
IF THEY APPEAL TO GOD FOR HELP...
THEN HE WILL EXTEND HIS HAND OF SALVATION TO THEM.
BUT WHEN HE DOES...
MANKIND WILL BE PLACED...
...UNDER HIS RULE.

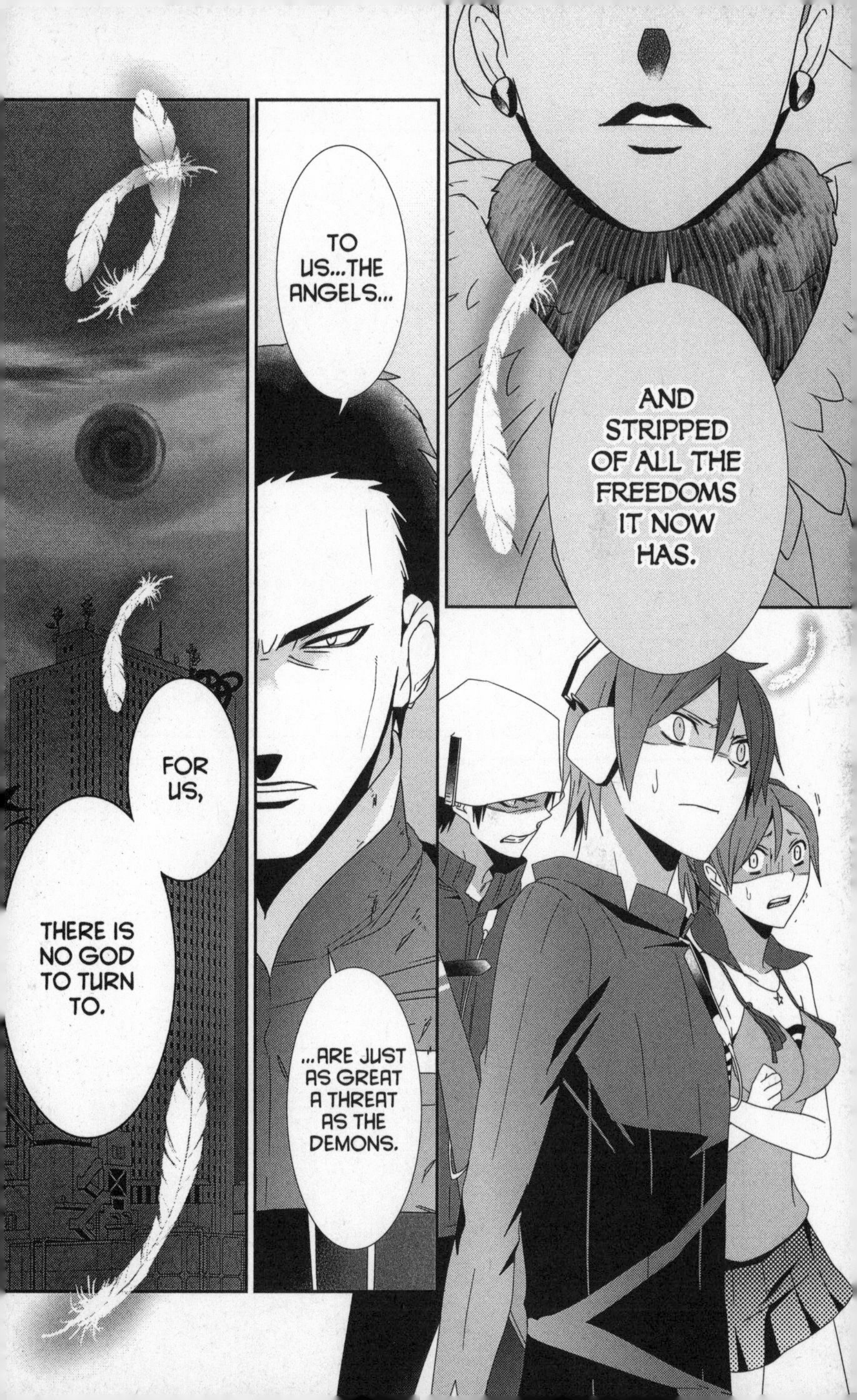
AND STRIPPED OF ALL THE FREEDOMS IT NOW HAS.
TO US...THE ANGELS...
...ARE JUST AS GREAT A THREAT AS THE DEMONS.
FOR US,
THERE IS NO GOD TO TURN TO.

DEVIL SURVIVOR デビルサバイバー

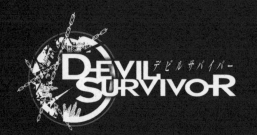

DEVIL SURVIVOR デビルサバイバー

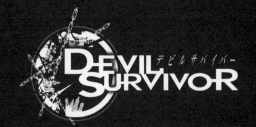

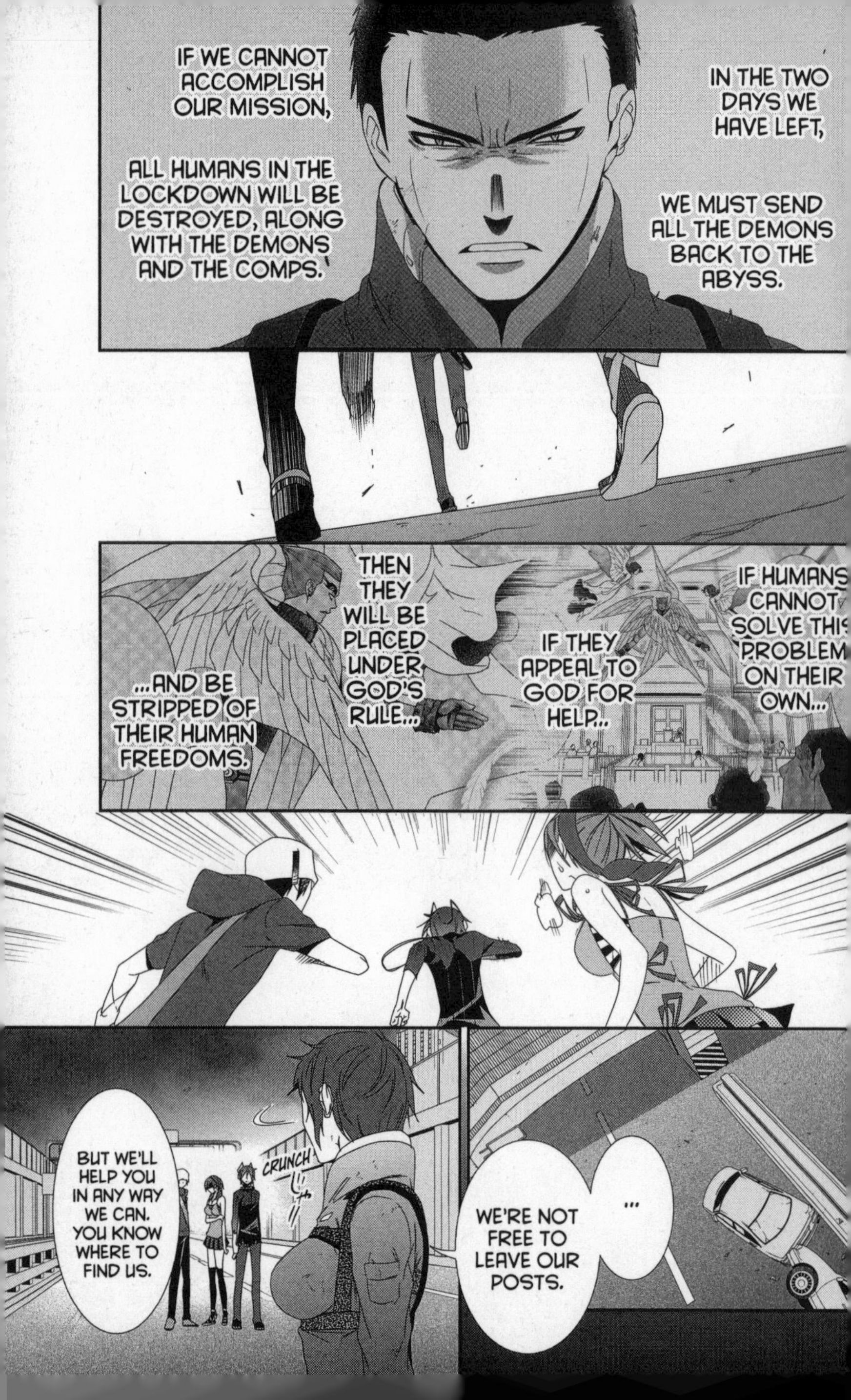
IN THE TWO DAYS WE HAVE LEFT,
WE MUST SEND ALL THE DEMONS BACK TO THE ABYSS.
IF WE CANNOT ACCOMPLISH OUR MISSION,
ALL HUMANS IN THE LOCKDOWN WILL BE DESTROYED, ALONG WITH THE DEMONS AND THE COMPS.
IF HUMANS CANNOT SOLVE THIS PROBLEM ON THEIR OWN...
IF THEY APPEAL TO GOD FOR HELP...
THEN THEY WILL BE PLACED UNDER GOD'S RULE...
...AND BE STRIPPED OF THEIR HUMAN FREEDOMS.
...
WE'RE NOT FREE TO LEAVE OUR POSTS.
CRUNCH
BUT WE'LL HELP YOU IN ANY WAY WE CAN. YOU KNOW WHERE TO FIND US.

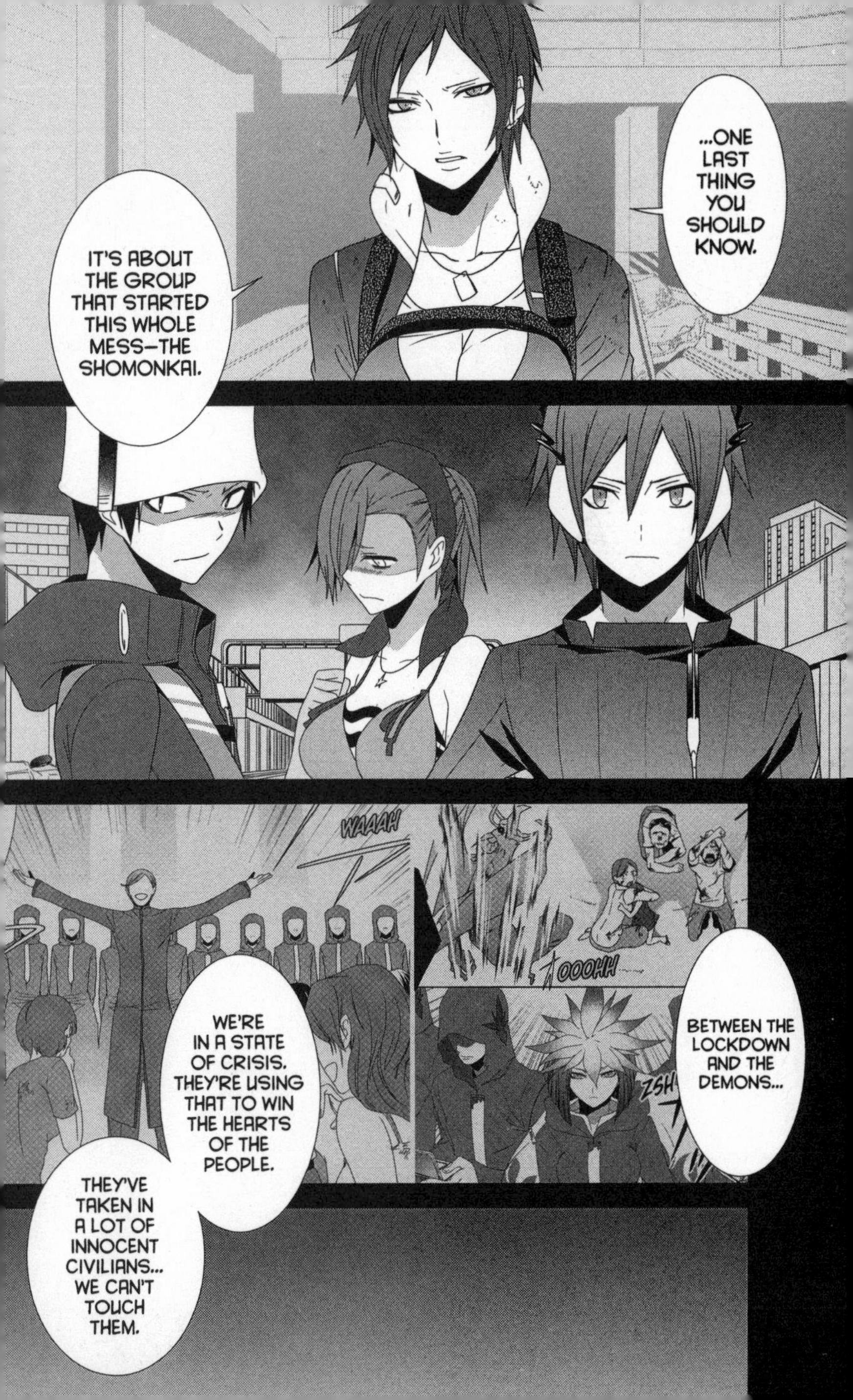
...ONE LAST THING YOU SHOULD KNOW.
IT'S ABOUT THE GROUP THAT STARTED THIS WHOLE MESS—THE SHOMONKAI.
OOOHH
ZSH
BETWEEN THE LOCKDOWN AND THE DEMONS...
WAAAH
WE'RE IN A STATE OF CRISIS. THEY'RE USING THAT TO WIN THE HEARTS OF THE PEOPLE.
THEY'VE TAKEN IN A LOT OF INNOCENT CIVILIANS... WE CAN'T TOUCH THEM.

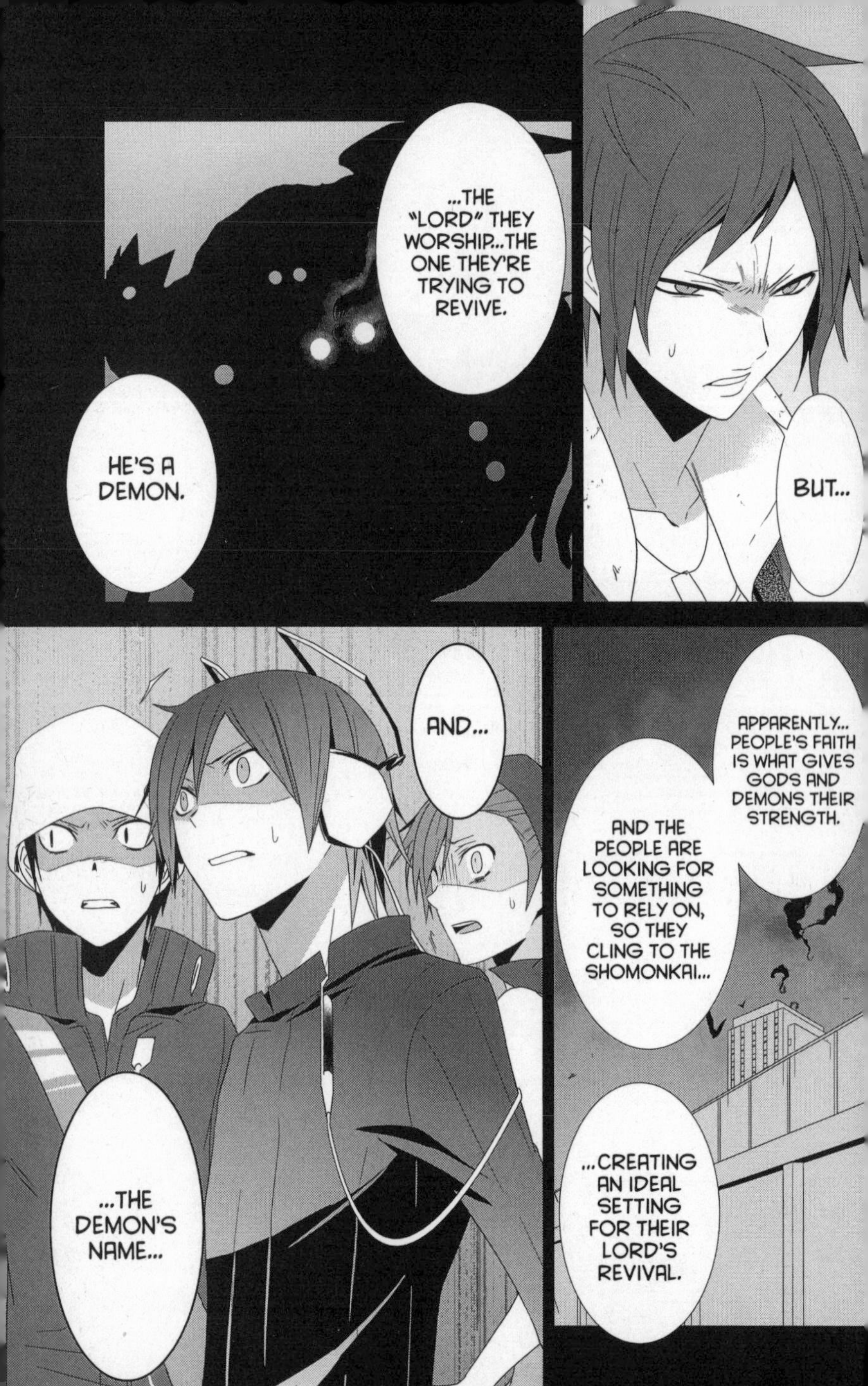
BUT...
...THE "LORD" THEY WORSHIP...THE ONE THEY'RE TRYING TO REVIVE.
HE'S A DEMON.
APPARENTLY... PEOPLE'S FAITH IS WHAT GIVES GODS AND DEMONS THEIR STRENGTH.
AND THE PEOPLE ARE LOOKING FOR SOMETHING TO RELY ON, SO THEY CLING TO THE SHOMONKAI...
...CREATING AN IDEAL SETTING FOR THEIR LORD'S REVIVAL.
AND...
...THE DEMON'S NAME...

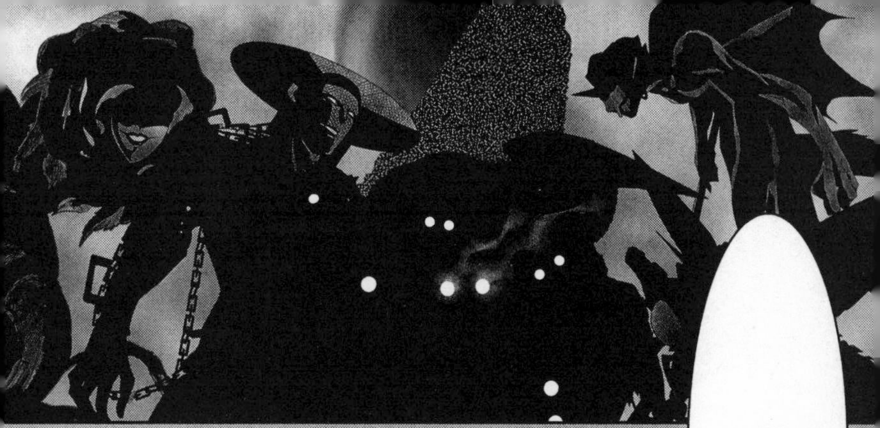
...IS BELBERITH.

SURVIVAL : 28

THE CALL OF THE ANGEL REMIEL

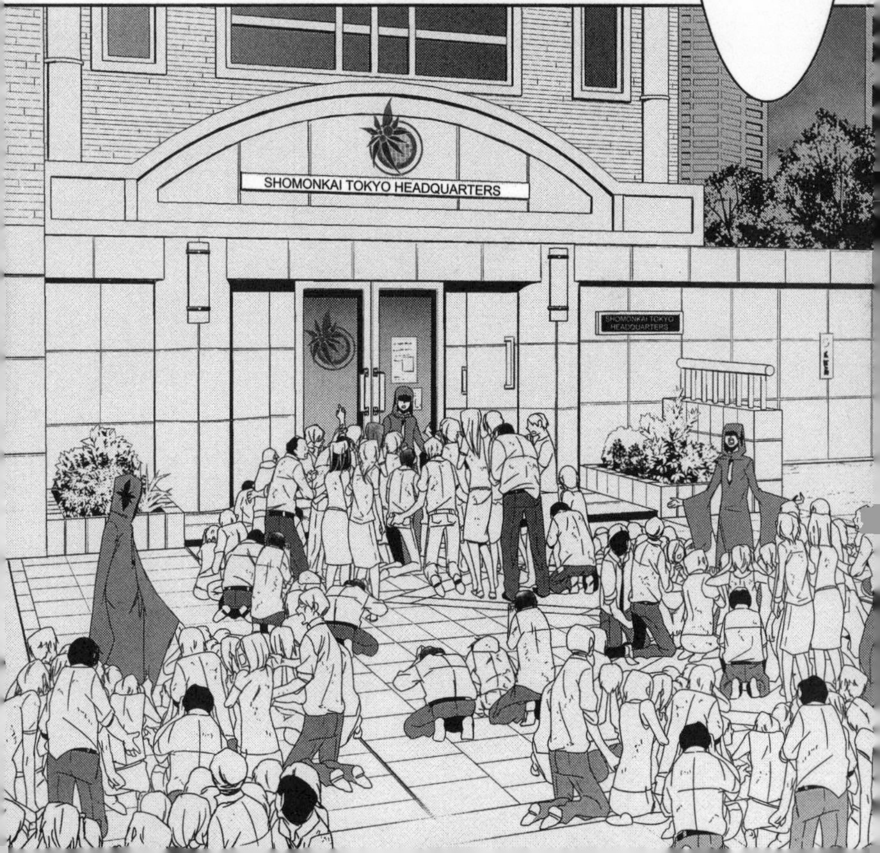
SHOMONKAI TOKYO HEADQUARTERS
SHOMONKAI TOKYO HEADQUARTERS

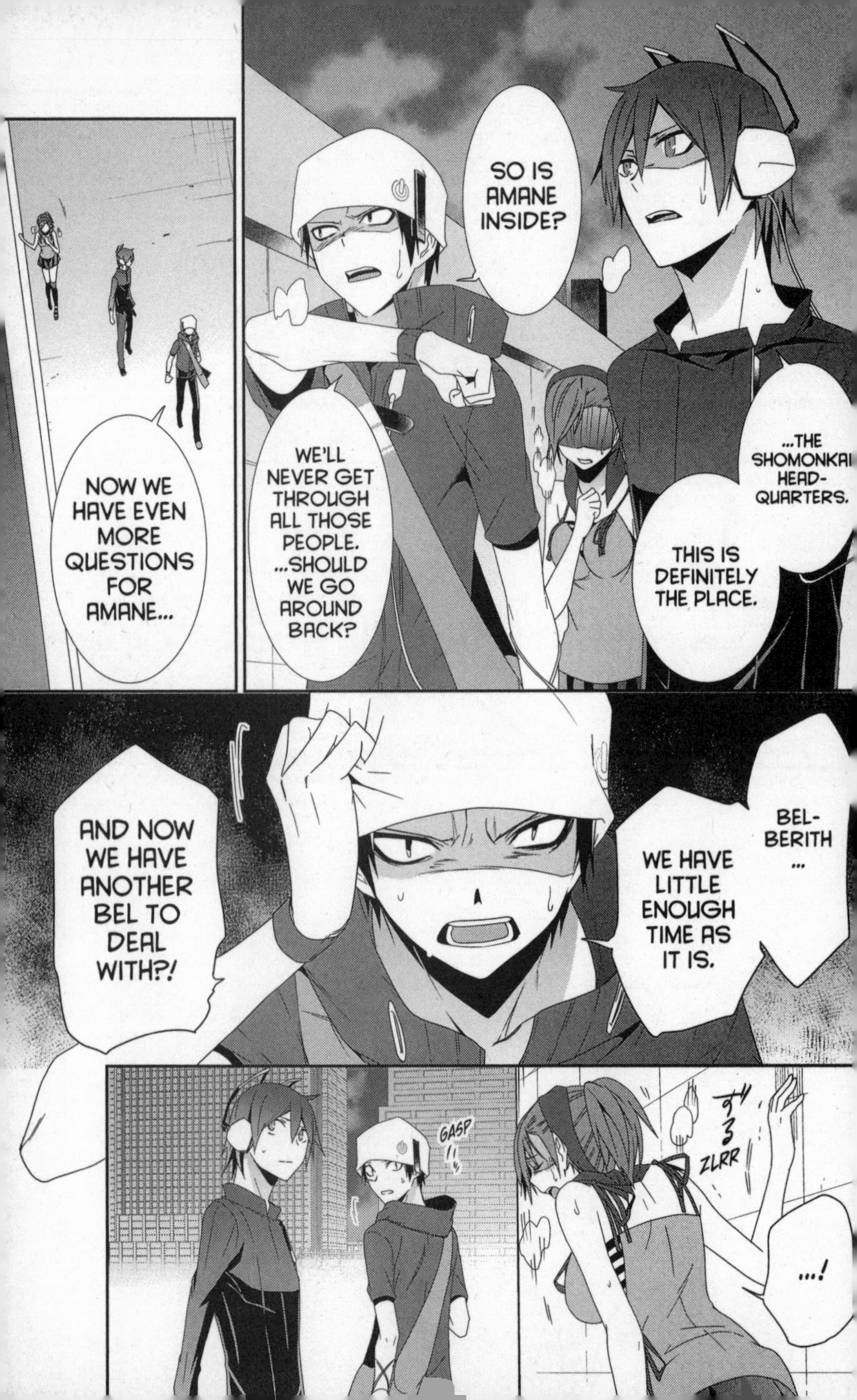
THIS IS DEFINITELY THE PLACE.
...THE SHOMONKAI HEAD-QUARTERS.
SO IS AMANE INSIDE?
WE'LL NEVER GET THROUGH ALL THOSE PEOPLE. ...SHOULD WE GO AROUND BACK?
NOW WE HAVE EVEN MORE QUESTIONS FOR AMANE...
BEL-BERITH...
WE HAVE LITTLE ENOUGH TIME AS IT IS.
AND NOW WE HAVE ANOTHER BEL TO DEAL WITH?!
ずる
ZLRR
...!
GASP!!

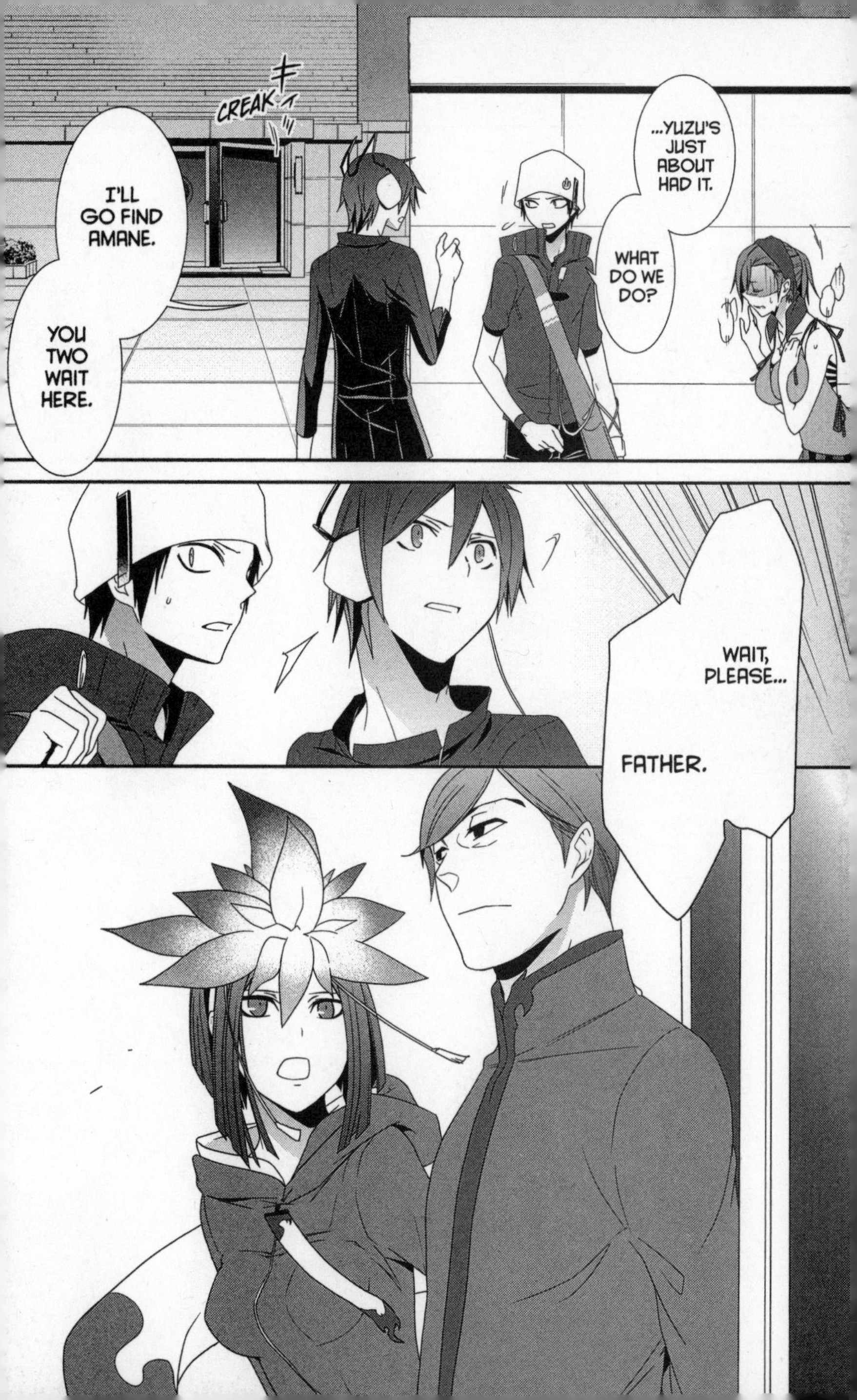
...YUZU'S JUST ABOUT HAD IT.
WHAT DO WE DO?
CREAK
I'LL GO FIND AMANE.
YOU TWO WAIT HERE.
WAIT, PLEASE...
FATHER.

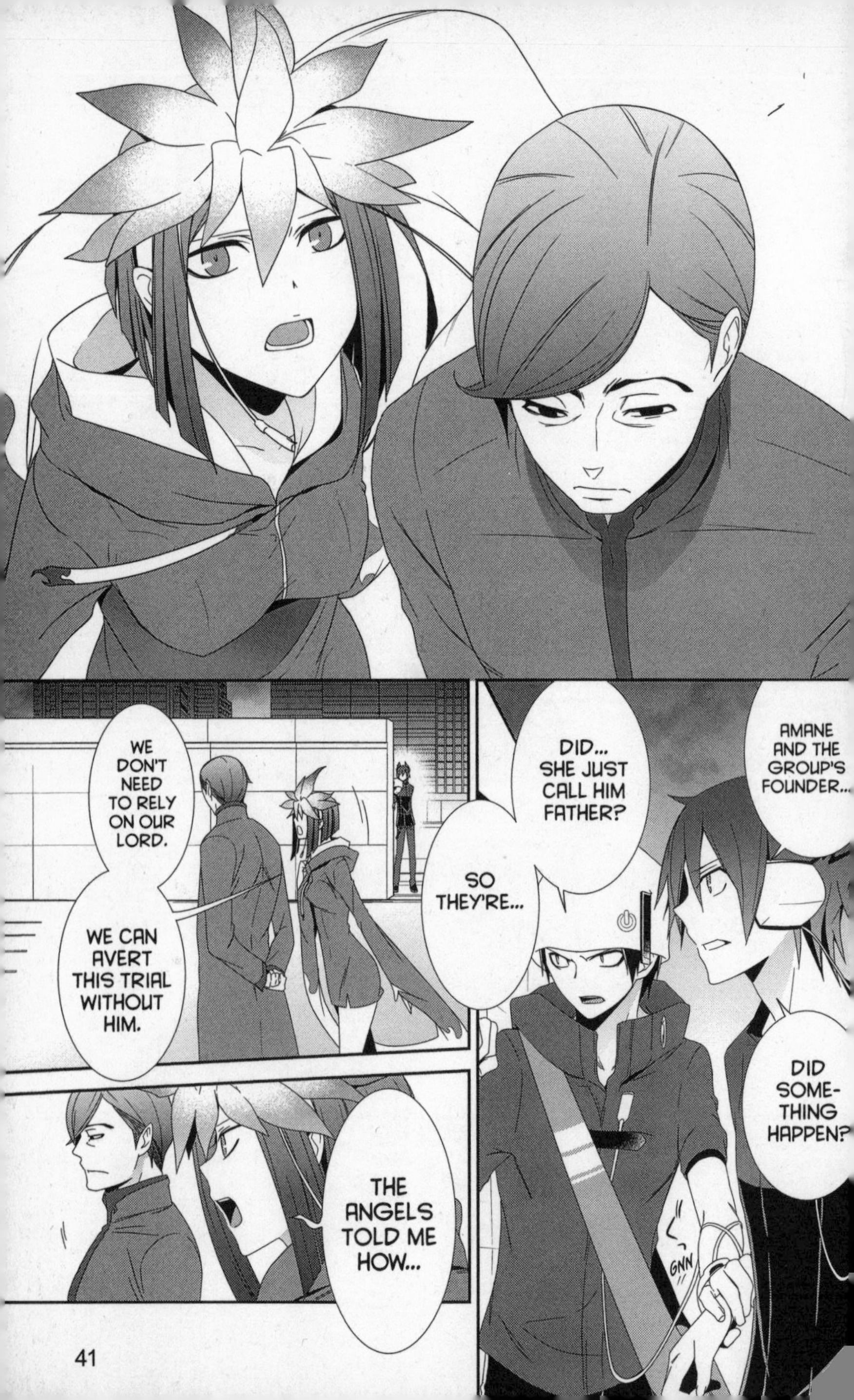
AMANE AND THE GROUP'S FOUNDER...
DID... SHE JUST CALL HIM FATHER?
SO THEY'RE...
DID SOME-THING HAPPEN?
GNN
WE DON'T NEED TO RELY ON OUR LORD.
WE CAN AVERT THIS TRIAL WITHOUT HIM.
THE ANGELS TOLD ME HOW...

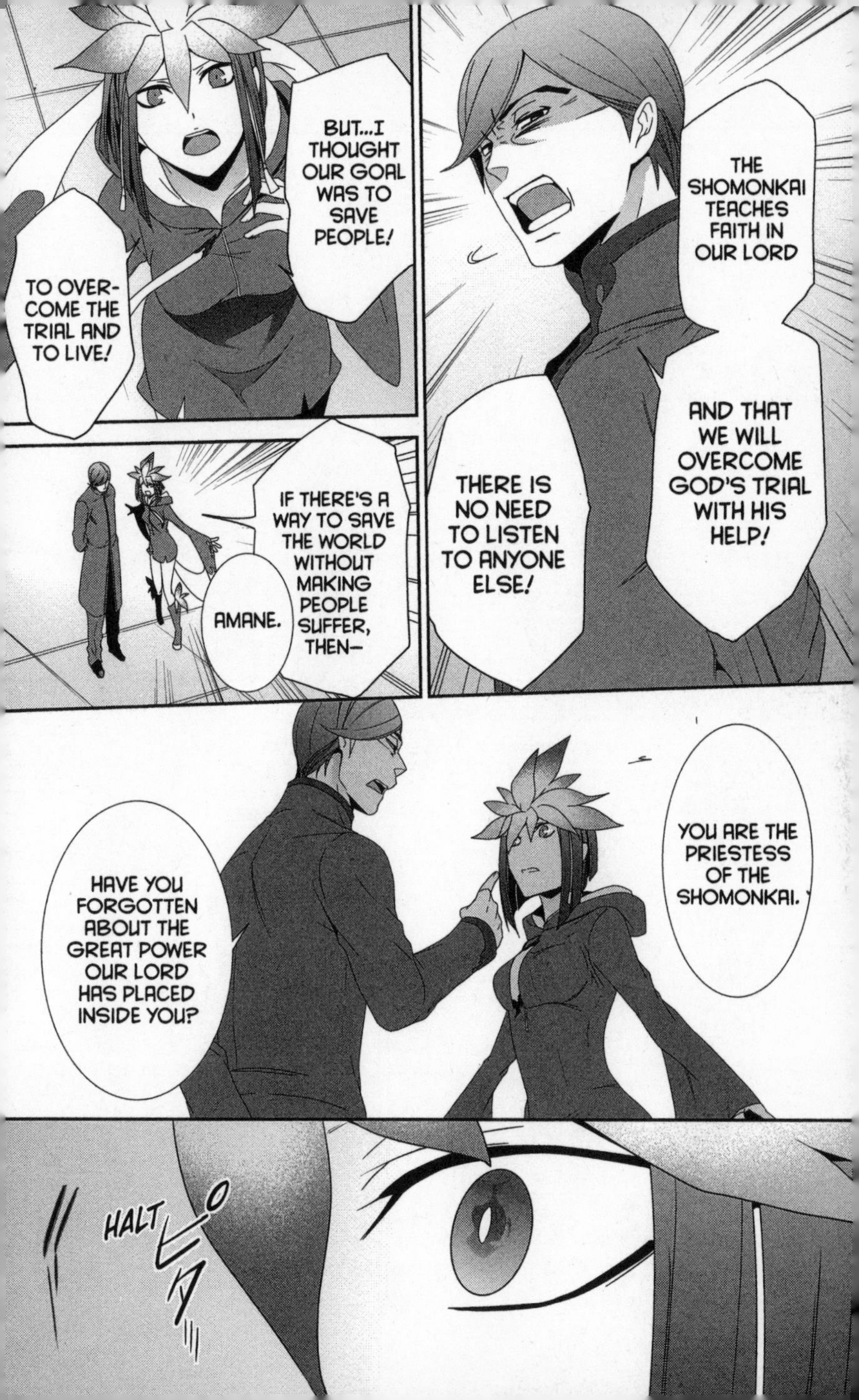
THE SHOMONKAI TEACHES FAITH IN OUR LORD
AND THAT WE WILL OVERCOME GOD'S TRIAL WITH HIS HELP!
THERE IS NO NEED TO LISTEN TO ANYONE ELSE!
BUT...I THOUGHT OUR GOAL WAS TO SAVE PEOPLE!
TO OVER-COME THE TRIAL AND TO LIVE!
IF THERE'S A WAY TO SAVE THE WORLD WITHOUT MAKING PEOPLE SUFFER, THEN—
AMANE.
YOU ARE THE PRIESTESS OF THE SHOMONKAI.
HAVE YOU FORGOTTEN ABOUT THE GREAT POWER OUR LORD HAS PLACED INSIDE YOU?
HALT

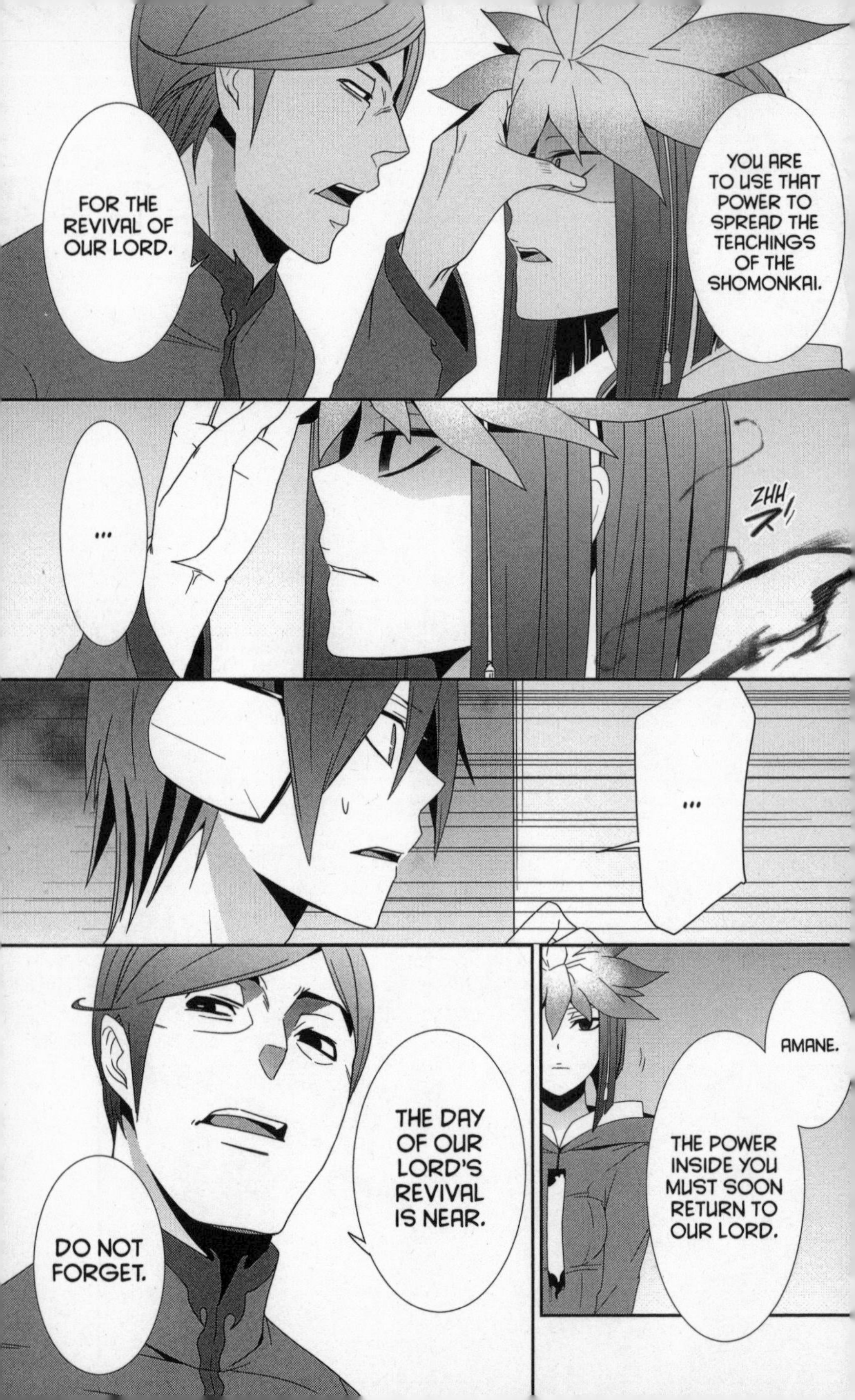
YOU ARE TO USE THAT POWER TO SPREAD THE TEACHINGS OF THE SHOMONKAI.
FOR THE REVIVAL OF OUR LORD.
ZHH
...
...
AMANE.
THE POWER INSIDE YOU MUST SOON RETURN TO OUR LORD.
THE DAY OF OUR LORD'S REVIVAL IS NEAR.
DO NOT FORGET.

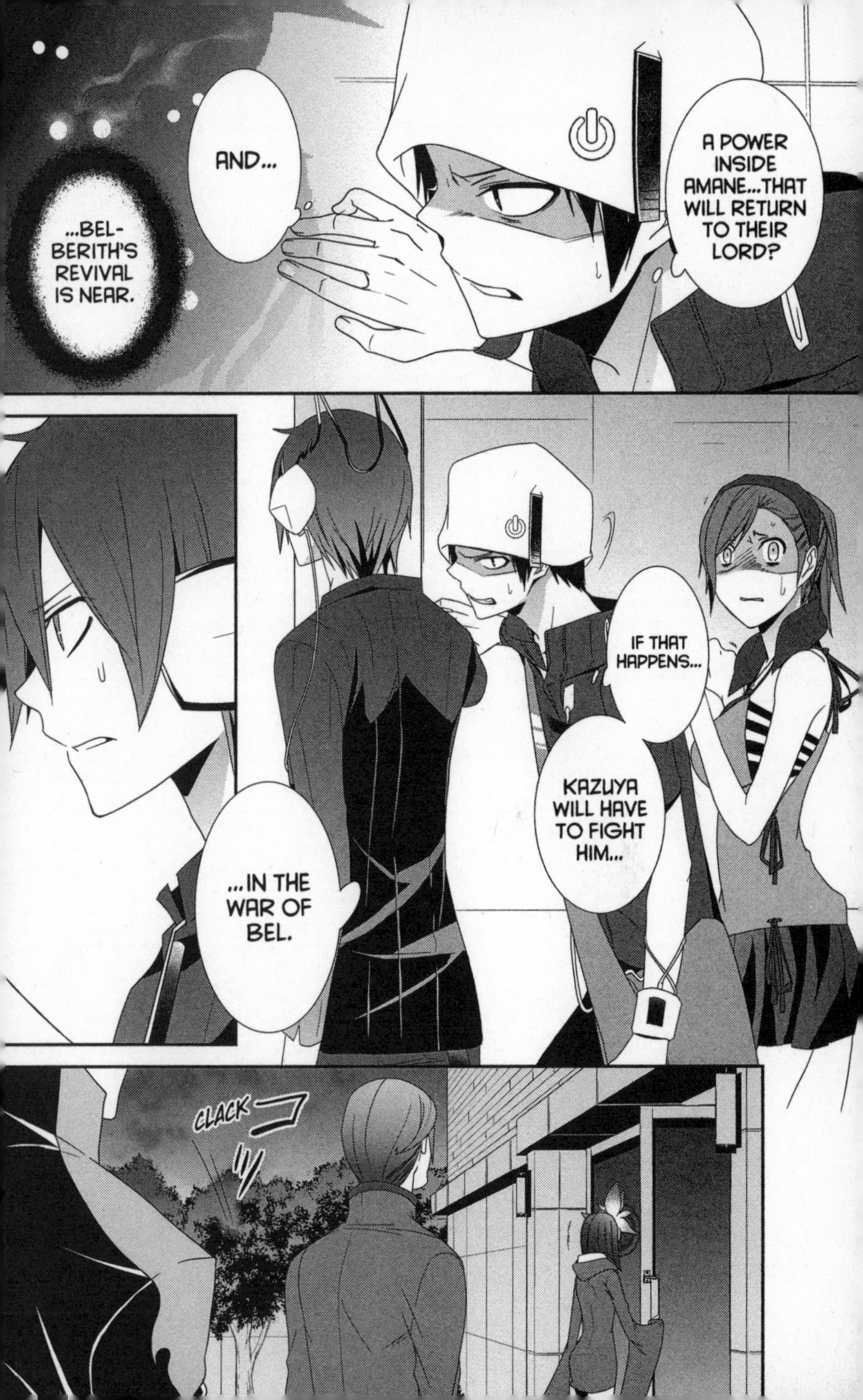
A POWER INSIDE AMANE...THAT WILL RETURN TO THEIR LORD?
AND...
...BEL-BERITH'S REVIVAL IS NEAR.
IF THAT HAPPENS...
KAZUYA WILL HAVE TO FIGHT HIM...
...IN THE WAR OF BEL.
CLACK

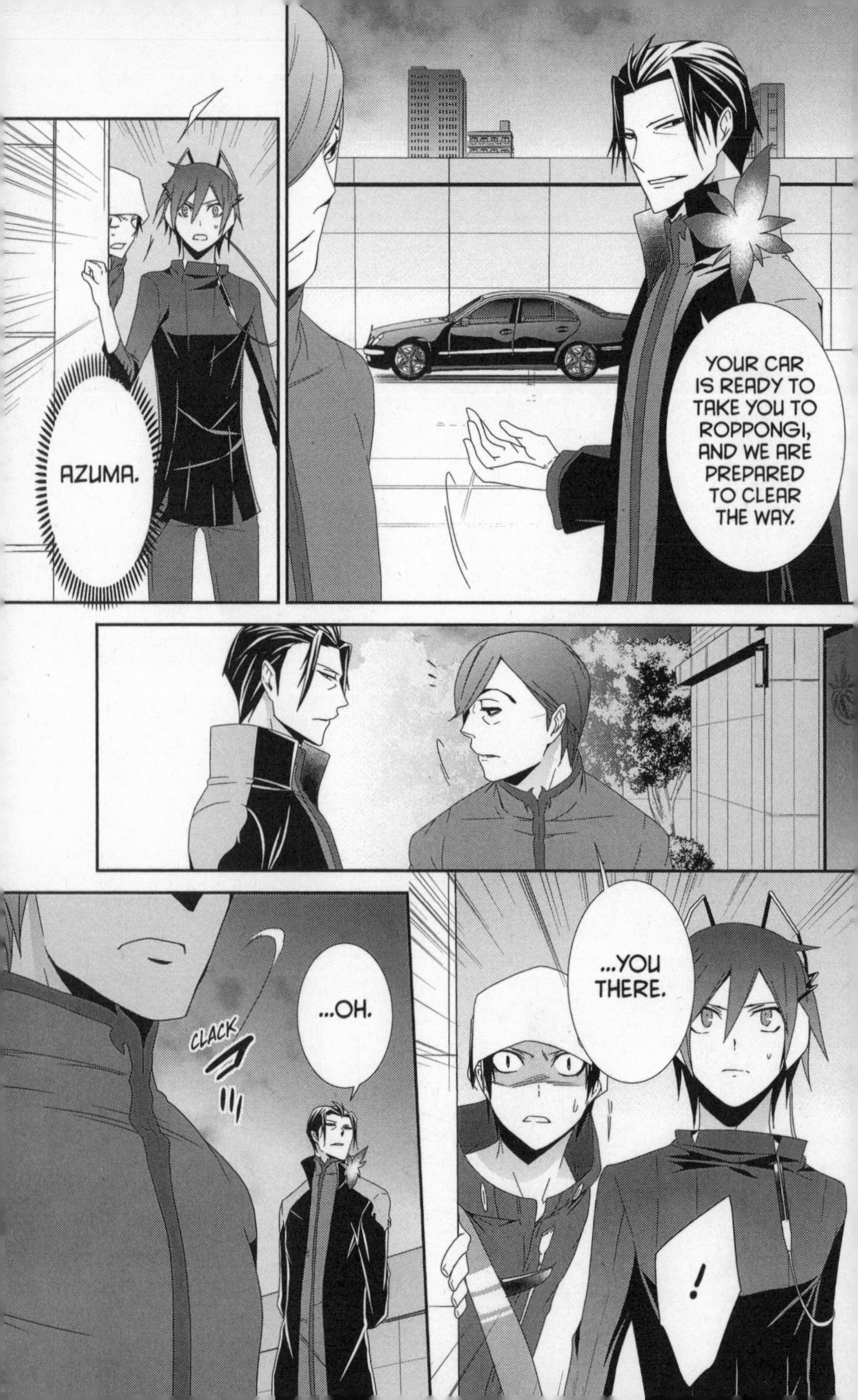
YOUR CAR IS READY TO TAKE YOU TO ROPPONGI, AND WE ARE PREPARED TO CLEAR THE WAY.
AZUMA.
...YOU THERE.
!
...OH.
CLACK

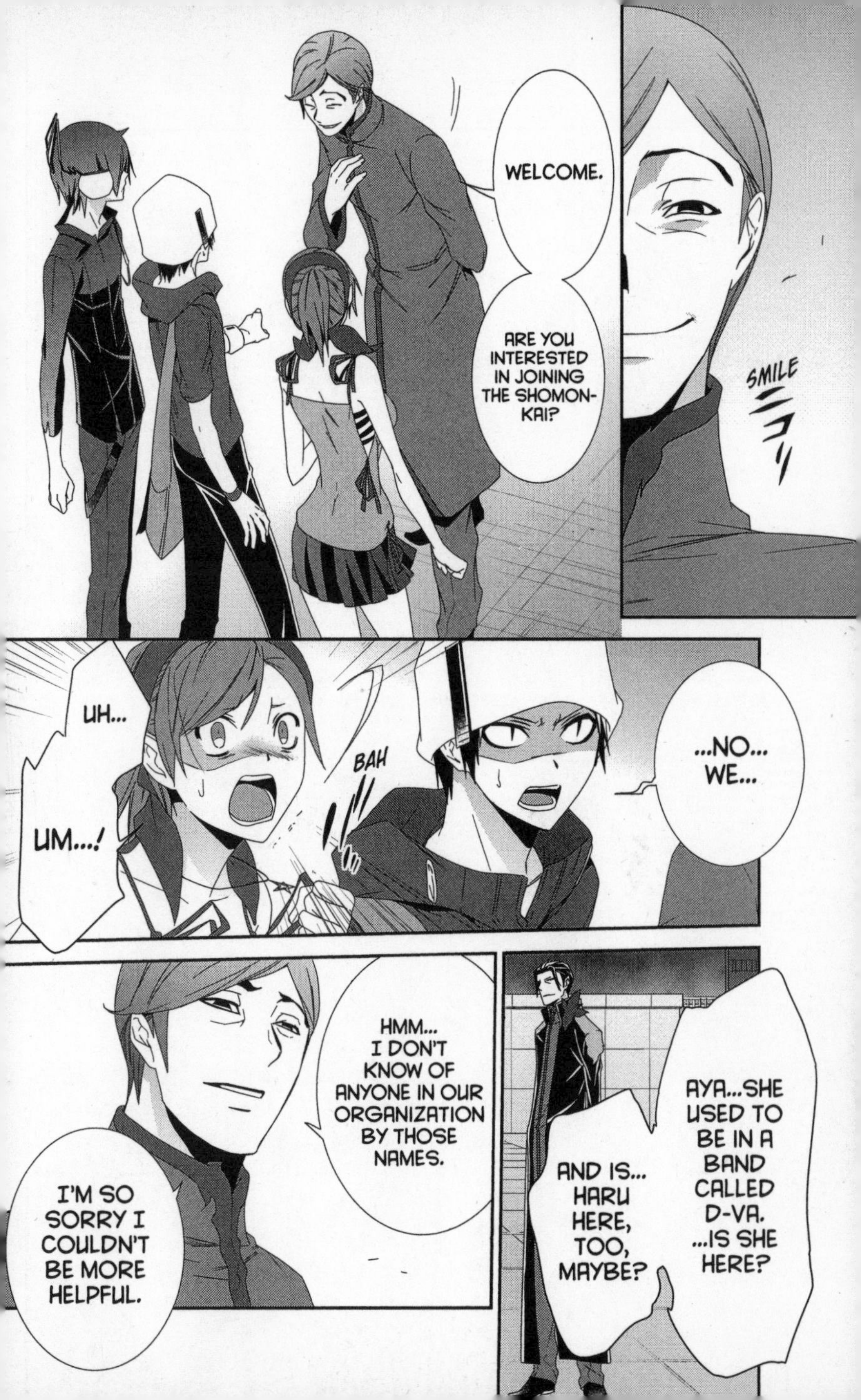
SMILE
WELCOME.
ARE YOU INTERESTED IN JOINING THE SHOMON-KAI?
...NO... WE...
BAH
UH...
UM...!
AYA...SHE USED TO BE IN A BAND CALLED D-VA. ...IS SHE HERE?
AND IS... HARU HERE, TOO, MAYBE?
HMM... I DON'T KNOW OF ANYONE IN OUR ORGANIZATION BY THOSE NAMES.
I'M SO SORRY I COULDN'T BE MORE HELPFUL.

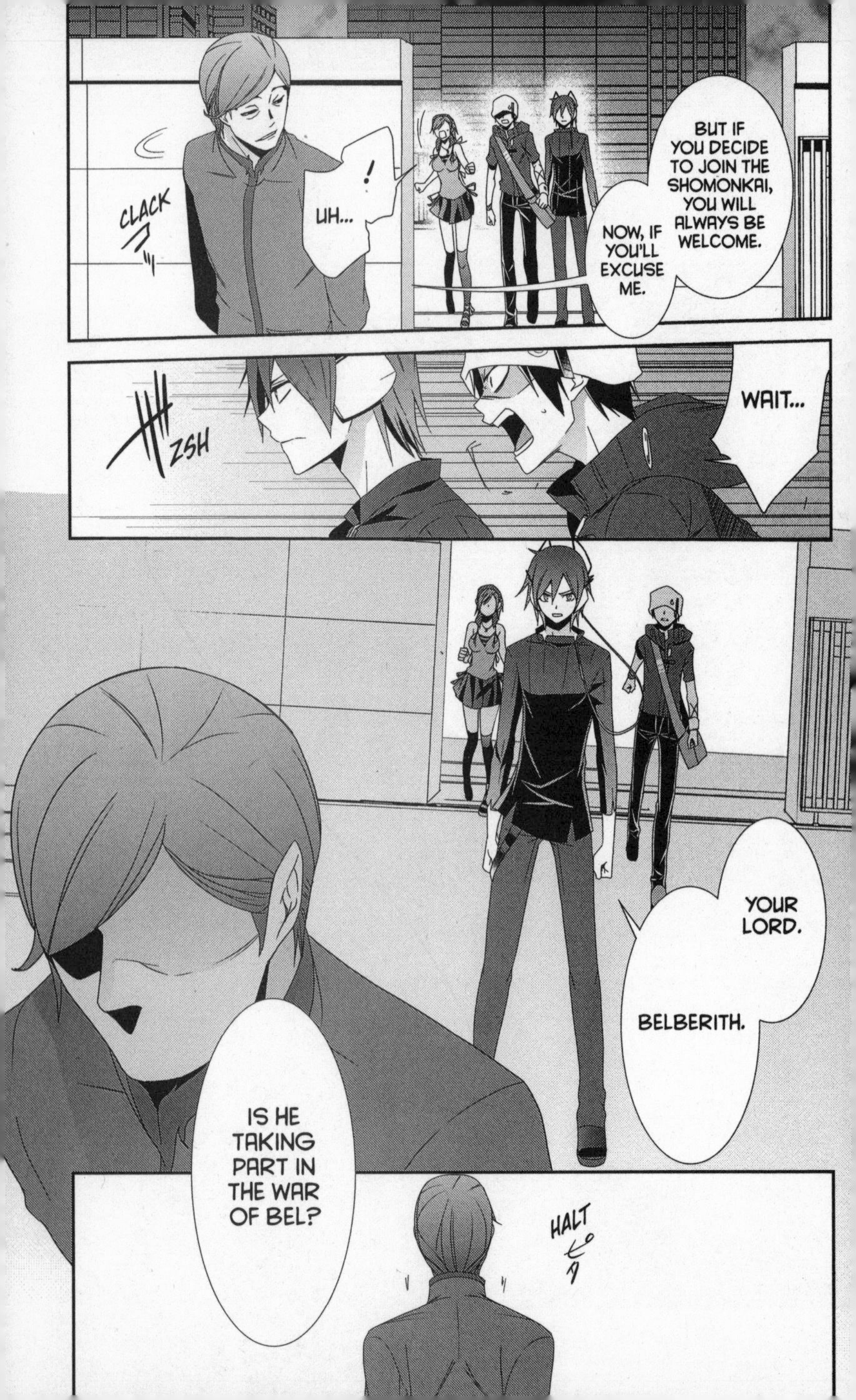
BUT IF YOU DECIDE TO JOIN THE SHOMONKAI, YOU WILL ALWAYS BE WELCOME.
NOW, IF YOU'LL EXCUSE ME.
!
UH...
CLACK
WAIT...
ZSH
YOUR LORD.
BELBERITH.
IS HE TAKING PART IN THE WAR OF BEL?
HALT

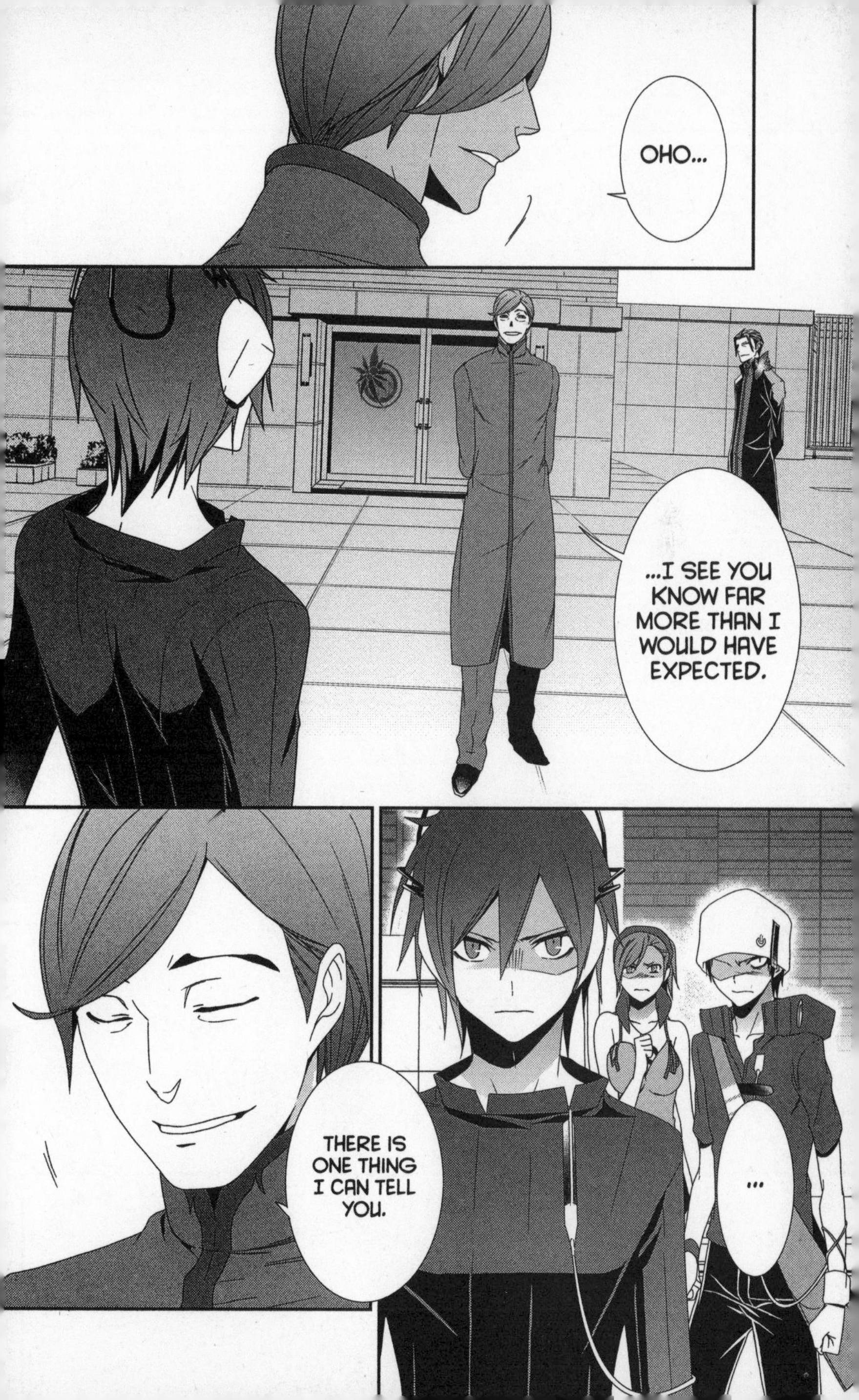
OHO...
...I SEE YOU KNOW FAR MORE THAN I WOULD HAVE EXPECTED.
...
THERE IS ONE THING I CAN TELL YOU.

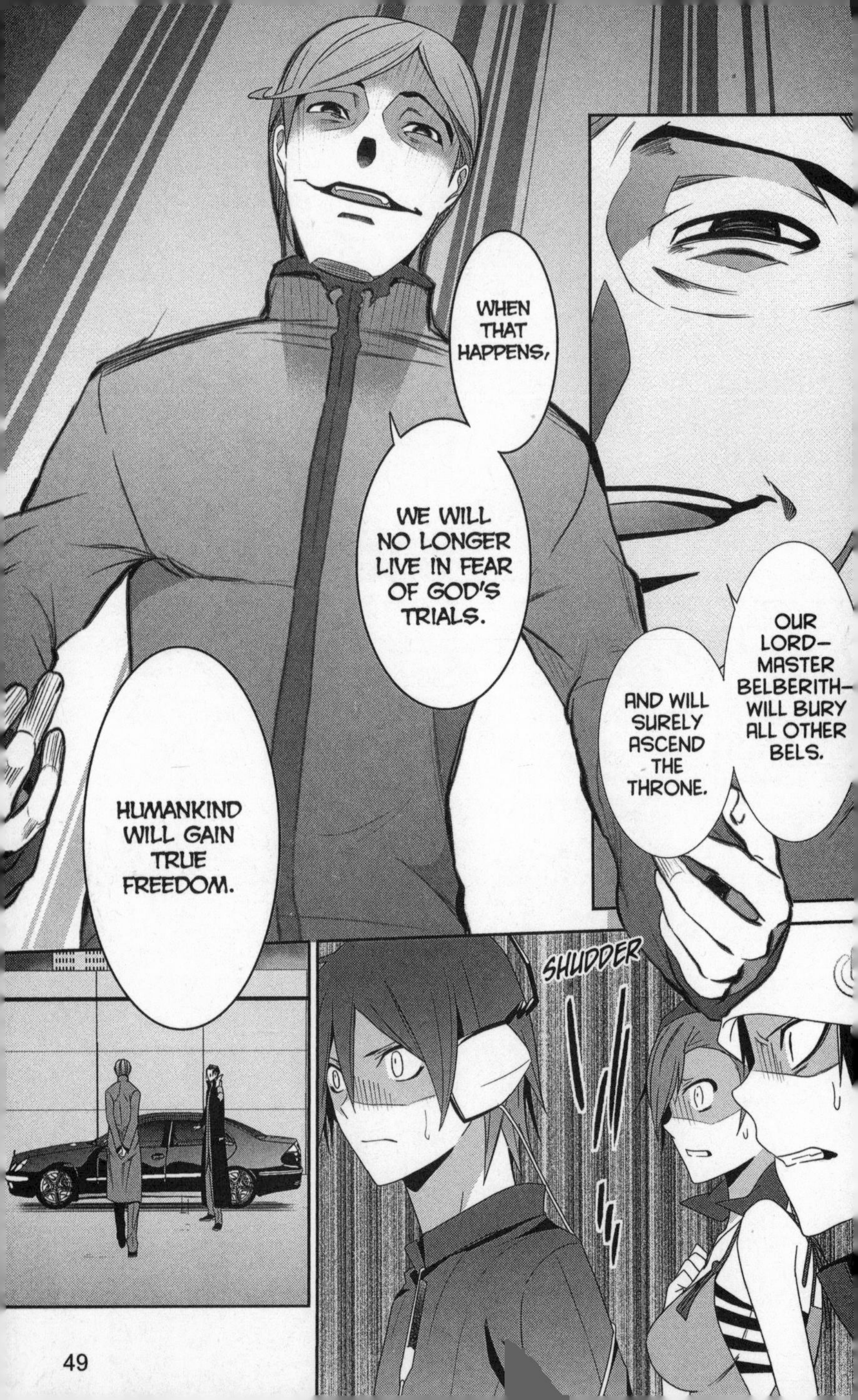
OUR LORD—MASTER BELBERITH—WILL BURY ALL OTHER BELS.
AND WILL SURELY ASCEND THE THRONE.
WHEN THAT HAPPENS,
WE WILL NO LONGER LIVE IN FEAR OF GOD'S TRIALS.
HUMANKIND WILL GAIN TRUE FREEDOM.
SHUDDER

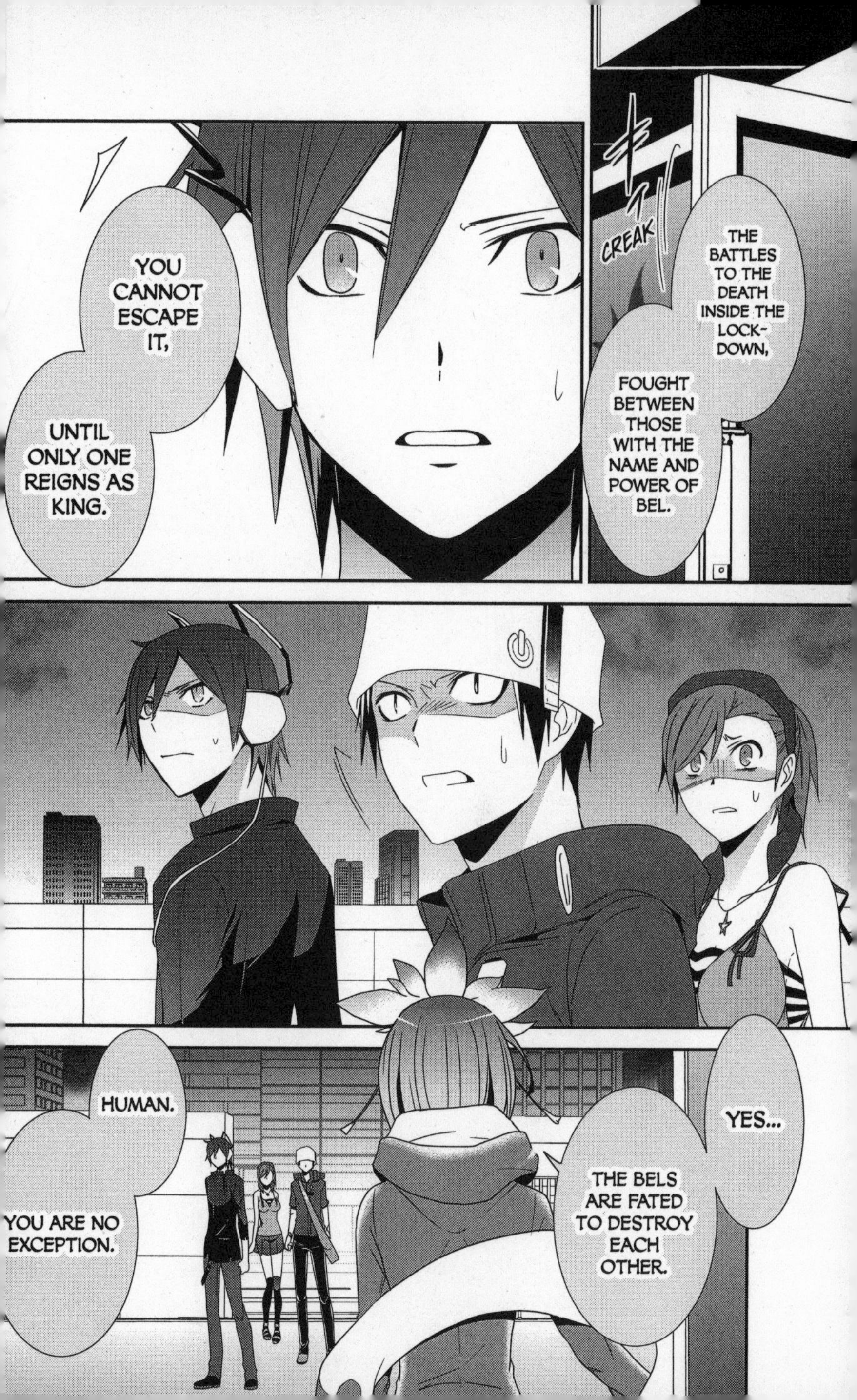
キィ
CREAK
THE BATTLES TO THE DEATH INSIDE THE LOCK-DOWN,
FOUGHT BETWEEN THOSE WITH THE NAME AND POWER OF BEL.
YOU CANNOT ESCAPE IT,
UNTIL ONLY ONE REIGNS AS KING.
YES...
THE BELS ARE FATED TO DESTROY EACH OTHER.
HUMAN.
YOU ARE NO EXCEPTION.

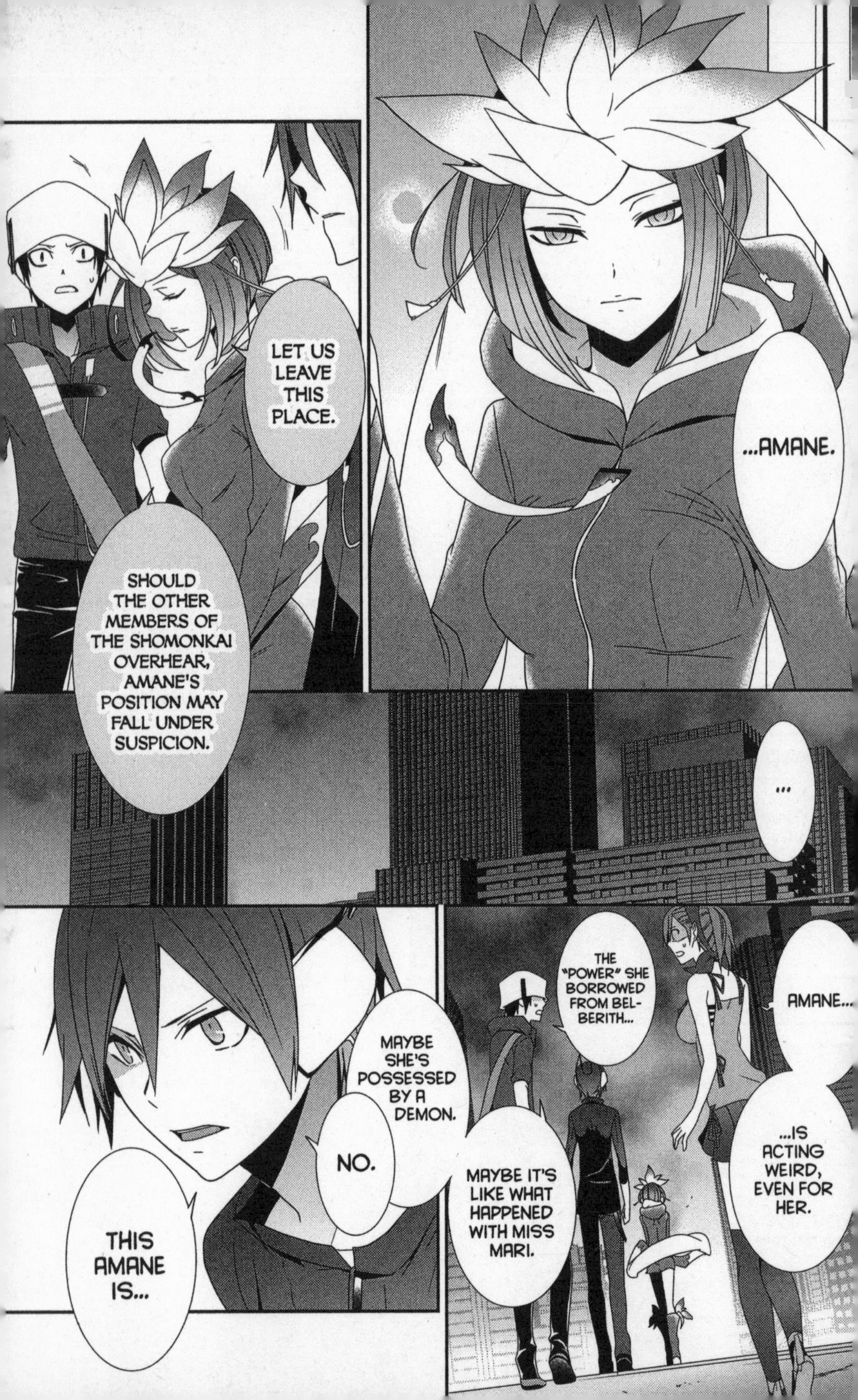

...AMANE.
LET US LEAVE THIS PLACE.
SHOULD THE OTHER MEMBERS OF THE SHOMONKAI OVERHEAR, AMANE'S POSITION MAY FALL UNDER SUSPICION.
...
AMANE...
...IS ACTING WEIRD, EVEN FOR HER.
THE "POWER" SHE BORROWED FROM BEL-BERITH...
MAYBE IT'S LIKE WHAT HAPPENED WITH MISS MARI.
MAYBE SHE'S POSSESSED BY A DEMON.
NO.
THIS AMANE IS...

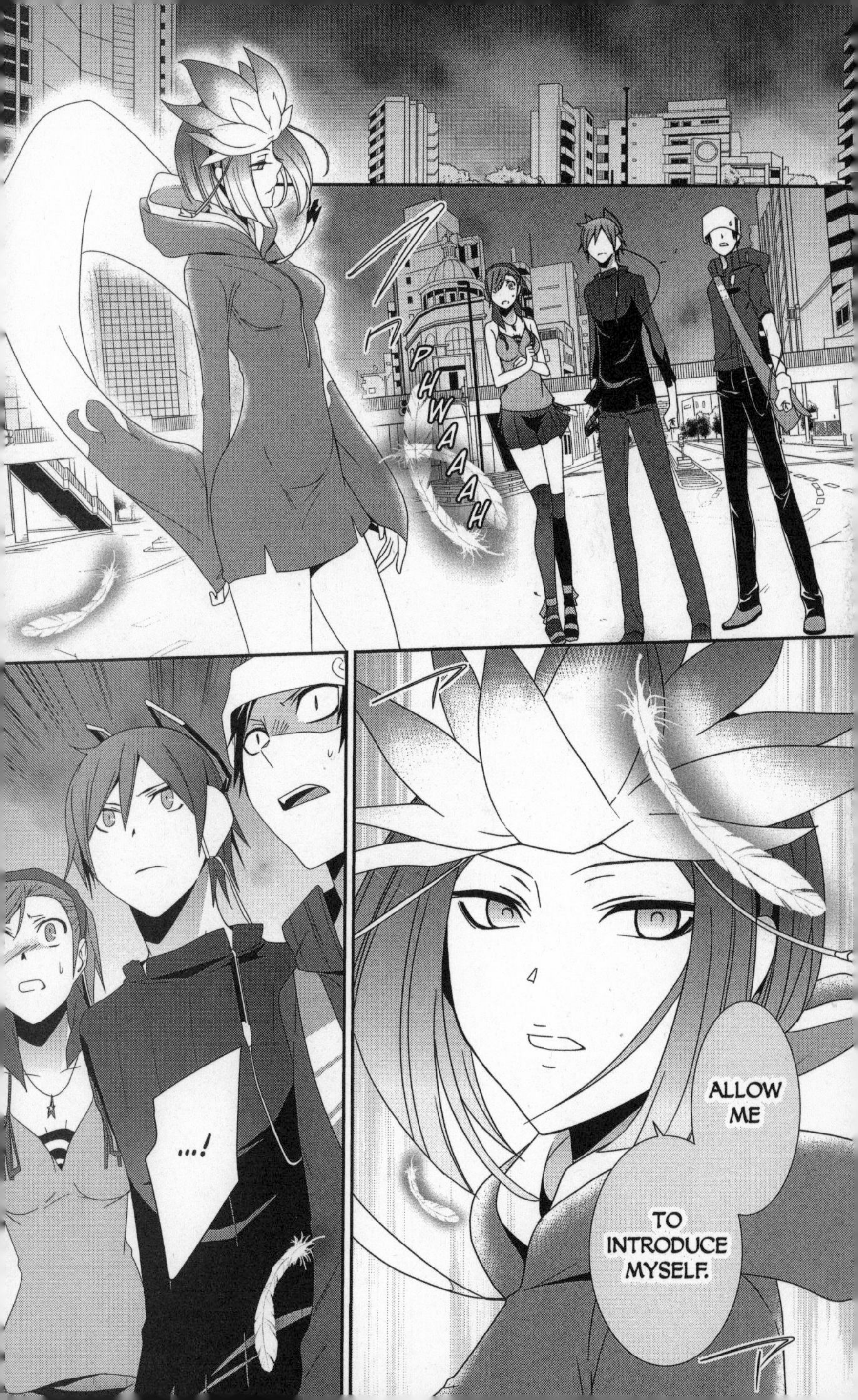
PHWAAAAH
ALLOW ME
TO INTRODUCE MYSELF.
...!

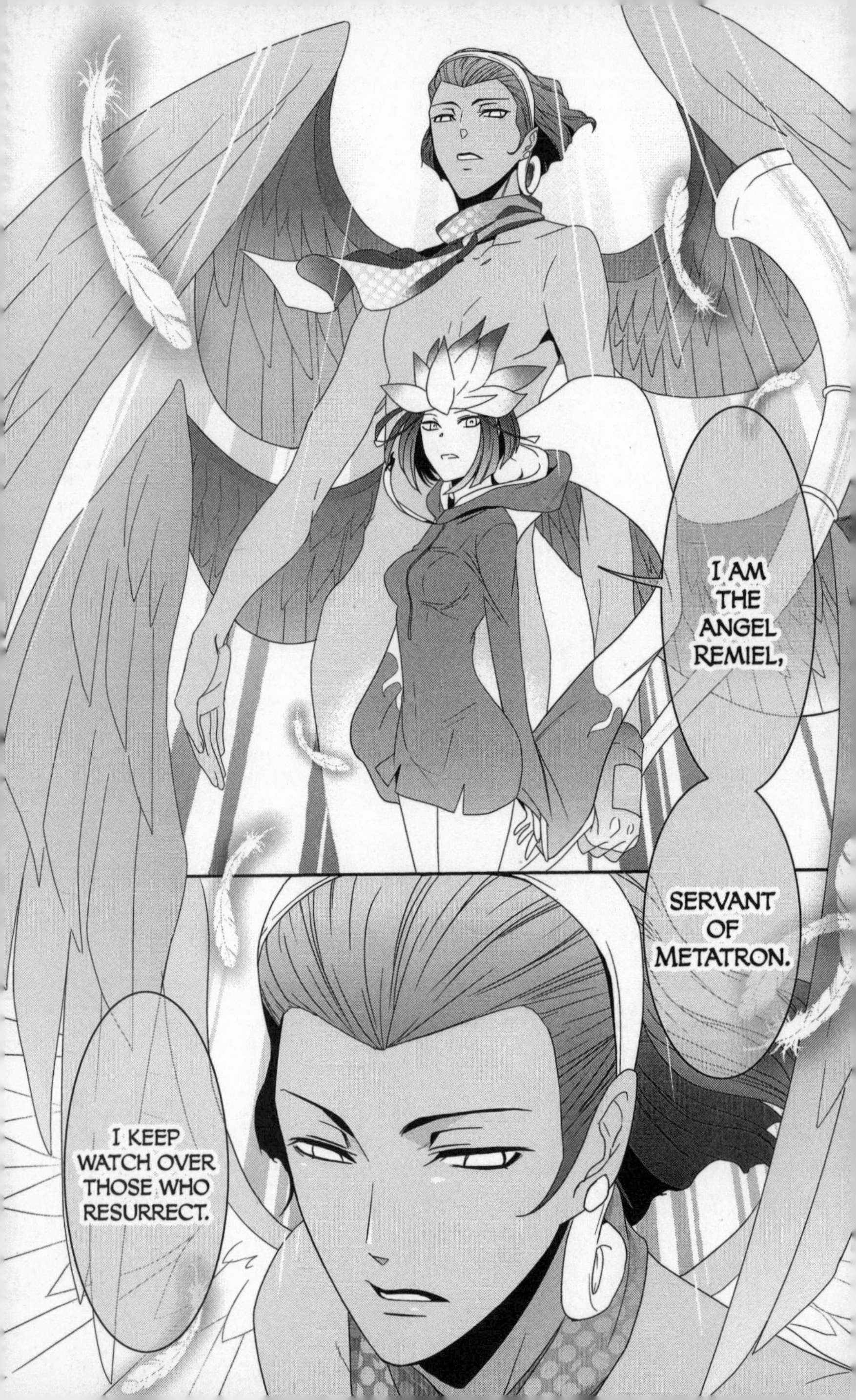
I AM THE ANGEL REMIEL,
SERVANT OF METATRON.
I KEEP WATCH OVER THOSE WHO RESURRECT.

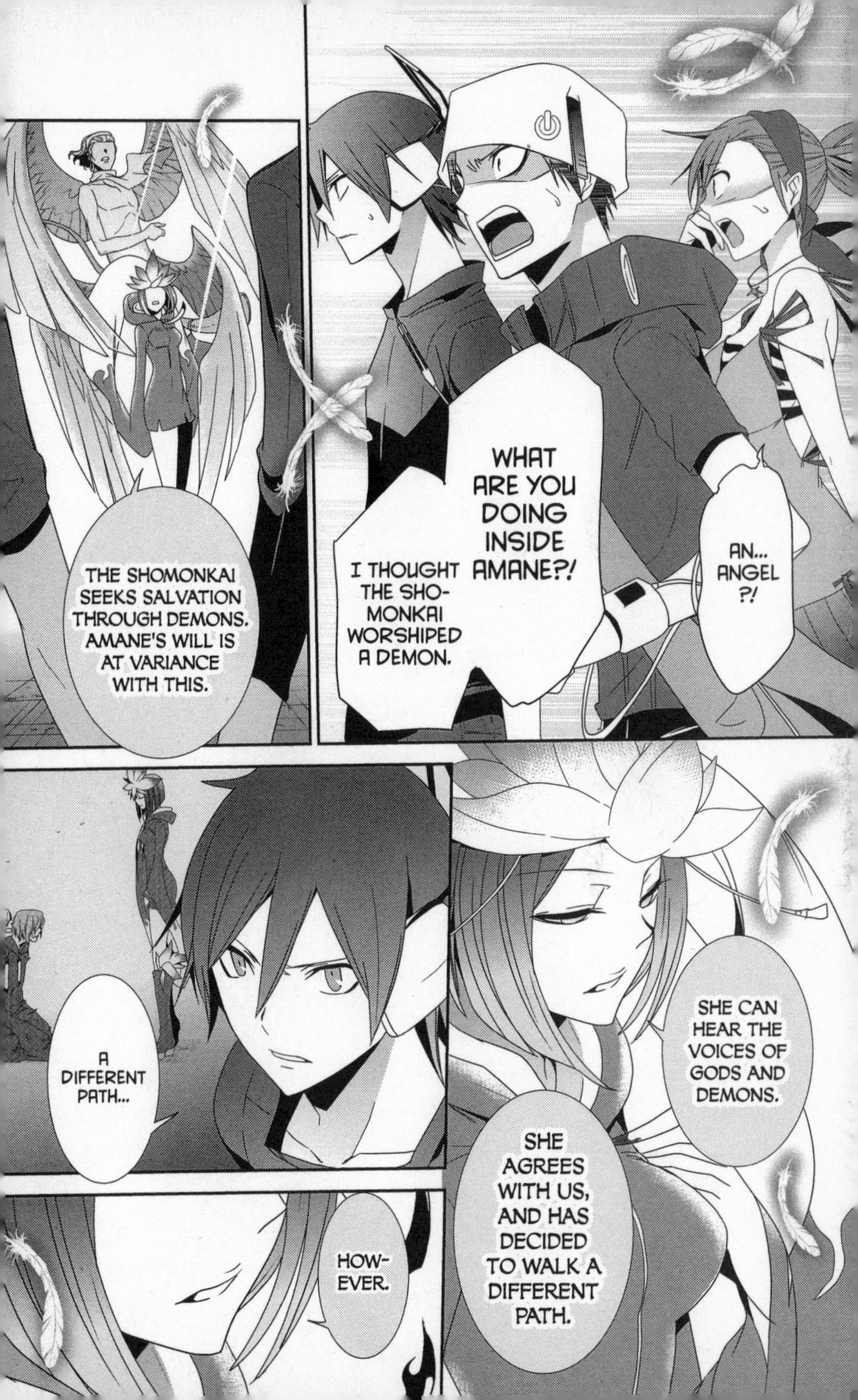
AN... ANGEL ?!
WHAT ARE YOU DOING INSIDE AMANE?!
I THOUGHT THE SHO-MONKAI WORSHIPED A DEMON.
THE SHOMONKAI SEEKS SALVATION THROUGH DEMONS. AMANE'S WILL IS AT VARIANCE WITH THIS.
SHE CAN HEAR THE VOICES OF GODS AND DEMONS.
SHE AGREES WITH US, AND HAS DECIDED TO WALK A DIFFERENT PATH.
A DIFFERENT PATH...
HOW-EVER.

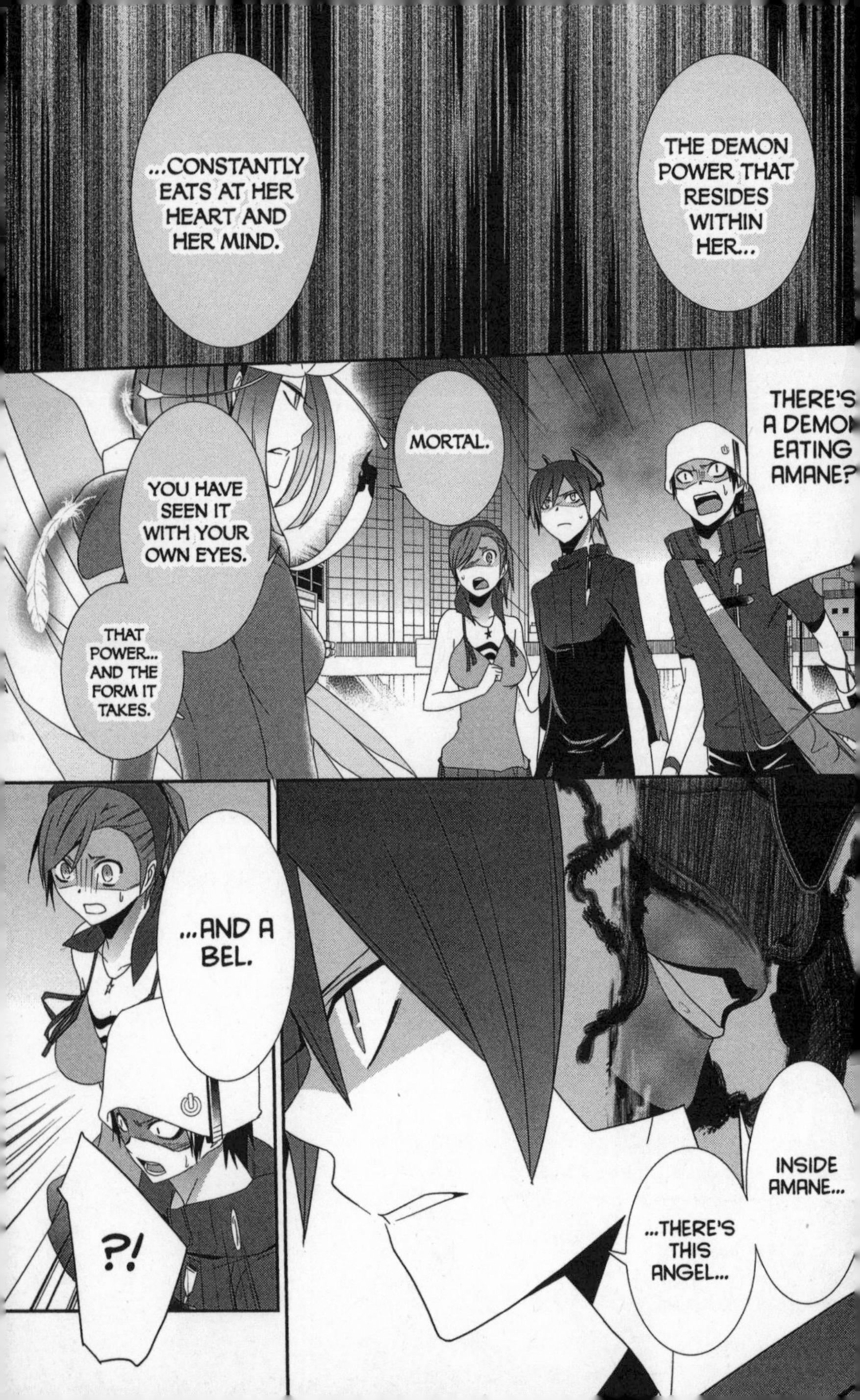
THE DEMON POWER THAT RESIDES WITHIN HER...
...CONSTANTLY EATS AT HER HEART AND HER MIND.
THERE'S A DEMON EATING AMANE?
MORTAL.
YOU HAVE SEEN IT WITH YOUR OWN EYES.
THAT POWER... AND THE FORM IT TAKES.
INSIDE AMANE...
...THERE'S THIS ANGEL...
...AND A BEL.
?!

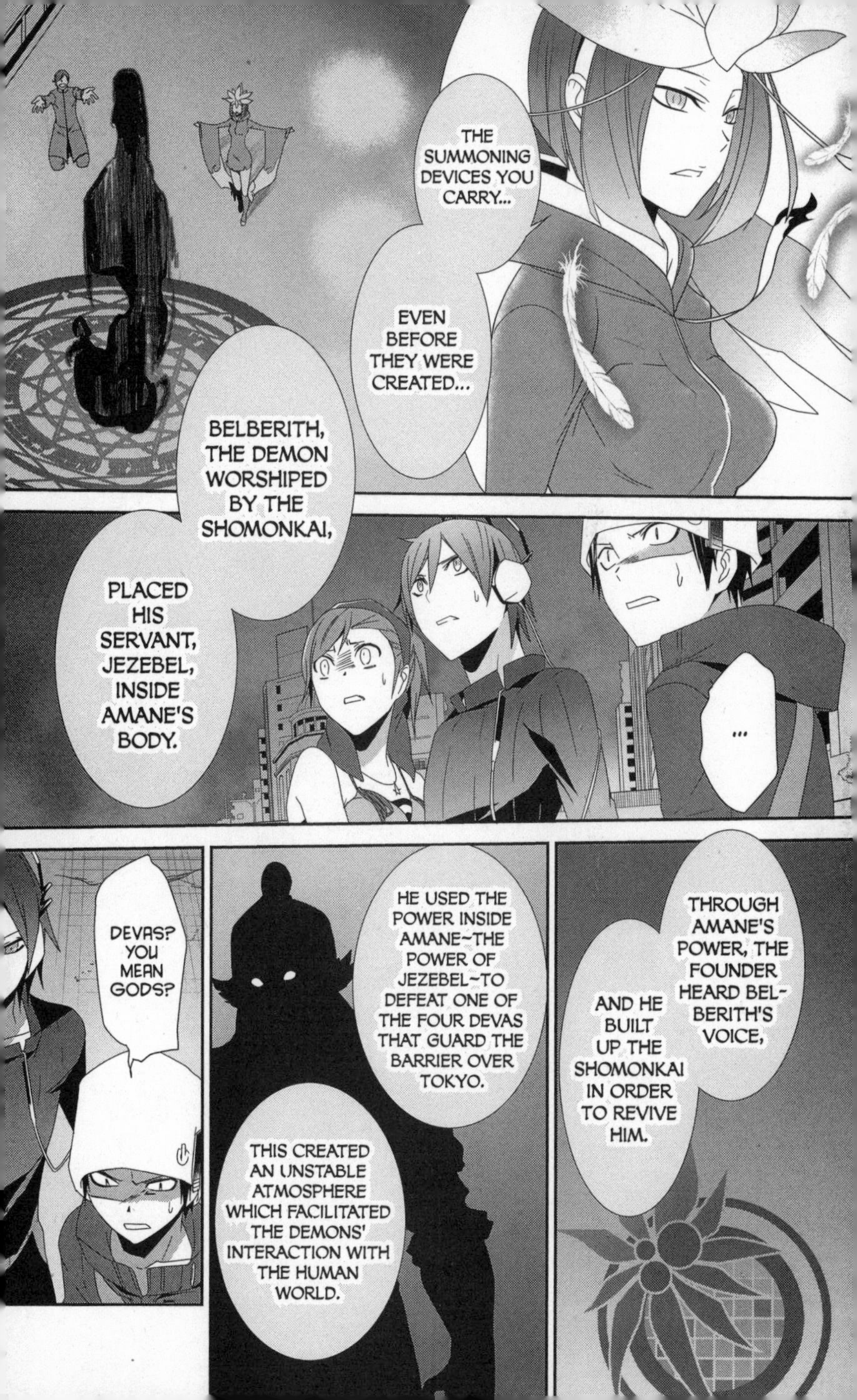
THE SUMMONING DEVICES YOU CARRY...
EVEN BEFORE THEY WERE CREATED...
BELBERITH, THE DEMON WORSHIPED BY THE SHOMONKAI,
PLACED HIS SERVANT, JEZEBEL, INSIDE AMANE'S BODY.
...
THROUGH AMANE'S POWER, THE FOUNDER HEARD BEL-BERITH'S VOICE,
AND HE BUILT UP THE SHOMONKAI IN ORDER TO REVIVE HIM.
HE USED THE POWER INSIDE AMANE~THE POWER OF JEZEBEL~TO DEFEAT ONE OF THE FOUR DEVAS THAT GUARD THE BARRIER OVER TOKYO.
THIS CREATED AN UNSTABLE ATMOSPHERE WHICH FACILITATED THE DEMONS' INTERACTION WITH THE HUMAN WORLD.
DEVAS? YOU MEAN GODS?

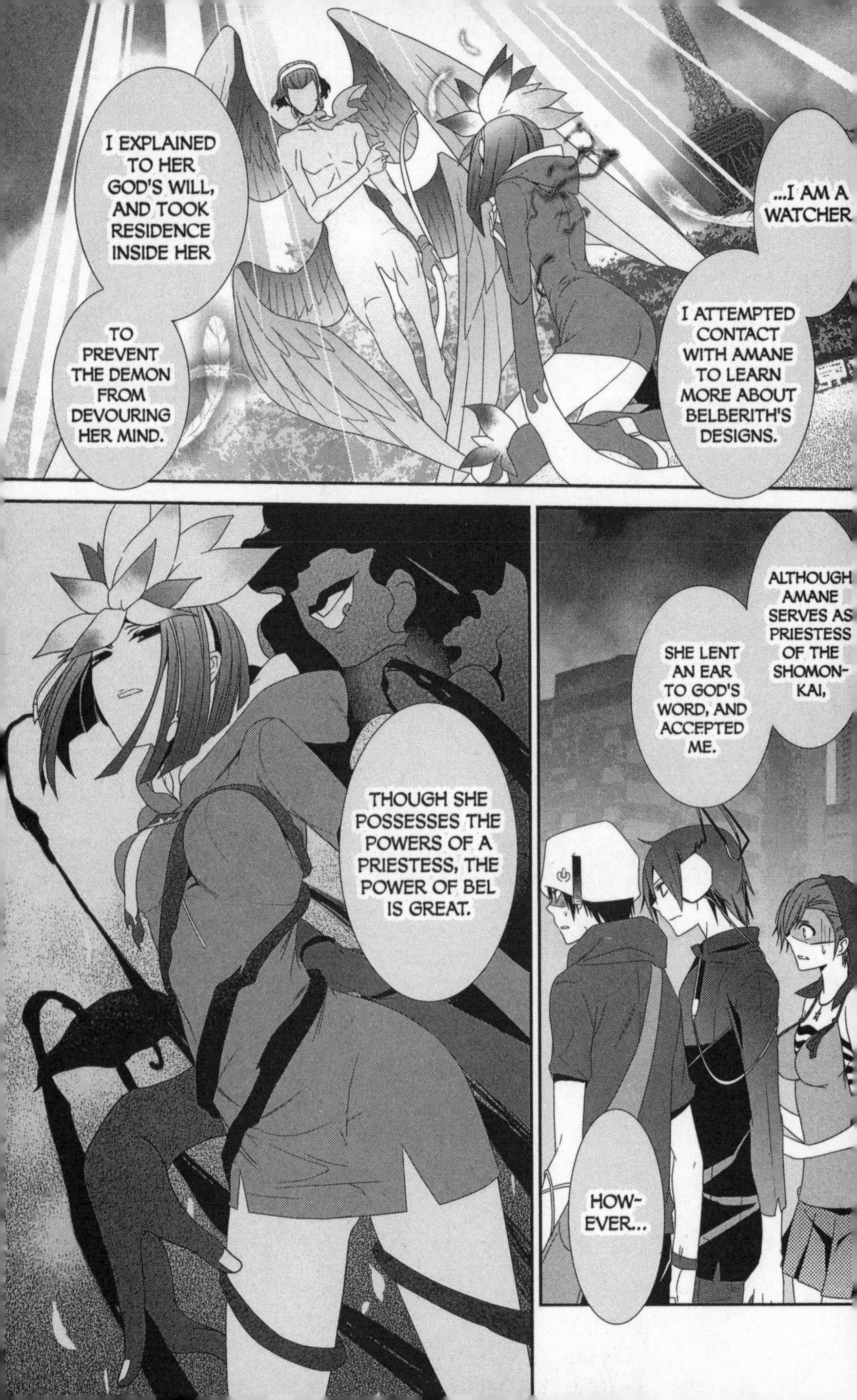
...I AM A WATCHER
I ATTEMPTED CONTACT WITH AMANE TO LEARN MORE ABOUT BELBERITH'S DESIGNS.
I EXPLAINED TO HER GOD'S WILL, AND TOOK RESIDENCE INSIDE HER
TO PREVENT THE DEMON FROM DEVOURING HER MIND.
ALTHOUGH AMANE SERVES AS PRIESTESS OF THE SHOMON-KAI,
SHE LENT AN EAR TO GOD'S WORD, AND ACCEPTED ME.
HOW-EVER...
THOUGH SHE POSSESSES THE POWERS OF A PRIESTESS, THE POWER OF BEL IS GREAT.

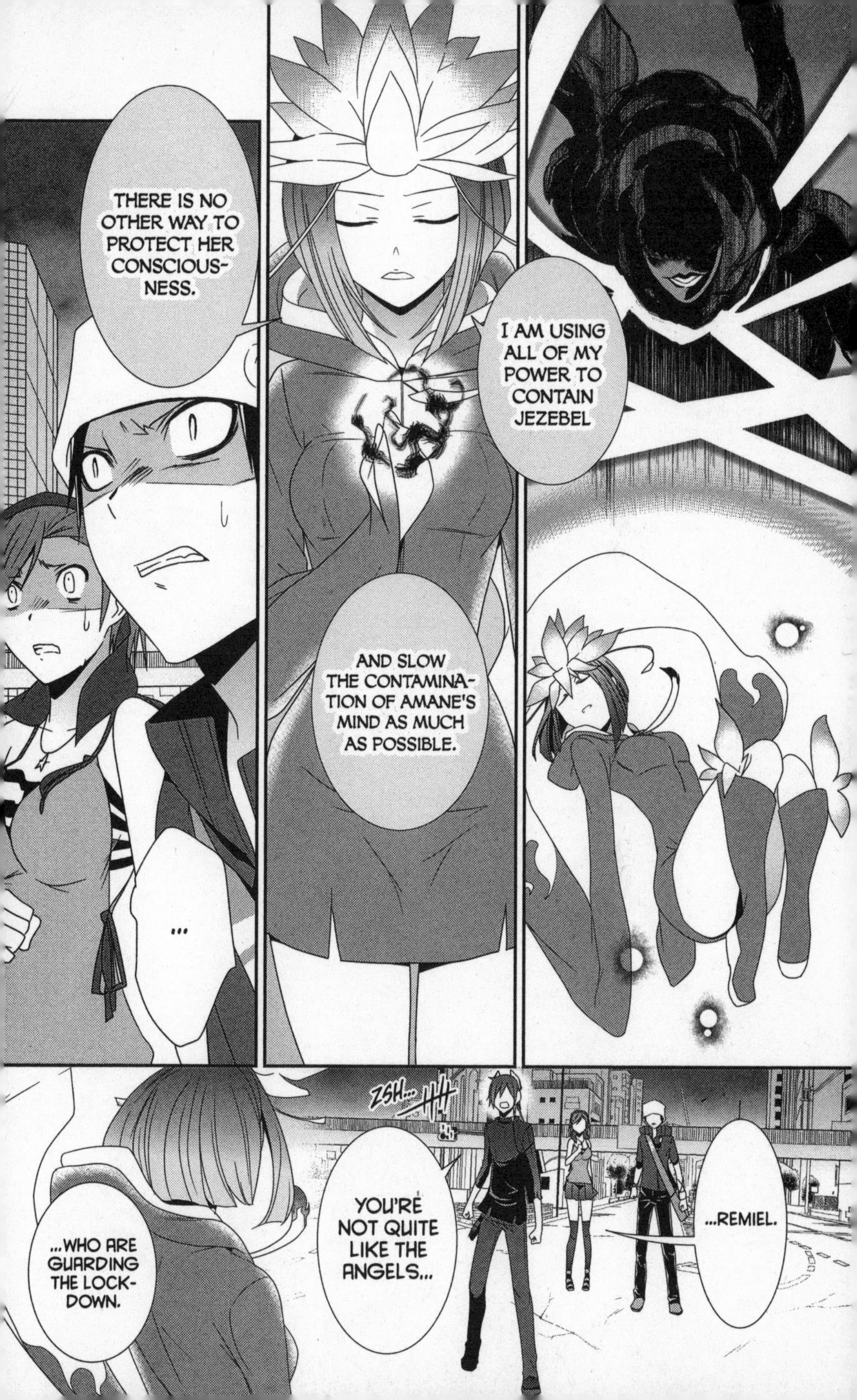
I AM USING ALL OF MY POWER TO CONTAIN JEZEBEL
AND SLOW THE CONTAMINATION OF AMANE'S MIND AS MUCH AS POSSIBLE.
THERE IS NO OTHER WAY TO PROTECT HER CONSCIOUSNESS.
...
...REMIEL.
ZSH...HH
YOU'RE NOT QUITE LIKE THE ANGELS...
...WHO ARE GUARDING THE LOCK-DOWN.

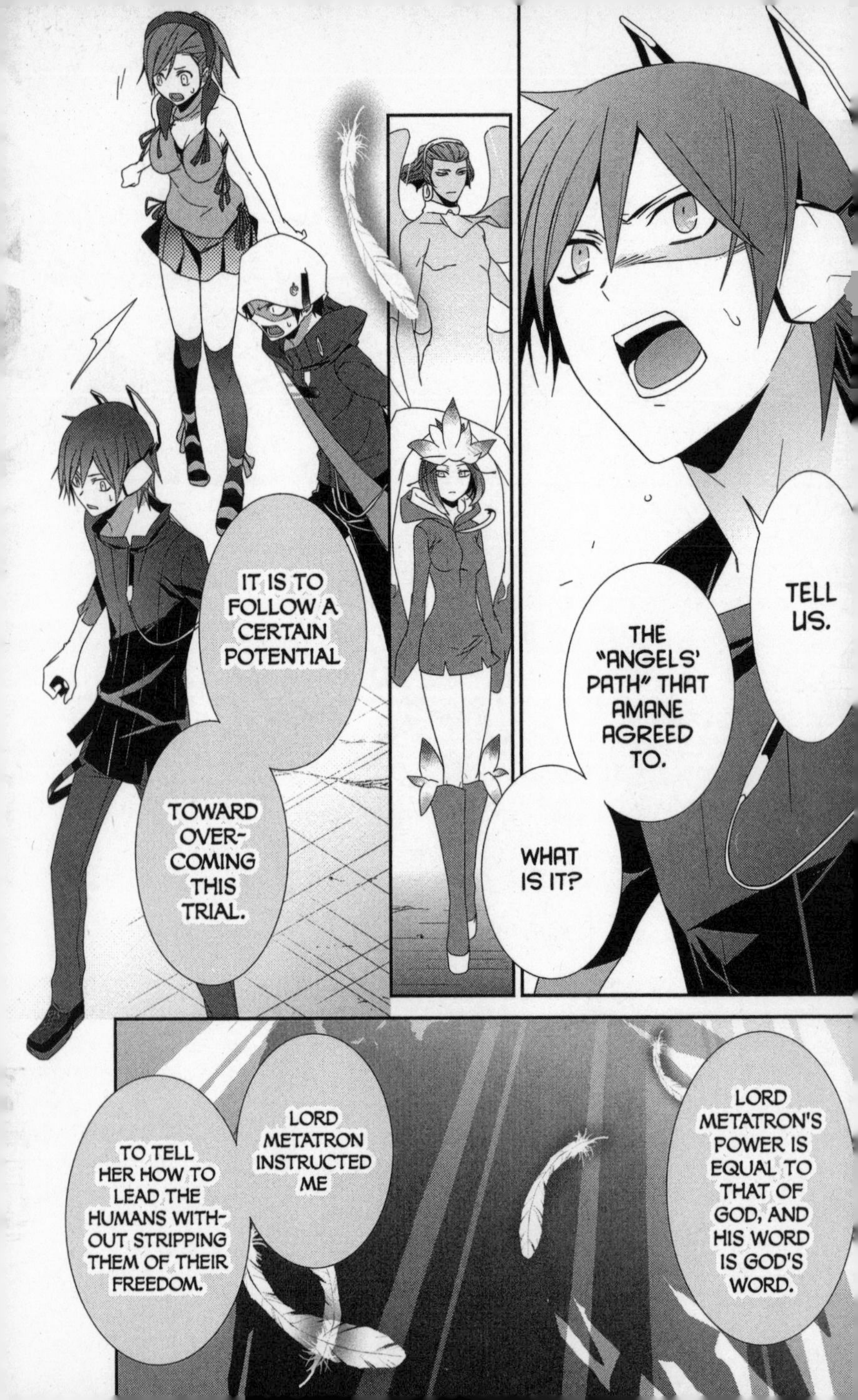
TELL US.
THE "ANGELS' PATH" THAT AMANE AGREED TO.
WHAT IS IT?
IT IS TO FOLLOW A CERTAIN POTENTIAL
TOWARD OVER-COMING THIS TRIAL.
LORD METATRON'S POWER IS EQUAL TO THAT OF GOD, AND HIS WORD IS GOD'S WORD.
LORD METATRON INSTRUCTED ME
TO TELL HER HOW TO LEAD THE HUMANS WITH-OUT STRIPPING THEM OF THEIR FREEDOM.

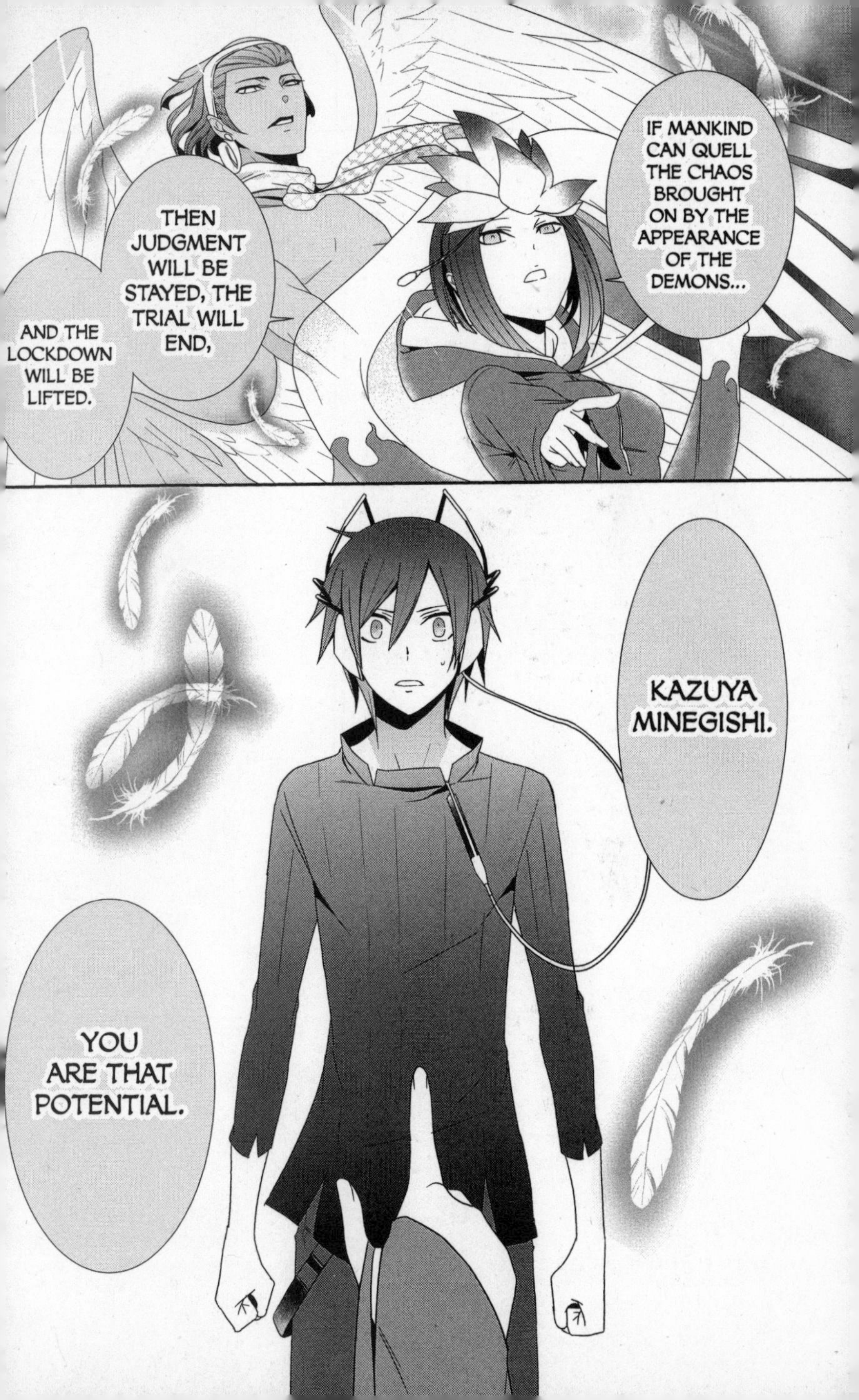
IF MANKIND CAN QUELL THE CHAOS BROUGHT ON BY THE APPEARANCE OF THE DEMONS...
THEN JUDGMENT WILL BE STAYED, THE TRIAL WILL END,
AND THE LOCKDOWN WILL BE LIFTED.
KAZUYA MINEGISHI.
YOU ARE THAT POTENTIAL.

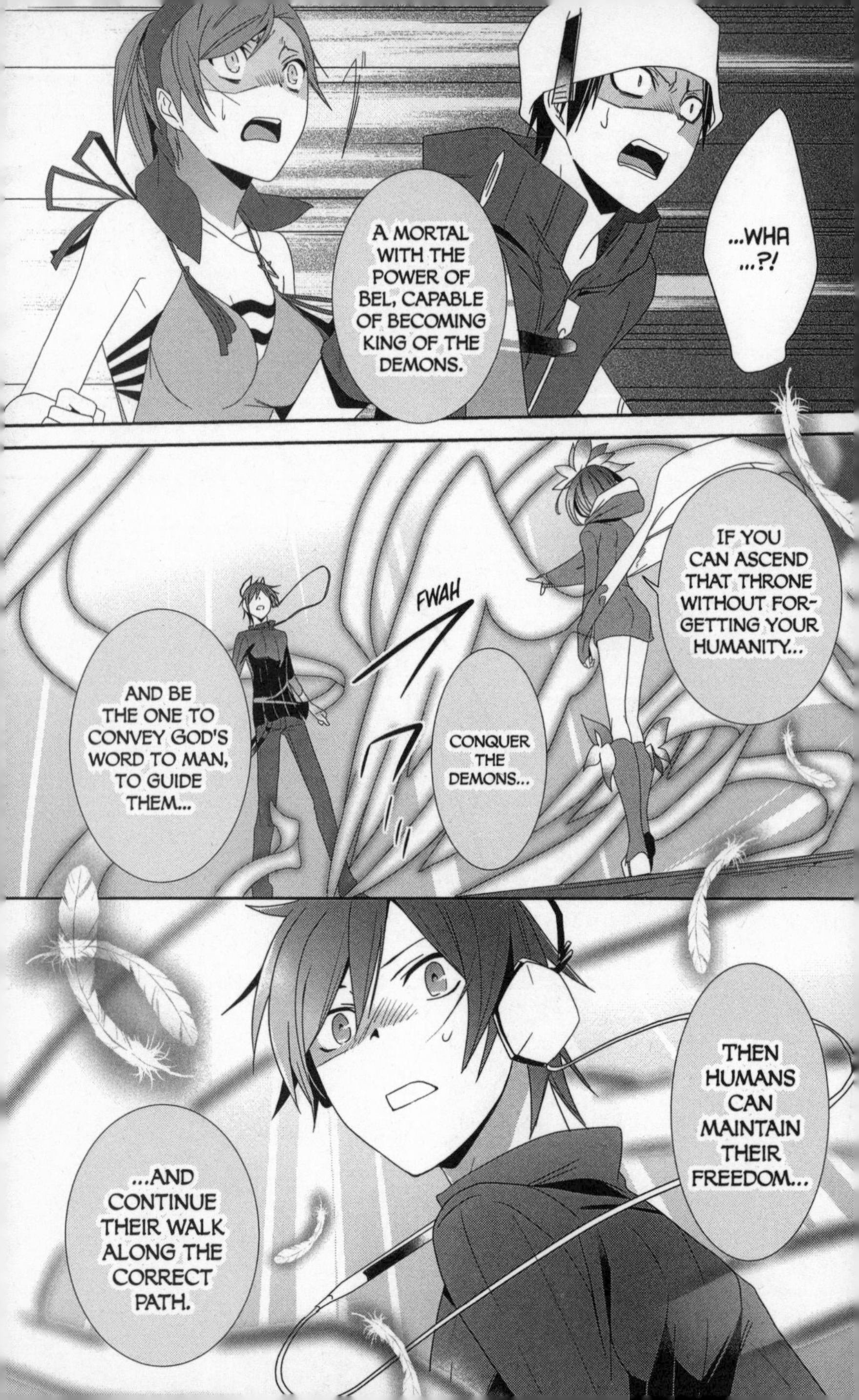
...WHA ...?!
A MORTAL WITH THE POWER OF BEL, CAPABLE OF BECOMING KING OF THE DEMONS.
IF YOU CAN ASCEND THAT THRONE WITHOUT FOR-GETTING YOUR HUMANITY...
FWAH
CONQUER THE DEMONS...
AND BE THE ONE TO CONVEY GOD'S WORD TO MAN, TO GUIDE THEM...
THEN HUMANS CAN MAINTAIN THEIR FREEDOM...
...AND CONTINUE THEIR WALK ALONG THE CORRECT PATH.

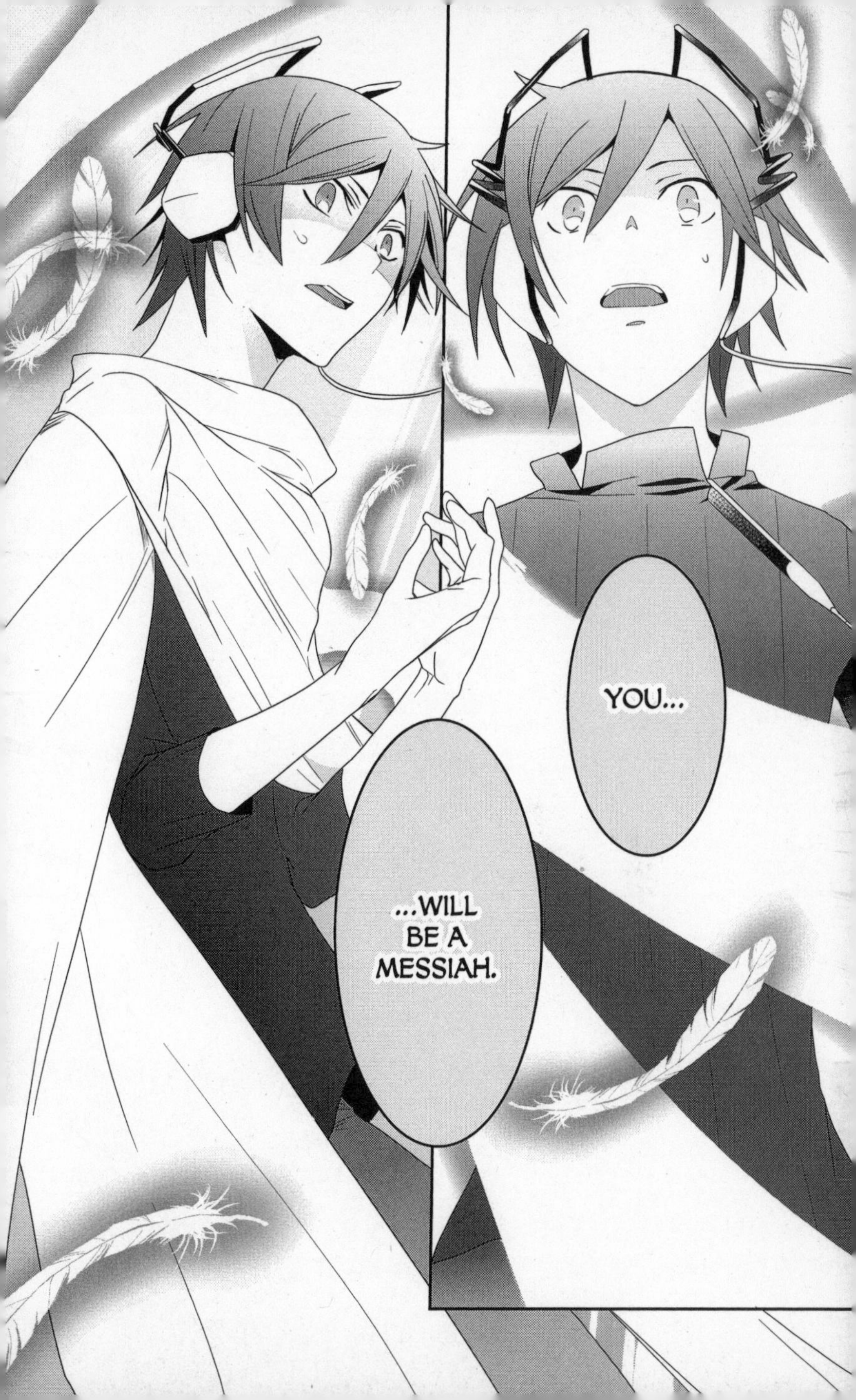
YOU...
...WILL BE A MESSIAH.

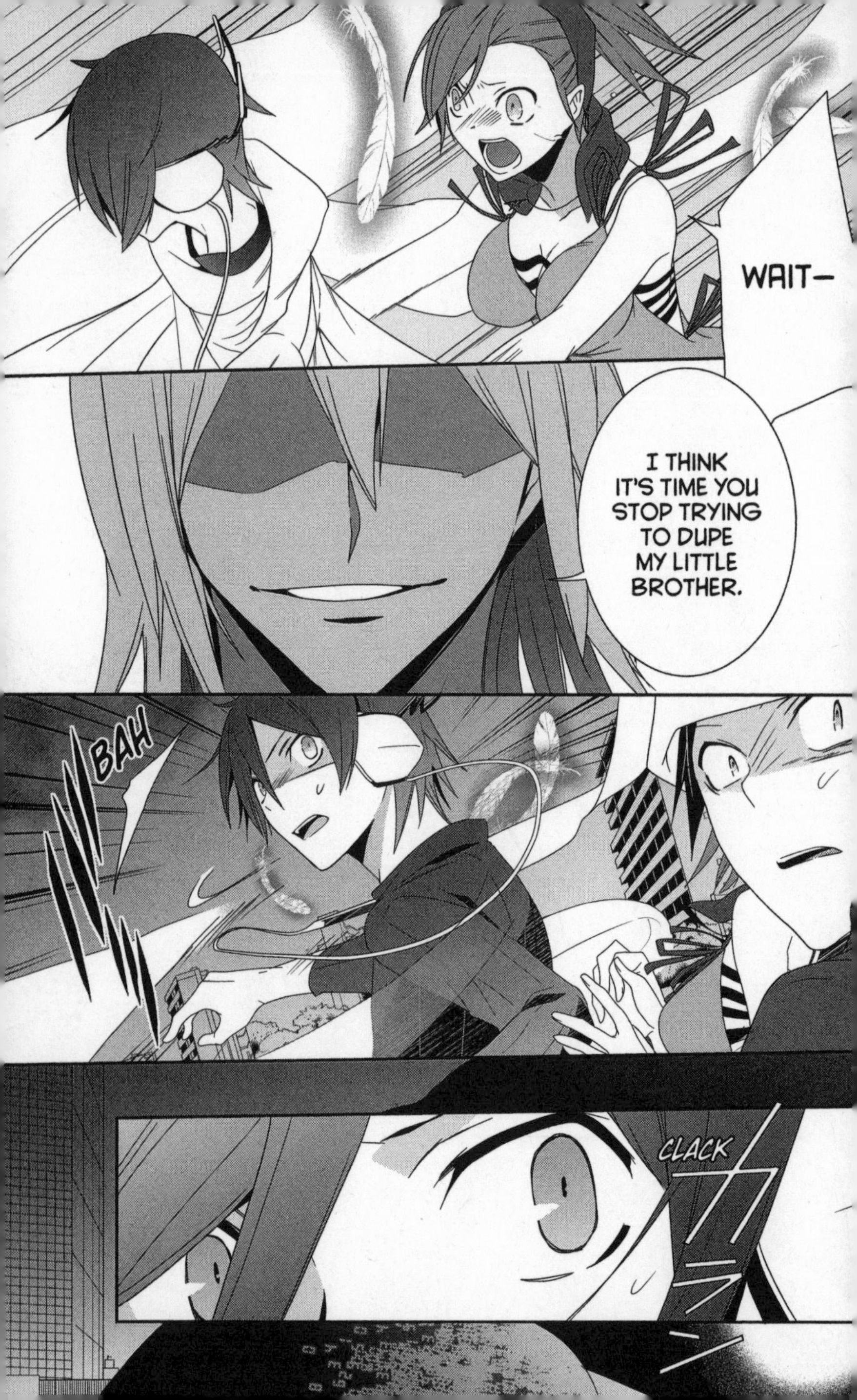
WAIT–
I THINK IT'S TIME YOU STOP TRYING TO DUPE MY LITTLE BROTHER.
BAH
CLACK

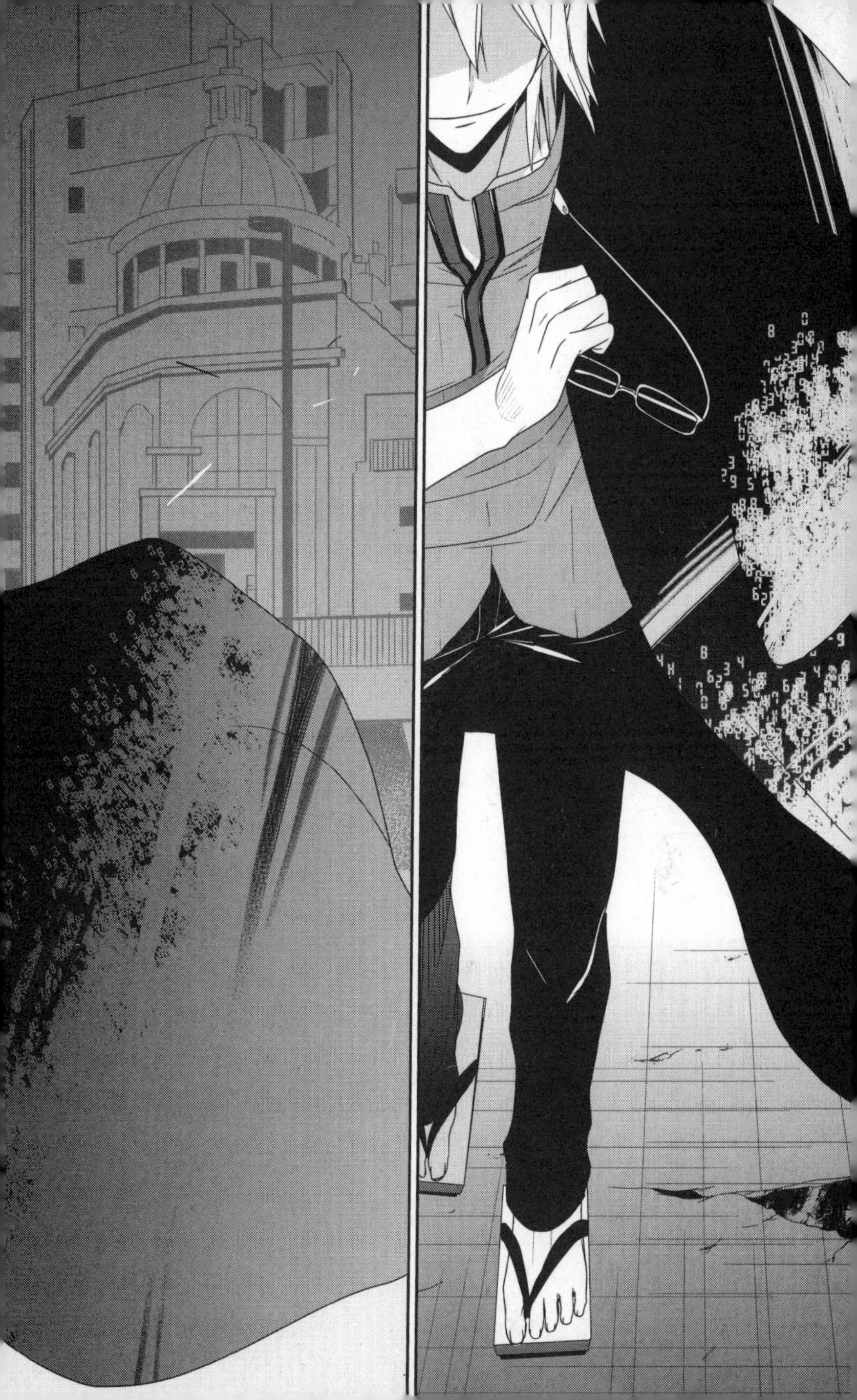

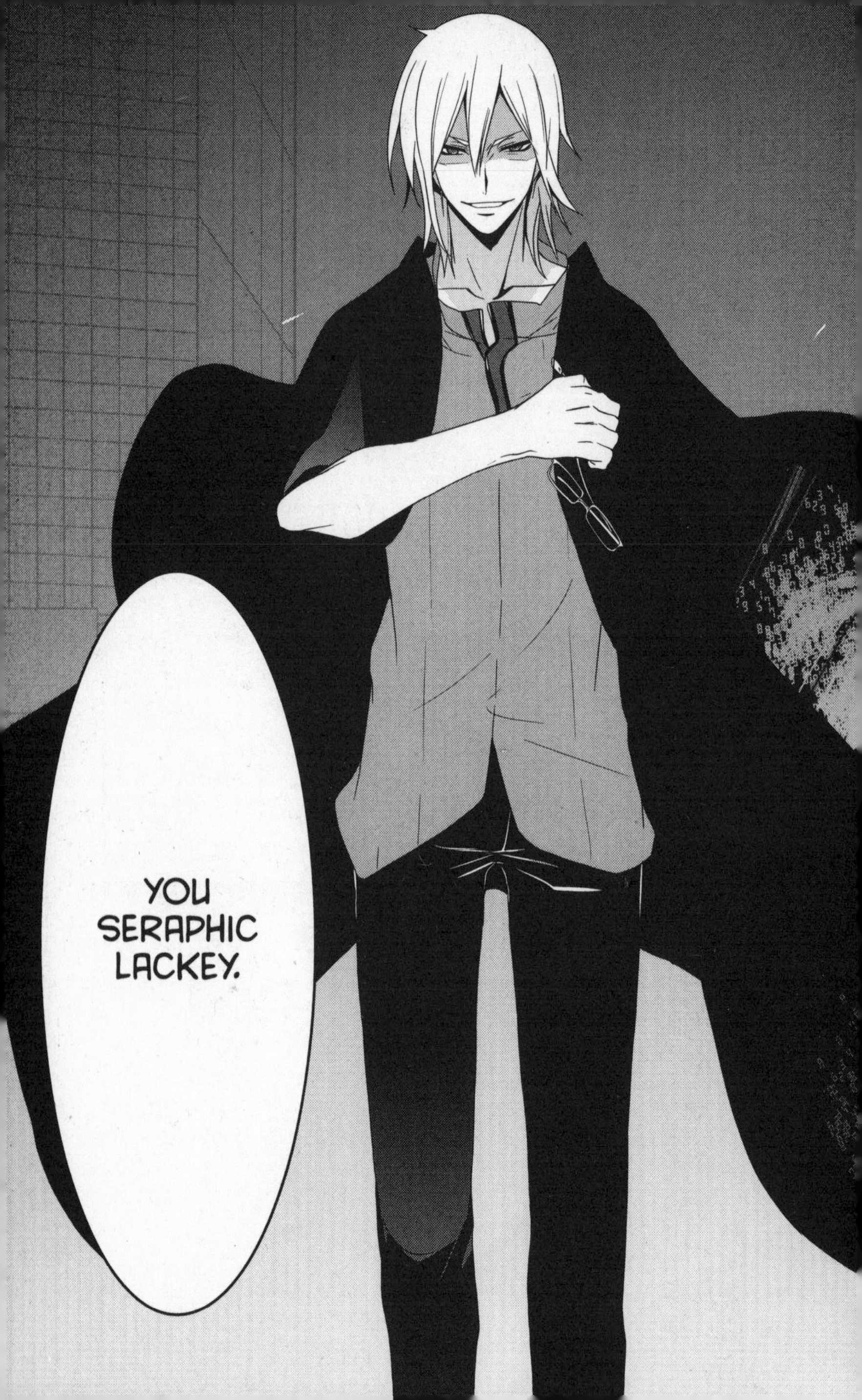
YOU SERAPHIC LACKEY.

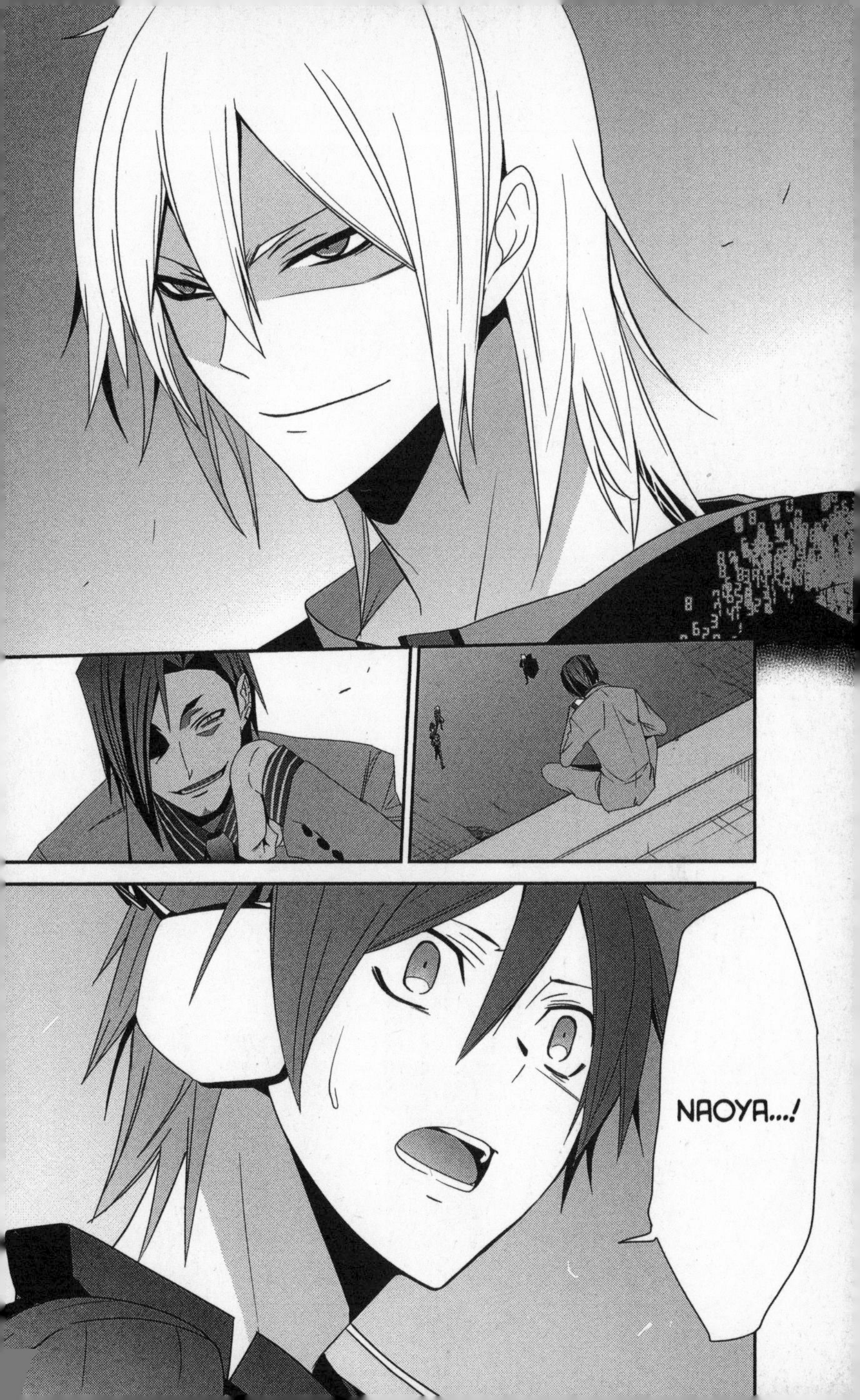
NAOYA...!

PROFILE

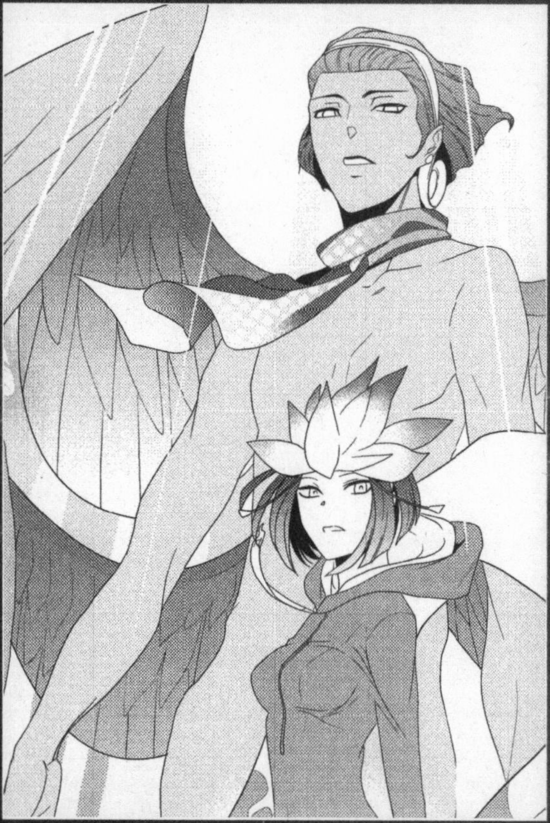

REMIEL

ALSO KNOWN AS RAMIEL. ONE OF THE SEVEN ARCHANGELS THAT SERVES GOD, HIS DUTY IS TO CARRY THEIR INSTRUCTIONS ABROAD. THE WORDS HE CONVEYS APPEAR BEFORE MANKIND AS "VISIONS." HE KNOWS WHICH SOULS WILL BE SAVED AND WHICH WILL BE DESTROYED WHEN THE FINAL JUDGMENT COMES. HE IS RESPONSIBLE FOR GUIDING THE SOULS THAT WILL BE SAVED.

DEVIL SURVIVOR
デビルサバイバー

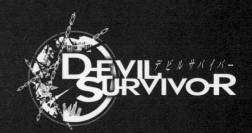

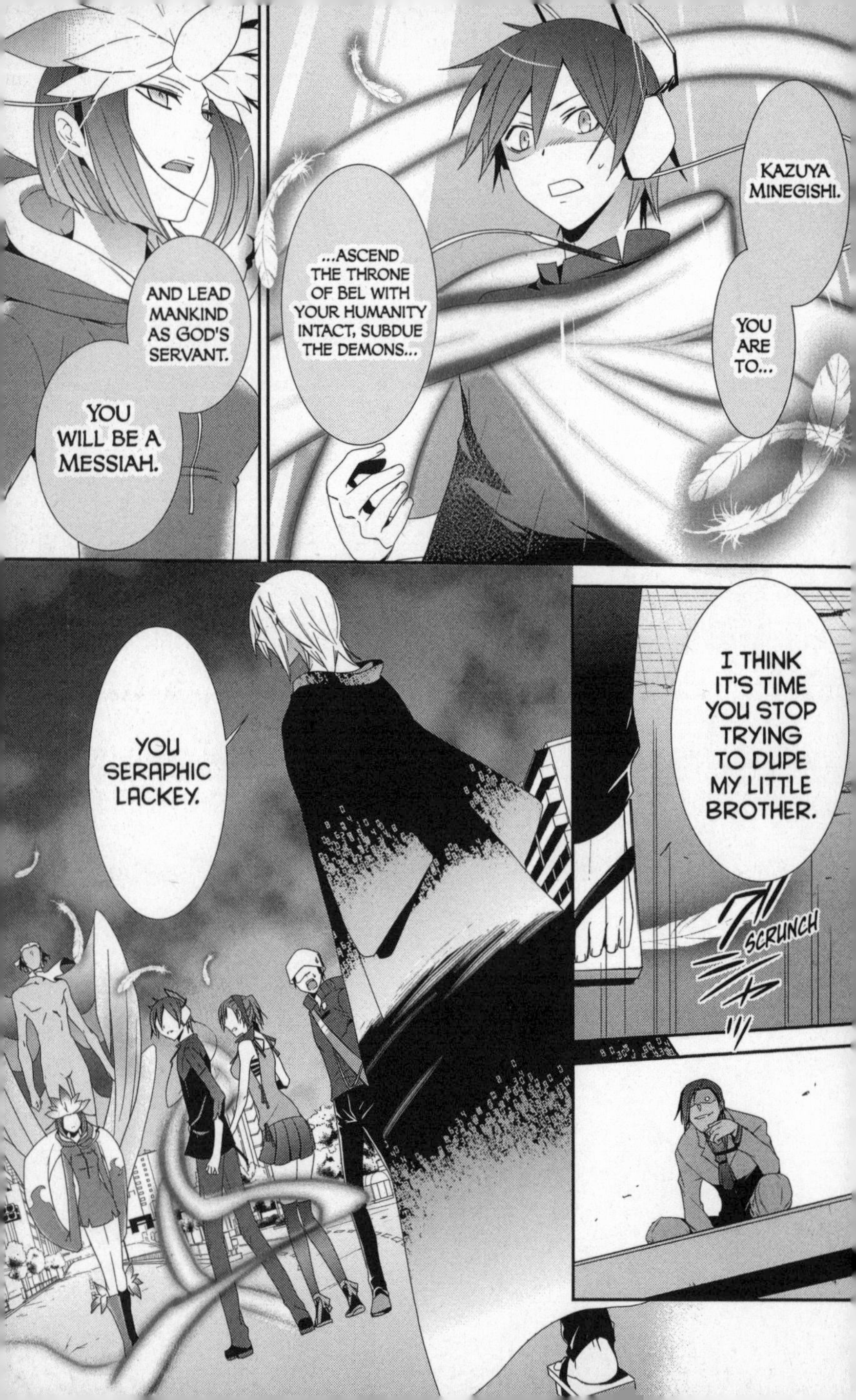

KAZUYA MINEGISHI.
YOU ARE TO...
...ASCEND THE THRONE OF BEL WITH YOUR HUMANITY INTACT, SUBDUE THE DEMONS...
AND LEAD MANKIND AS GOD'S SERVANT.
YOU WILL BE A MESSIAH.
I THINK IT'S TIME YOU STOP TRYING TO DUPE MY LITTLE BROTHER.
SCRUNCH
YOU SERAPHIC LACKEY.

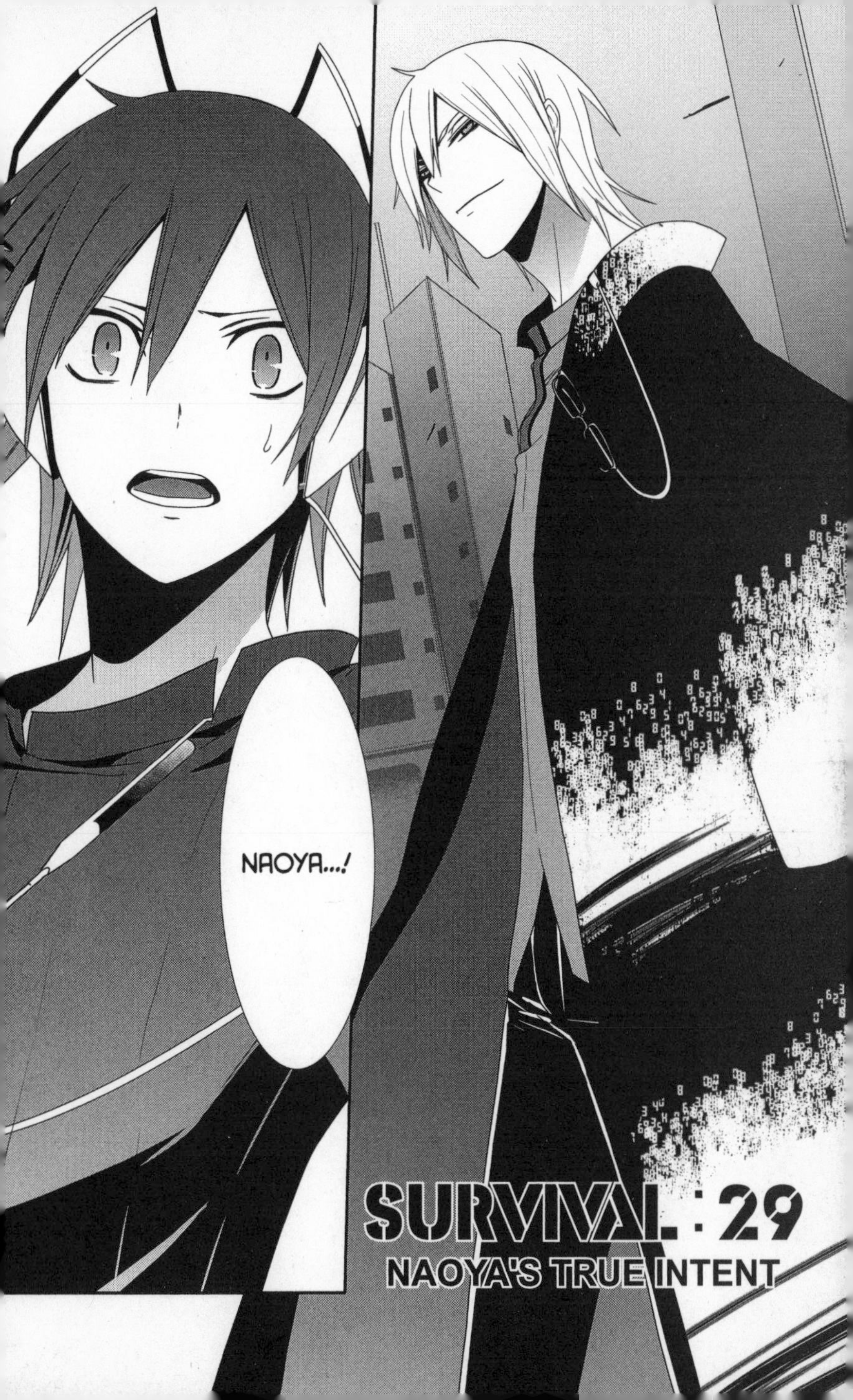
NAOYA...!
SURVIVAL : 29
NAOYA'S TRUE INTENT

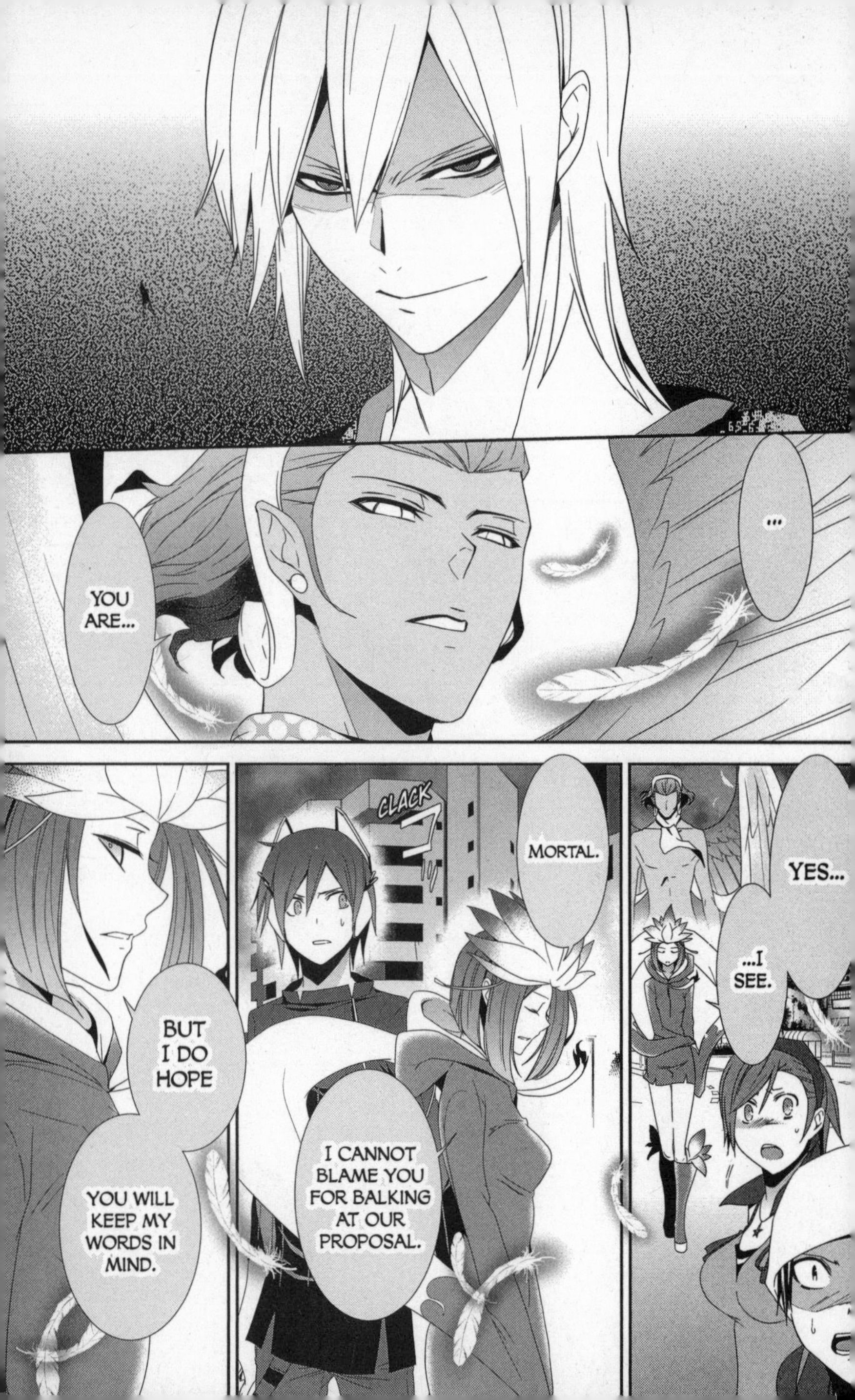
...
YOU ARE...
YES...
...I SEE.
CLACK
MORTAL.
I CANNOT BLAME YOU FOR BALKING AT OUR PROPOSAL.
BUT I DO HOPE
YOU WILL KEEP MY WORDS IN MIND.

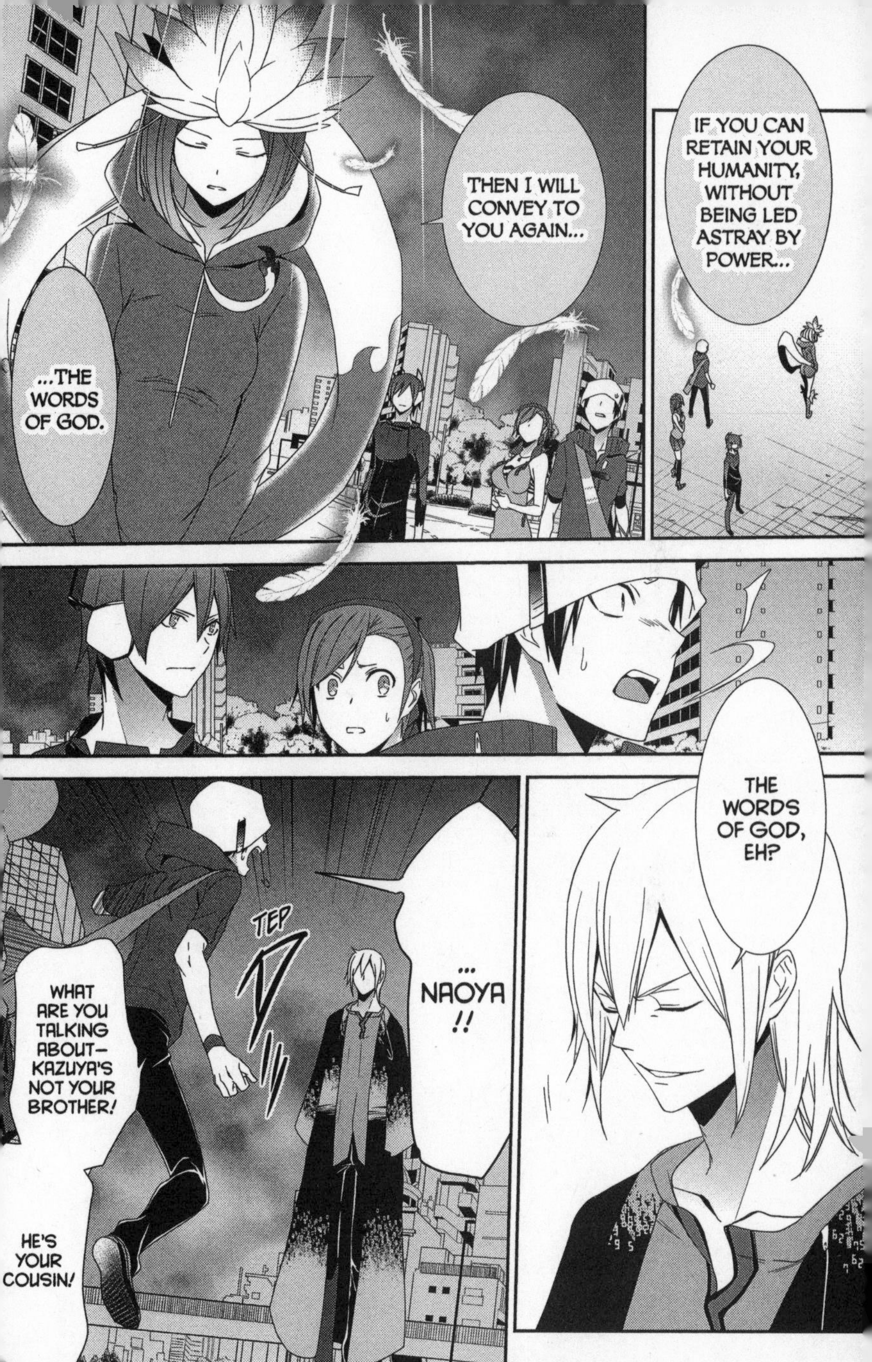
IF YOU CAN RETAIN YOUR HUMANITY, WITHOUT BEING LED ASTRAY BY POWER...
THEN I WILL CONVEY TO YOU AGAIN...
...THE WORDS OF GOD.
THE WORDS OF GOD, EH?
...NAOYA!!
TEP
WHAT ARE YOU TALKING ABOUT—KAZUYA'S NOT YOUR BROTHER!
HE'S YOUR COUSIN!

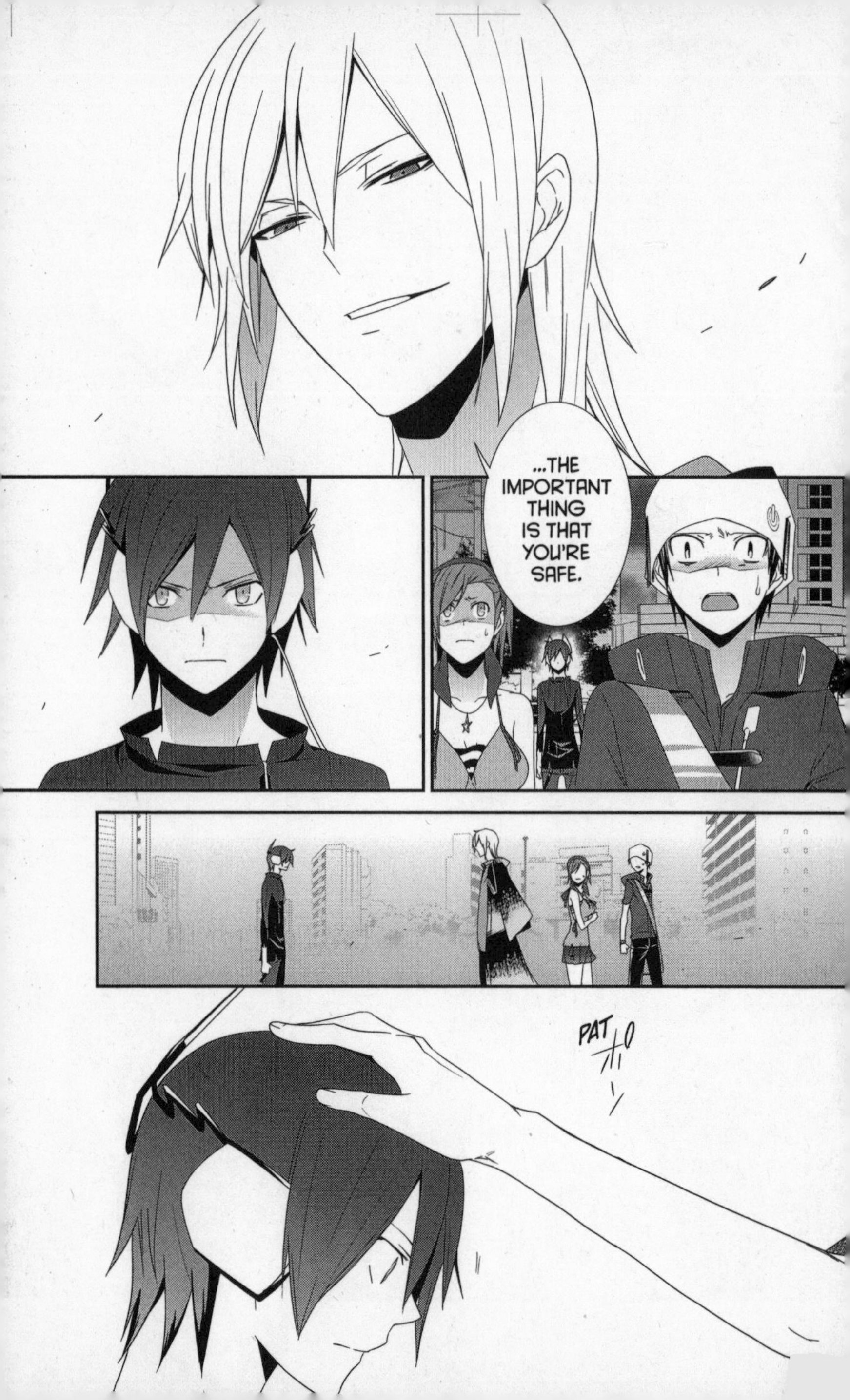
...THE IMPORTANT THING IS THAT YOU'RE SAFE.
PAT

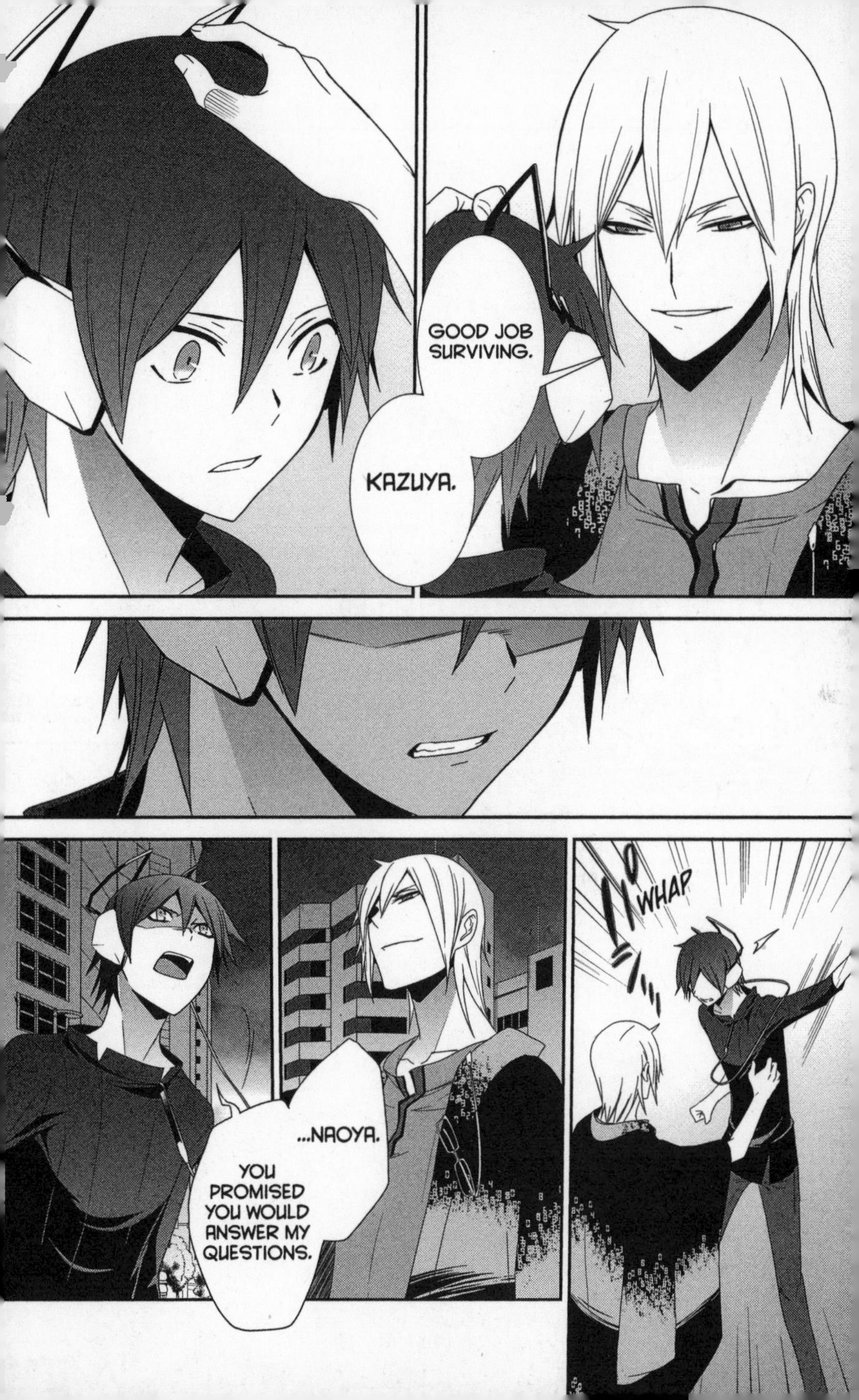
GOOD JOB SURVIVING.
KAZUYA.
WHAP
...NAOYA.
YOU PROMISED YOU WOULD ANSWER MY QUESTIONS.

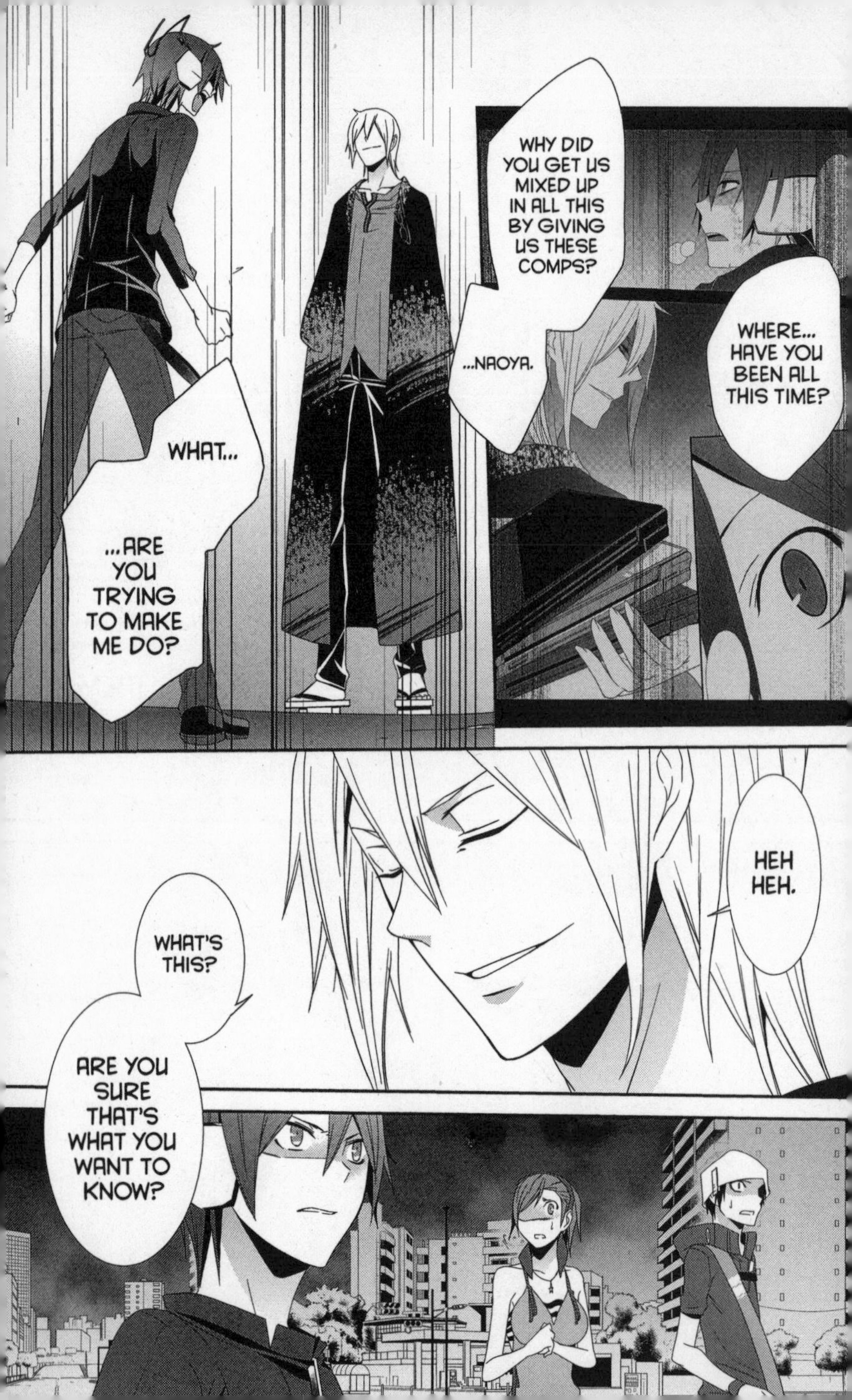
WHY DID YOU GET US MIXED UP IN ALL THIS BY GIVING US THESE COMPS?
WHERE... HAVE YOU BEEN ALL THIS TIME?
...NAOYA.
WHAT...
...ARE YOU TRYING TO MAKE ME DO?
HEH HEH.
WHAT'S THIS?
ARE YOU SURE THAT'S WHAT YOU WANT TO KNOW?

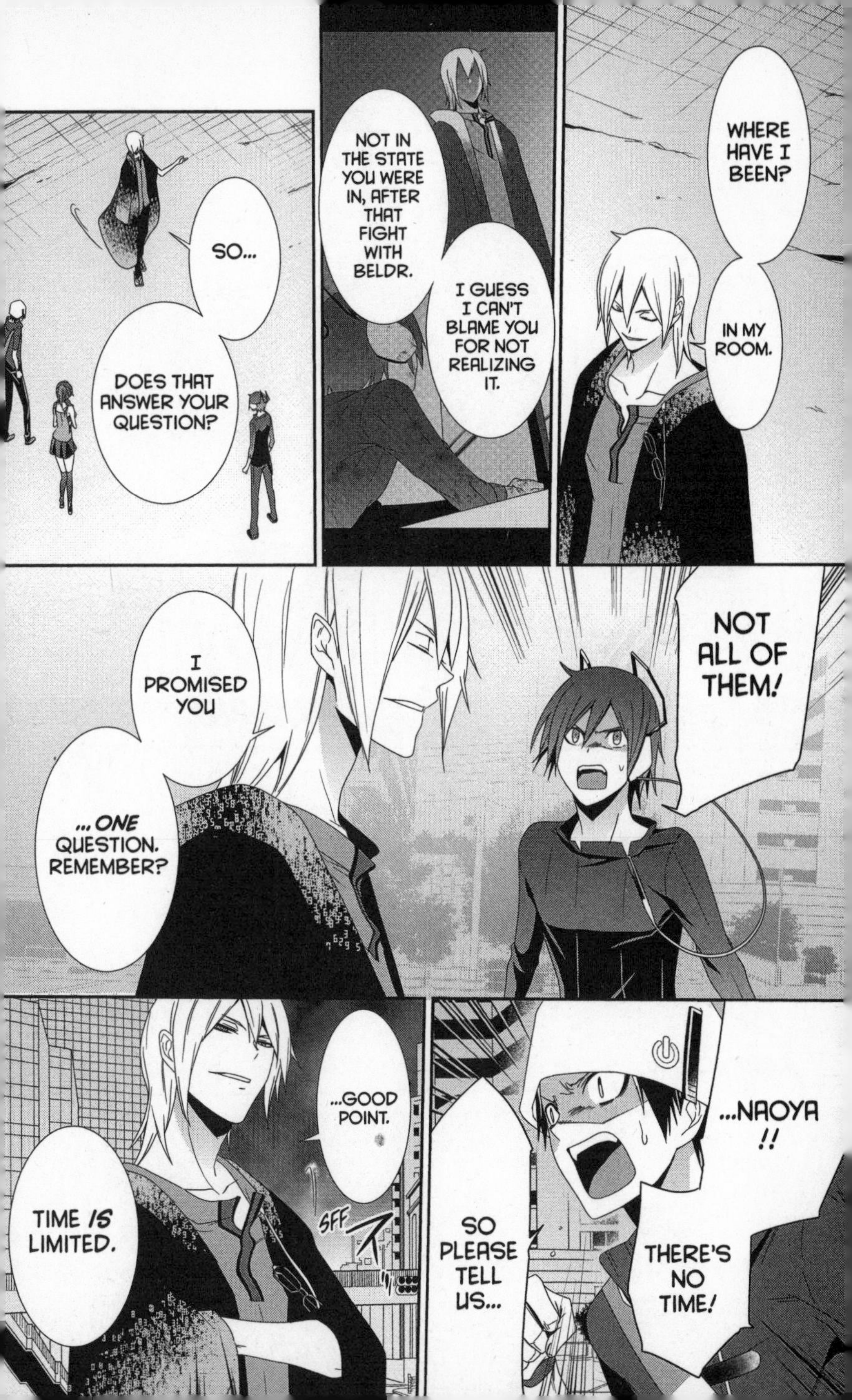
WHERE HAVE I BEEN?
IN MY ROOM.
NOT IN THE STATE YOU WERE IN, AFTER THAT FIGHT WITH BELDR.
I GUESS I CAN'T BLAME YOU FOR NOT REALIZING IT.
SO...
DOES THAT ANSWER YOUR QUESTION?
NOT ALL OF THEM!
I PROMISED YOU
...*ONE* QUESTION. REMEMBER?
...NAOYA!!
THERE'S NO TIME!
SO PLEASE TELL US...
...GOOD POINT.
SFF
TIME *IS* LIMITED.

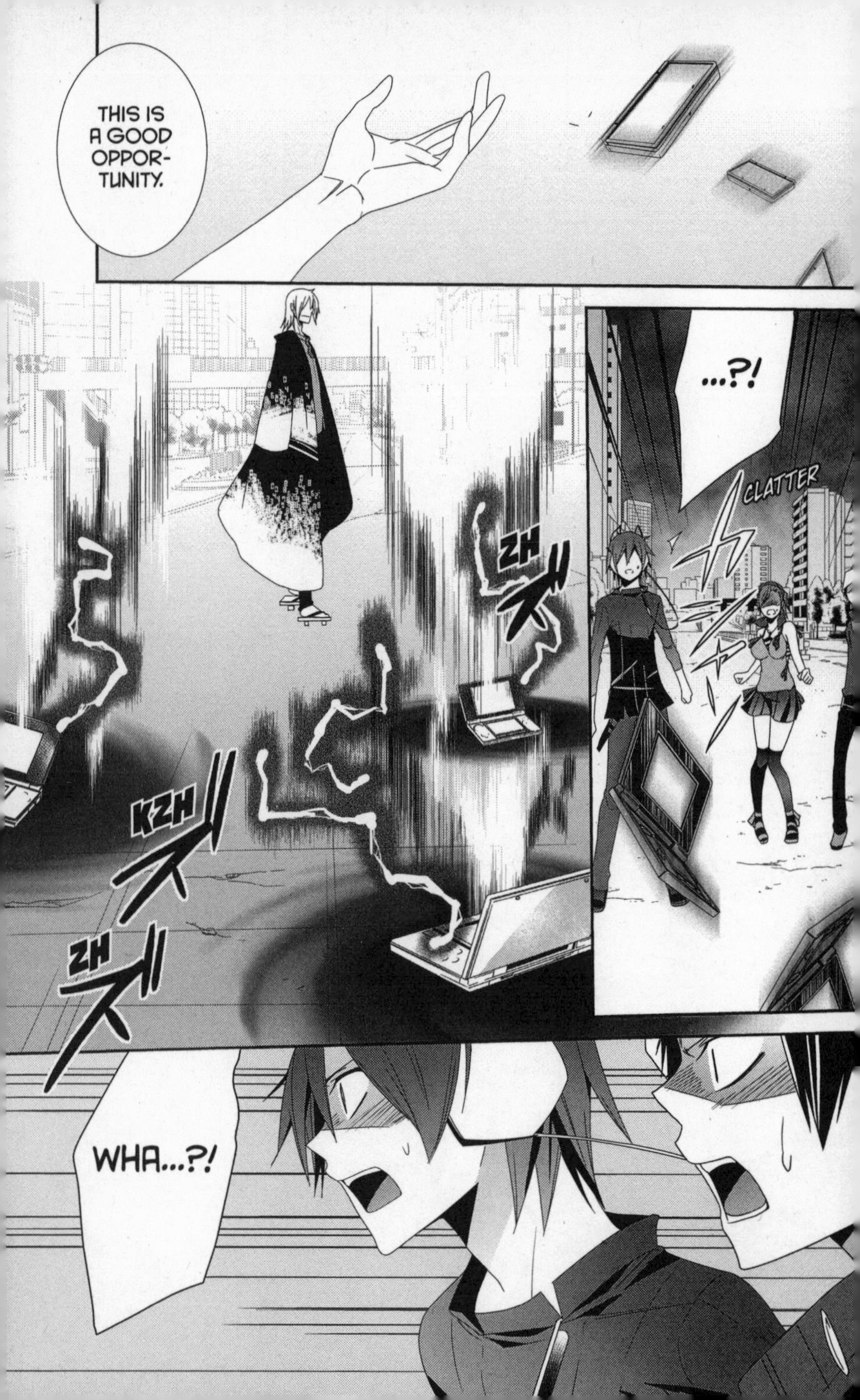
THIS IS A GOOD OPPORTUNITY.
...?!
CLATTER
ZH
KZH
ZH
WHA...?!

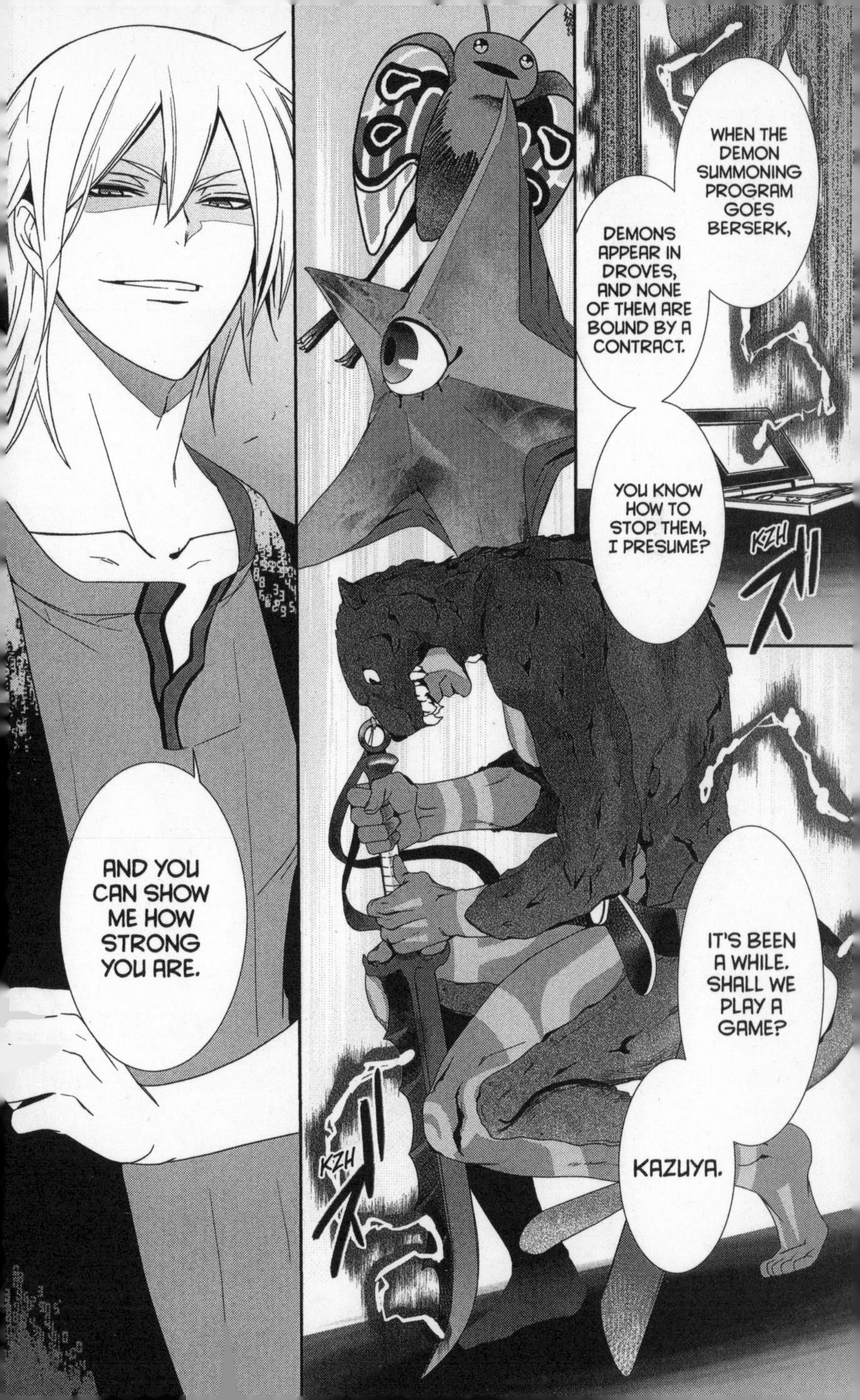
WHEN THE DEMON SUMMONING PROGRAM GOES BERSERK,
DEMONS APPEAR IN DROVES, AND NONE OF THEM ARE BOUND BY A CONTRACT.
YOU KNOW HOW TO STOP THEM, I PRESUME?
KZH
IT'S BEEN A WHILE. SHALL WE PLAY A GAME?
KAZUYA.
KZH
AND YOU CAN SHOW ME HOW STRONG YOU ARE.

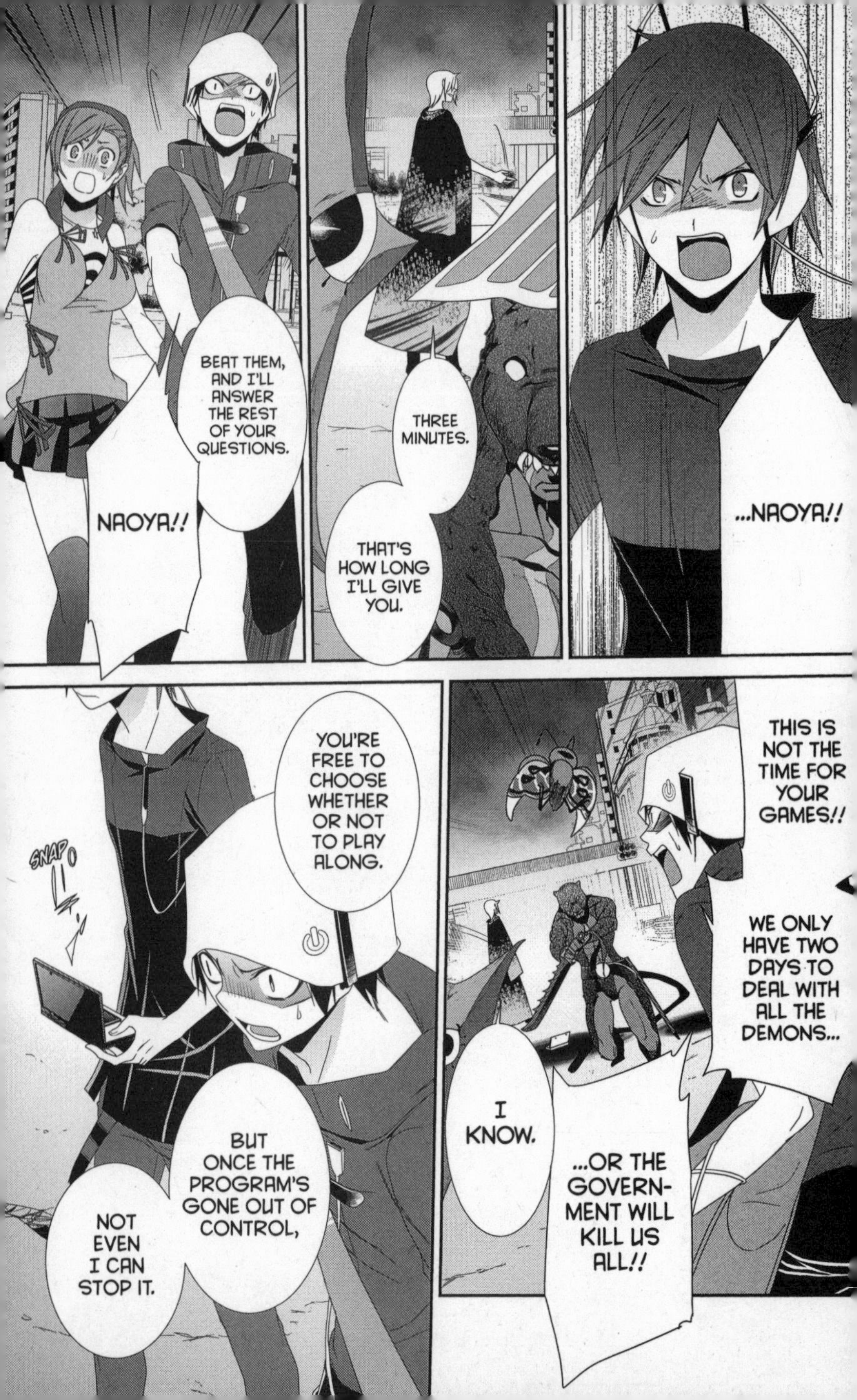
...NAOYA!!
THREE MINUTES.
THAT'S HOW LONG I'LL GIVE YOU.
BEAT THEM, AND I'LL ANSWER THE REST OF YOUR QUESTIONS.
NAOYA!!
THIS IS NOT THE TIME FOR YOUR GAMES!!
WE ONLY HAVE TWO DAYS TO DEAL WITH ALL THE DEMONS...
...OR THE GOVERNMENT WILL KILL US ALL!!
I KNOW.
YOU'RE FREE TO CHOOSE WHETHER OR NOT TO PLAY ALONG.
SNAP
BUT ONCE THE PROGRAM'S GONE OUT OF CONTROL,
NOT EVEN I CAN STOP IT.

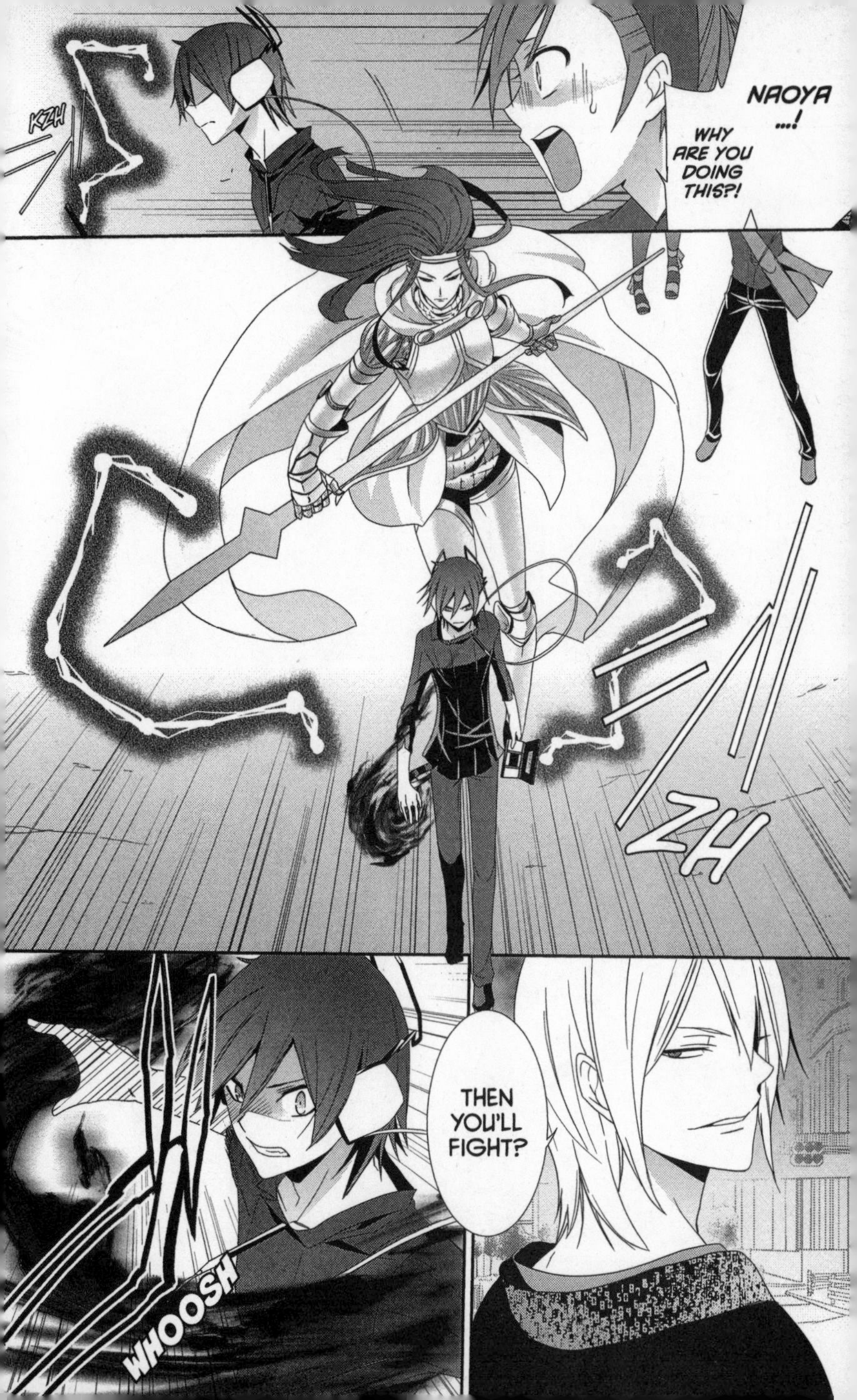
NAOYA ...!
WHY ARE YOU DOING THIS?!
KZH
ZH
THEN YOU'LL FIGHT?
WHOOSH

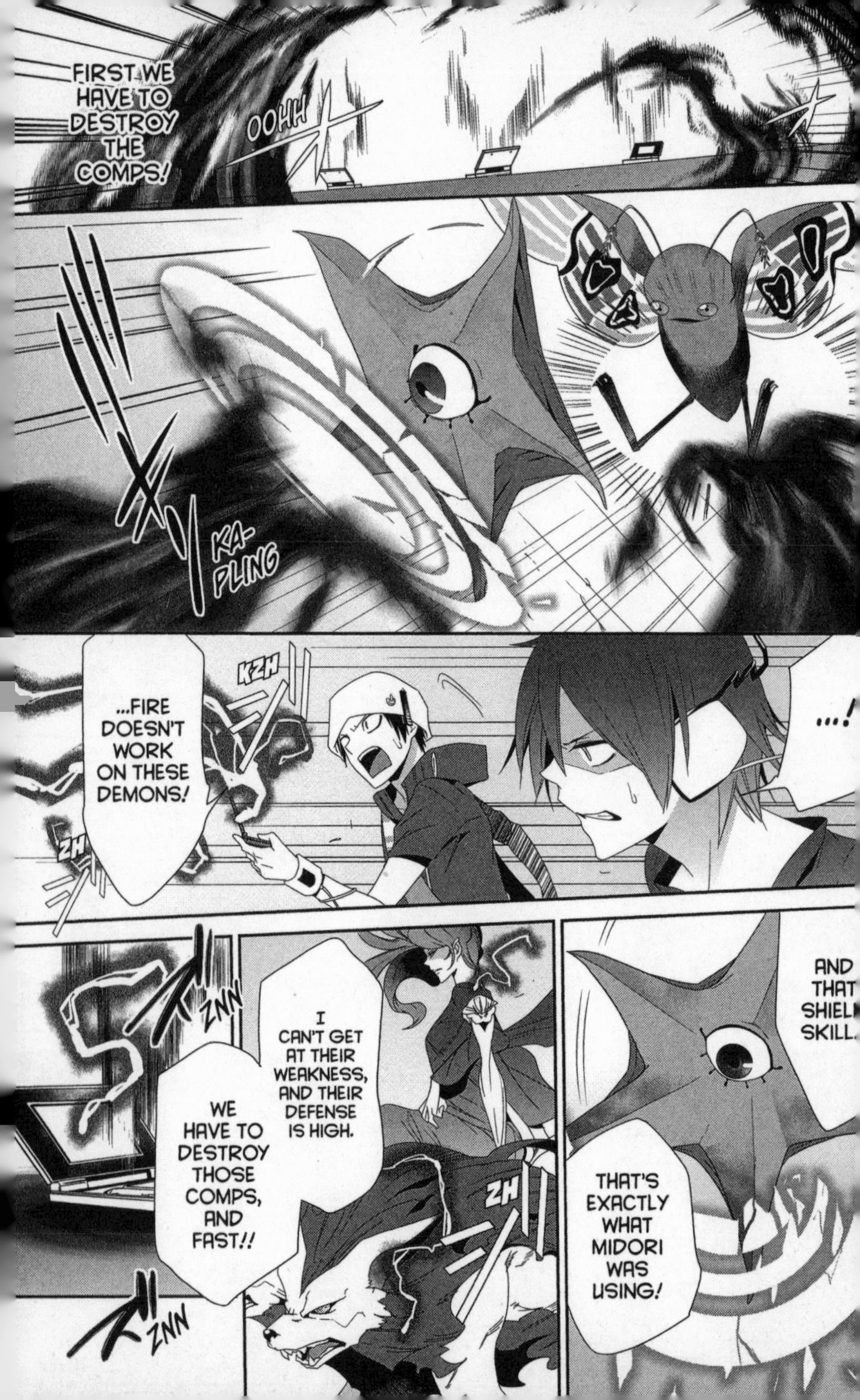
FIRST WE HAVE TO DESTROY THE COMPS!
OOHH
KA-PLING
...!
KZH
...FIRE DOESN'T WORK ON THESE DEMONS!
ZH
AND THAT SHIEL SKILL.
THAT'S EXACTLY WHAT MIDORI WAS USING!
I CAN'T GET AT THEIR WEAKNESS, AND THEIR DEFENSE IS HIGH.
ZNN
WE HAVE TO DESTROY THOSE COMPS, AND FAST!!
ZH
ZNN

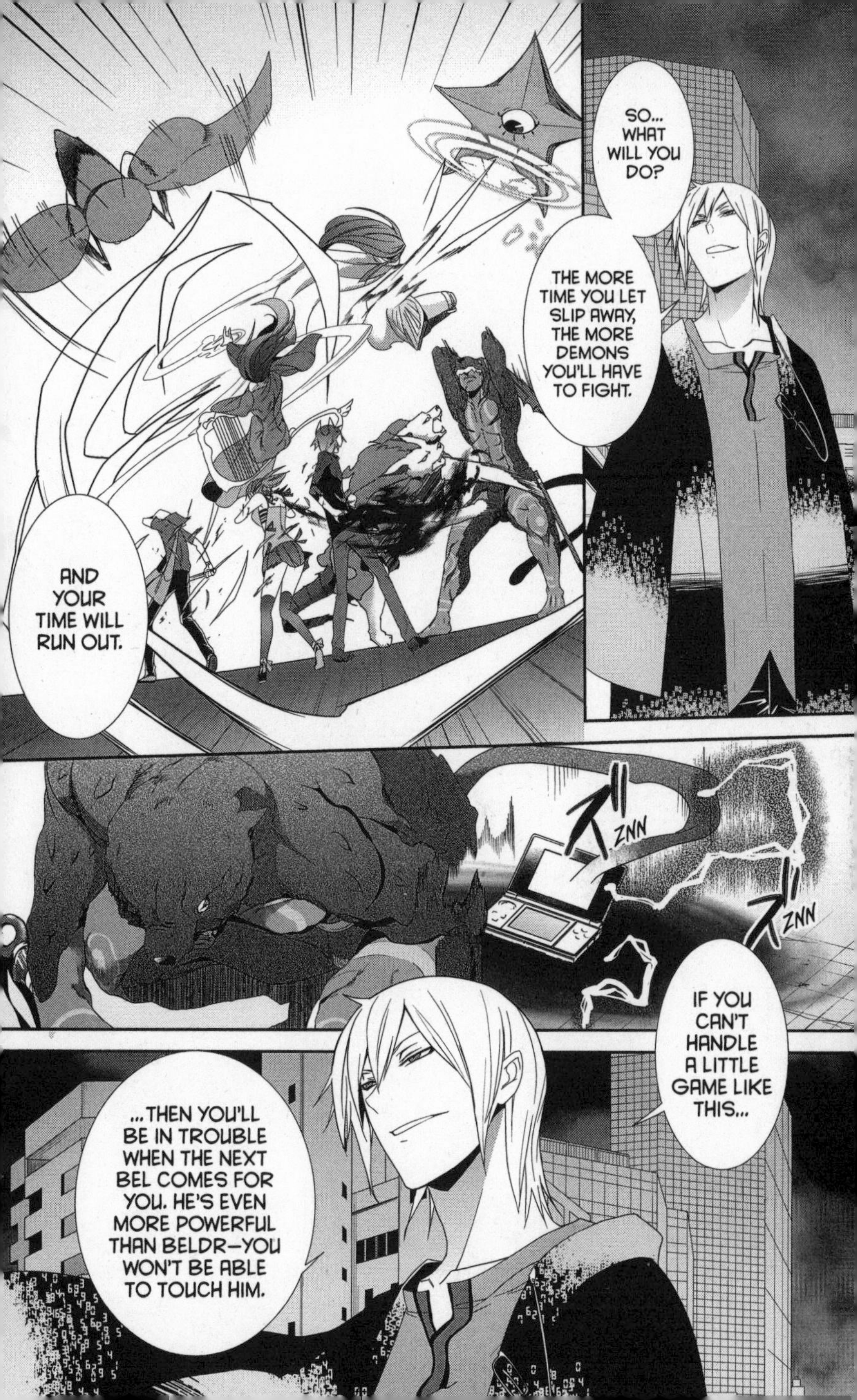
SO... WHAT WILL YOU DO?
THE MORE TIME YOU LET SLIP AWAY, THE MORE DEMONS YOU'LL HAVE TO FIGHT.
AND YOUR TIME WILL RUN OUT.
ZNN
ZNN
IF YOU CAN'T HANDLE A LITTLE GAME LIKE THIS...
...THEN YOU'LL BE IN TROUBLE WHEN THE NEXT BEL COMES FOR YOU. HE'S EVEN MORE POWERFUL THAN BELDR—YOU WON'T BE ABLE TO TOUCH HIM.

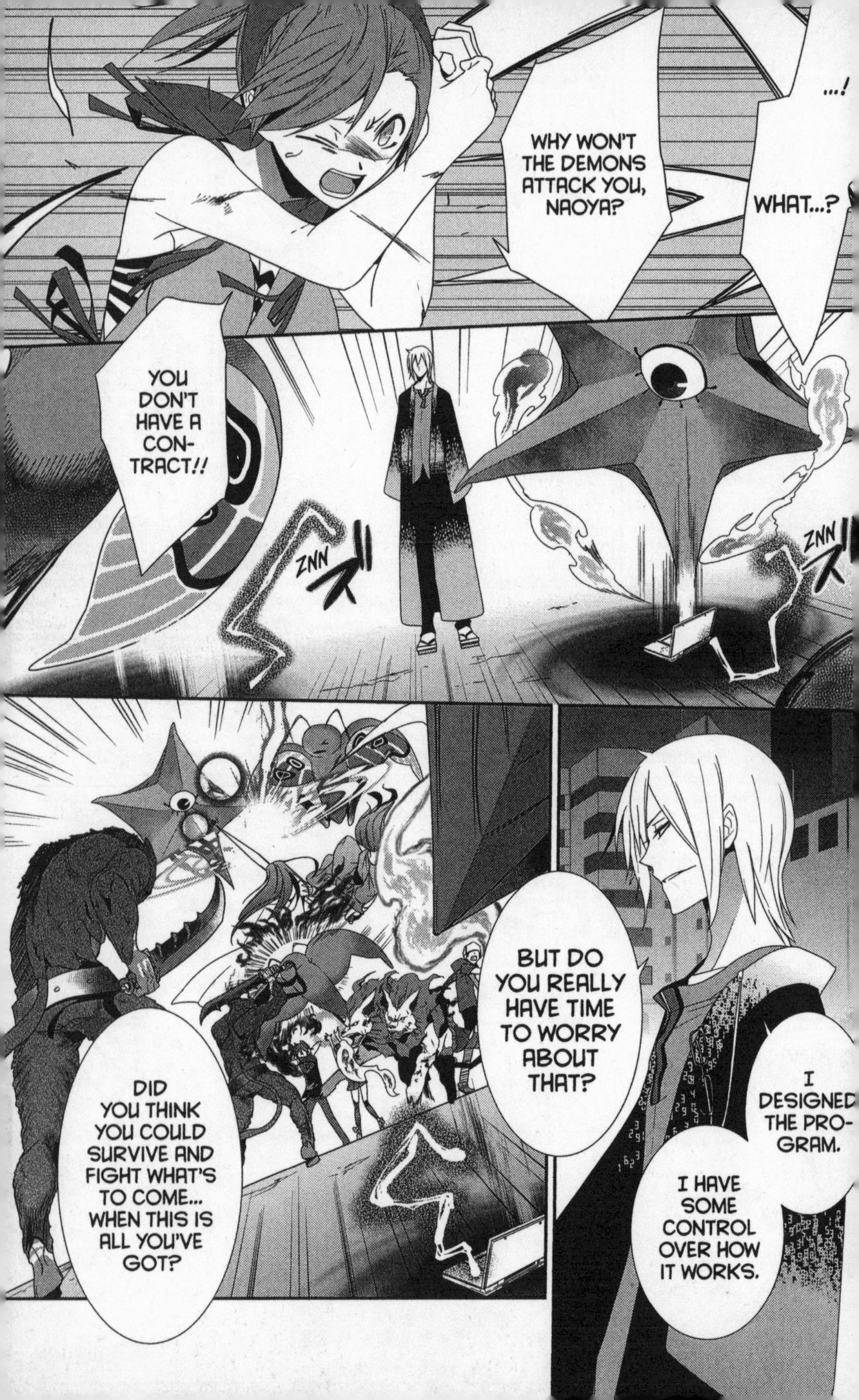
...!
WHAT...?
WHY WON'T THE DEMONS ATTACK YOU, NAOYA?
YOU DON'T HAVE A CONTRACT!!
ZNN
ZNN
I DESIGNED THE PROGRAM.
I HAVE SOME CONTROL OVER HOW IT WORKS.
BUT DO YOU REALLY HAVE TIME TO WORRY ABOUT THAT?
DID YOU THINK YOU COULD SURVIVE AND FIGHT WHAT'S TO COME... WHEN THIS IS ALL YOU'VE GOT?

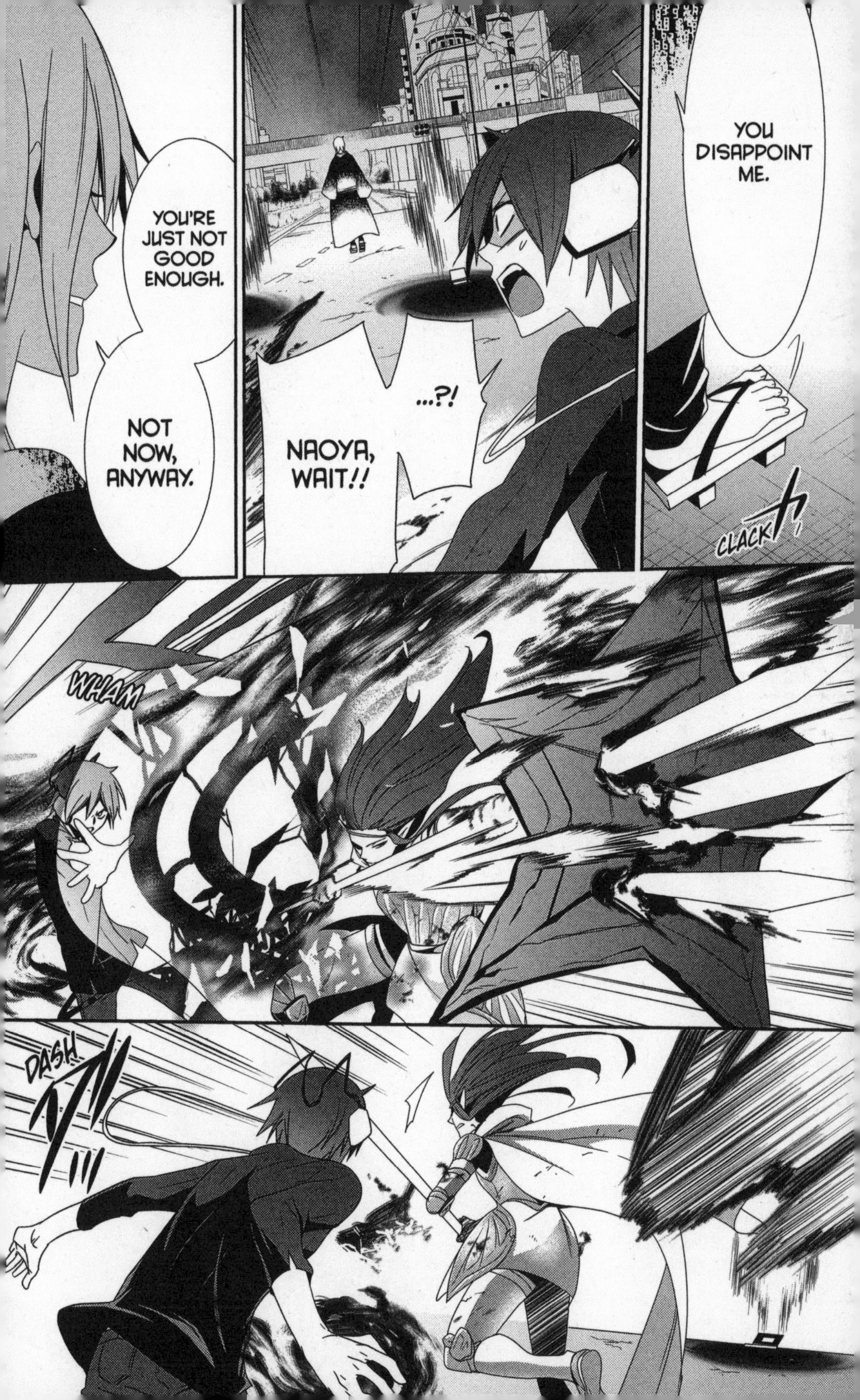
YOU DISAPPOINT ME.
CLACK
...?!
NAOYA, WAIT!!
YOU'RE JUST NOT GOOD ENOUGH.
NOT NOW, ANYWAY.
WHAM
DASH

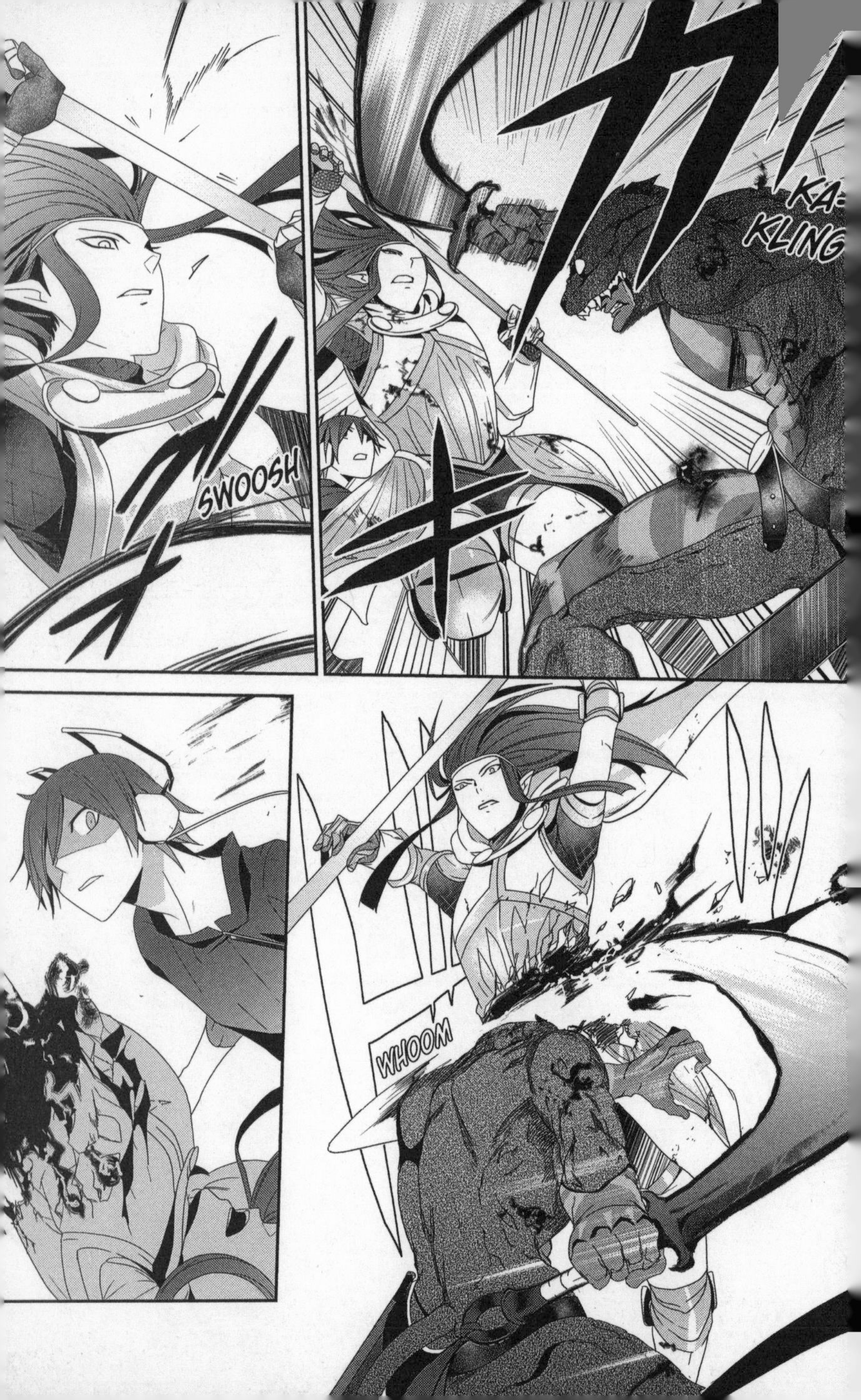
KA-
KLING
SWOOSH
WHOOM

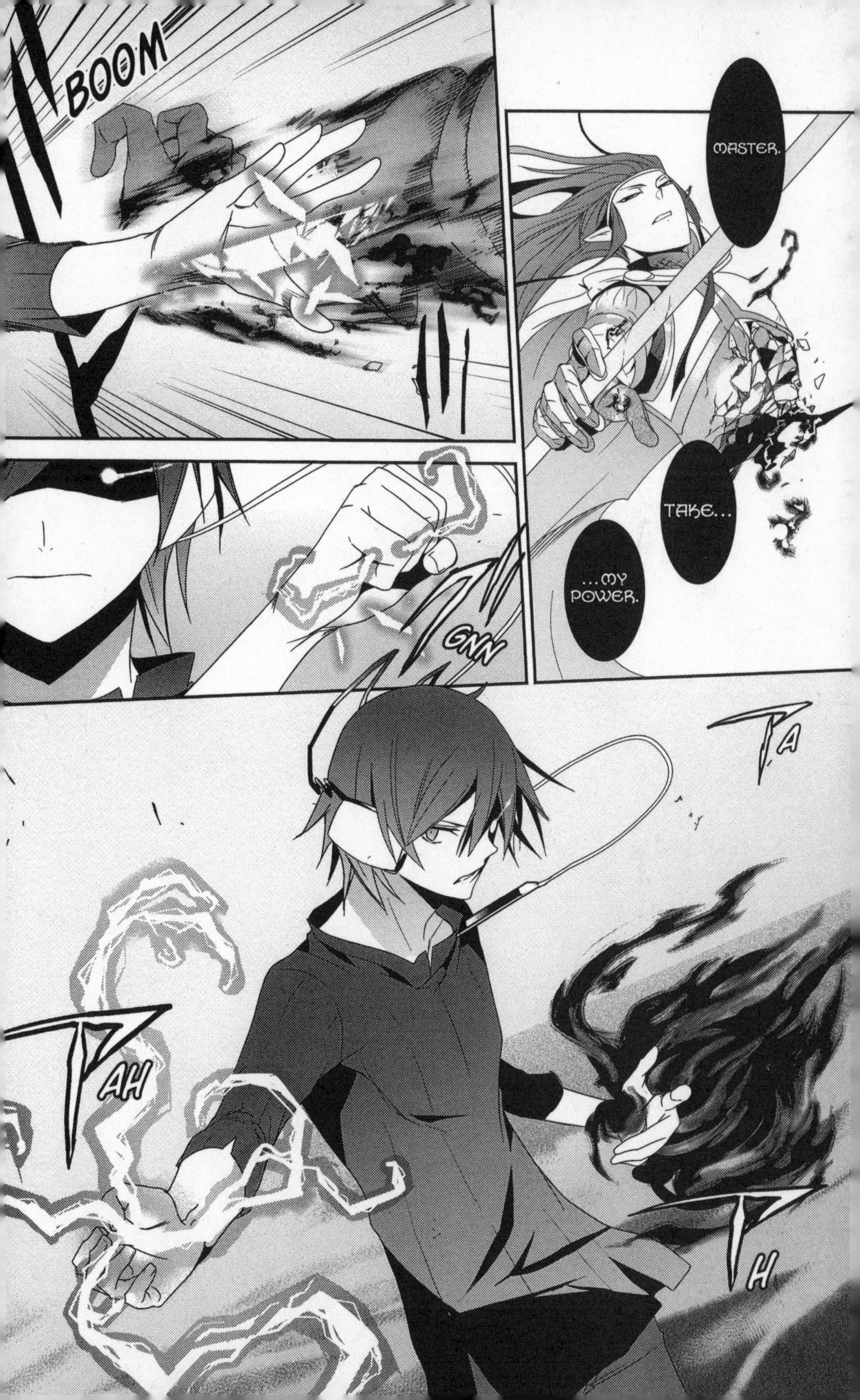
MASTER.
TAKE...
...MY POWER.
BOOM
GNN
PA
PAH
PH

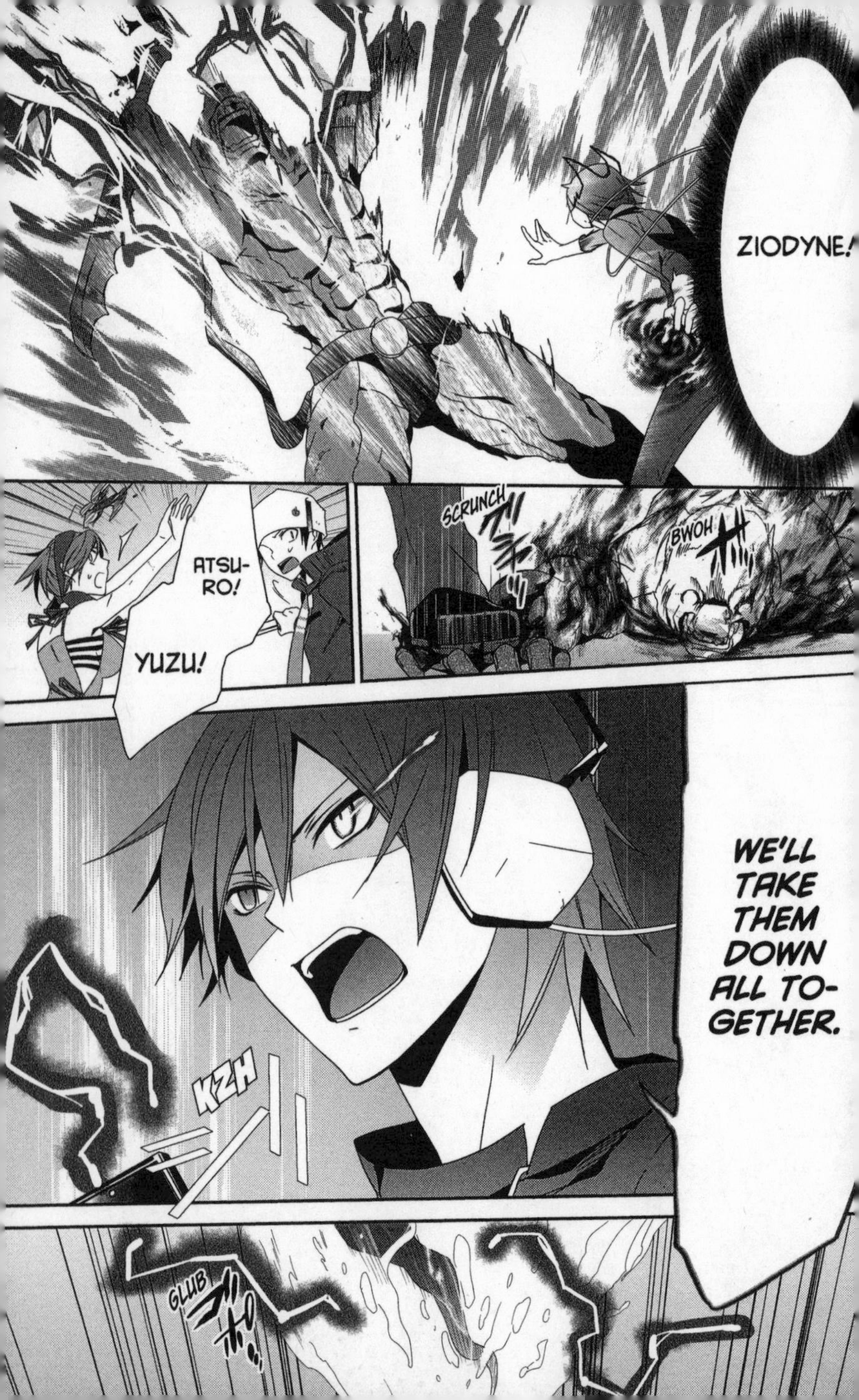
ZIODYNE!
SCRUNCH
BWOH
ATSU-RO!
YUZU!
WE'LL TAKE THEM DOWN ALL TO-GETHER.
KZH
GLUB

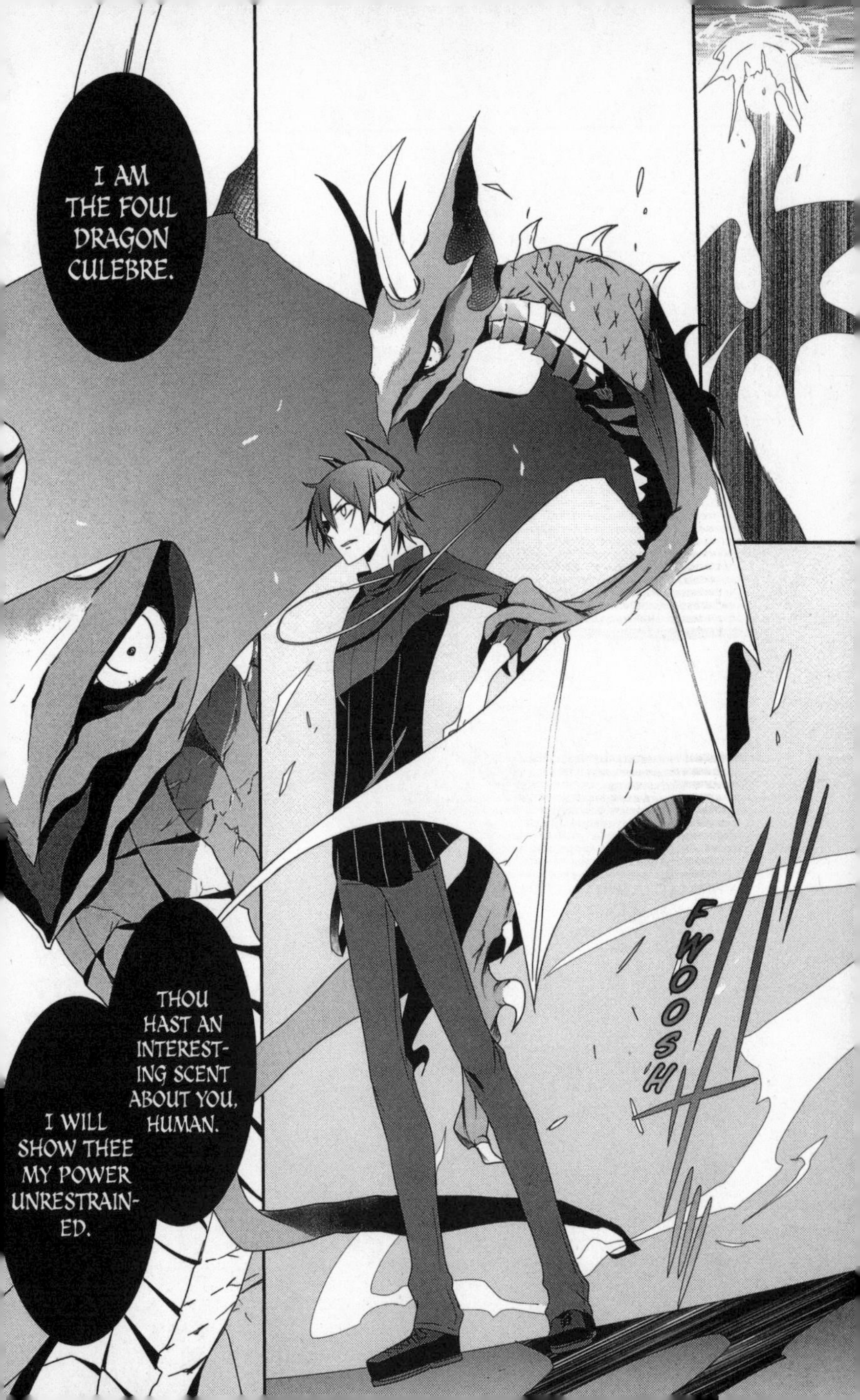
FWOOSH
I AM THE FOUL DRAGON CULEBRE.
THOU HAST AN INTEREST-ING SCENT ABOUT YOU, HUMAN.
I WILL SHOW THEE MY POWER UNRESTRAIN-ED.

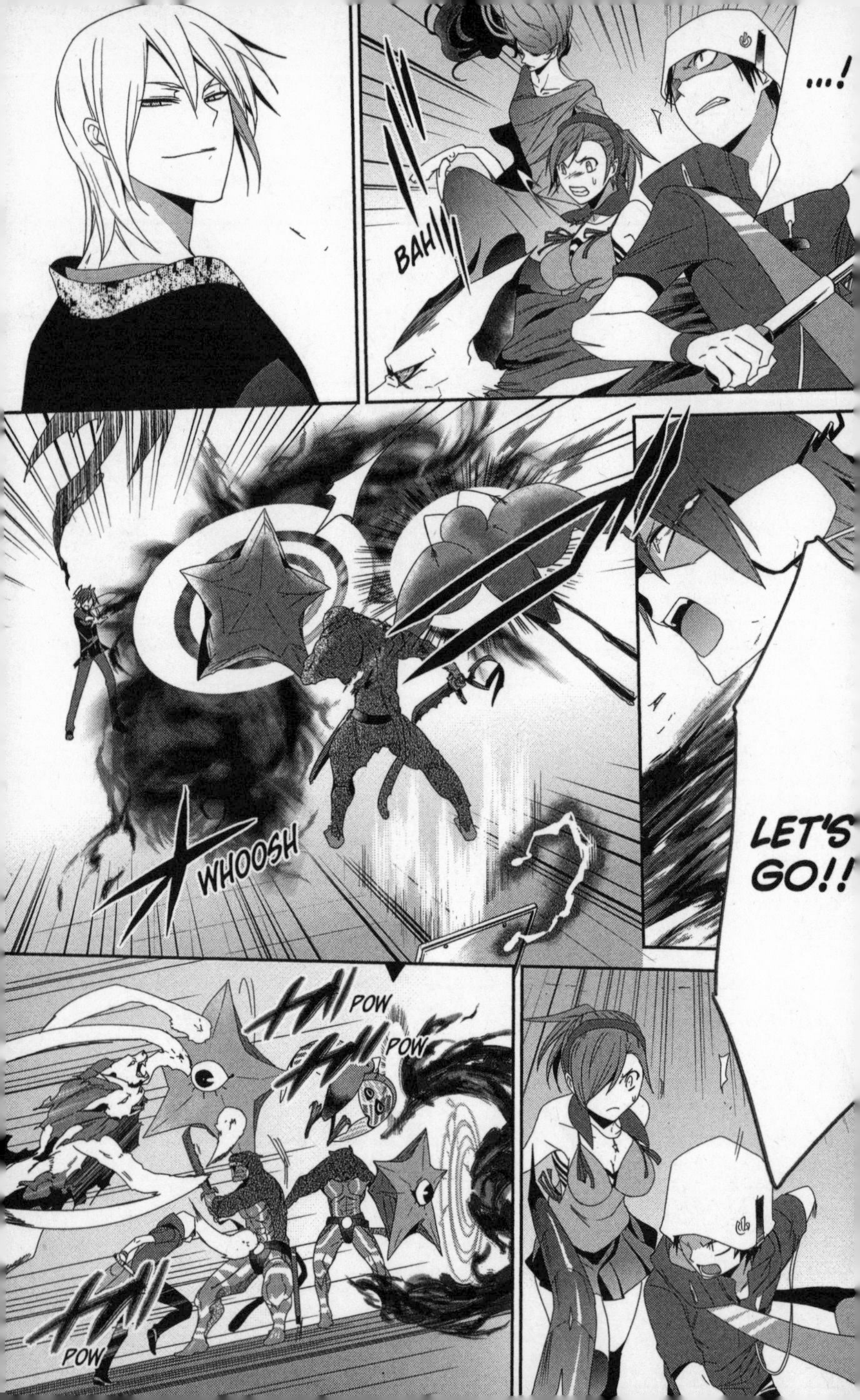

...!
BAH
LET'S GO!!
WHOOSH
POW
POW
POW

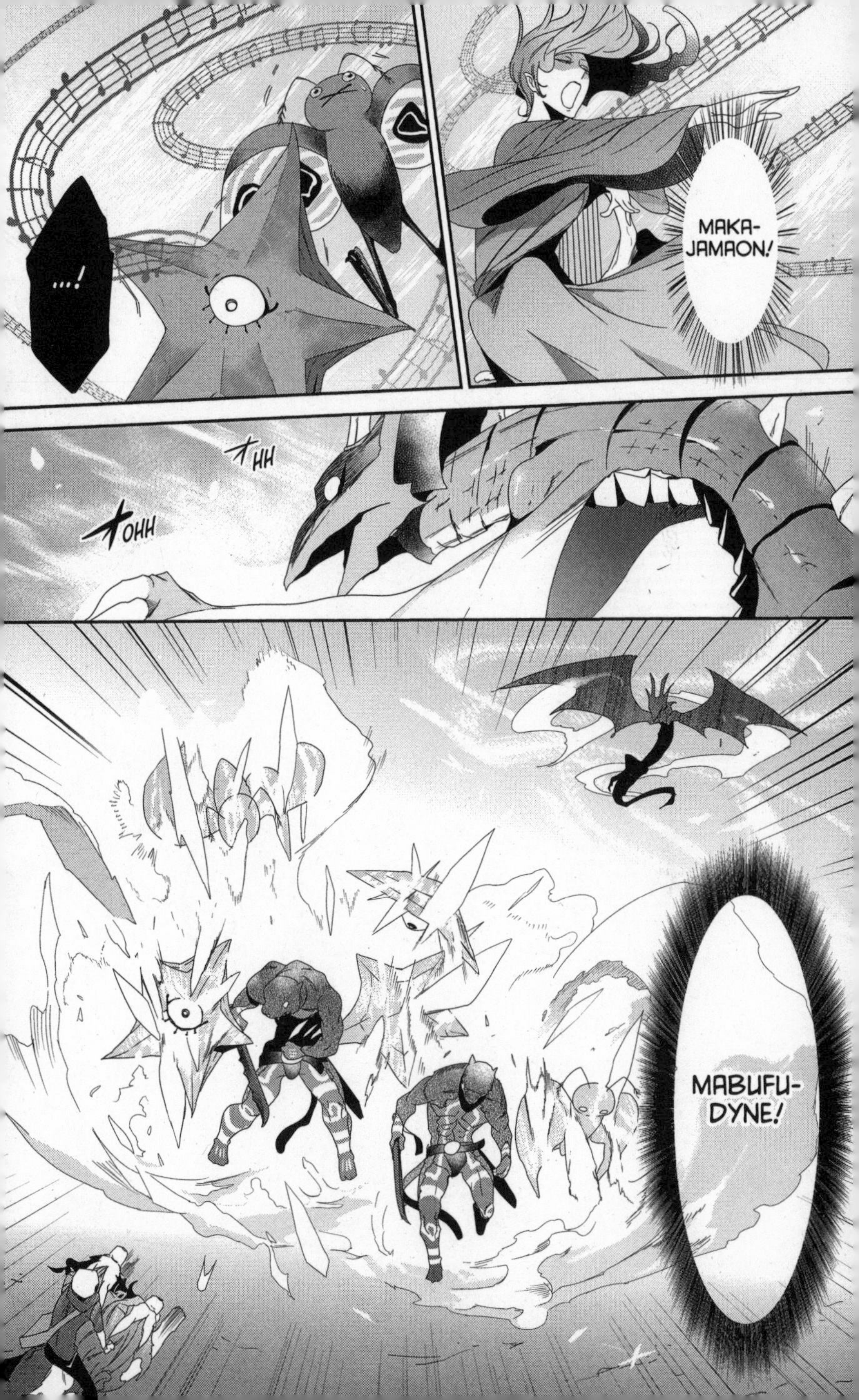
MAKA-JAMAON!
...!
HH
OHH
MABUFU-DYNE!

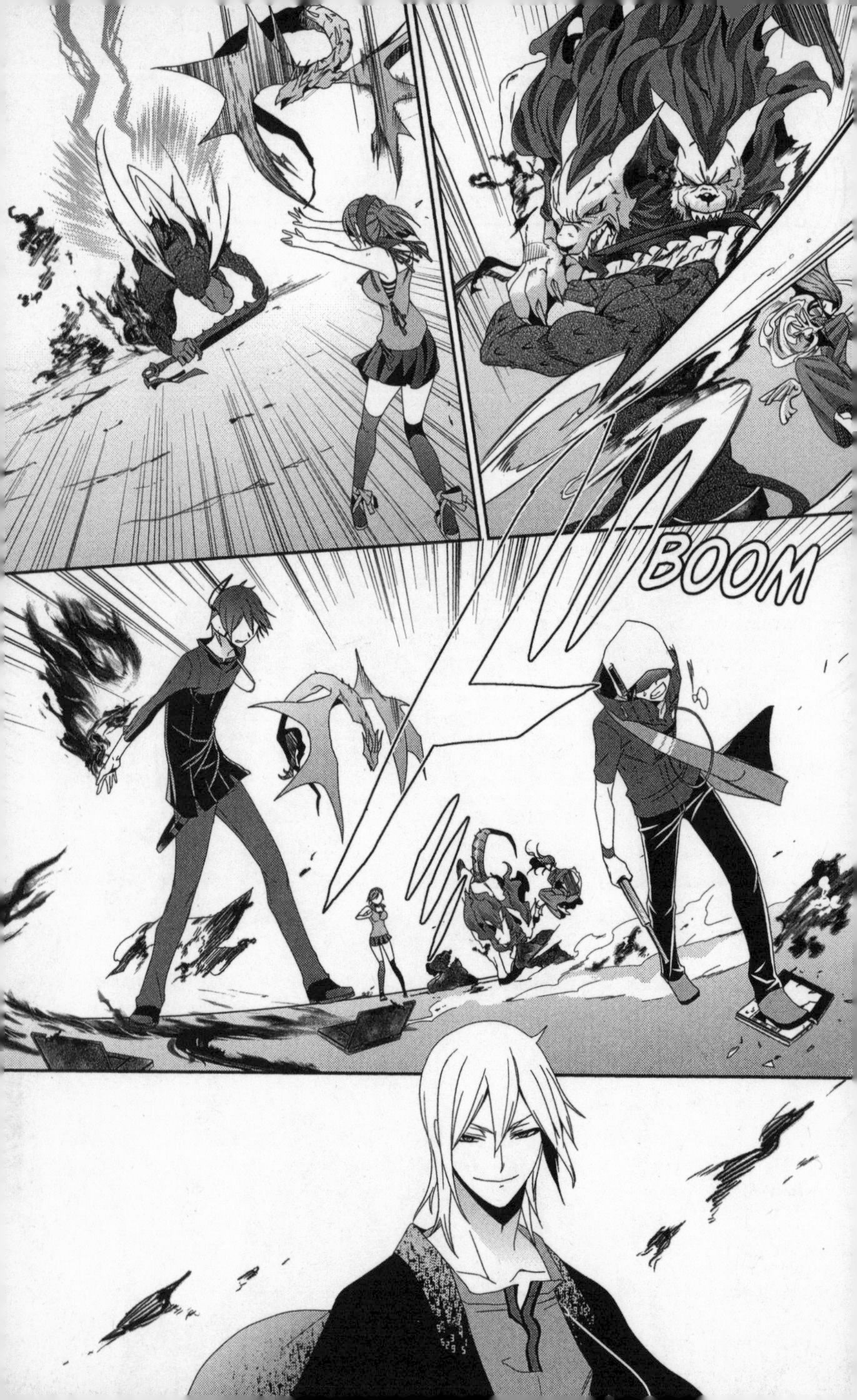
BOOM

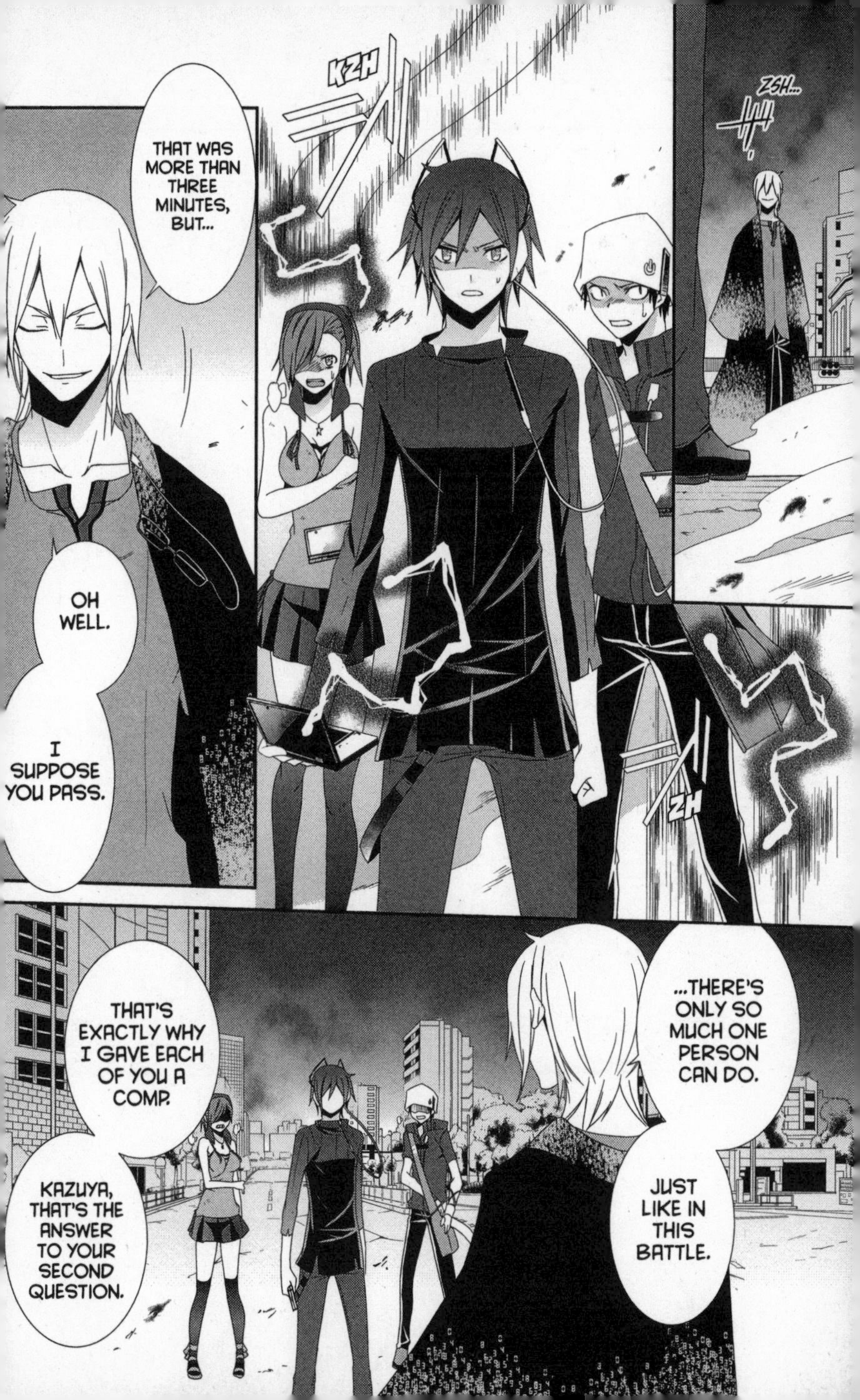
ZSH...
KZH
ZH
THAT WAS MORE THAN THREE MINUTES, BUT...
OH WELL.
I SUPPOSE YOU PASS.
...THERE'S ONLY SO MUCH ONE PERSON CAN DO.
JUST LIKE IN THIS BATTLE.
THAT'S EXACTLY WHY I GAVE EACH OF YOU A COMP.
KAZUYA, THAT'S THE ANSWER TO YOUR SECOND QUESTION.

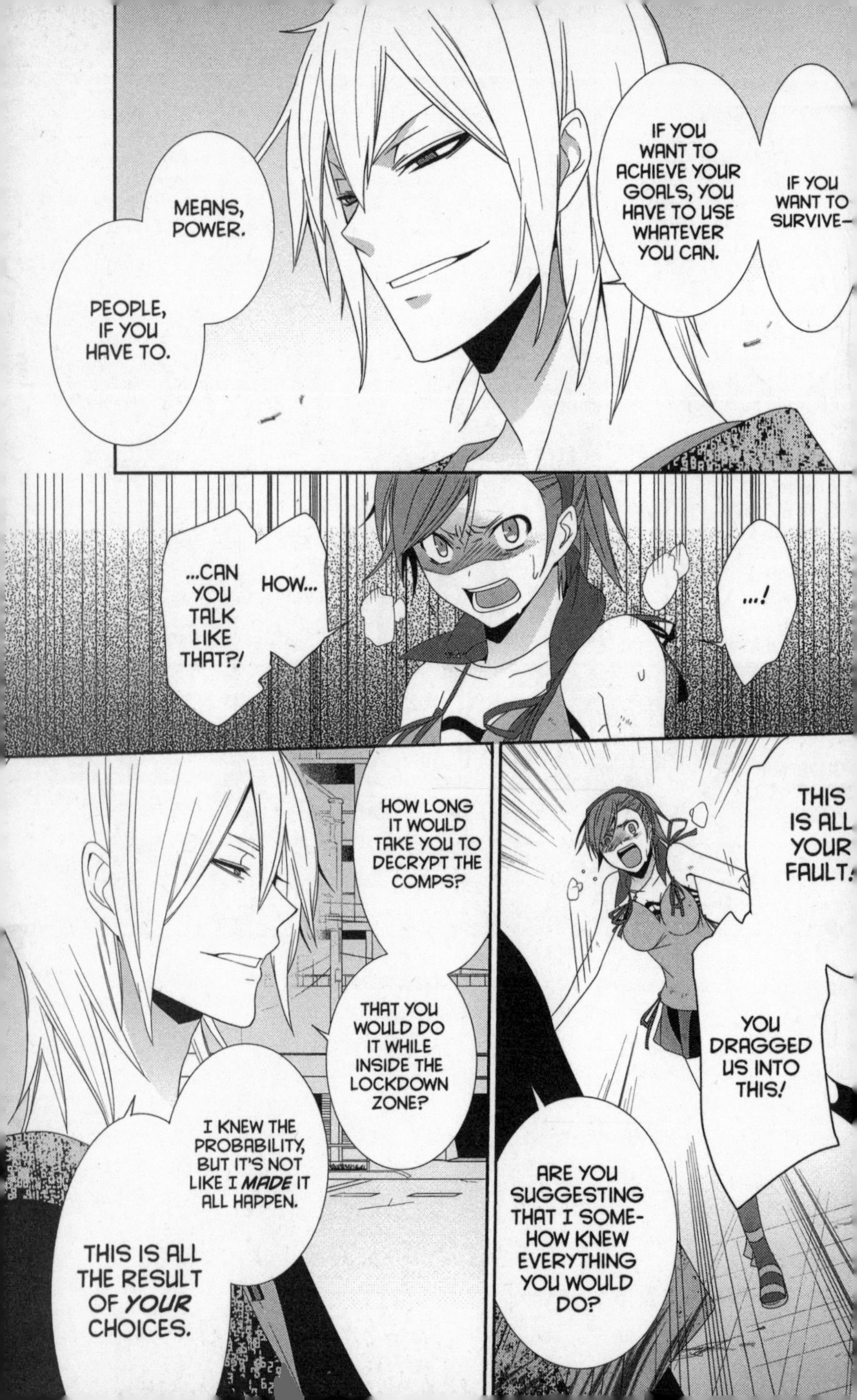
IF YOU WANT TO SURVIVE—
IF YOU WANT TO ACHIEVE YOUR GOALS, YOU HAVE TO USE WHATEVER YOU CAN.
MEANS, POWER.
PEOPLE, IF YOU HAVE TO.
...!
HOW...
...CAN YOU TALK LIKE THAT?!
THIS IS ALL YOUR FAULT.
YOU DRAGGED US INTO THIS!
ARE YOU SUGGESTING THAT I SOME-HOW KNEW EVERYTHING YOU WOULD DO?
HOW LONG IT WOULD TAKE YOU TO DECRYPT THE COMPS?
THAT YOU WOULD DO IT WHILE INSIDE THE LOCKDOWN ZONE?
I KNEW THE PROBABILITY, BUT IT'S NOT LIKE I *MADE* IT ALL HAPPEN.
THIS IS ALL THE RESULT OF *YOUR* CHOICES.

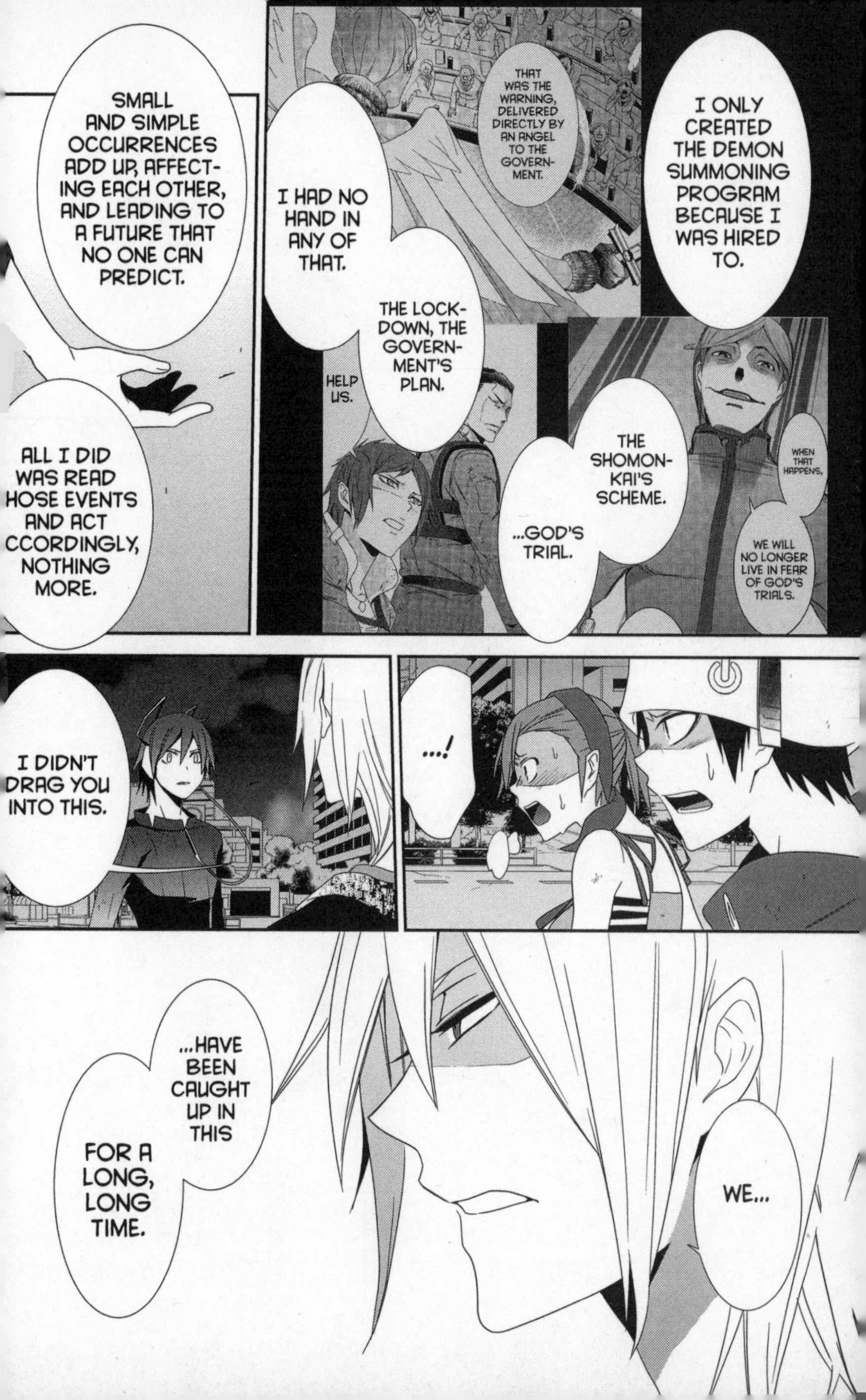
I ONLY CREATED THE DEMON SUMMONING PROGRAM BECAUSE I WAS HIRED TO.
THAT WAS THE WARNING, DELIVERED DIRECTLY BY AN ANGEL TO THE GOVERNMENT.
I HAD NO HAND IN ANY OF THAT.
WHEN THAT HAPPENS,
WE WILL NO LONGER LIVE IN FEAR OF GOD'S TRIALS.
THE SHOMONKAI'S SCHEME.
...GOD'S TRIAL.
THE LOCKDOWN, THE GOVERNMENT'S PLAN.
HELP US.
SMALL AND SIMPLE OCCURRENCES ADD UP, AFFECTING EACH OTHER, AND LEADING TO A FUTURE THAT NO ONE CAN PREDICT.
ALL I DID WAS READ HOSE EVENTS AND ACT CCORDINGLY, NOTHING MORE.
...!
I DIDN'T DRAG YOU INTO THIS.
WE...
...HAVE BEEN CAUGHT UP IN THIS
FOR A LONG, LONG TIME.

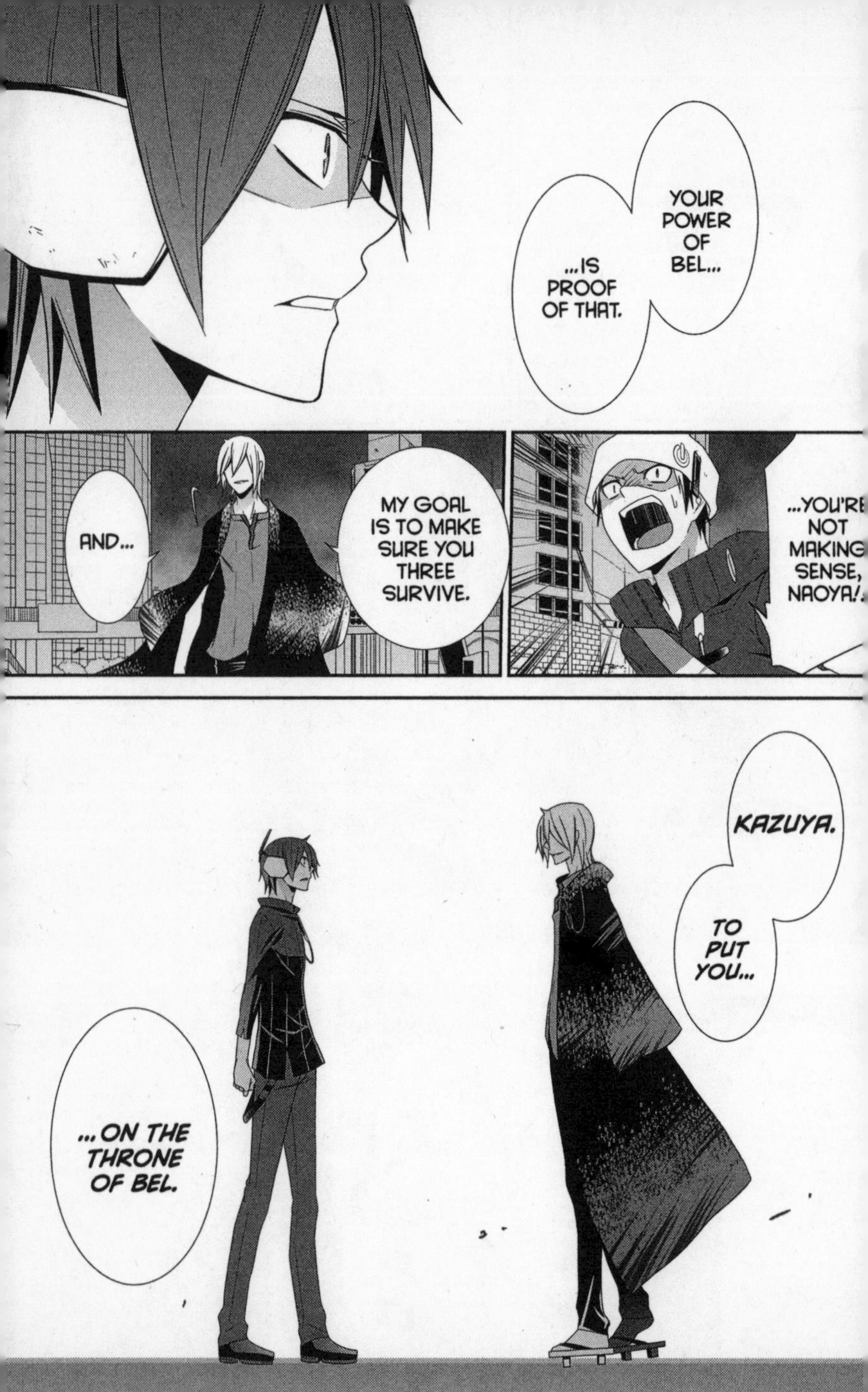
YOUR POWER OF BEL...
...IS PROOF OF THAT.
...YOU'RE NOT MAKING SENSE, NAOYA!.
MY GOAL IS TO MAKE SURE YOU THREE SURVIVE.
AND...
KAZUYA.
TO PUT YOU...
...ON THE THRONE OF BEL.

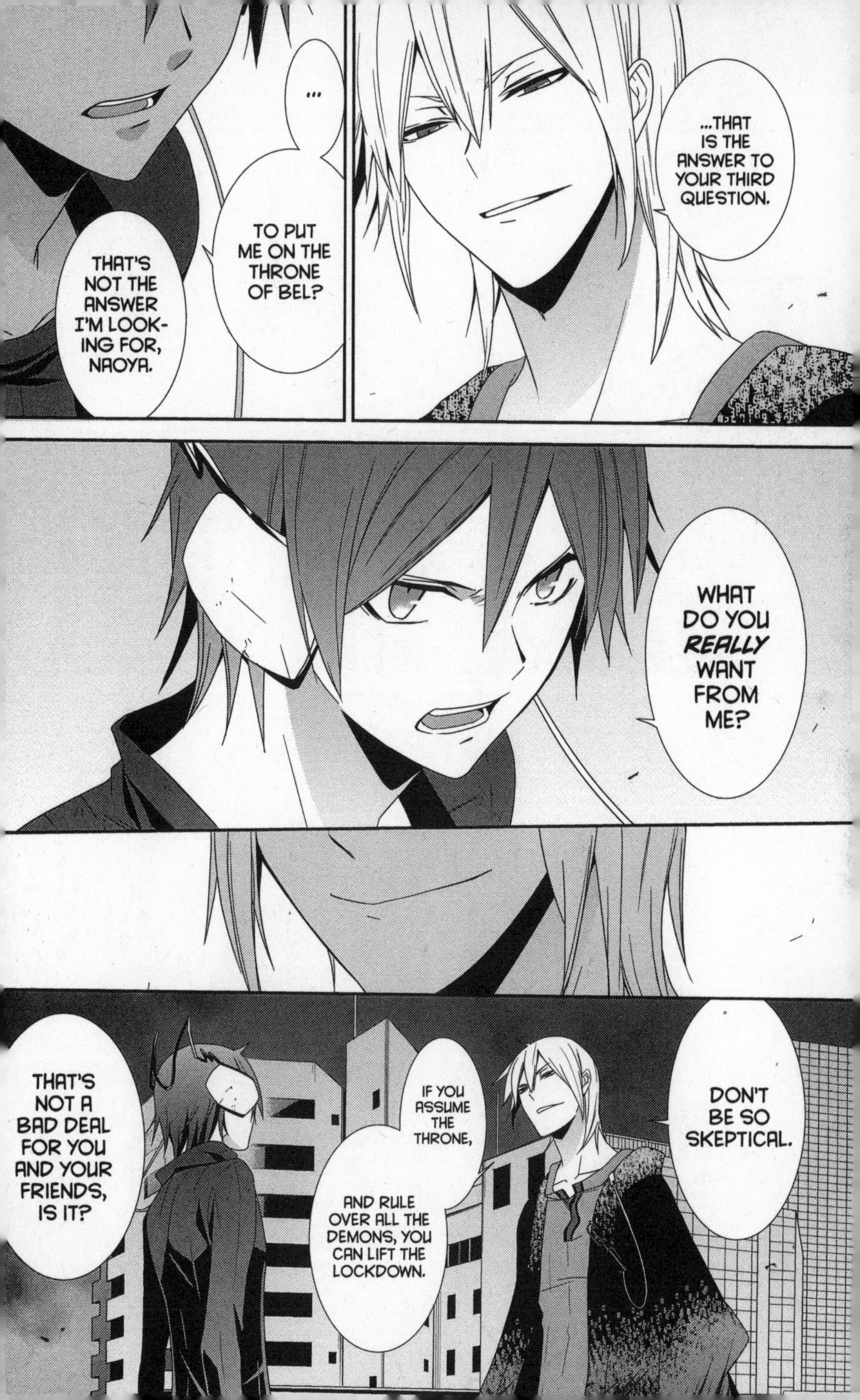
...THAT IS THE ANSWER TO YOUR THIRD QUESTION.
...
TO PUT ME ON THE THRONE OF BEL?
THAT'S NOT THE ANSWER I'M LOOKING FOR, NAOYA.
WHAT DO YOU *REALLY* WANT FROM ME?
DON'T BE SO SKEPTICAL.
IF YOU ASSUME THE THRONE,
AND RULE OVER ALL THE DEMONS, YOU CAN LIFT THE LOCKDOWN.
THAT'S NOT A BAD DEAL FOR YOU AND YOUR FRIENDS, IS IT?

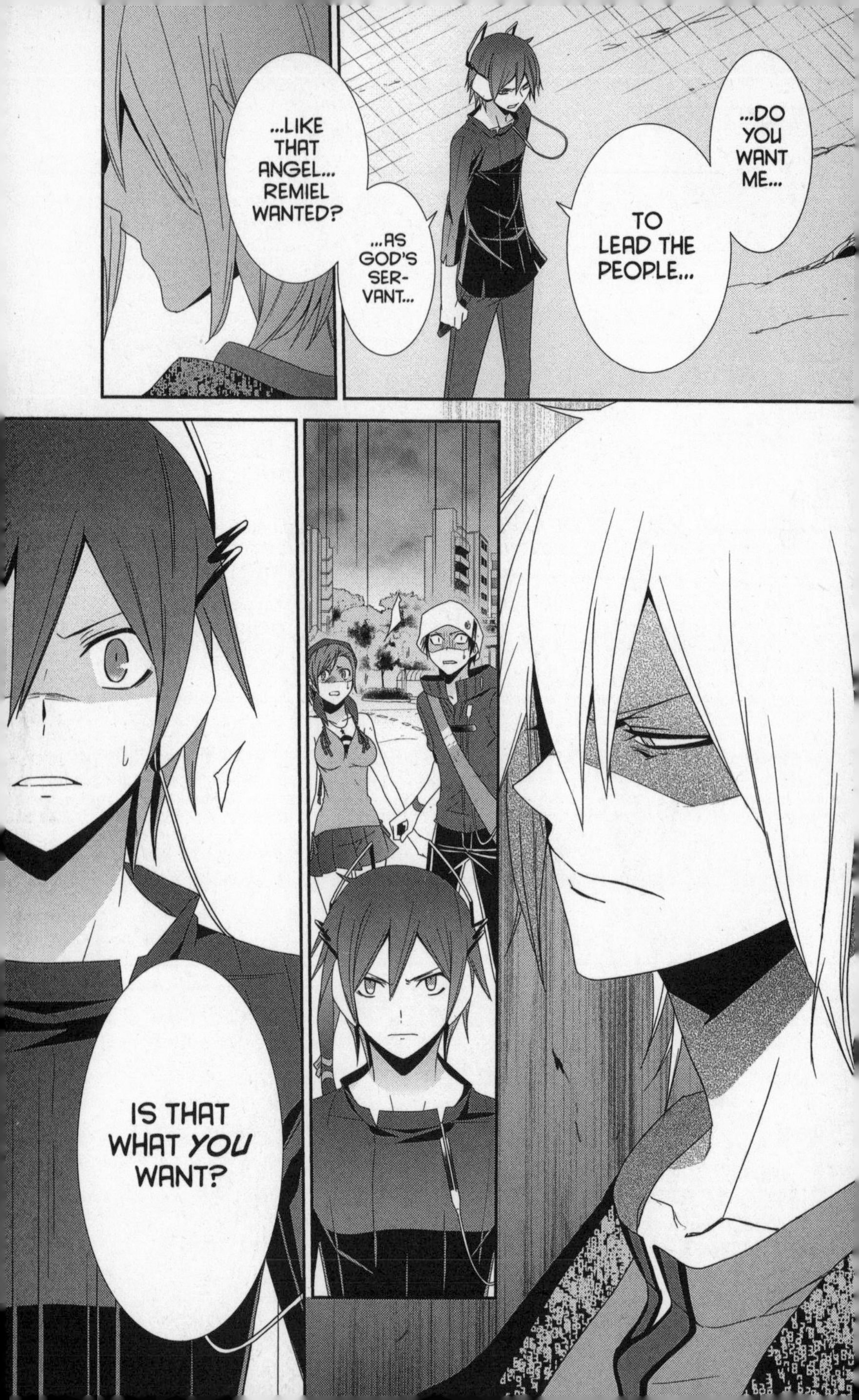
...DO YOU WANT ME...
TO LEAD THE PEOPLE...
...AS GOD'S SER-VANT...
...LIKE THAT ANGEL... REMIEL WANTED?
IS THAT WHAT *YOU* WANT?

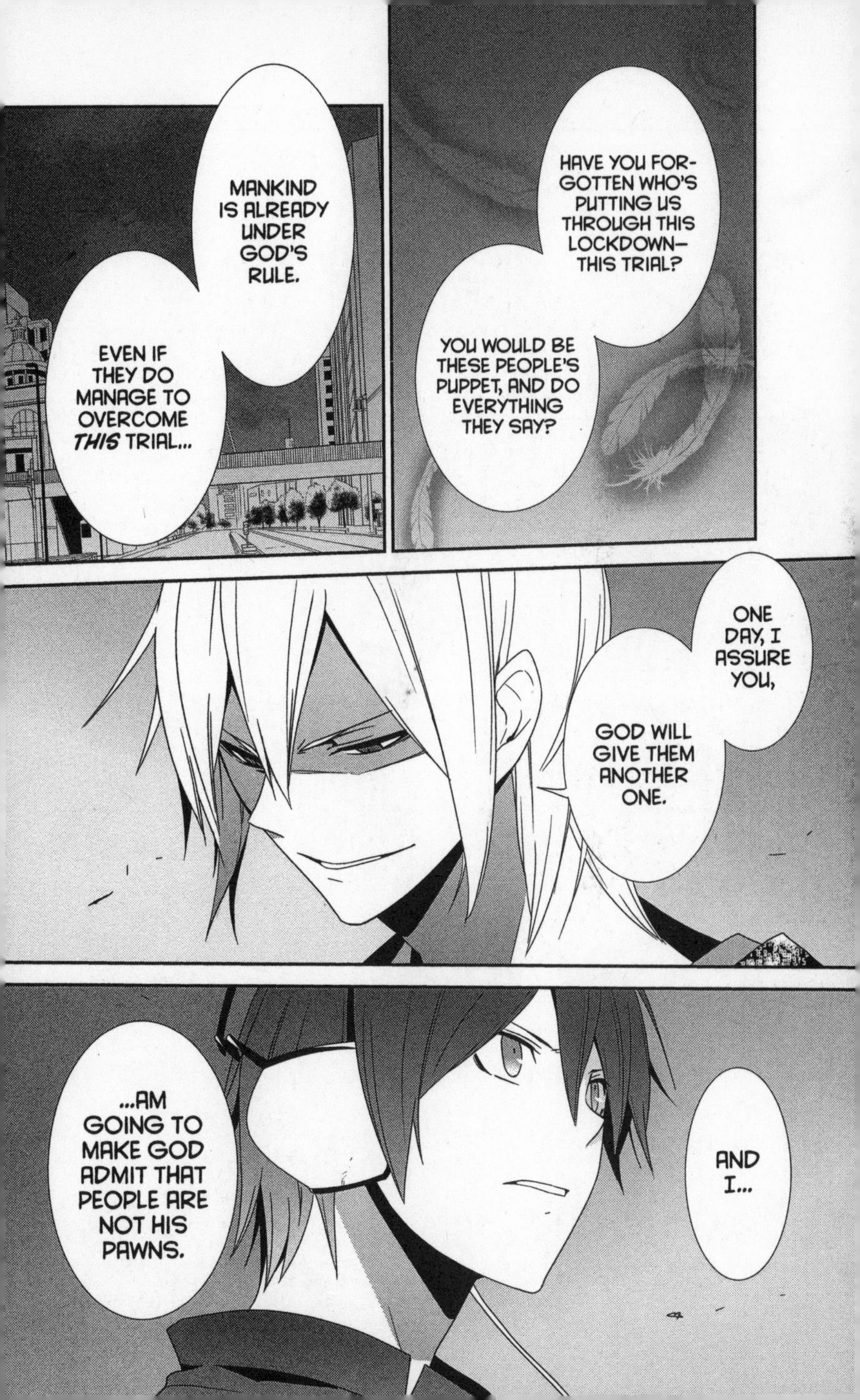
HAVE YOU FOR-GOTTEN WHO'S PUTTING US THROUGH THIS LOCKDOWN—THIS TRIAL?
YOU WOULD BE THESE PEOPLE'S PUPPET, AND DO EVERYTHING THEY SAY?
MANKIND IS ALREADY UNDER GOD'S RULE.
EVEN IF THEY DO MANAGE TO OVERCOME *THIS* TRIAL...
ONE DAY, I ASSURE YOU,
GOD WILL GIVE THEM ANOTHER ONE.
AND I...
...AM GOING TO MAKE GOD ADMIT THAT PEOPLE ARE NOT HIS PAWNS.

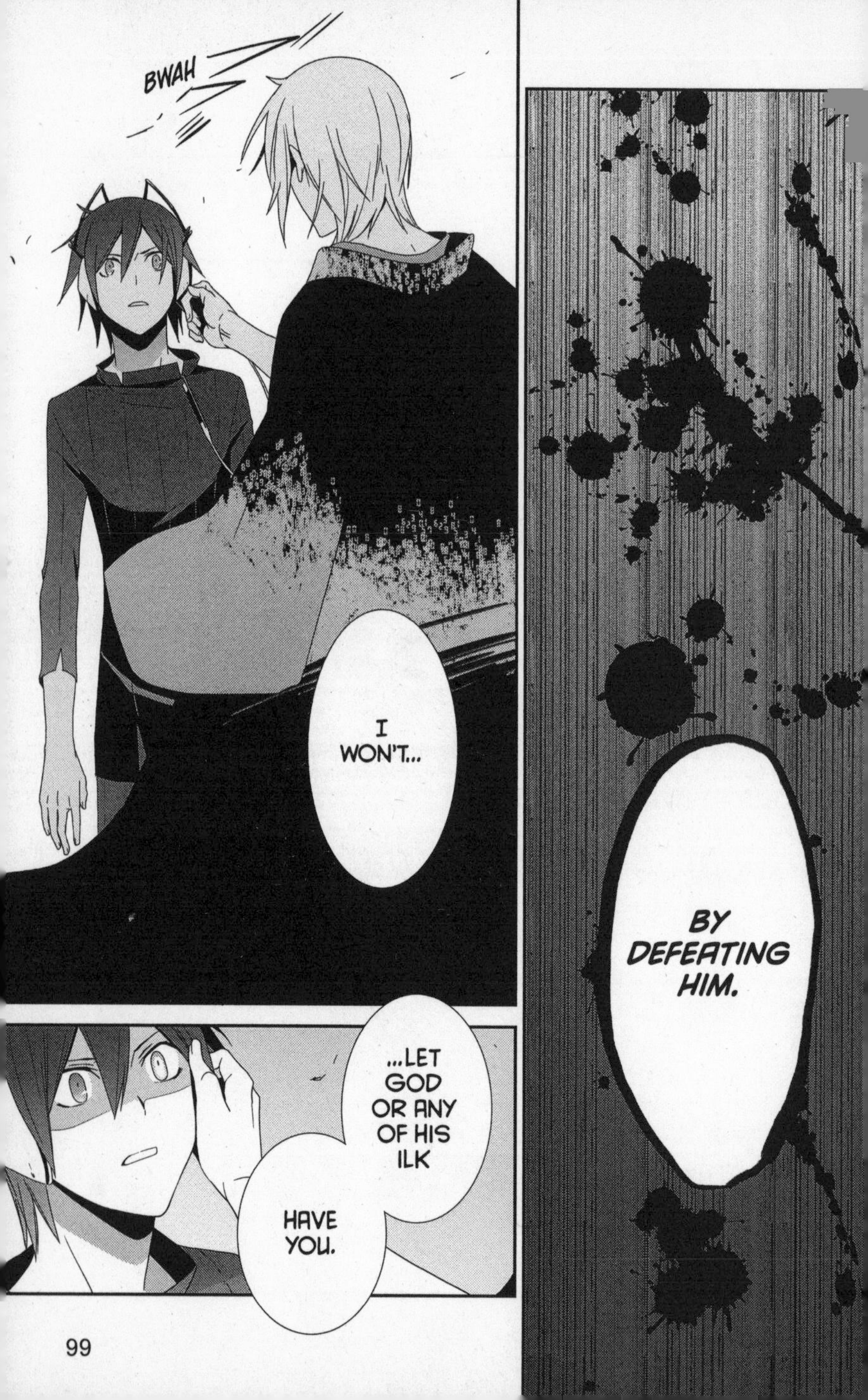
BY DEFEATING HIM.
BWAH
I WON'T...
...LET GOD OR ANY OF HIS ILK
HAVE YOU.

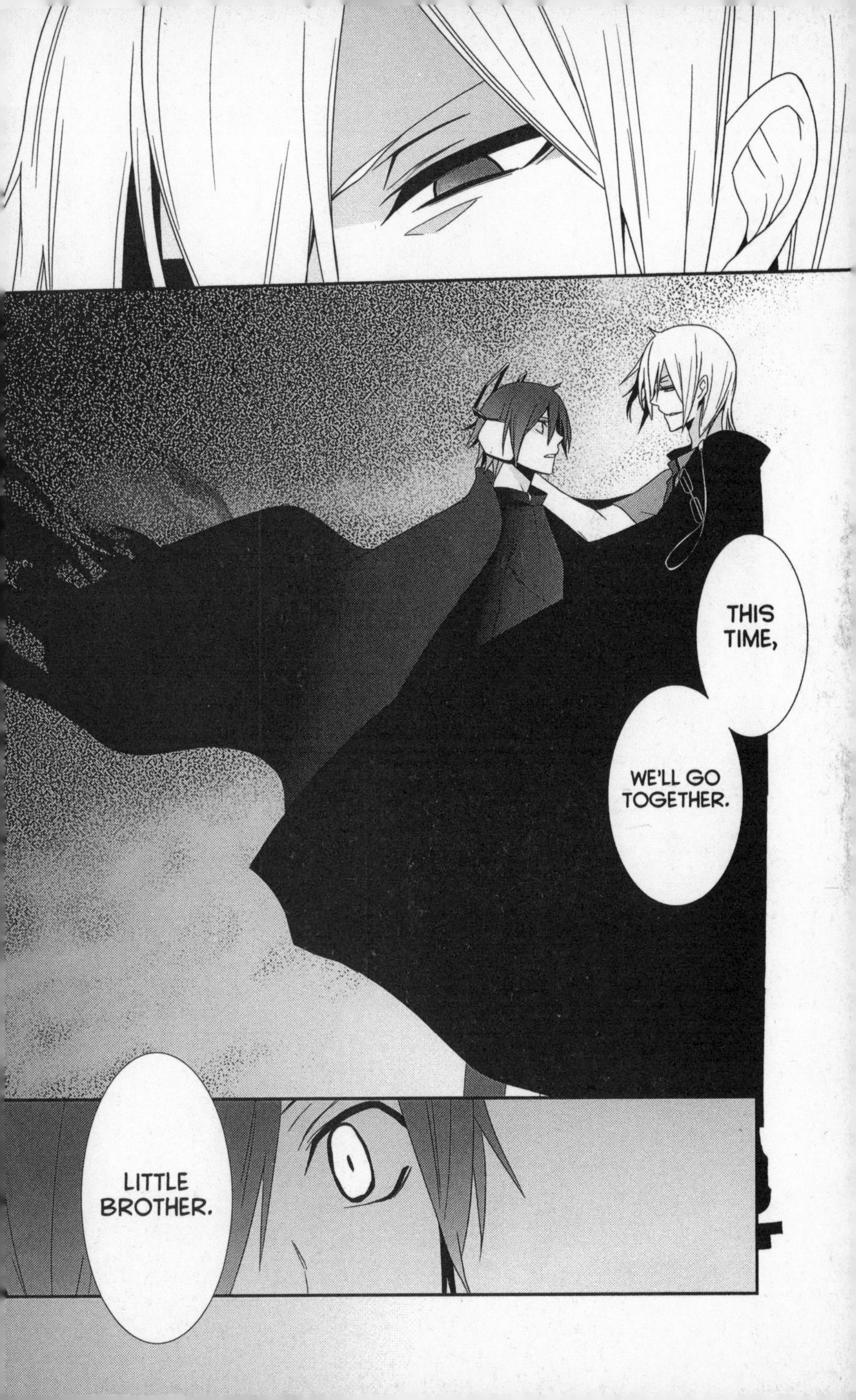
THIS TIME,
WE'LL GO TOGETHER.
LITTLE BROTHER.

PROFILE

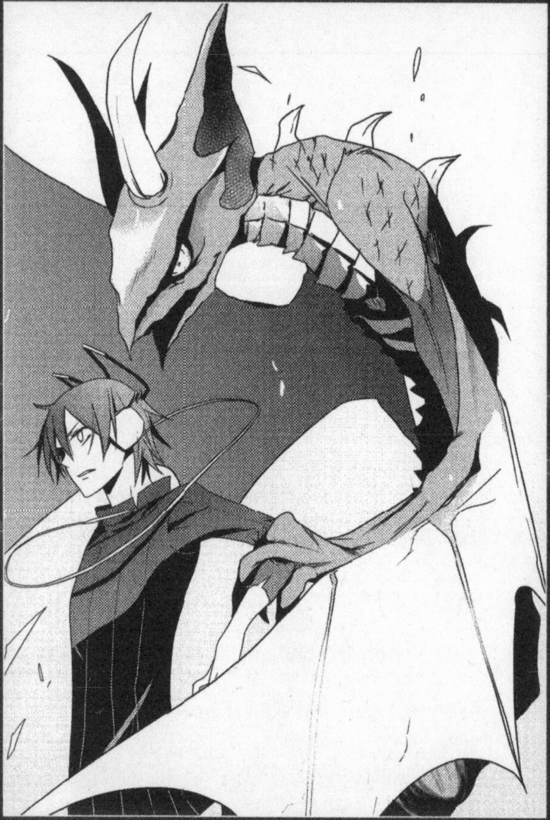

CULEBRE

A WINGED DRAGON THAT LIVES IN SPRINGS WHEN YOUNG, THEN RELOCATES TO THE OCEAN WHEN IT MATURES. A YOUNG CULEBRE LIVES IN SPRINGS THAT REACH DOWN TO THE DEPTHS OF THE EARTH, AND WON'T ATTACK UNLESS APPROACHED, BUT IT DOES DRINK THE BLOOD OF HUMANS AND LIVESTOCK. AS IT AGES AND ITS SCALES GROW AND HARDEN, IT MOVES FROM THE SPRING TO THE OCEAN, WHERE IT GUARDS THE TREASURES THAT LIE IN CAVES AT THE BOTTOM OF THE SEA. TO AVOID ATTACK, ONE SHOULD OFFER THE CULEBRE LOAVES OF BREAD MADE FROM BARLEY OR CORN.

DEVIL SURVIVOR
デビルサバイバー

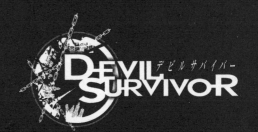

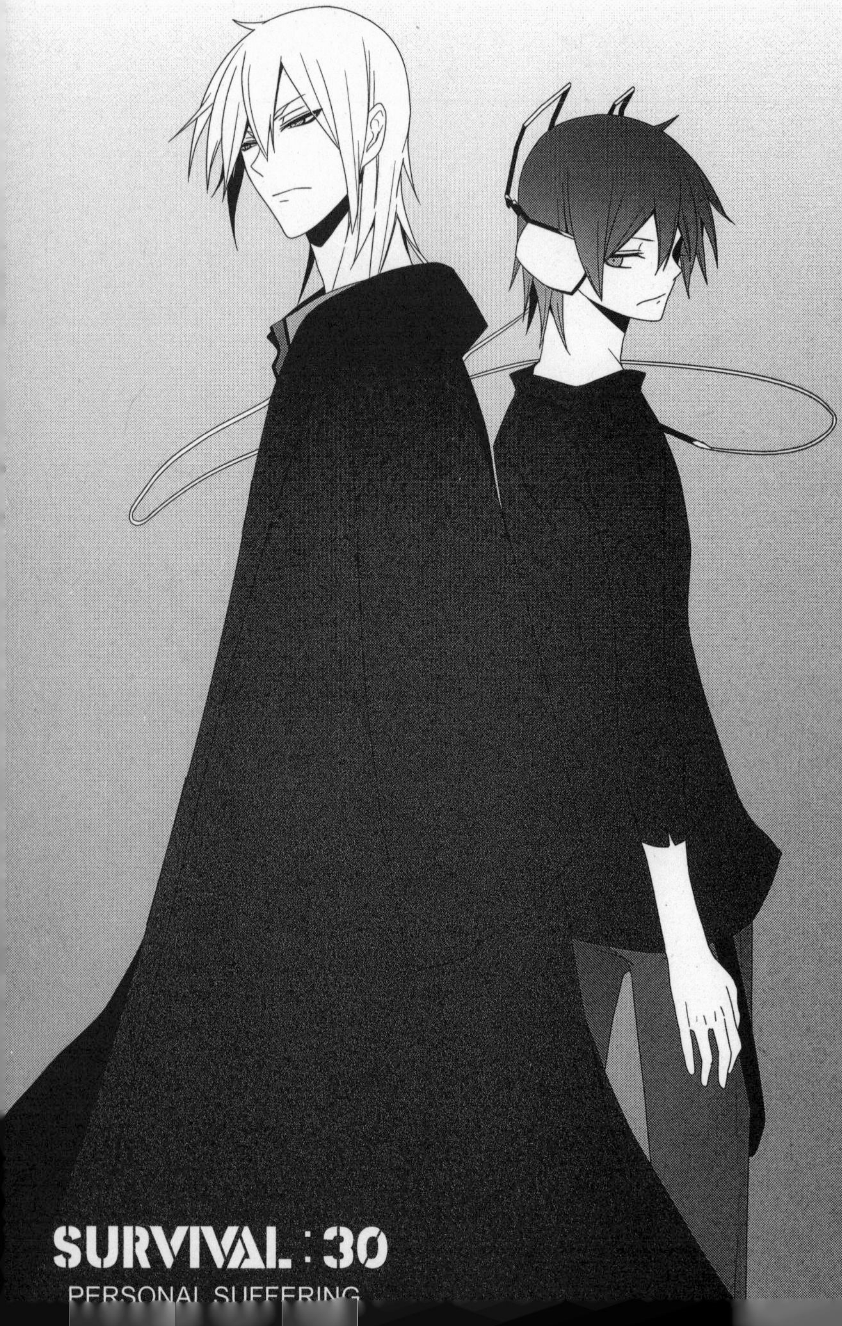

SURVIVAL : 30

PERSONAL SUFFERING

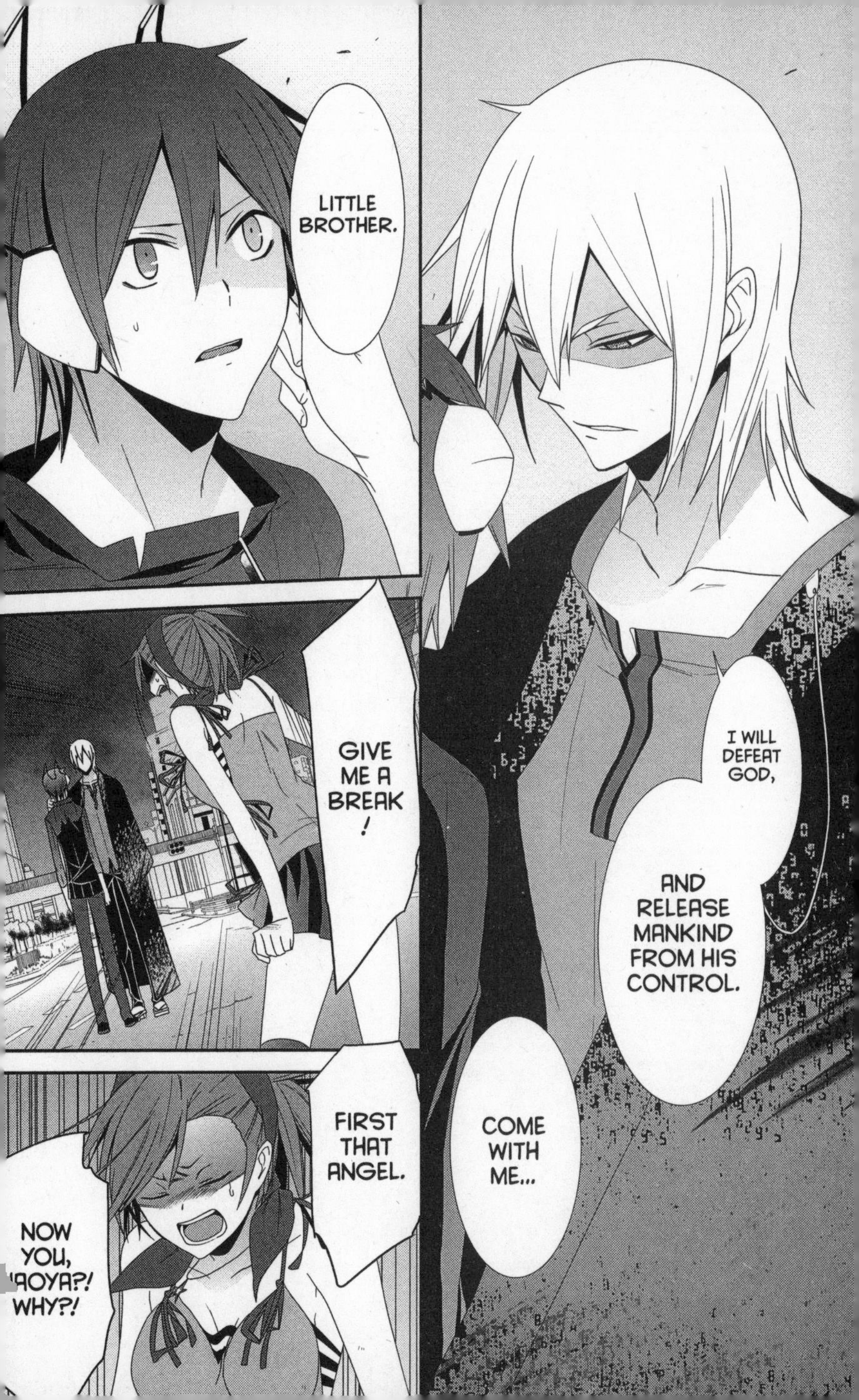

I WILL DEFEAT GOD,
AND RELEASE MANKIND FROM HIS CONTROL.
COME WITH ME...
LITTLE BROTHER.
GIVE ME A BREAK!
FIRST THAT ANGEL.
NOW YOU, AOYA?! WHY?!

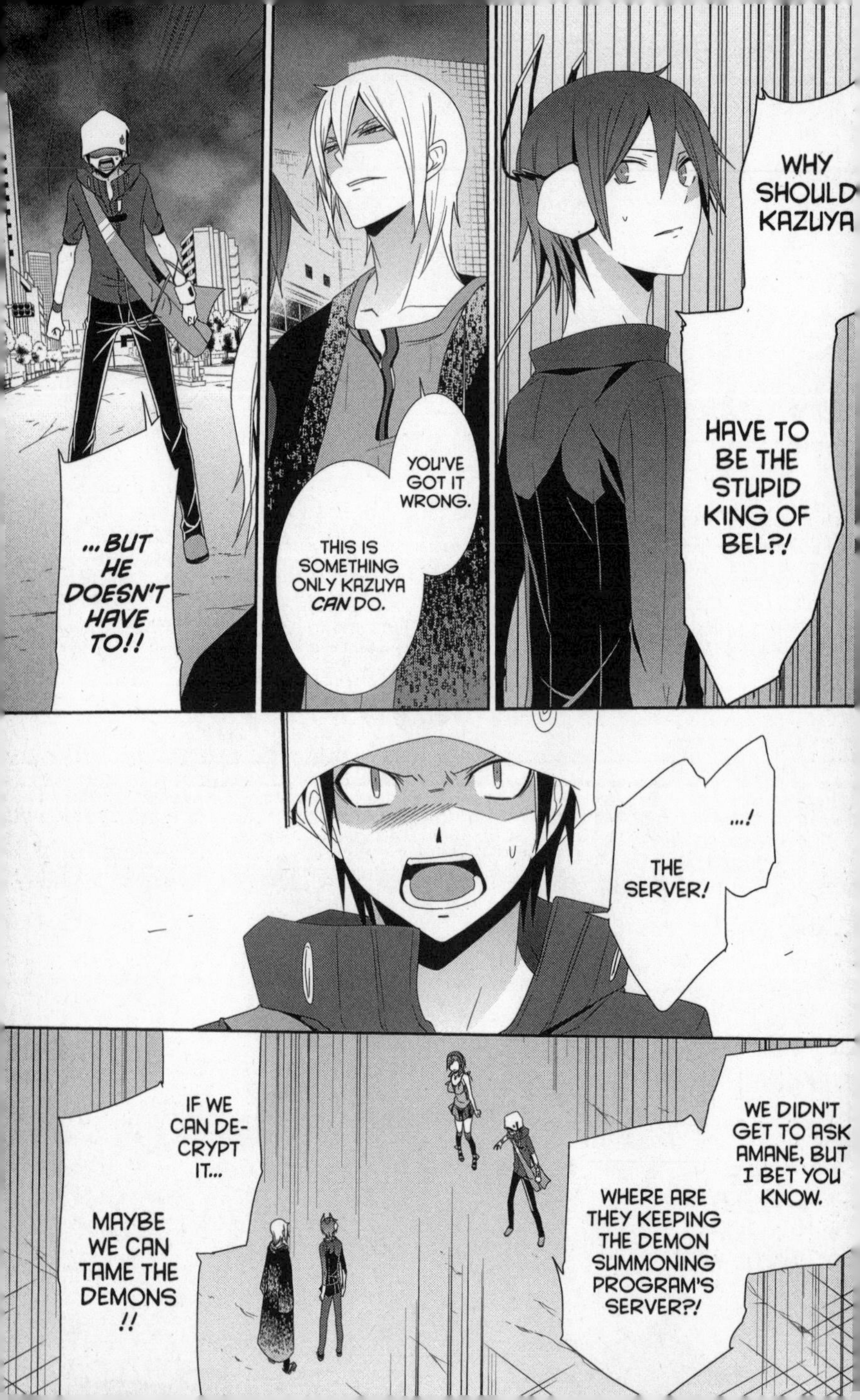
WHY SHOULD KAZUYA
HAVE TO BE THE STUPID KING OF BEL?!
YOU'VE GOT IT WRONG.
THIS IS SOMETHING ONLY KAZUYA *CAN* DO.
...BUT HE DOESN'T HAVE TO!!
...!
THE SERVER!
WE DIDN'T GET TO ASK AMANE, BUT I BET YOU KNOW.
WHERE ARE THEY KEEPING THE DEMON SUMMONING PROGRAM'S SERVER?!
IF WE CAN DE-CRYPT IT...
MAYBE WE CAN TAME THE DEMONS!!

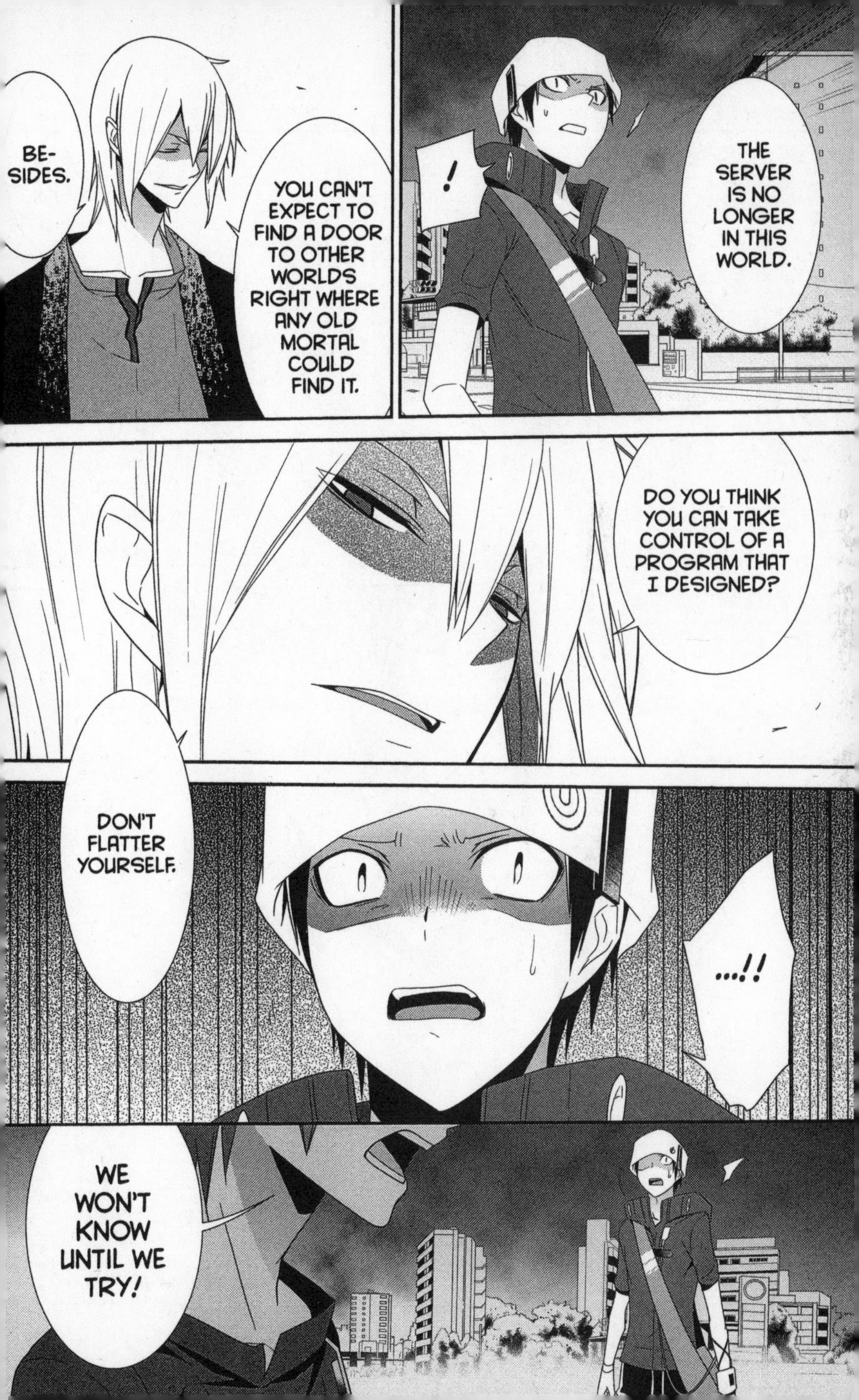
THE SERVER IS NO LONGER IN THIS WORLD.
!
YOU CAN'T EXPECT TO FIND A DOOR TO OTHER WORLDS RIGHT WHERE ANY OLD MORTAL COULD FIND IT.
BE-SIDES.
DO YOU THINK YOU CAN TAKE CONTROL OF A PROGRAM THAT I DESIGNED?
...!!
DON'T FLATTER YOURSELF.
WE WON'T KNOW UNTIL WE TRY!

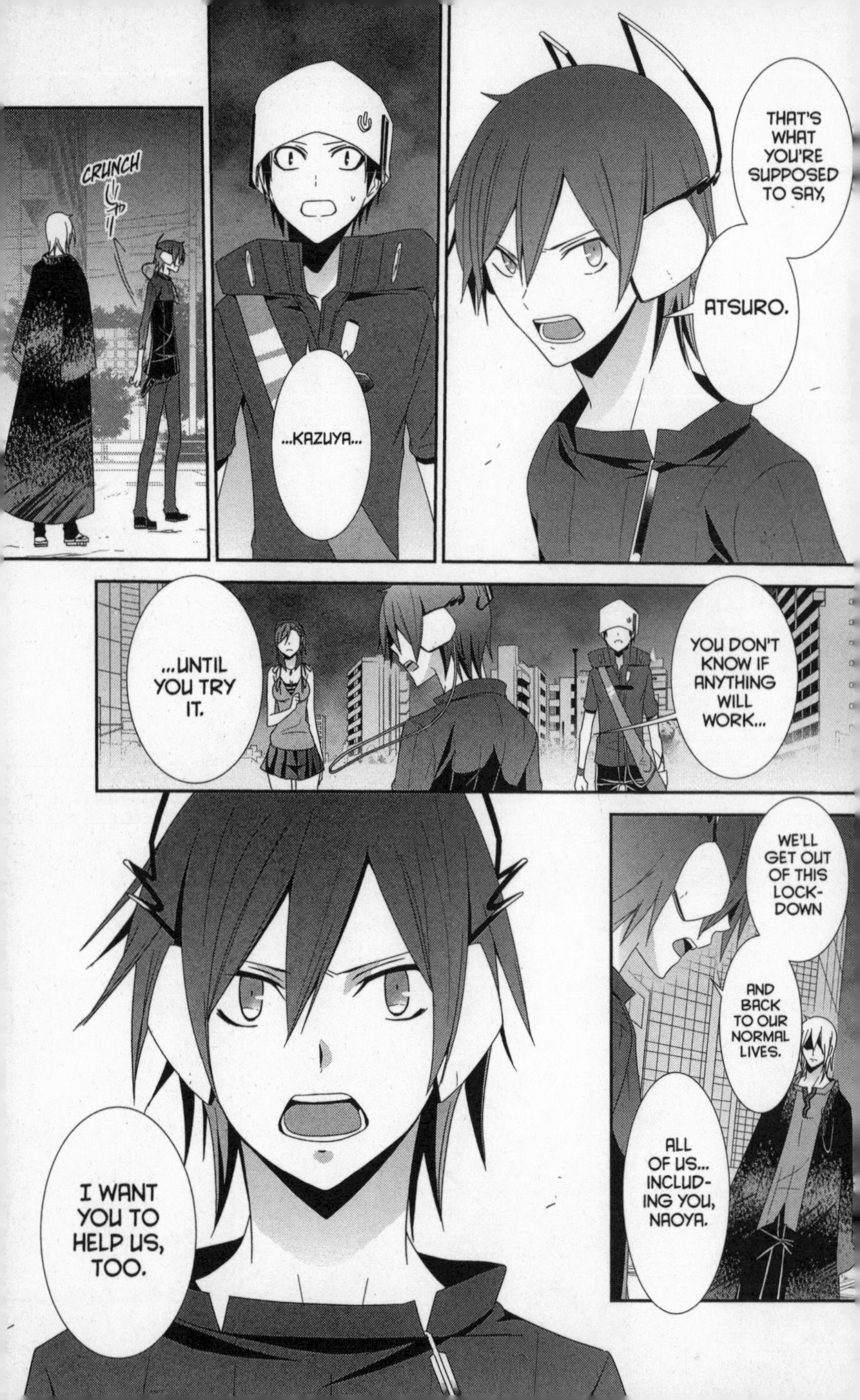
THAT'S WHAT YOU'RE SUPPOSED TO SAY,
ATSURO.
...KAZUYA...
CRUNCH
YOU DON'T KNOW IF ANYTHING WILL WORK...
...UNTIL YOU TRY IT.
WE'LL GET OUT OF THIS LOCK-DOWN
AND BACK TO OUR NORMAL LIVES.
ALL OF US... INCLUDING YOU, NAOYA.
I WANT YOU TO HELP US, TOO.

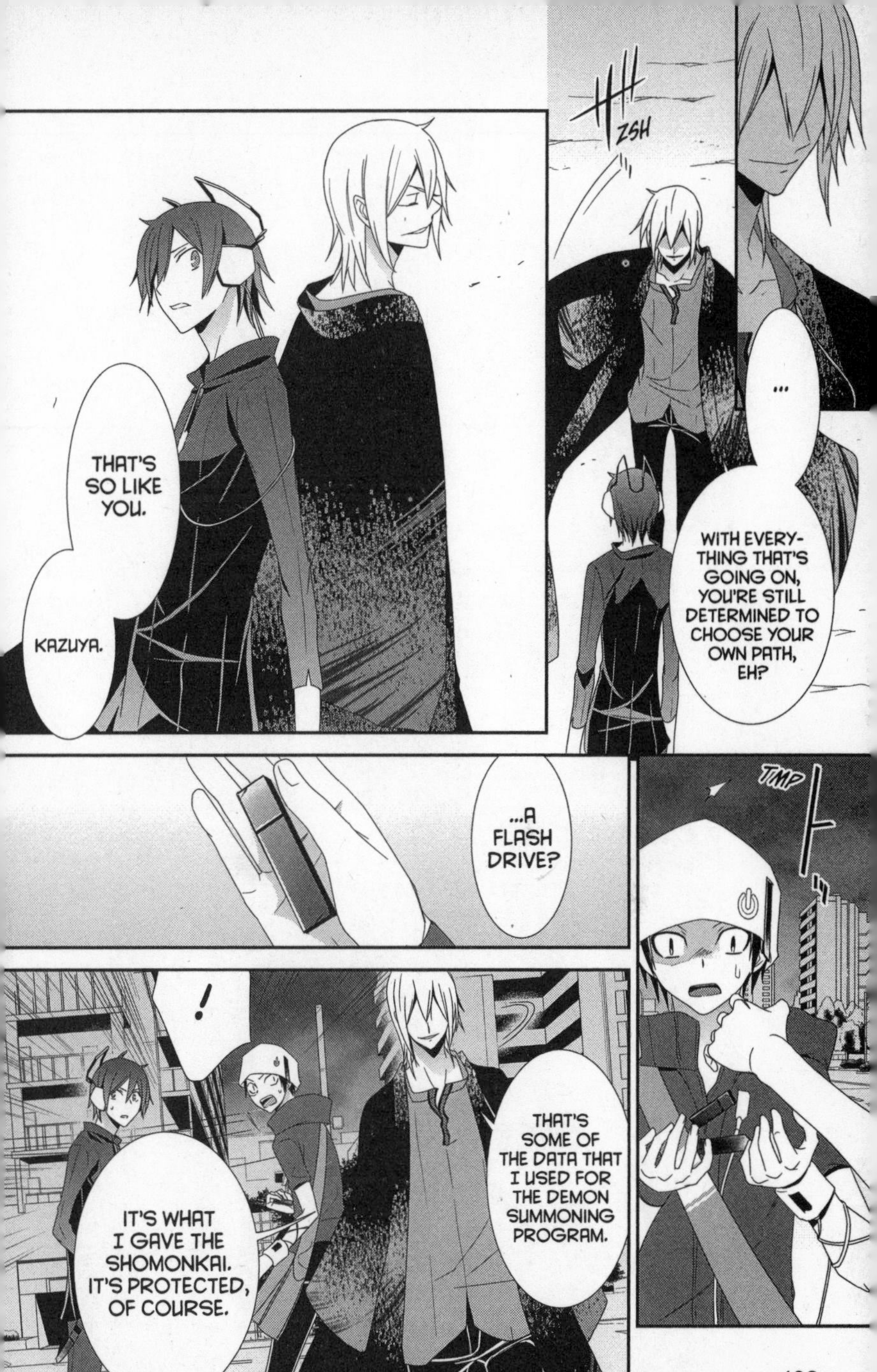
ZSH
...
WITH EVERY-THING THAT'S GOING ON, YOU'RE STILL DETERMINED TO CHOOSE YOUR OWN PATH, EH?
THAT'S SO LIKE YOU.
KAZUYA.
TMP
...A FLASH DRIVE?
!
THAT'S SOME OF THE DATA THAT I USED FOR THE DEMON SUMMONING PROGRAM.
IT'S WHAT I GAVE THE SHOMONKAI. IT'S PROTECTED, OF COURSE.

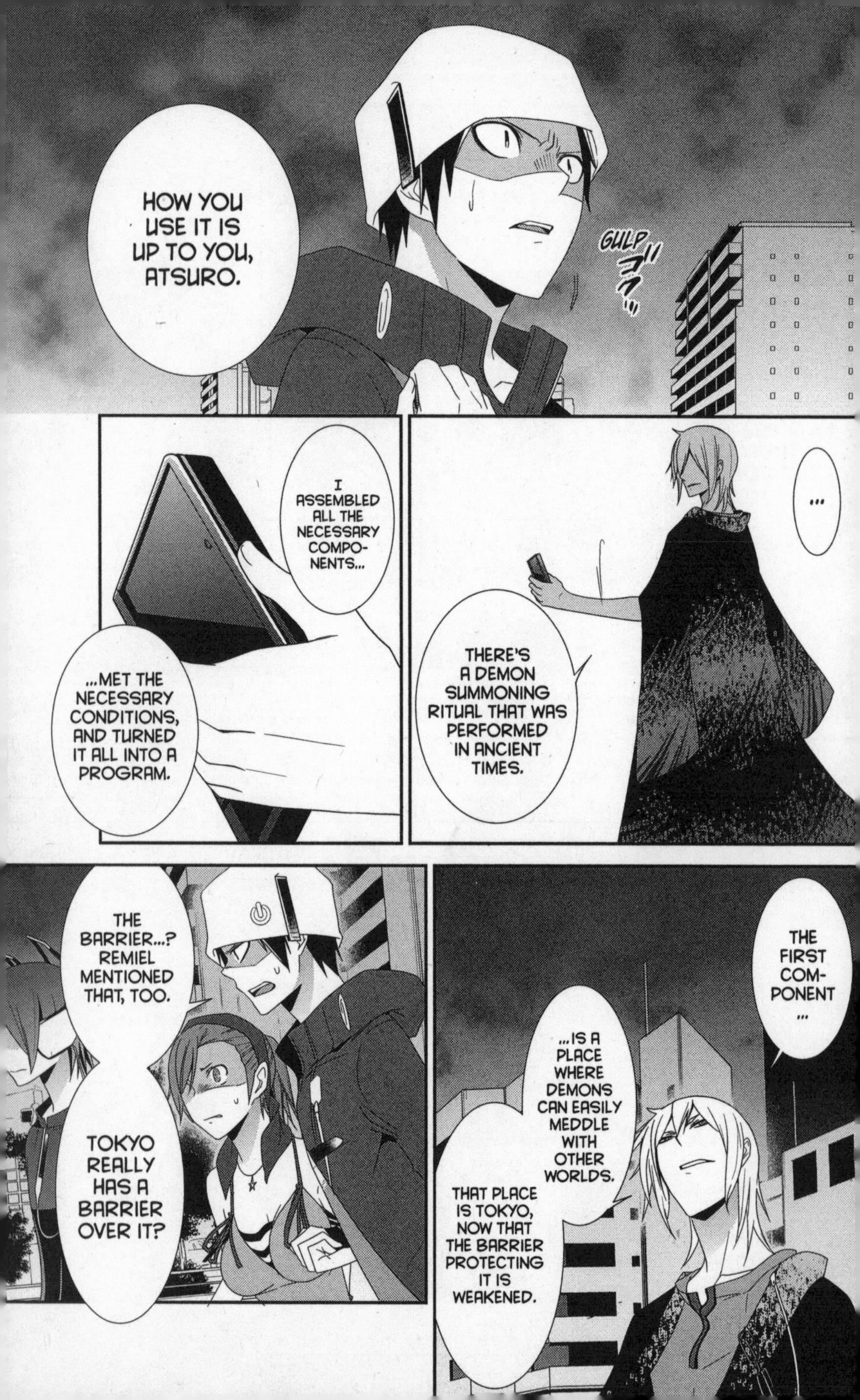

HOW YOU USE IT IS UP TO YOU, ATSURO.
GULP
...
THERE'S A DEMON SUMMONING RITUAL THAT WAS PERFORMED IN ANCIENT TIMES.
I ASSEMBLED ALL THE NECESSARY COMPONENTS...
...MET THE NECESSARY CONDITIONS, AND TURNED IT ALL INTO A PROGRAM.
THE FIRST COMPONENT...
...IS A PLACE WHERE DEMONS CAN EASILY MEDDLE WITH OTHER WORLDS.
THAT PLACE IS TOKYO, NOW THAT THE BARRIER PROTECTING IT IS WEAKENED.
THE BARRIER...? REMIEL MENTIONED THAT, TOO.
TOKYO REALLY HAS A BARRIER OVER IT?

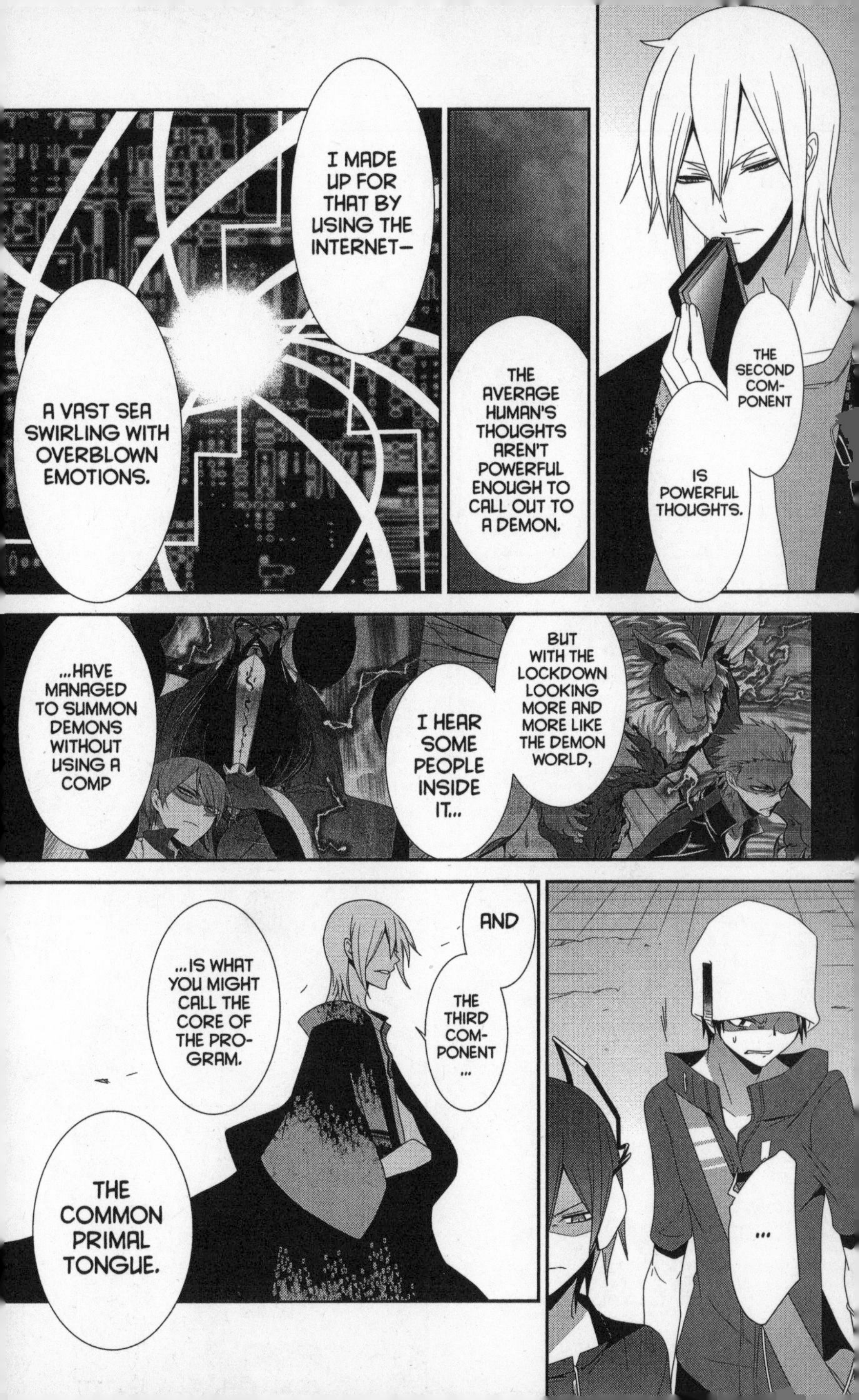
THE SECOND COMPONENT
IS POWERFUL THOUGHTS.
THE AVERAGE HUMAN'S THOUGHTS AREN'T POWERFUL ENOUGH TO CALL OUT TO A DEMON.
I MADE UP FOR THAT BY USING THE INTERNET—
A VAST SEA SWIRLING WITH OVERBLOWN EMOTIONS.
BUT WITH THE LOCKDOWN LOOKING MORE AND MORE LIKE THE DEMON WORLD,
I HEAR SOME PEOPLE INSIDE IT...
...HAVE MANAGED TO SUMMON DEMONS WITHOUT USING A COMP
...
AND
THE THIRD COMPONENT ...
...IS WHAT YOU MIGHT CALL THE CORE OF THE PROGRAM.
THE COMMON PRIMAL TONGUE.

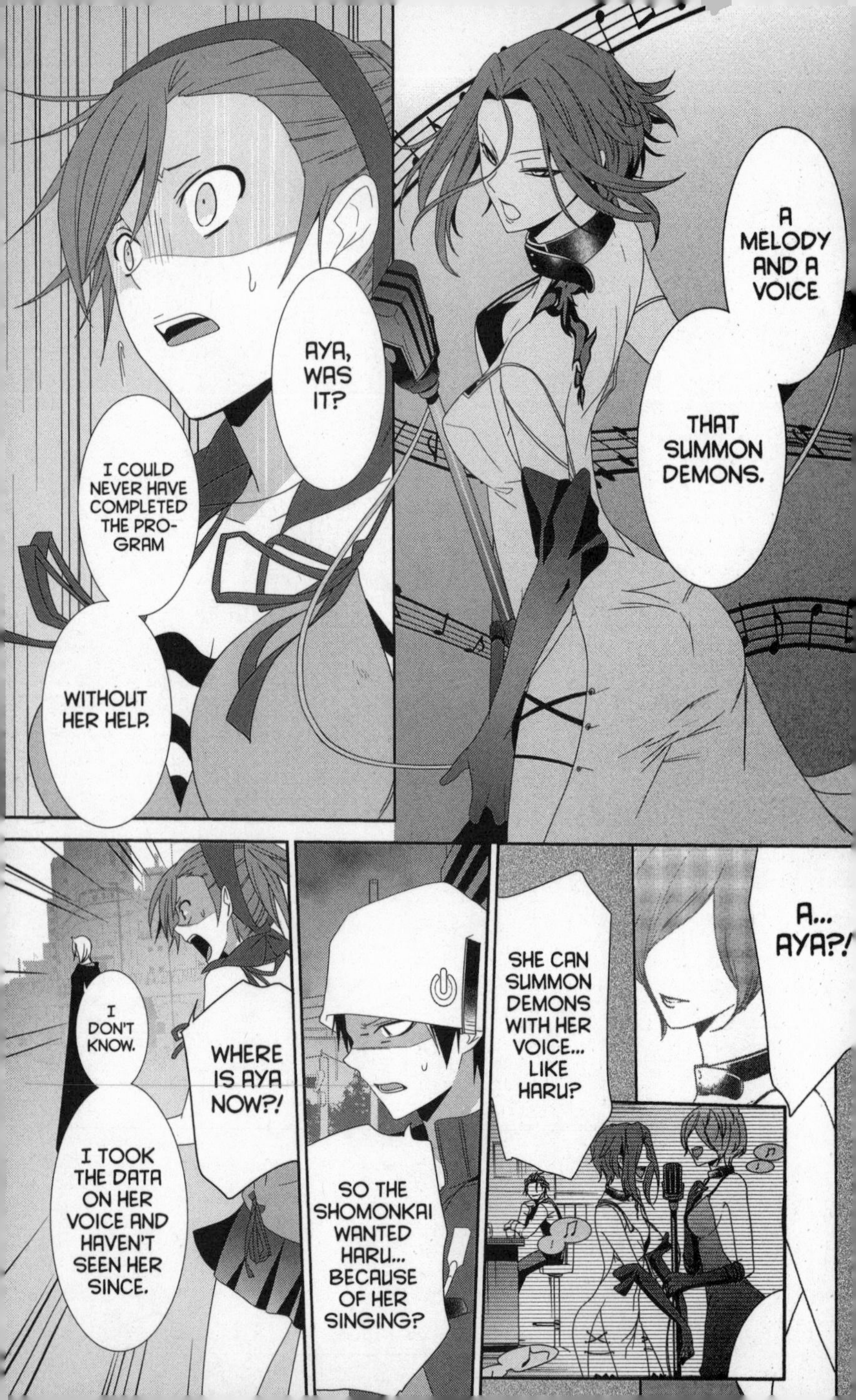
A MELODY AND A VOICE
THAT SUMMON DEMONS.
AYA, WAS IT?
I COULD NEVER HAVE COMPLETED THE PRO-GRAM
WITHOUT HER HELP.
A... AYA?!
SHE CAN SUMMON DEMONS WITH HER VOICE... LIKE HARU?
SO THE SHOMONKAI WANTED HARU... BECAUSE OF HER SINGING?
WHERE IS AYA NOW?!
I DON'T KNOW.
I TOOK THE DATA ON HER VOICE AND HAVEN'T SEEN HER SINCE.

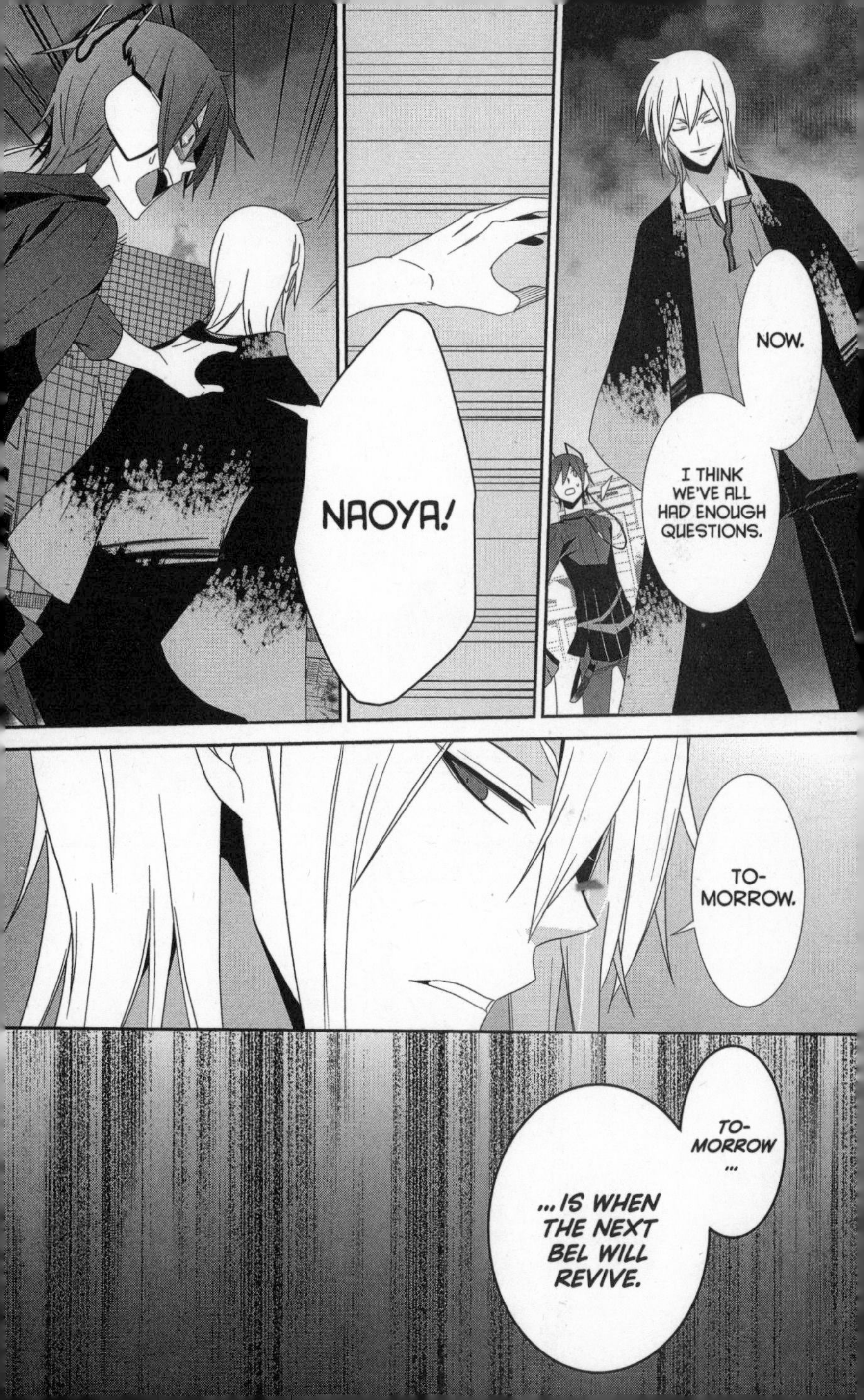
NOW.
I THINK WE'VE ALL HAD ENOUGH QUESTIONS.
NAOYA!
TO-MORROW.
TO-MORROW...
...IS WHEN THE NEXT BEL WILL REVIVE.

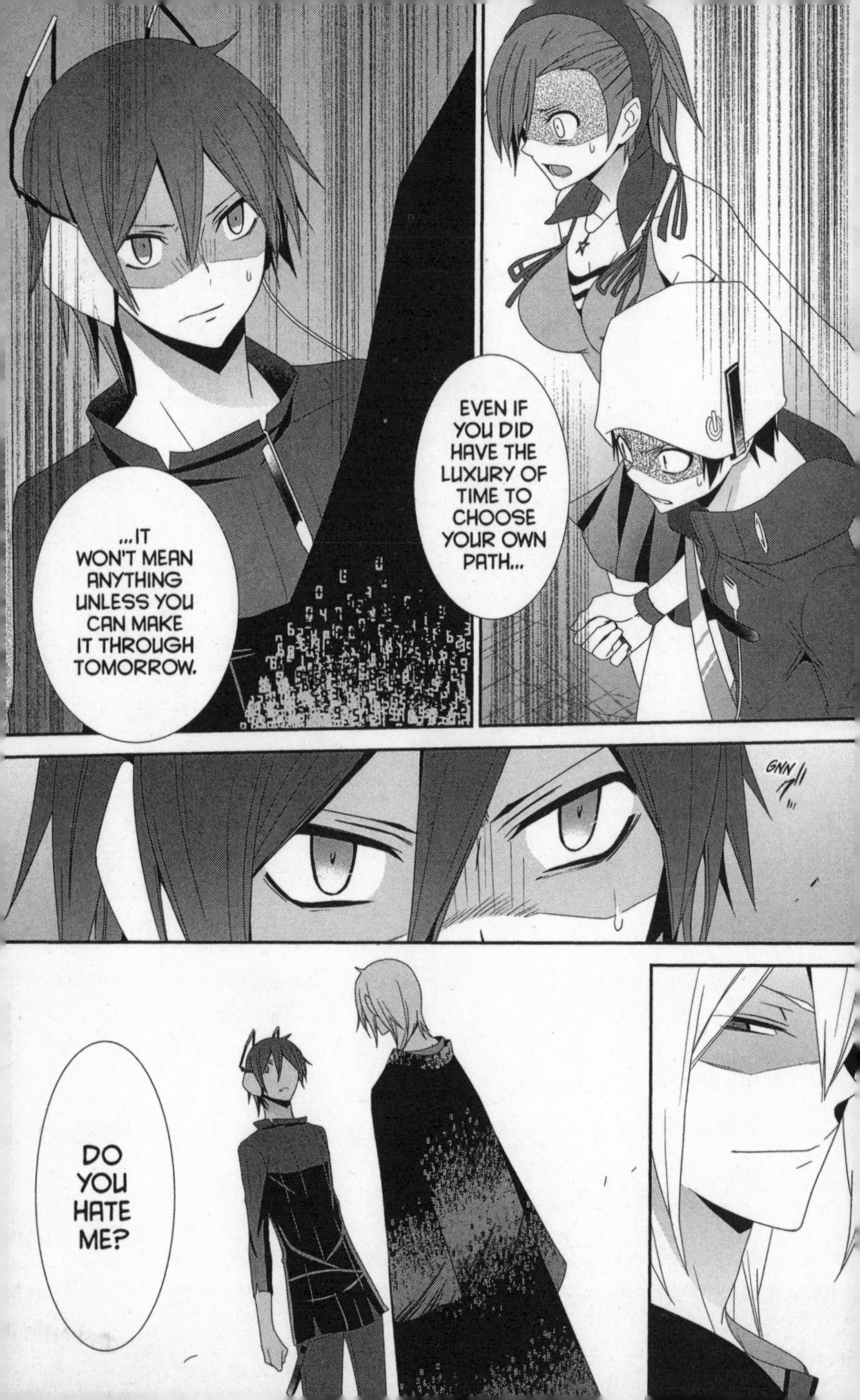
EVEN IF YOU DID HAVE THE LUXURY OF TIME TO CHOOSE YOUR OWN PATH...
...IT WON'T MEAN ANYTHING UNLESS YOU CAN MAKE IT THROUGH TOMORROW.
GNN
DO YOU HATE ME?

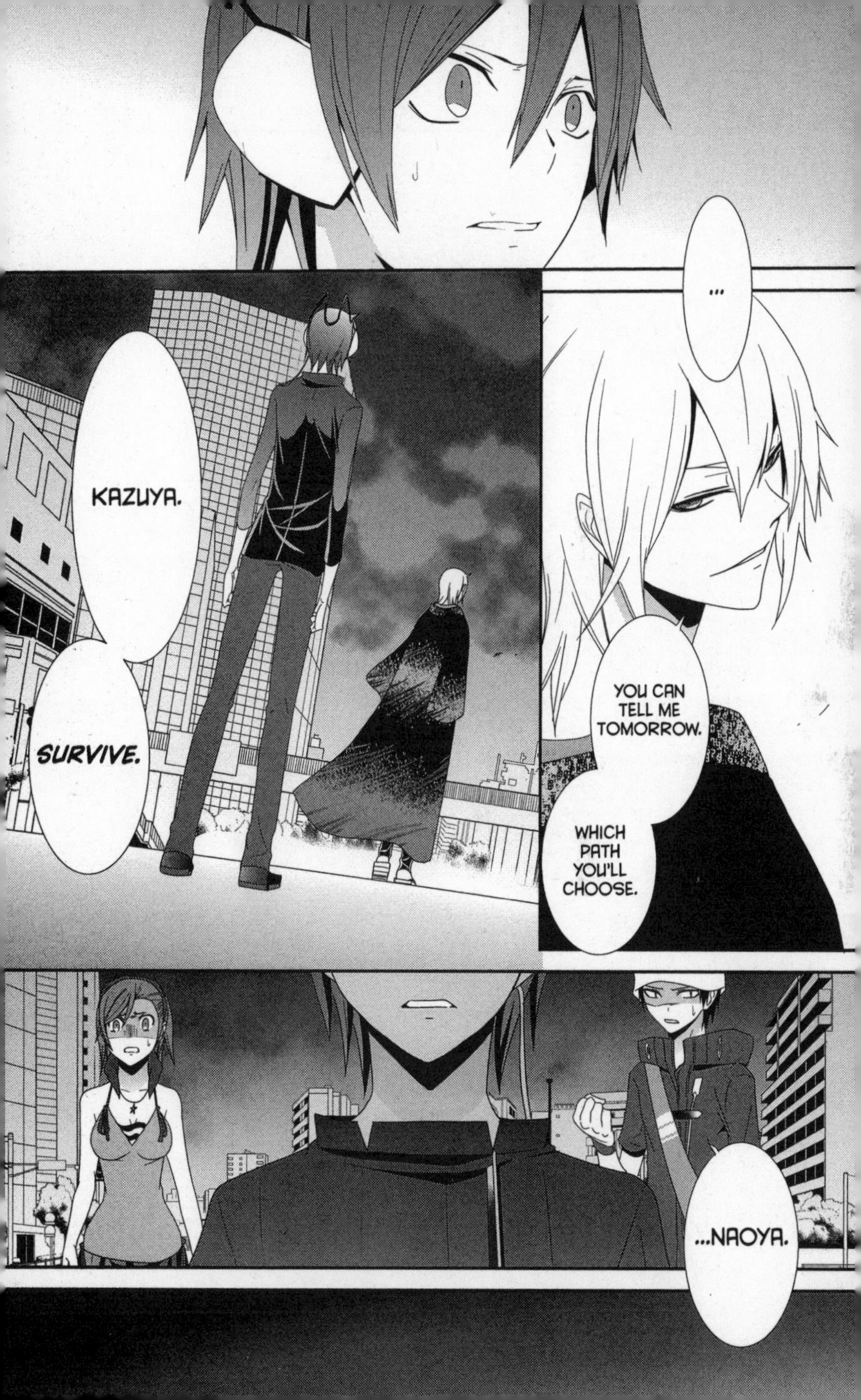
...
YOU CAN TELL ME TOMORROW.
WHICH PATH YOU'LL CHOOSE.
KAZUYA.
SURVIVE.
...NAOYA.

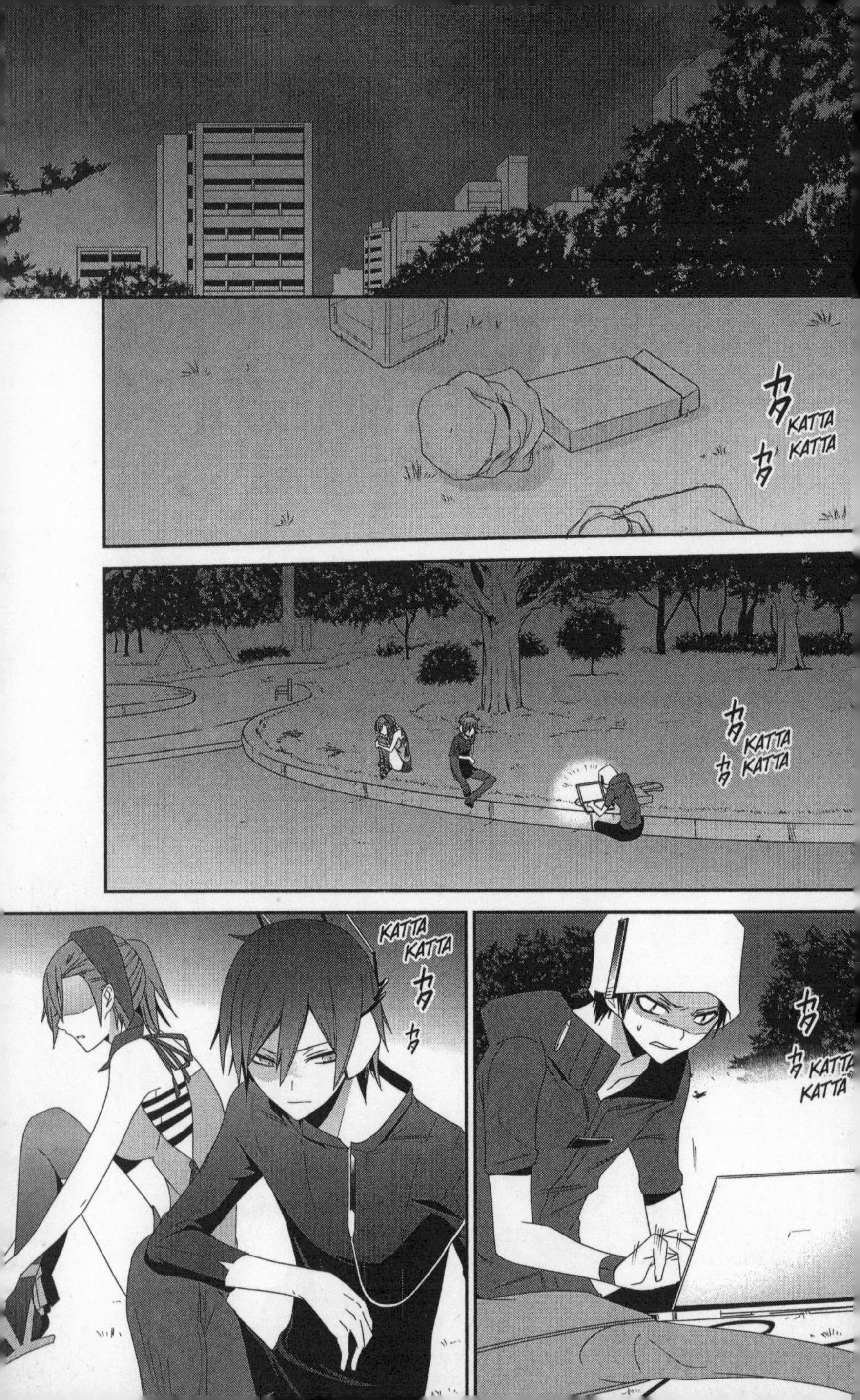
カタ
KATTA
KATTA
カタ
カタ
KATTA
カタ
KATTA
カタ
カタ
KATTA
KATTA
KATTA
KATTA
カタ
カタ

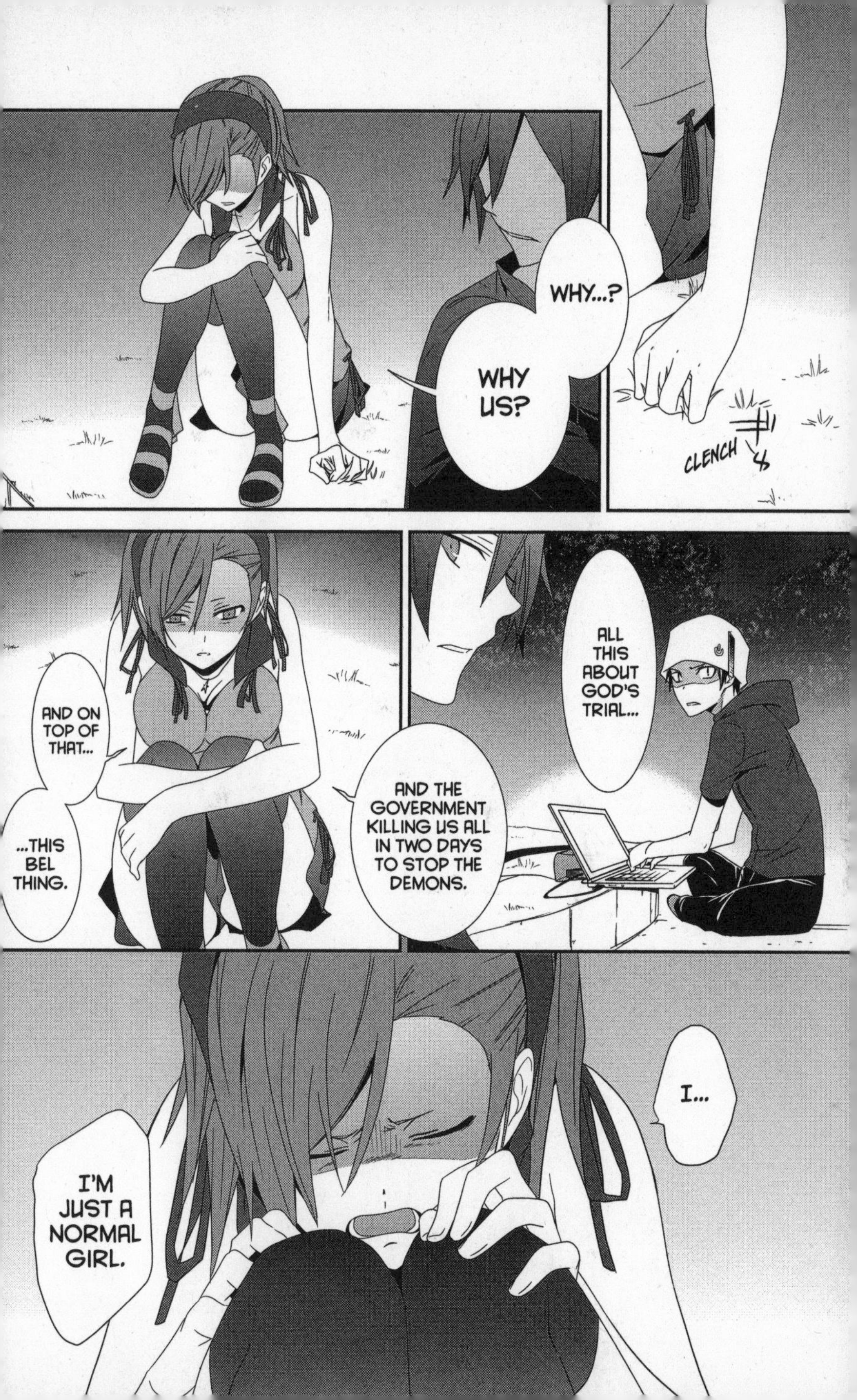
CLENCH
WHY...?
WHY US?
ALL THIS ABOUT GOD'S TRIAL...
AND THE GOVERNMENT KILLING US ALL IN TWO DAYS TO STOP THE DEMONS.
AND ON TOP OF THAT...
...THIS BEL THING.
I...
I'M JUST A NORMAL GIRL.

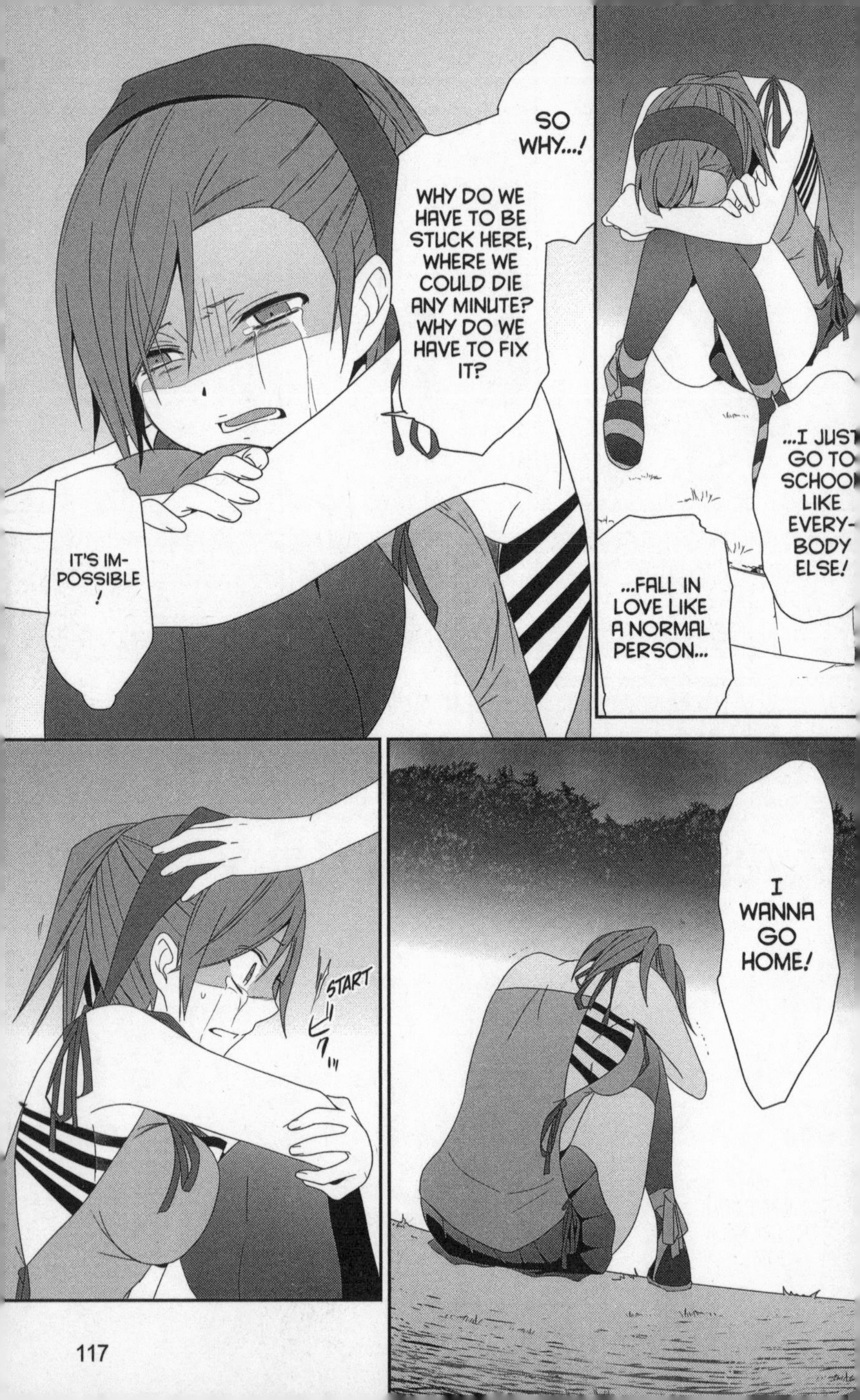
...I JUST GO TO SCHOO LIKE EVERY-BODY ELSE!
...FALL IN LOVE LIKE A NORMAL PERSON...
SO WHY...!
WHY DO WE HAVE TO BE STUCK HERE, WHERE WE COULD DIE ANY MINUTE? WHY DO WE HAVE TO FIX IT?
IT'S IM-POSSIBLE!
I WANNA GO HOME!
START

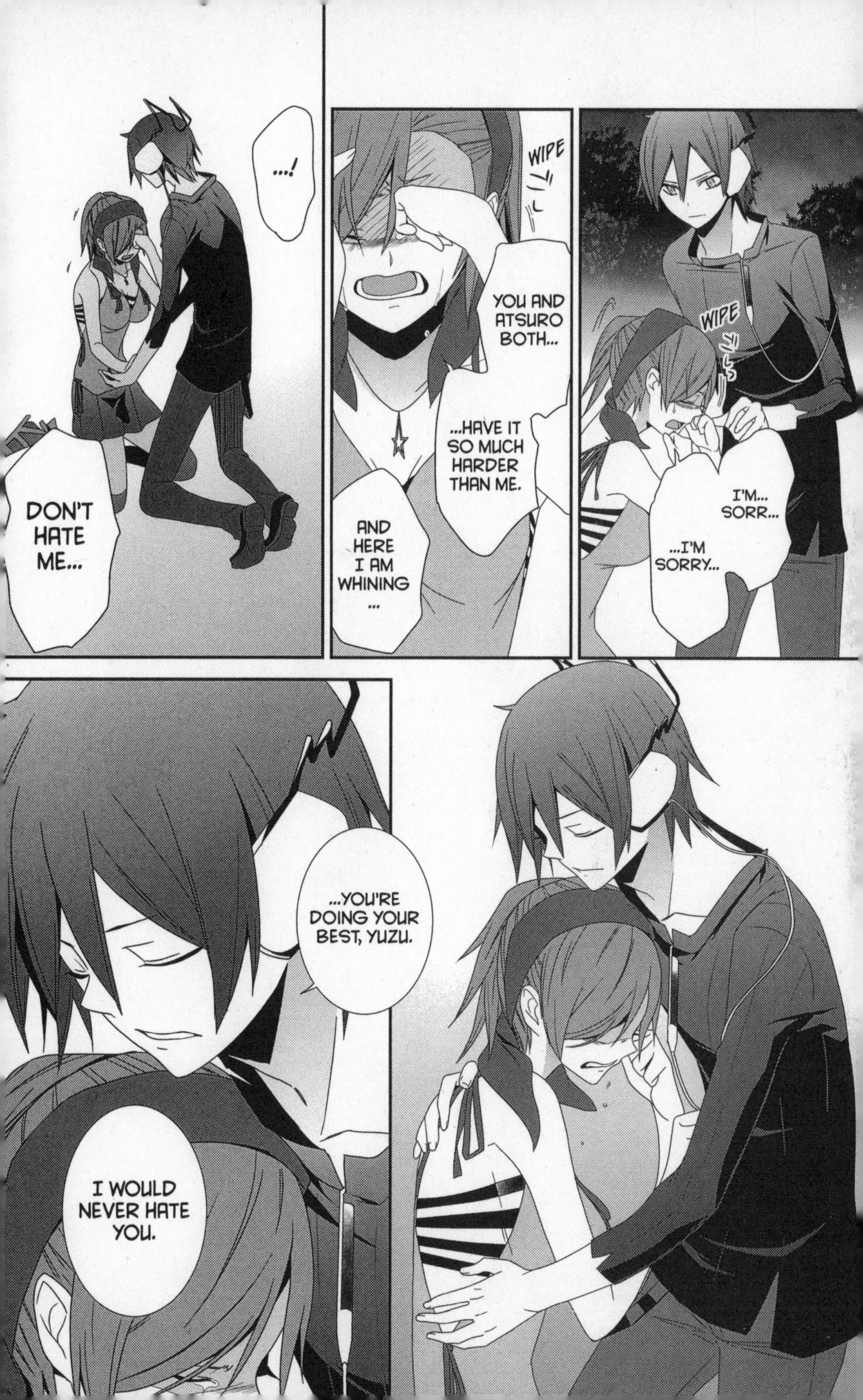
WIPE
I'M... SORR...
...I'M SORRY...
WIPE
YOU AND ATSURO BOTH...
...HAVE IT SO MUCH HARDER THAN ME.
AND HERE I AM WHINING ...
...!
DON'T HATE ME...
...YOU'RE DOING YOUR BEST, YUZU.
I WOULD NEVER HATE YOU.

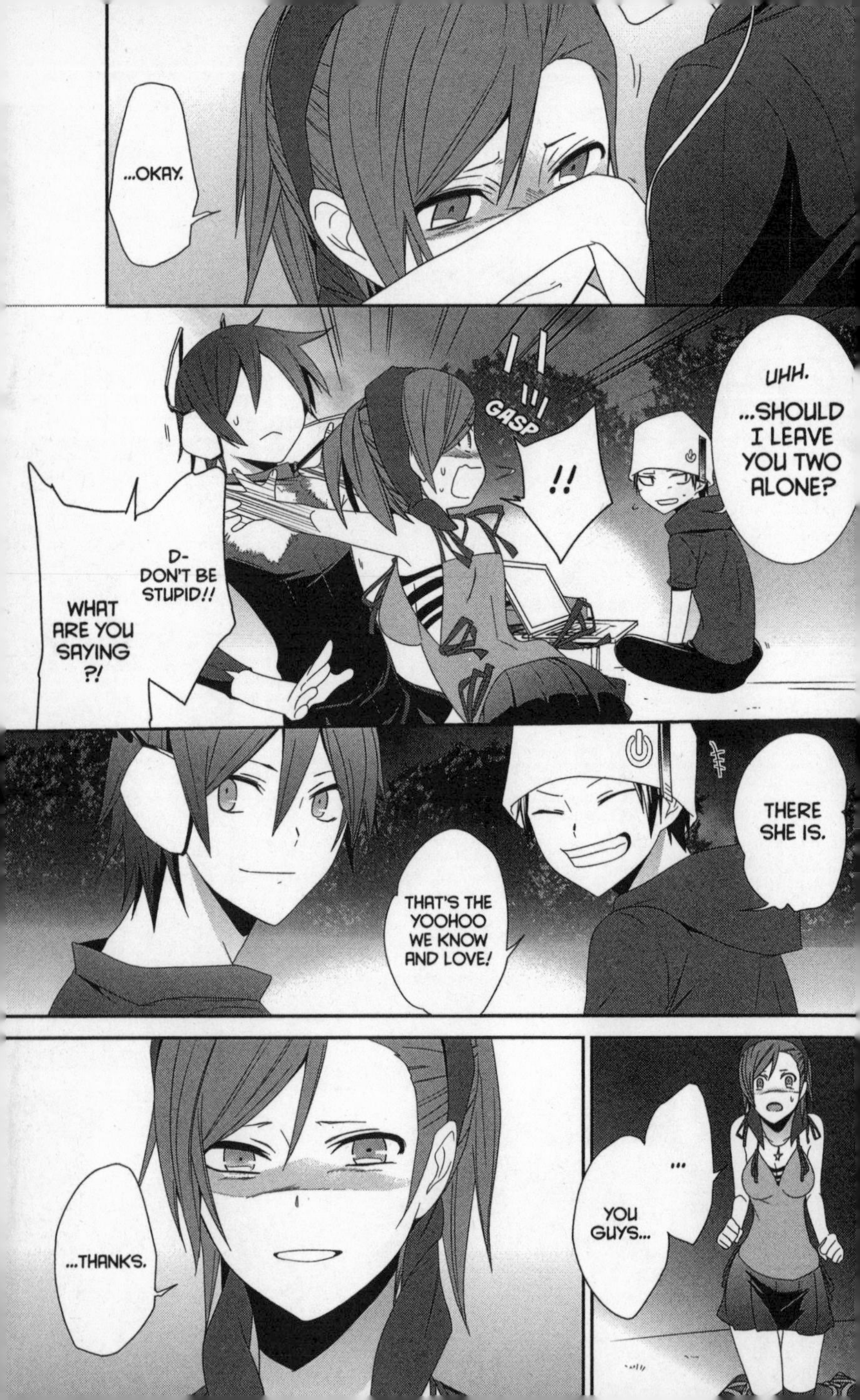
...OKAY.
UHH. ...SHOULD I LEAVE YOU TWO ALONE?
GASP
!!
D- DON'T BE STUPID!!
WHAT ARE YOU SAYING ?!
THERE SHE IS.
THAT'S THE YOOHOO WE KNOW AND LOVE!
...
YOU GUYS...
...THANKS.

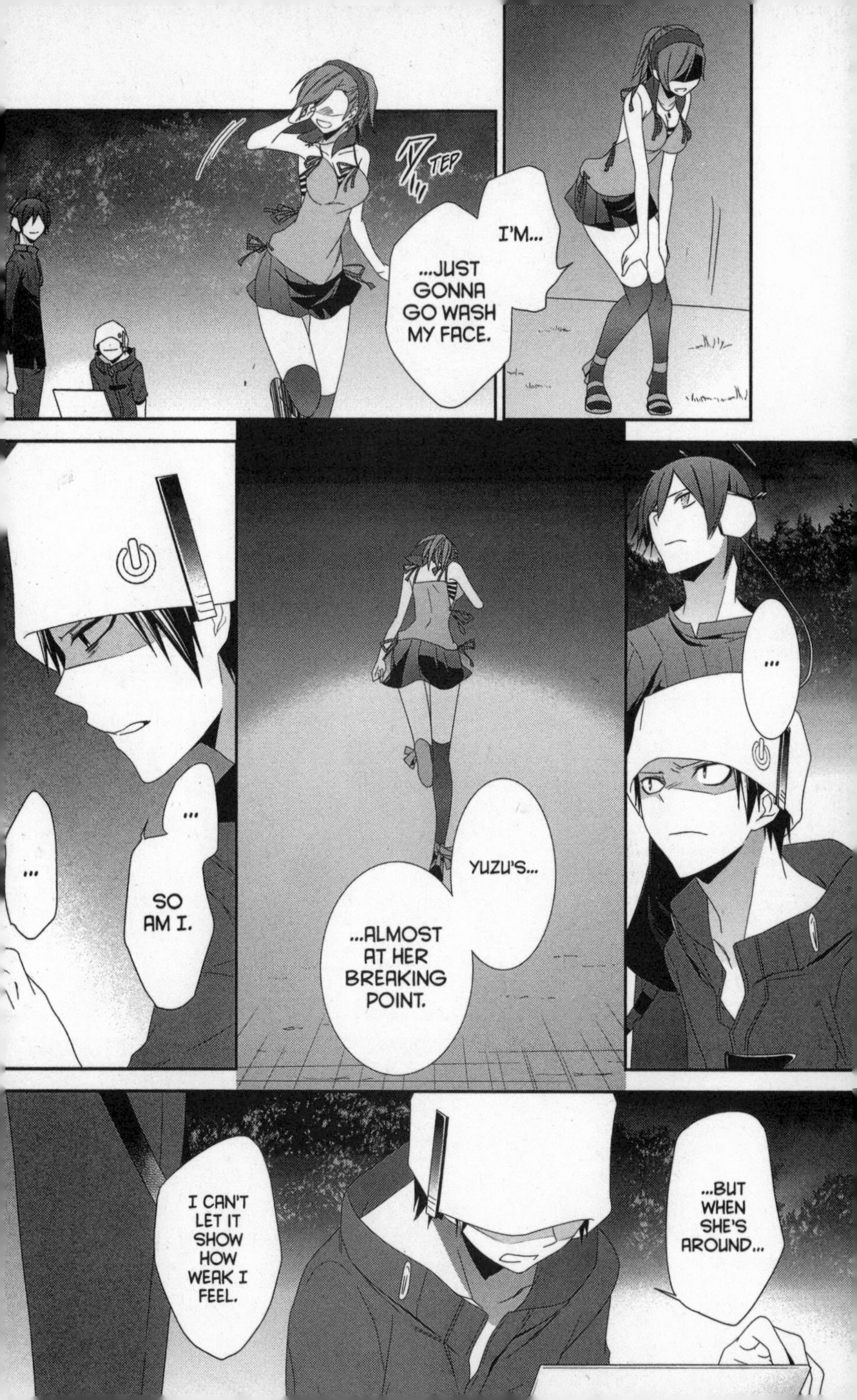
TEP
I'M...
...JUST GONNA GO WASH MY FACE.
...
YUZU'S...
...ALMOST AT HER BREAKING POINT.
...
SO AM I.
...
...BUT WHEN SHE'S AROUND...
I CAN'T LET IT SHOW HOW WEAK I FEEL.

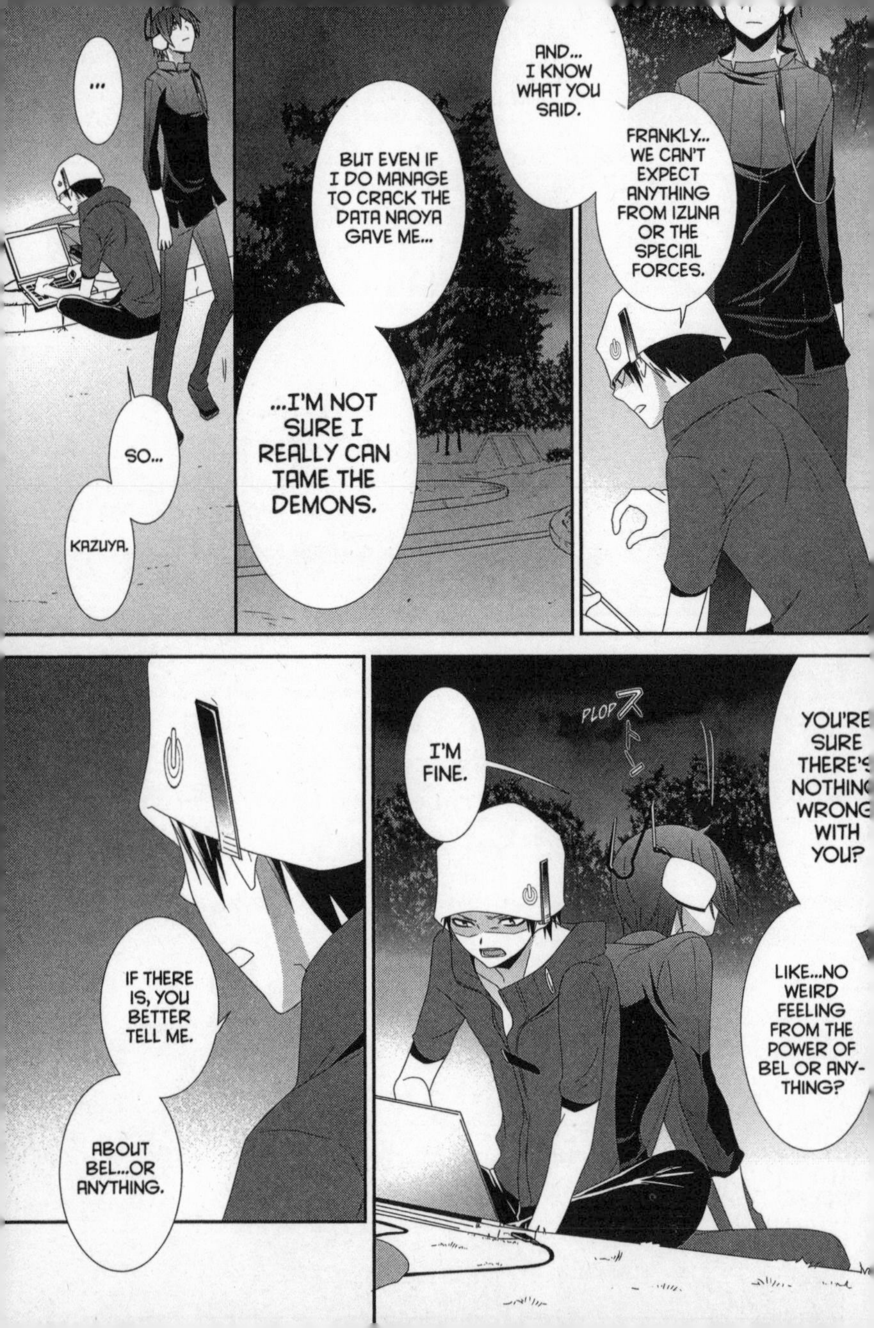
AND... I KNOW WHAT YOU SAID.
FRANKLY... WE CAN'T EXPECT ANYTHING FROM IZUNA OR THE SPECIAL FORCES.
BUT EVEN IF I DO MANAGE TO CRACK THE DATA NAOYA GAVE ME...
...I'M NOT SURE I REALLY CAN TAME THE DEMONS.
...
SO...
KAZUYA.
YOU'RE SURE THERE'S NOTHING WRONG WITH YOU?
LIKE...NO WEIRD FEELING FROM THE POWER OF BEL OR ANY-THING?
PLOP
I'M FINE.
IF THERE IS, YOU BETTER TELL ME.
ABOUT BEL...OR ANYTHING.

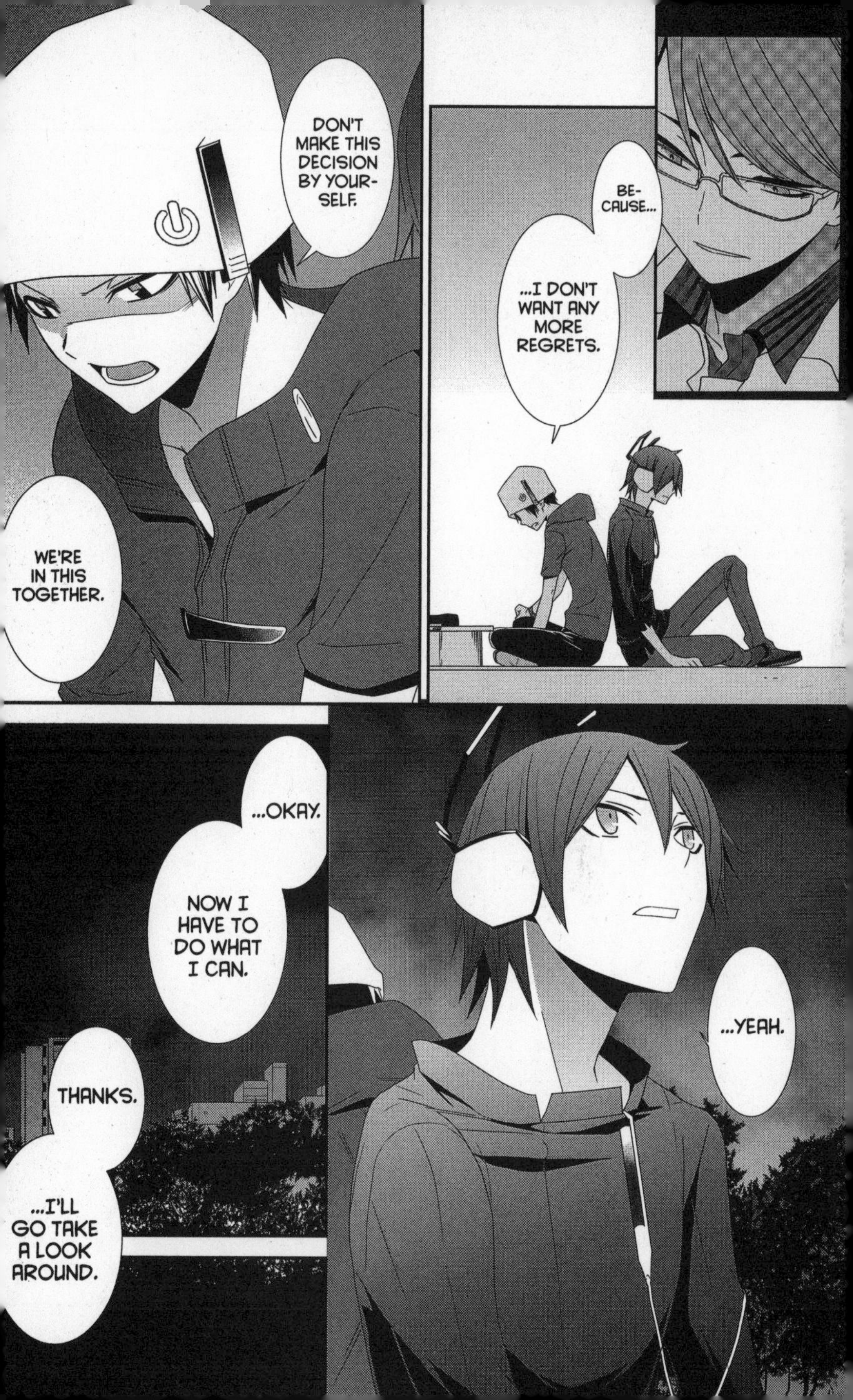
BE-CAUSE...
...I DON'T WANT ANY MORE REGRETS.
DON'T MAKE THIS DECISION BY YOUR-SELF.
WE'RE IN THIS TOGETHER.
...YEAH.
...OKAY.
NOW I HAVE TO DO WHAT I CAN.
THANKS.
...I'LL GO TAKE A LOOK AROUND.

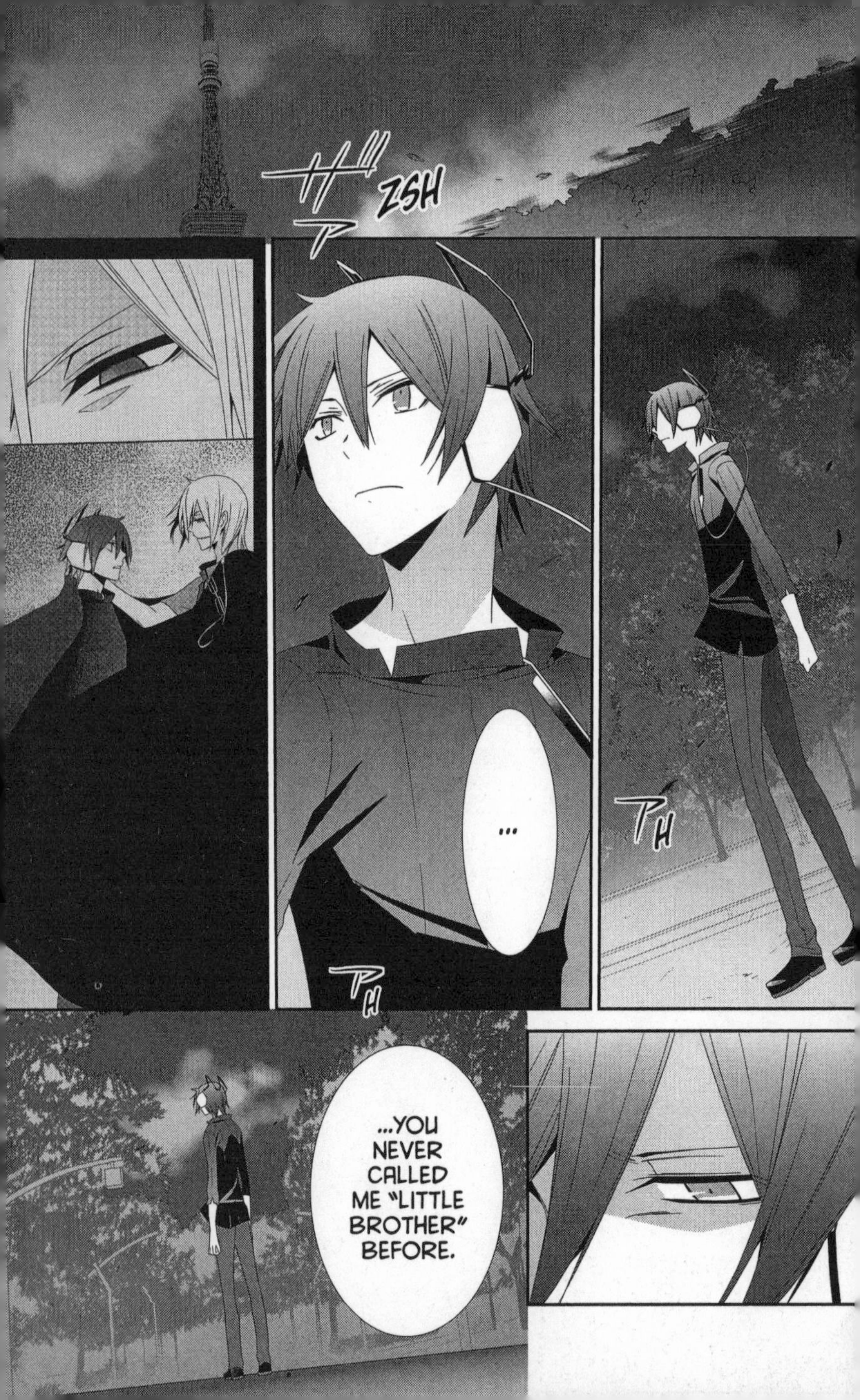
ZSH
PH
...
PH
...YOU NEVER CALLED ME "LITTLE BROTHER" BEFORE.

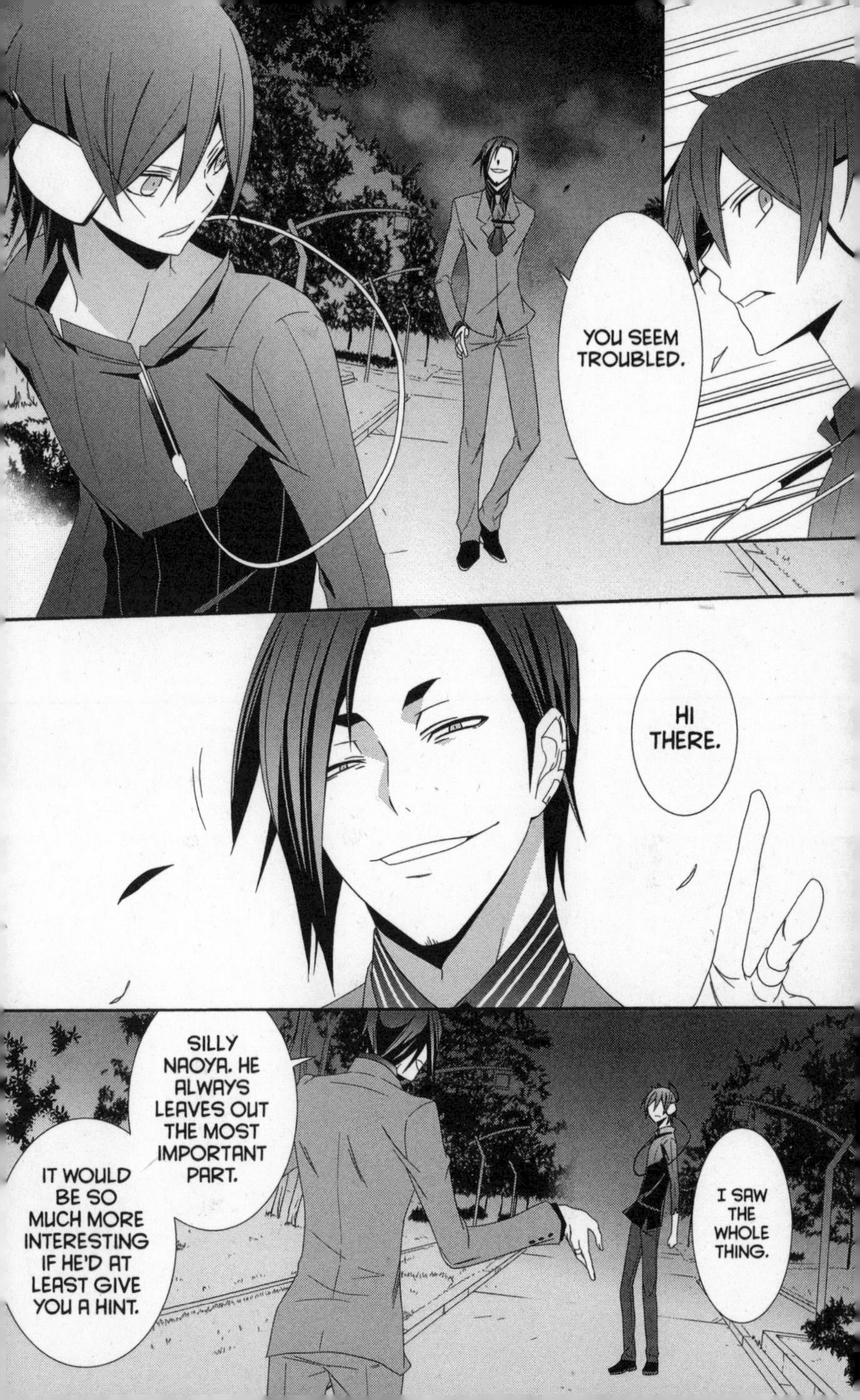
YOU SEEM TROUBLED.
HI THERE.
I SAW THE WHOLE THING.
SILLY NAOYA. HE ALWAYS LEAVES OUT THE MOST IMPORTANT PART.
IT WOULD BE SO MUCH MORE INTERESTING IF HE'D AT LEAST GIVE YOU A HINT.

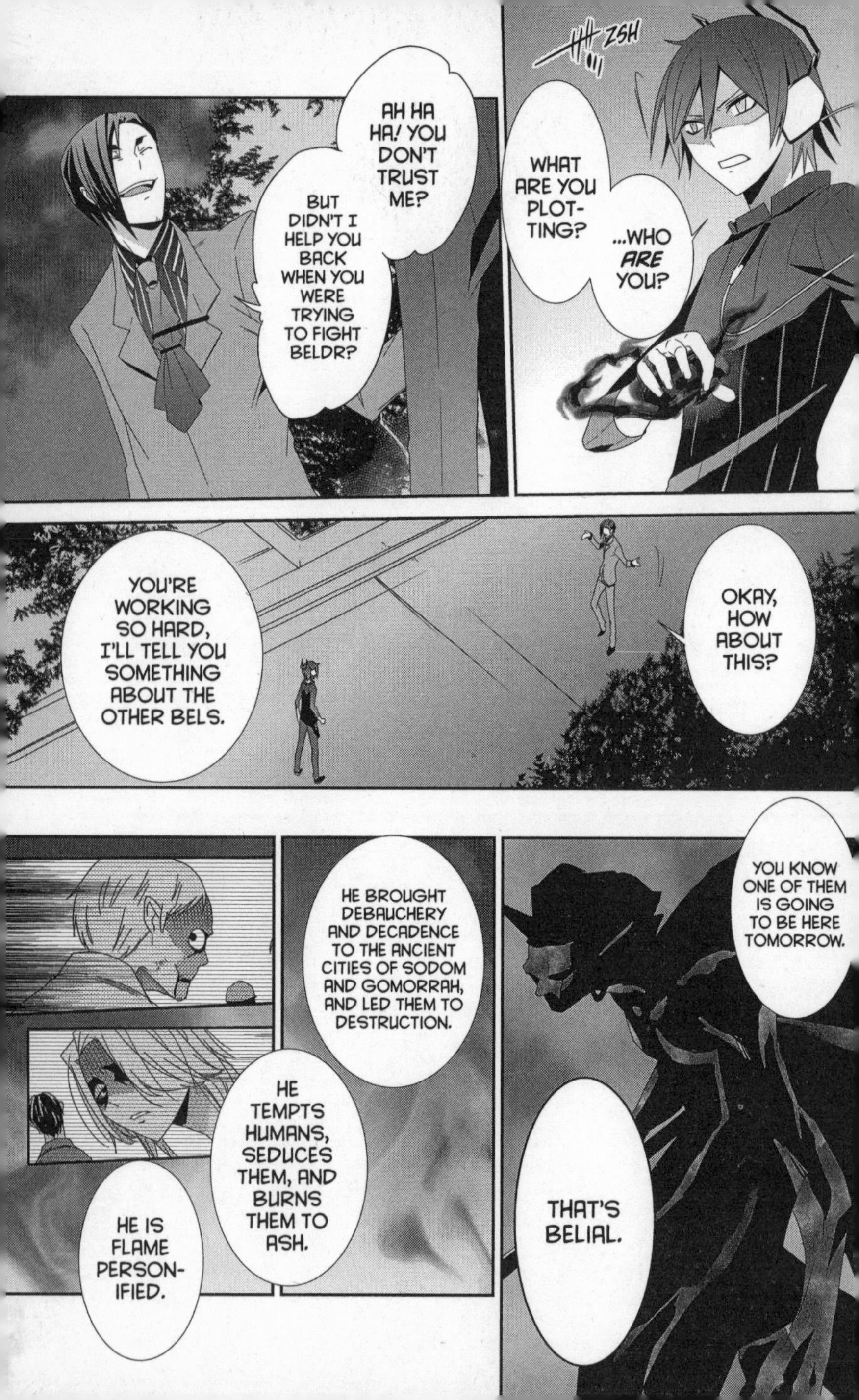
ZSH
WHAT ARE YOU PLOTTING?
...WHO *ARE* YOU?
AH HA HA! YOU DON'T TRUST ME?
BUT DIDN'T I HELP YOU BACK WHEN YOU WERE TRYING TO FIGHT BELDR?
OKAY, HOW ABOUT THIS?
YOU'RE WORKING SO HARD, I'LL TELL YOU SOMETHING ABOUT THE OTHER BELS.
YOU KNOW ONE OF THEM IS GOING TO BE HERE TOMORROW.
THAT'S BELIAL.
HE BROUGHT DEBAUCHERY AND DECADENCE TO THE ANCIENT CITIES OF SODOM AND GOMORRAH, AND LED THEM TO DESTRUCTION.
HE TEMPTS HUMANS, SEDUCES THEM, AND BURNS THEM TO ASH.
HE IS FLAME PERSONIFIED.

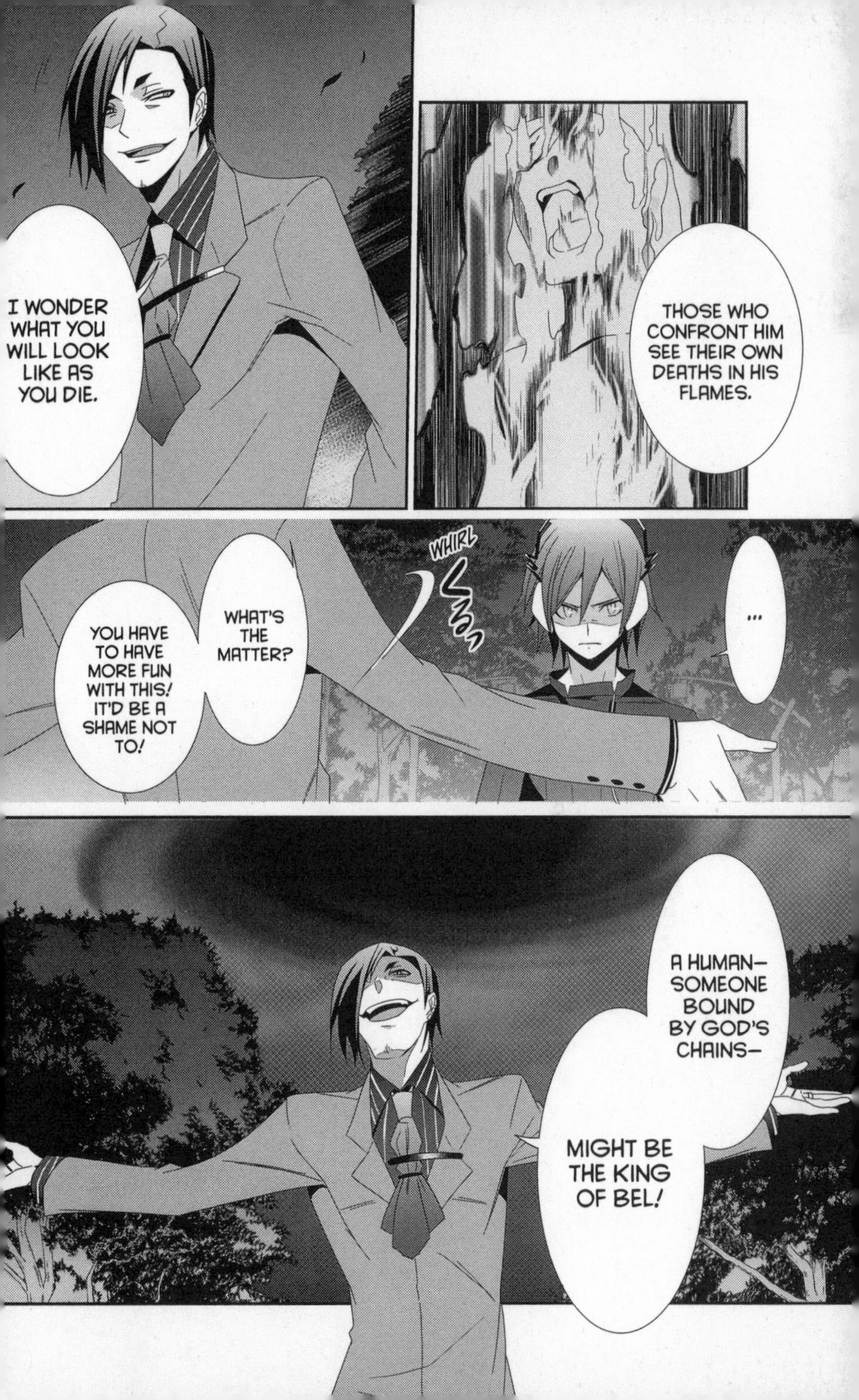
THOSE WHO CONFRONT HIM SEE THEIR OWN DEATHS IN HIS FLAMES.
I WONDER WHAT YOU WILL LOOK LIKE AS YOU DIE.
...
WHIRL
WHAT'S THE MATTER?
YOU HAVE TO HAVE MORE FUN WITH THIS! IT'D BE A SHAME NOT TO!
A HUMAN—SOMEONE BOUND BY GOD'S CHAINS—
MIGHT BE THE KING OF BEL!

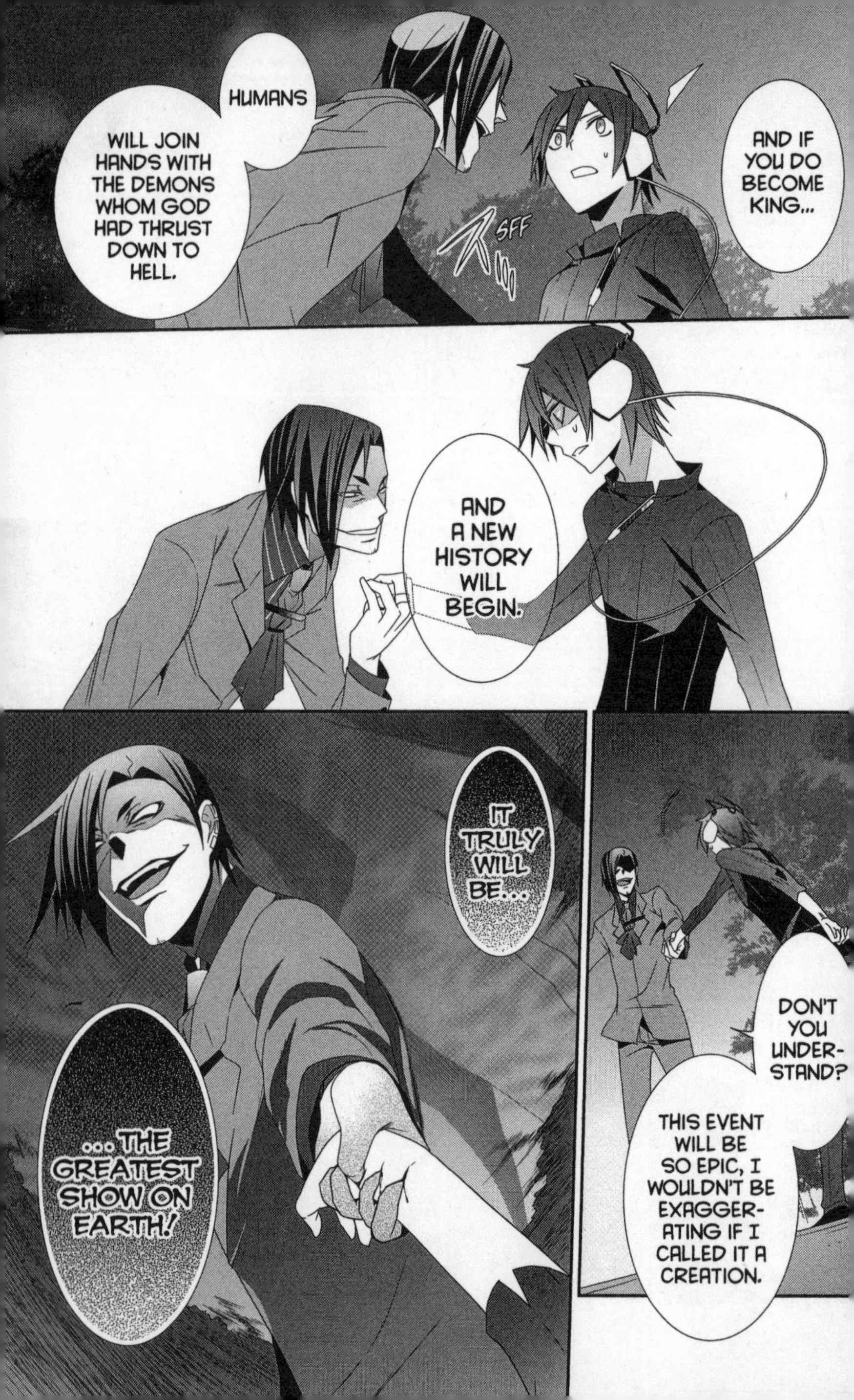
AND IF YOU DO BECOME KING...
HUMANS
WILL JOIN HANDS WITH THE DEMONS WHOM GOD HAD THRUST DOWN TO HELL.
SFF
AND A NEW HISTORY WILL BEGIN.
DON'T YOU UNDER-STAND?
THIS EVENT WILL BE SO EPIC, I WOULDN'T BE EXAGGER-ATING IF I CALLED IT A CREATION.
IT TRULY WILL BE...
...THE GREATEST SHOW ON EARTH!

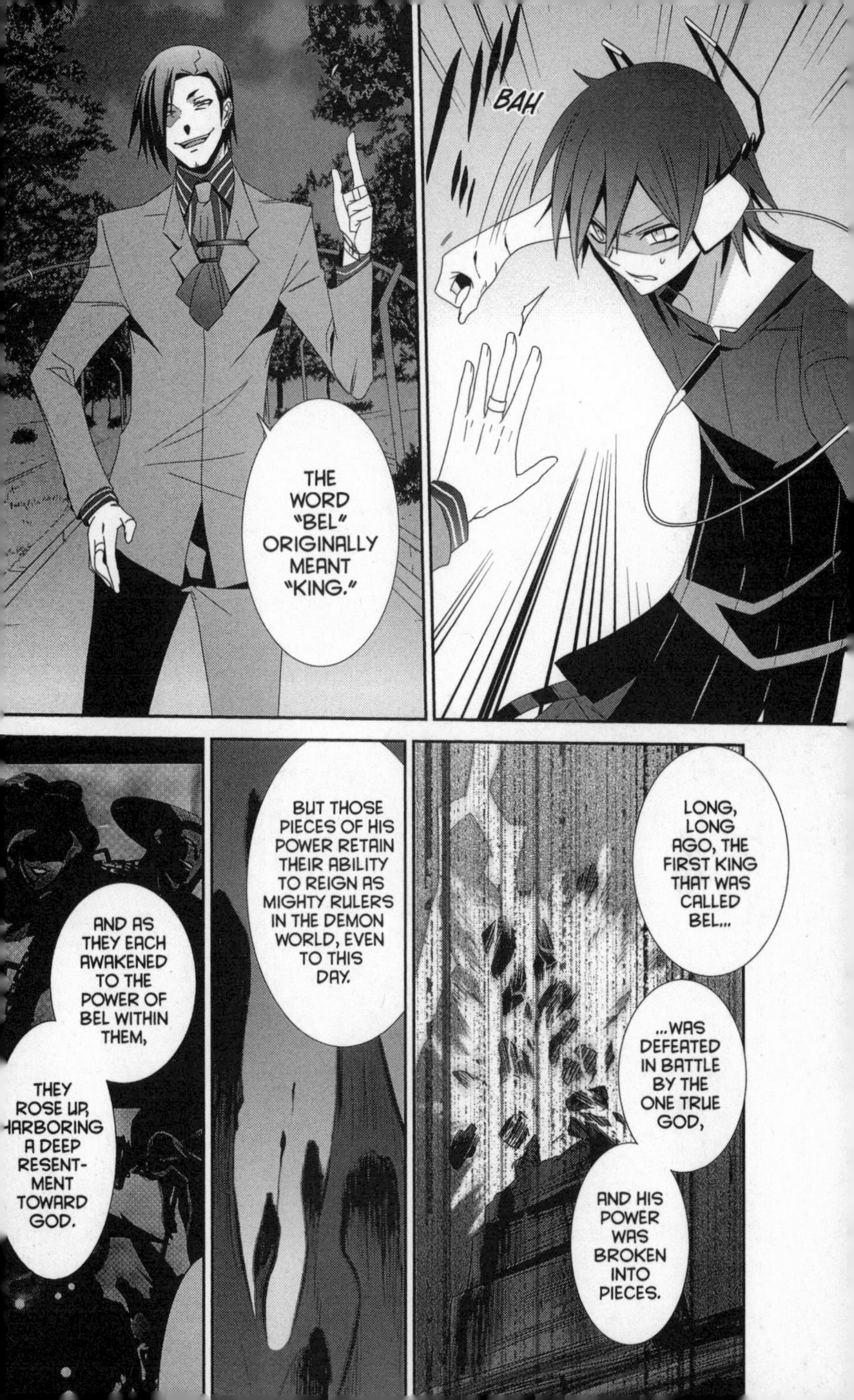
BAH
THE WORD "BEL" ORIGINALLY MEANT "KING."
LONG, LONG AGO, THE FIRST KING THAT WAS CALLED BEL...
...WAS DEFEATED IN BATTLE BY THE ONE TRUE GOD,
AND HIS POWER WAS BROKEN INTO PIECES.
BUT THOSE PIECES OF HIS POWER RETAIN THEIR ABILITY TO REIGN AS MIGHTY RULERS IN THE DEMON WORLD, EVEN TO THIS DAY.
AND AS THEY EACH AWAKENED TO THE POWER OF BEL WITHIN THEM,
THEY ROSE UP, HARBORING A DEEP RESENTMENT TOWARD GOD.

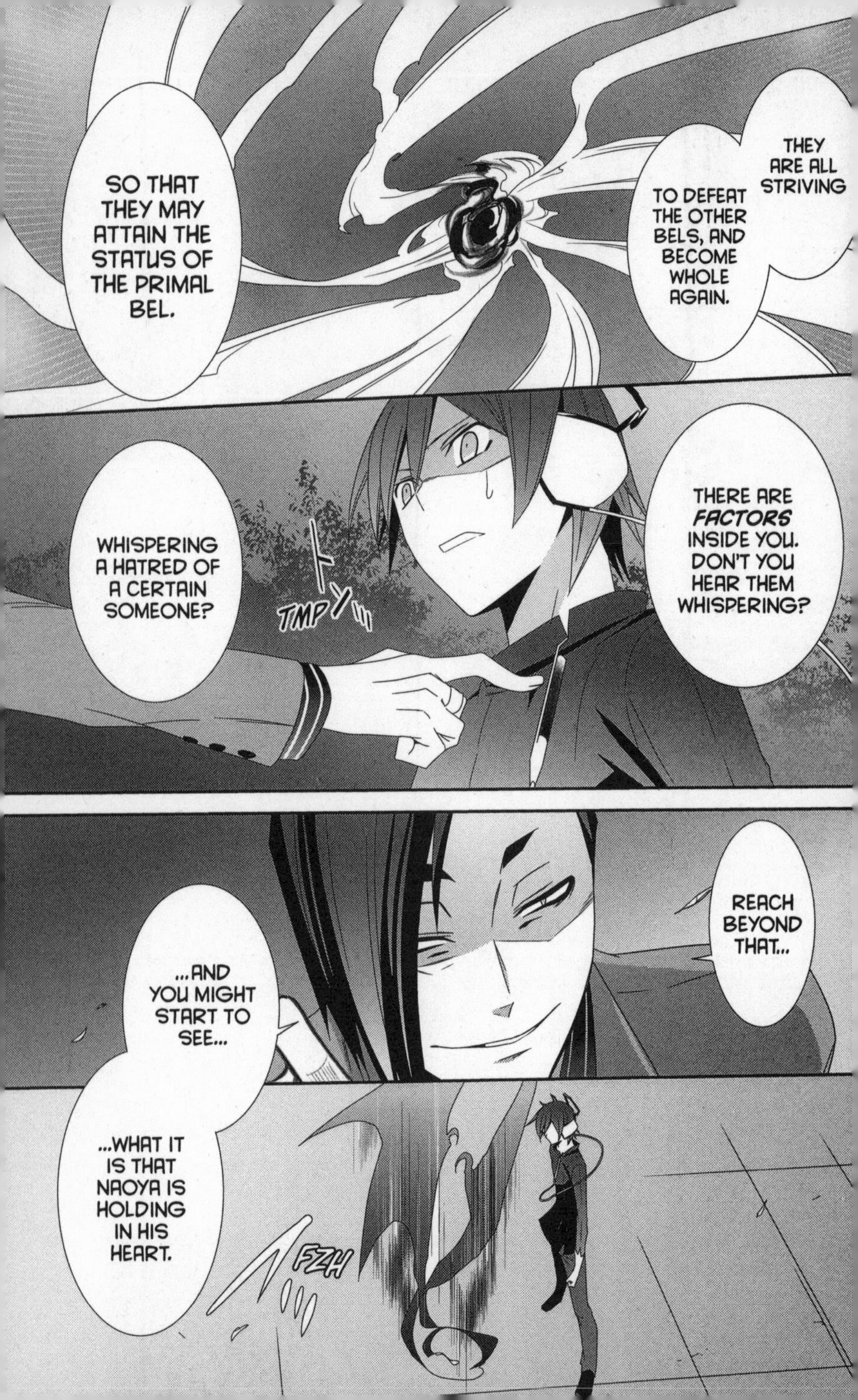
THEY ARE ALL STRIVING
TO DEFEAT THE OTHER BELS, AND BECOME WHOLE AGAIN.
SO THAT THEY MAY ATTAIN THE STATUS OF THE PRIMAL BEL.
THERE ARE *FACTORS* INSIDE YOU. DON'T YOU HEAR THEM WHISPERING?
TMP
WHISPERING A HATRED OF A CERTAIN SOMEONE?
REACH BEYOND THAT...
...AND YOU MIGHT START TO SEE...
...WHAT IT IS THAT NAOYA IS HOLDING IN HIS HEART.
FZH

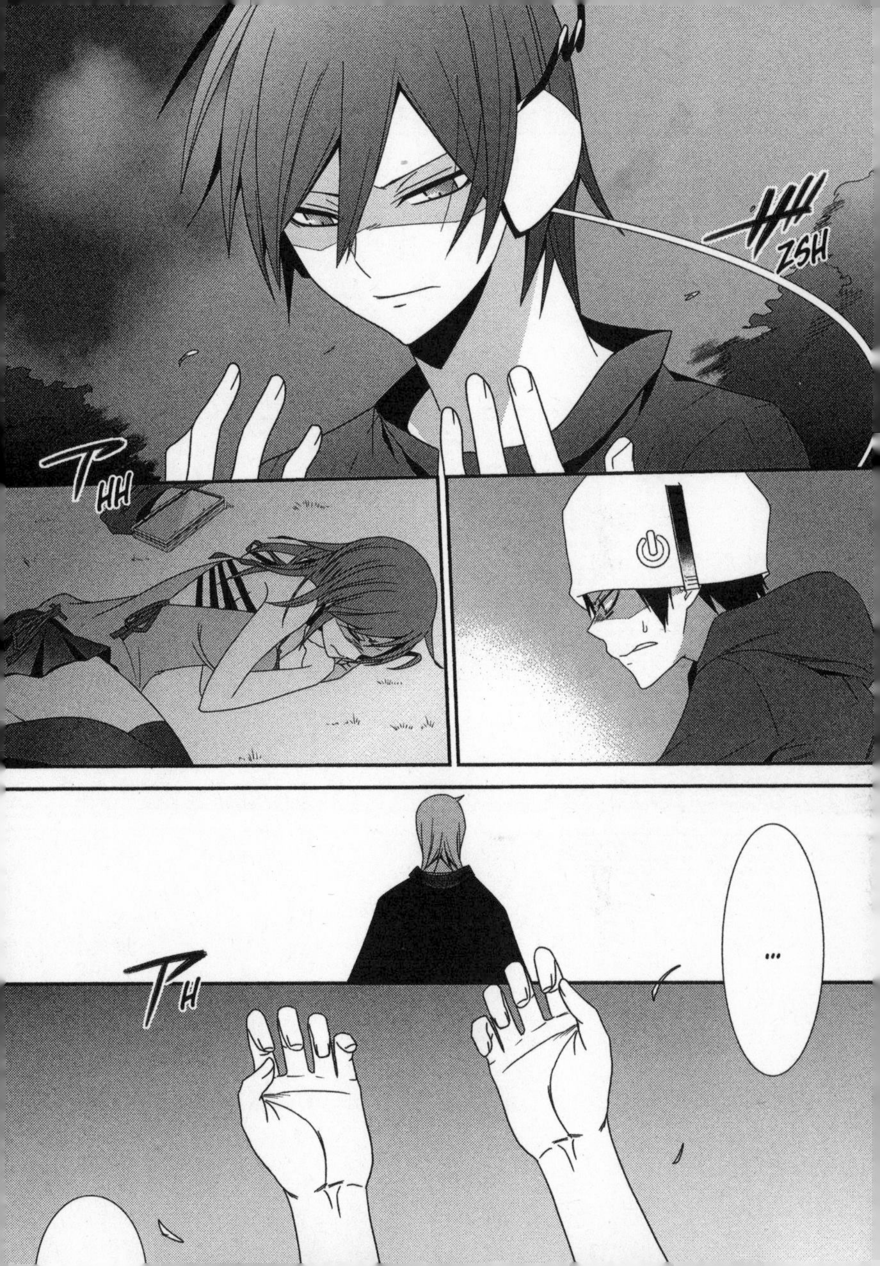
ZSH
THH
...
TH

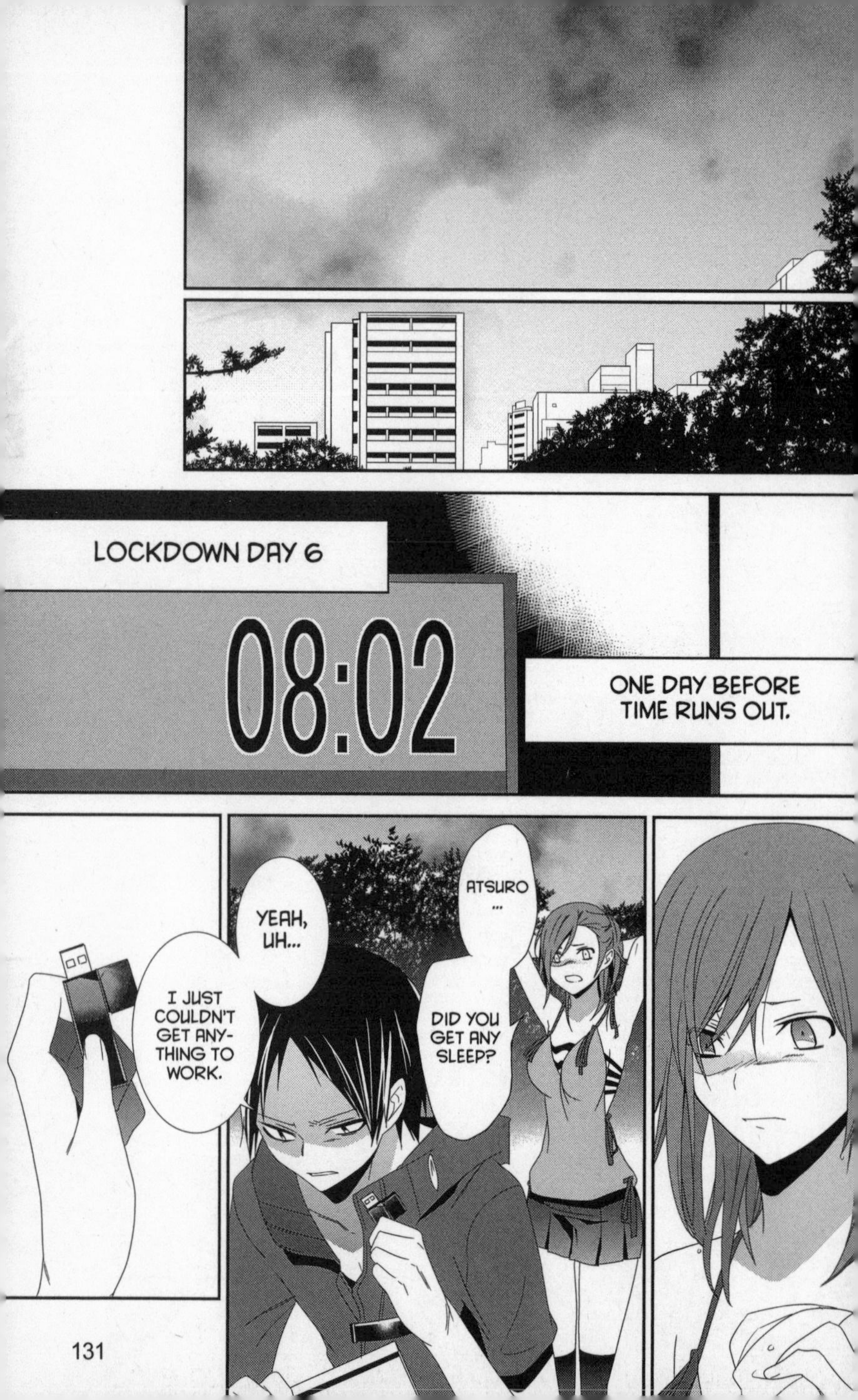
LOCKDOWN DAY 6
08:02
ONE DAY BEFORE TIME RUNS OUT.
ATSURO ...
DID YOU GET ANY SLEEP?
YEAH, UH...
I JUST COULDN'T GET ANY-THING TO WORK.

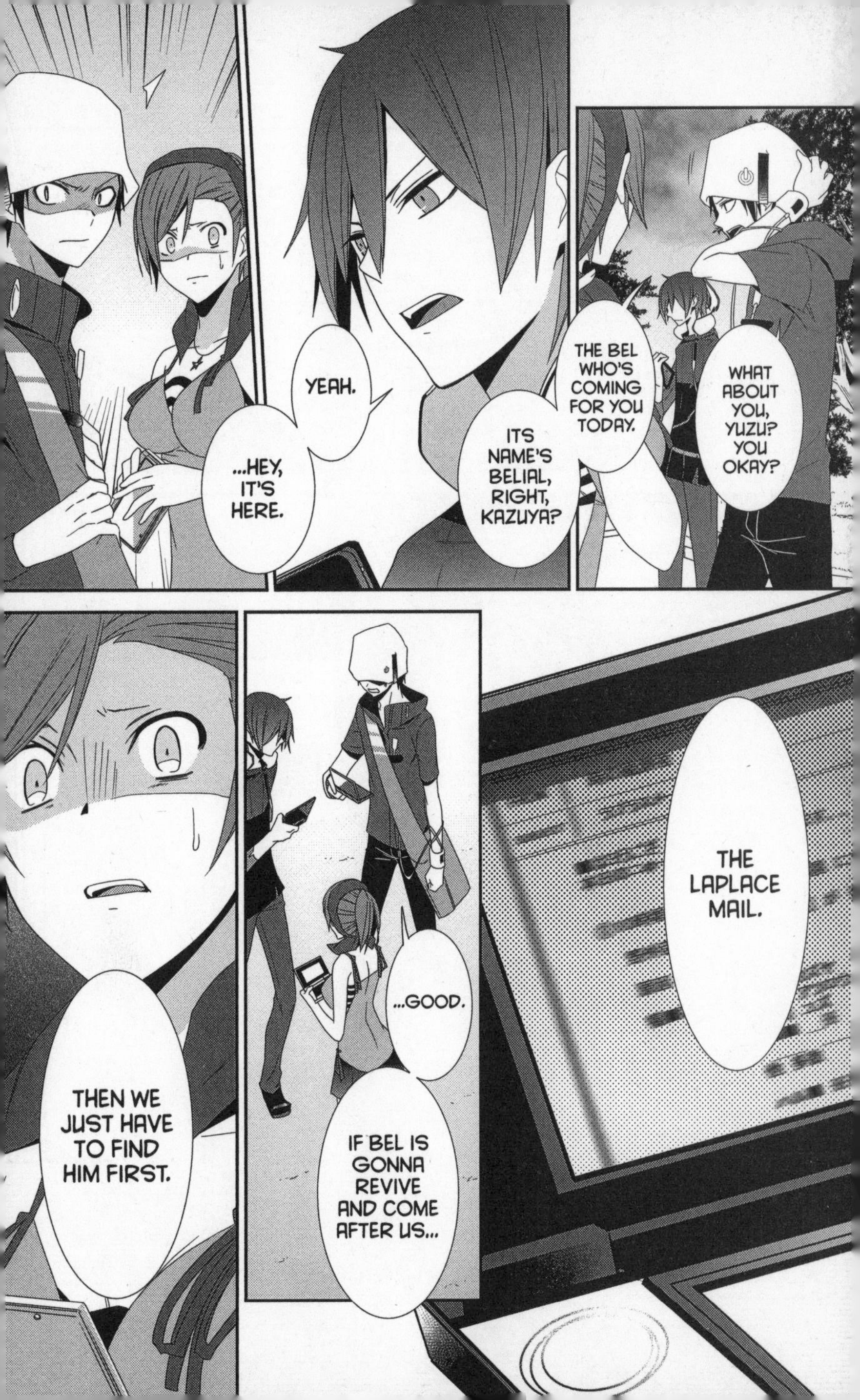
WHAT ABOUT YOU, YUZU? YOU OKAY?
THE BEL WHO'S COMING FOR YOU TODAY.
ITS NAME'S BELIAL, RIGHT, KAZUYA?
YEAH.
...HEY, IT'S HERE.
THE LAPLACE MAIL.
...GOOD.
IF BEL IS GONNA REVIVE AND COME AFTER US...
THEN WE JUST HAVE TO FIND HIM FIRST.

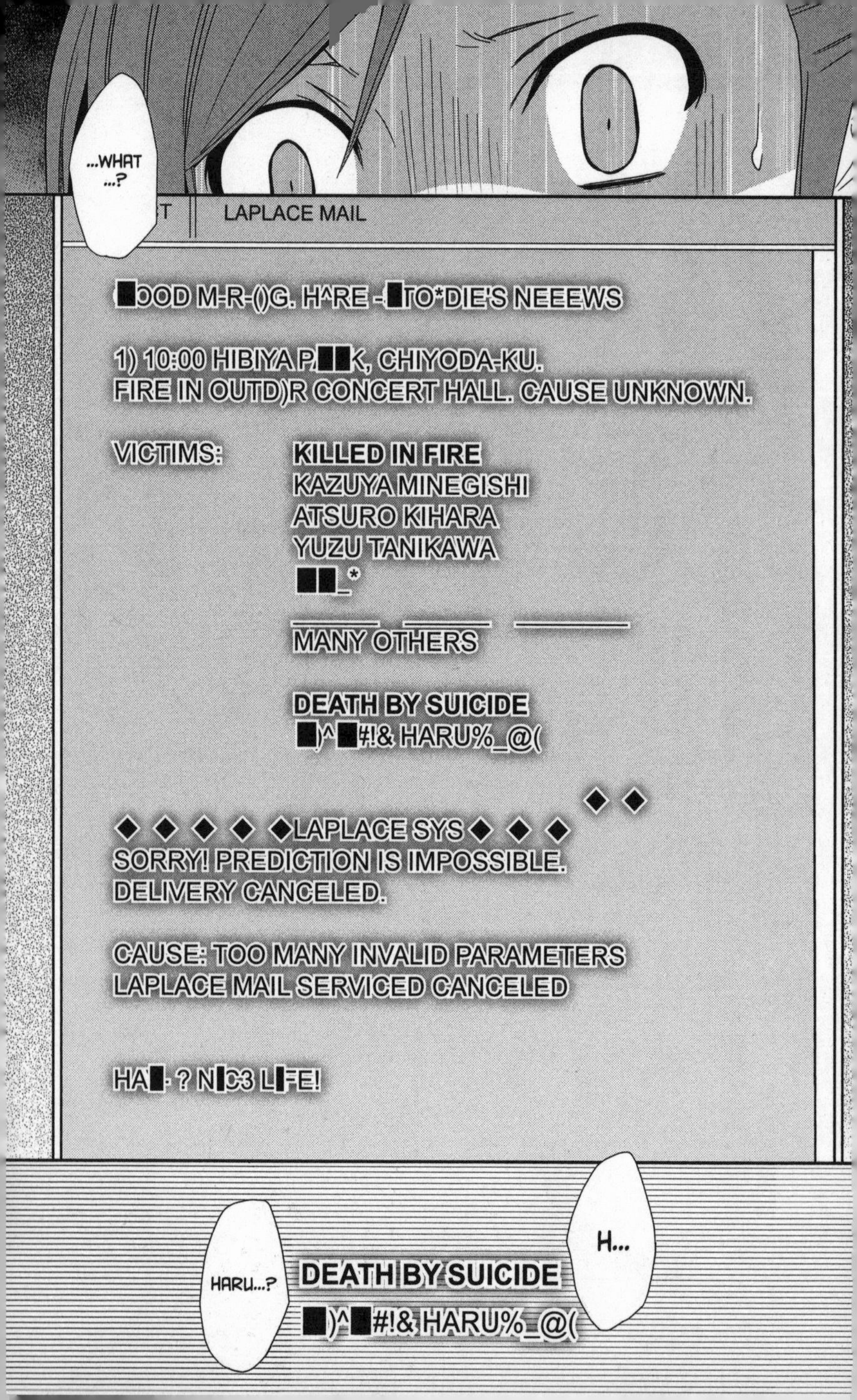

...WHAT ...?
LAPLACE MAIL
[redacted]OOD M-R-()G. H^RE -[redacted]TO*DIE'S NEEEWS
1) 10:00 HIBIYA P.[redacted]K, CHIYODA-KU.
FIRE IN OUTD)R CONCERT HALL. CAUSE UNKNOWN.
VICTIMS: KILLED IN FIRE
KAZUYA MINEGISHI
ATSURO KIHARA
YUZU TANIKAWA
[redacted]_*
MANY OTHERS
DEATH BY SUICIDE
[redacted])^[redacted]#!& HARU%_@(
◆ ◆ ◆ ◆ ◆LAPLACE SYS◆ ◆ ◆ ◆ ◆
SORRY! PREDICTION IS IMPOSSIBLE.
DELIVERY CANCELED.
CAUSE: TOO MANY INVALID PARAMETERS
LAPLACE MAIL SERVICED CANCELED
HA[redacted]- ? N[redacted]C3 L[redacted]FE!
H...
DEATH BY SUICIDE
[redacted])^[redacted]#!& HARU%_@(
HARU...?

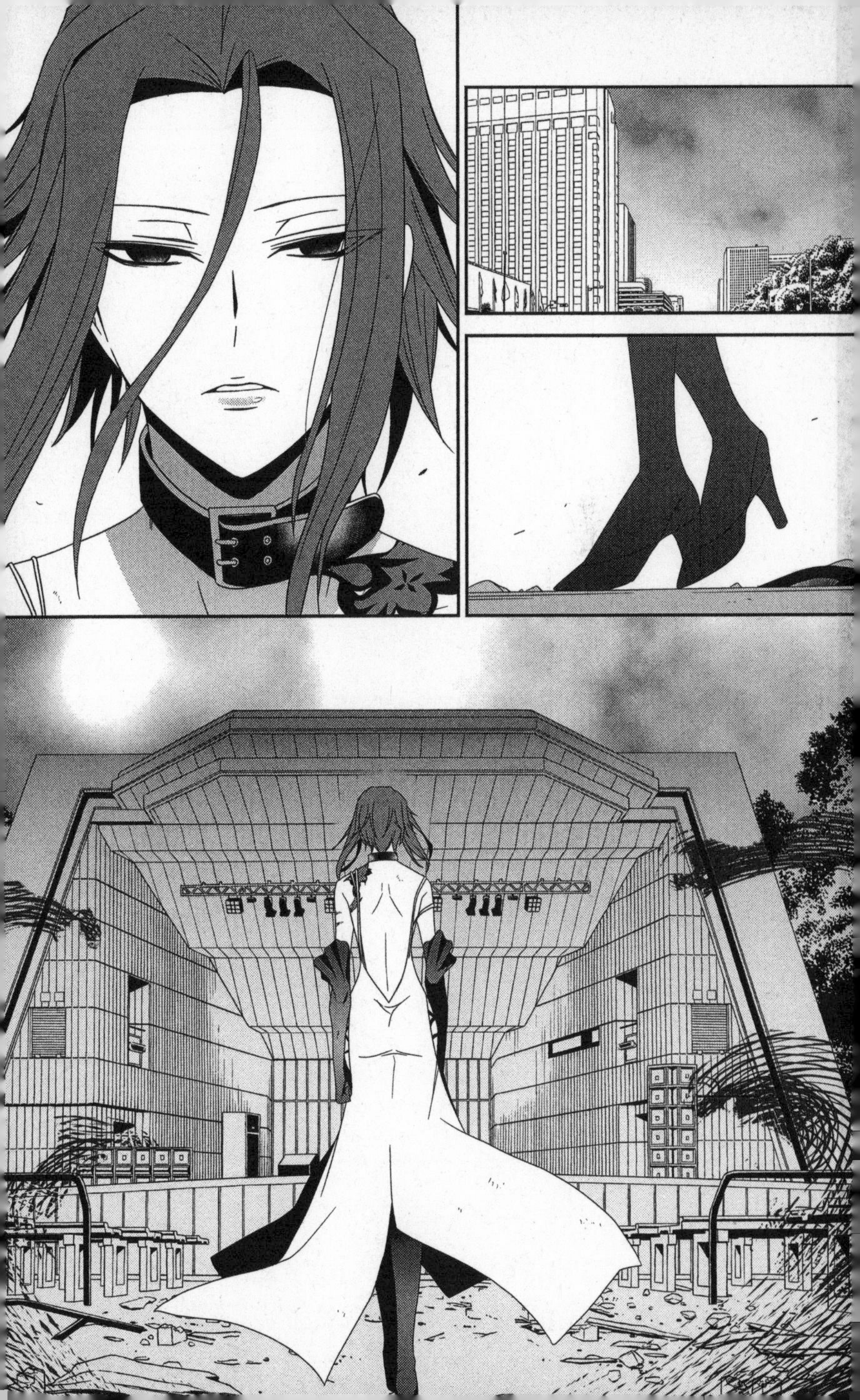

DEVIL SURVIVOR
デビルサバイバー

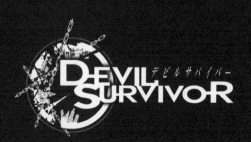

DEVIL デビルサバイバー
SURVIVOR

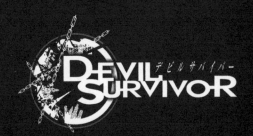

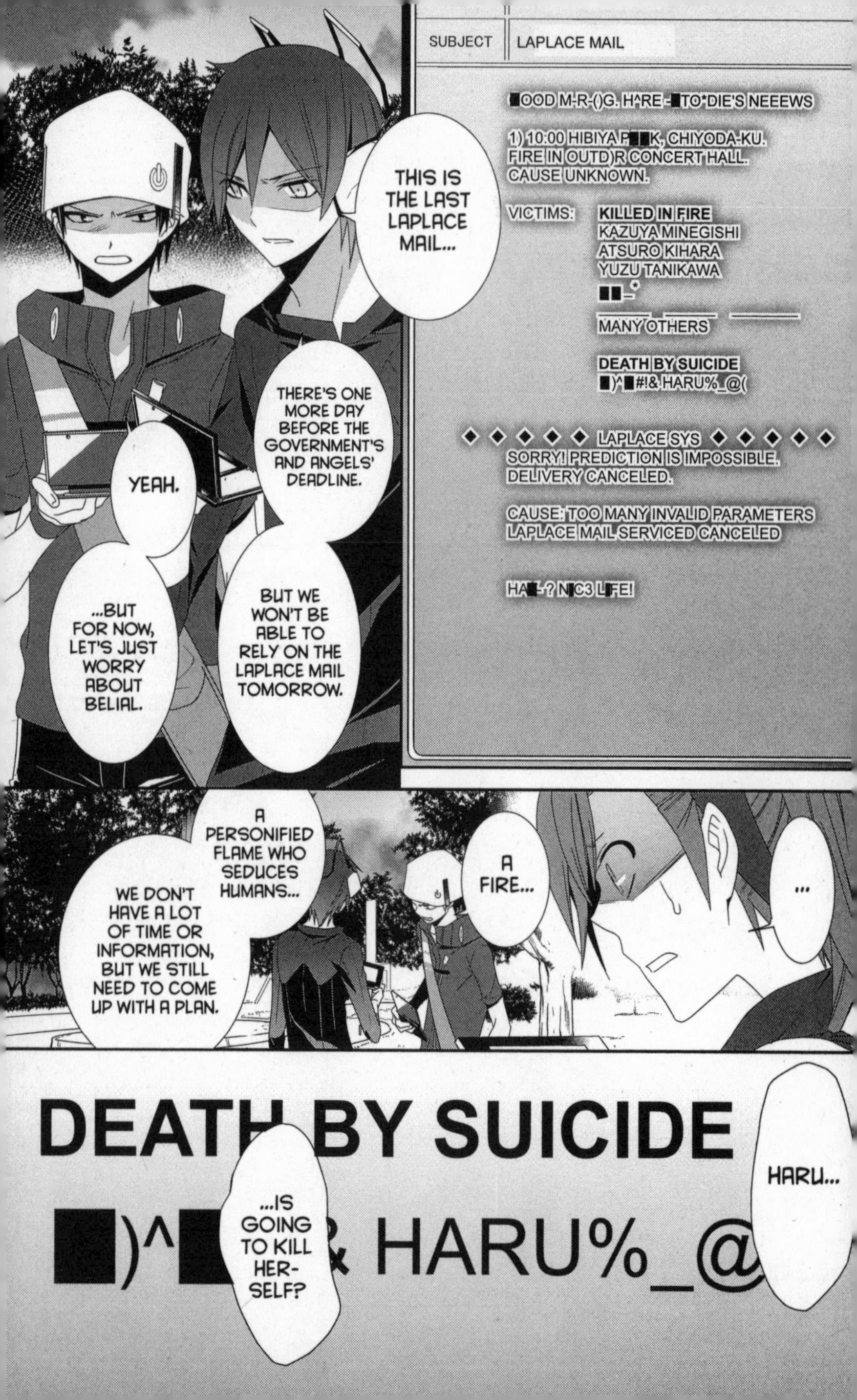
SUBJECT LAPLACE MAIL
[redacted]OOD M-R-()G. H^RE -[redacted]TO*DIE'S NEEEWS
1) 10:00 HIBIYA P[redacted]K, CHIYODA-KU.
FIRE IN OUTD)R CONCERT HALL.
CAUSE UNKNOWN.
VICTIMS: KILLED IN FIRE
KAZUYA MINEGISHI
ATSURO KIHARA
YUZU TANIKAWA
[redacted]–*
MANY OTHERS
DEATH BY SUICIDE
[redacted])^[redacted]#!& HARU%_@(
◆ ◆ ◆ ◆ ◆ LAPLACE SYS ◆ ◆ ◆ ◆ ◆
SORRY! PREDICTION IS IMPOSSIBLE.
DELIVERY CANCELED.
CAUSE: TOO MANY INVALID PARAMETERS
LAPLACE MAIL SERVICED CANCELED
HA[redacted]-? N[redacted]C3 L[redacted]FE!
THIS IS THE LAST LAPLACE MAIL...
THERE'S ONE MORE DAY BEFORE THE GOVERNMENT'S AND ANGELS' DEADLINE.
YEAH.
BUT WE WON'T BE ABLE TO RELY ON THE LAPLACE MAIL TOMORROW.
...BUT FOR NOW, LET'S JUST WORRY ABOUT BELIAL.
...
A FIRE...
A PERSONIFIED FLAME WHO SEDUCES HUMANS...
WE DON'T HAVE A LOT OF TIME OR INFORMATION, BUT WE STILL NEED TO COME UP WITH A PLAN.
HARU...
DEATH BY SUICIDE
[redacted])^[redacted]& HARU%_@
...IS GOING TO KILL HER-SELF?

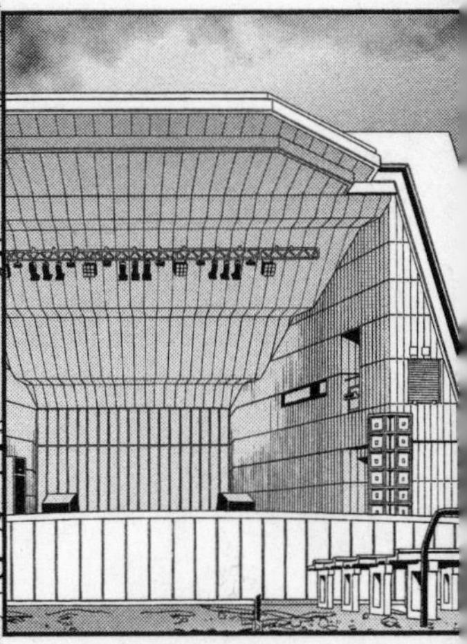
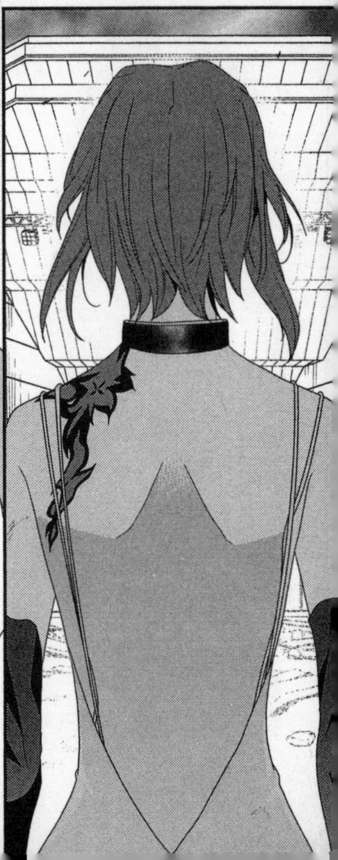
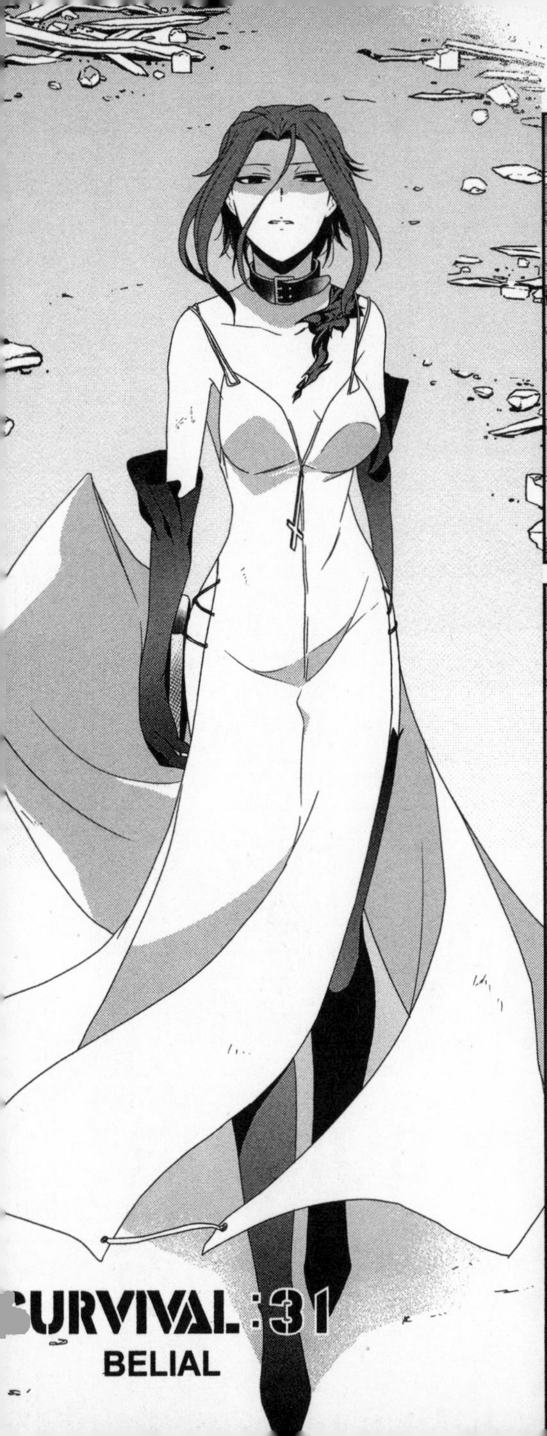
SURVIVAL :31
BELIAL

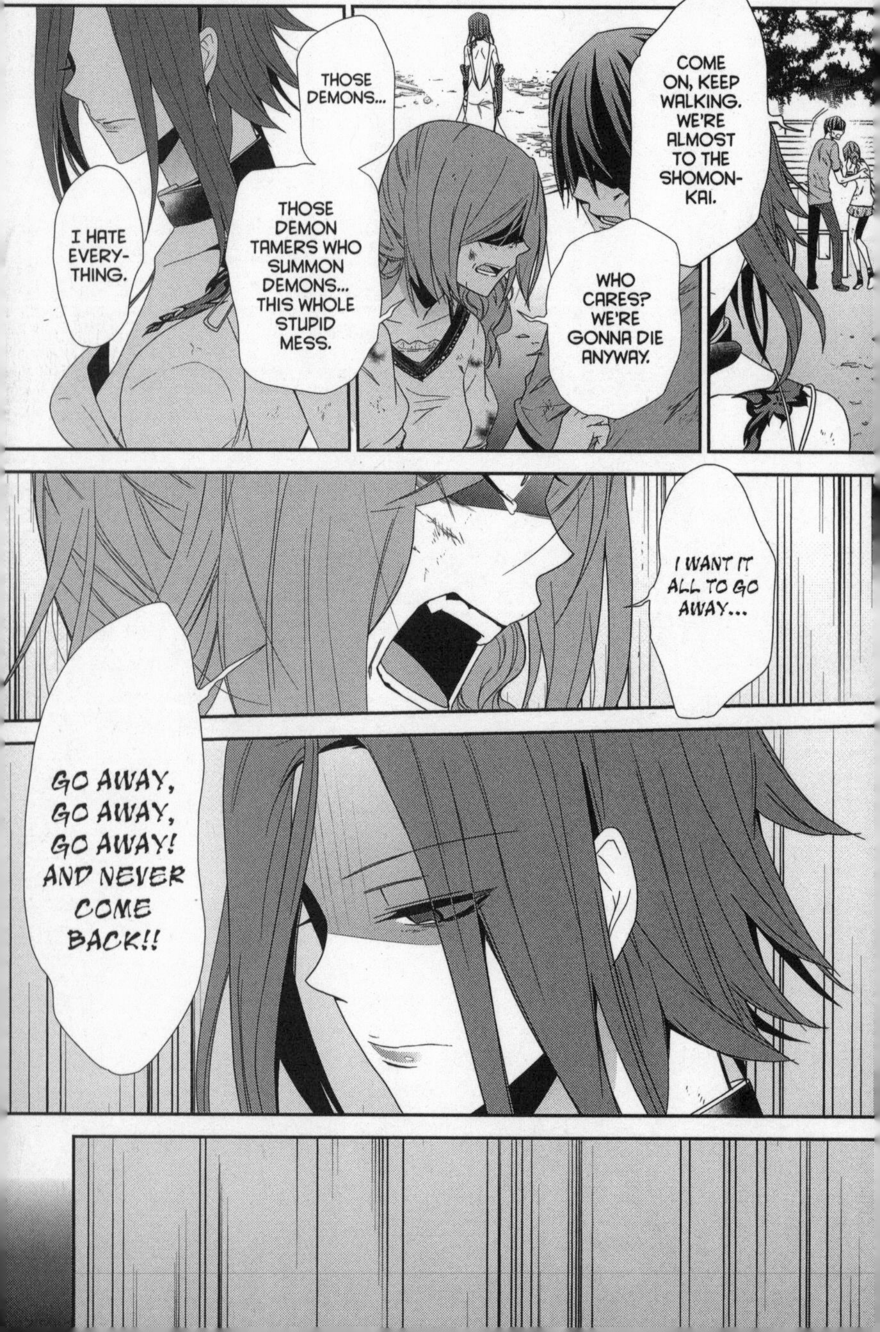
COME ON, KEEP WALKING. WE'RE ALMOST TO THE SHOMON-KAI.
THOSE DEMONS...
THOSE DEMON TAMERS WHO SUMMON DEMONS... THIS WHOLE STUPID MESS.
WHO CARES? WE'RE GONNA DIE ANYWAY.
I HATE EVERY-THING.
I WANT IT ALL TO GO AWAY...
GO AWAY, GO AWAY, GO AWAY! AND NEVER COME BACK!!

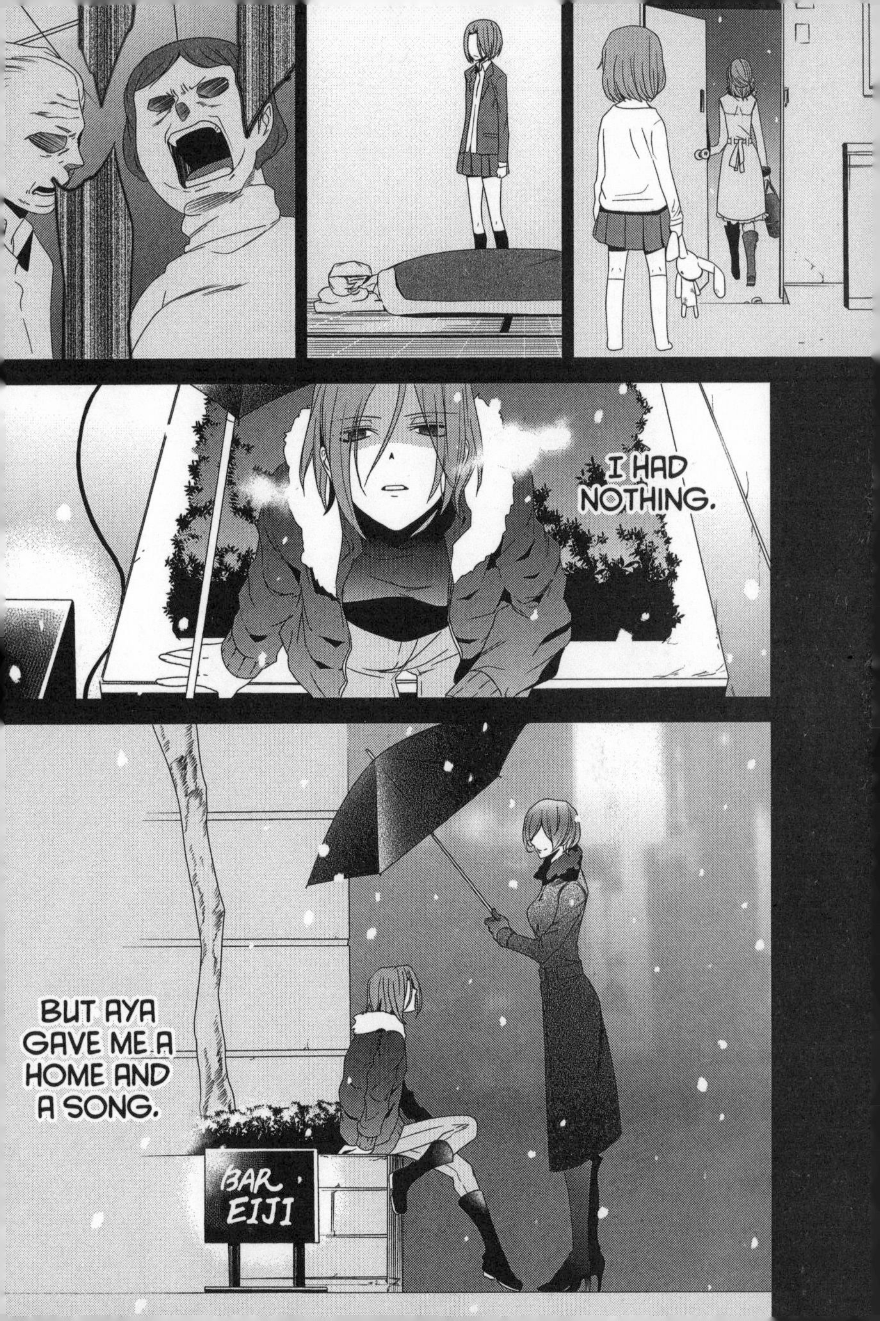
I HAD NOTHING.
BUT AYA GAVE ME A HOME AND A SONG.
BAR EIJI

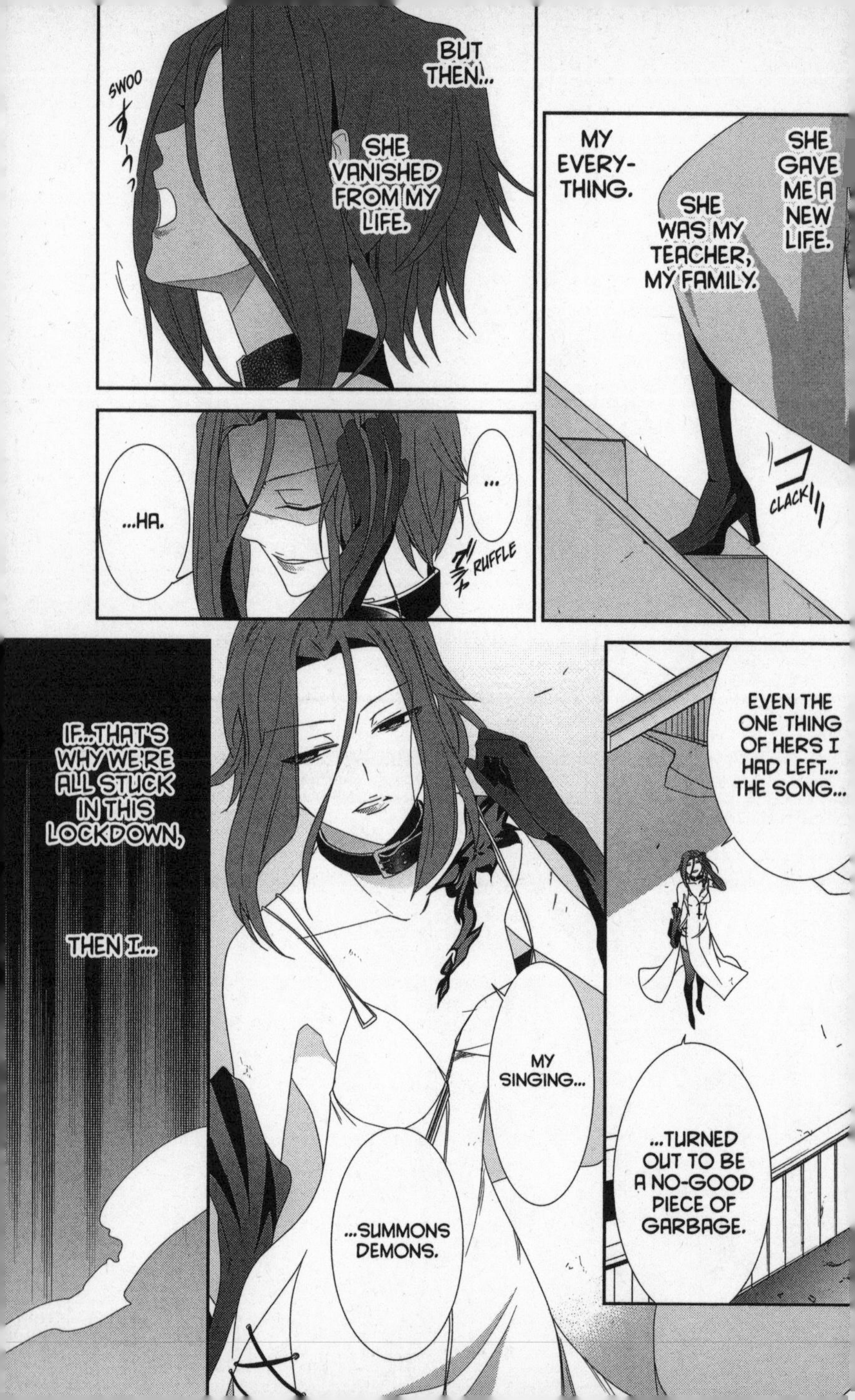

SHE GAVE ME A NEW LIFE.
SHE WAS MY TEACHER, MY FAMILY.
MY EVERY-THING.
CLACK
BUT THEN...
SHE VANISHED FROM MY LIFE.
SWOO
...
RUFFLE
...HA.
EVEN THE ONE THING OF HERS I HAD LEFT... THE SONG...
...TURNED OUT TO BE A NO-GOOD PIECE OF GARBAGE.
MY SINGING...
...SUMMONS DEMONS.
IF... THAT'S WHY WE'RE ALL STUCK IN THIS LOCKDOWN,
THEN I...

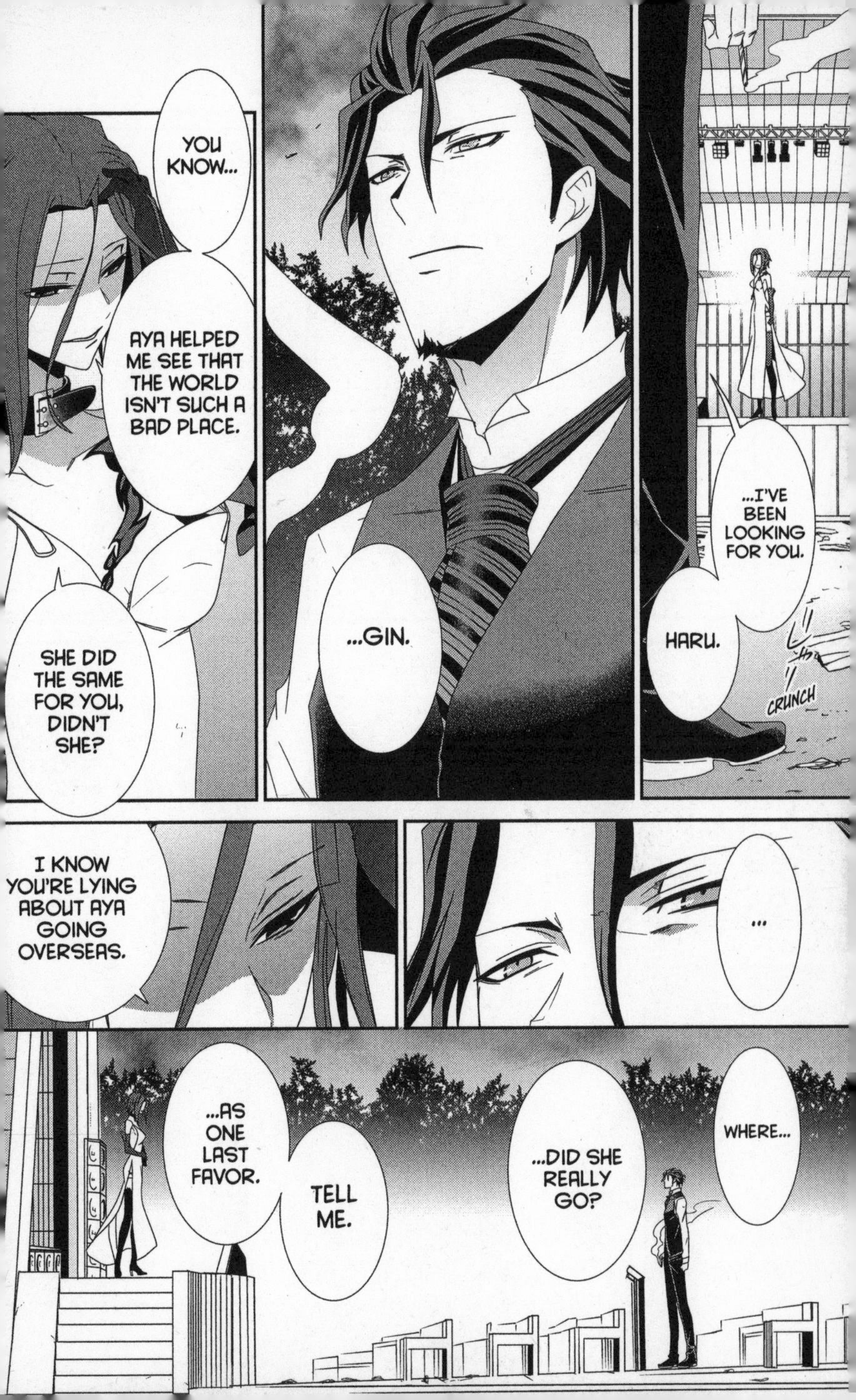
...I'VE BEEN LOOKING FOR YOU.
HARU.
CRUNCH
...GIN.
YOU KNOW...
AYA HELPED ME SEE THAT THE WORLD ISN'T SUCH A BAD PLACE.
SHE DID THE SAME FOR YOU, DIDN'T SHE?
...
I KNOW YOU'RE LYING ABOUT AYA GOING OVERSEAS.
WHERE...
...DID SHE REALLY GO?
TELL ME.
...AS ONE LAST FAVOR.

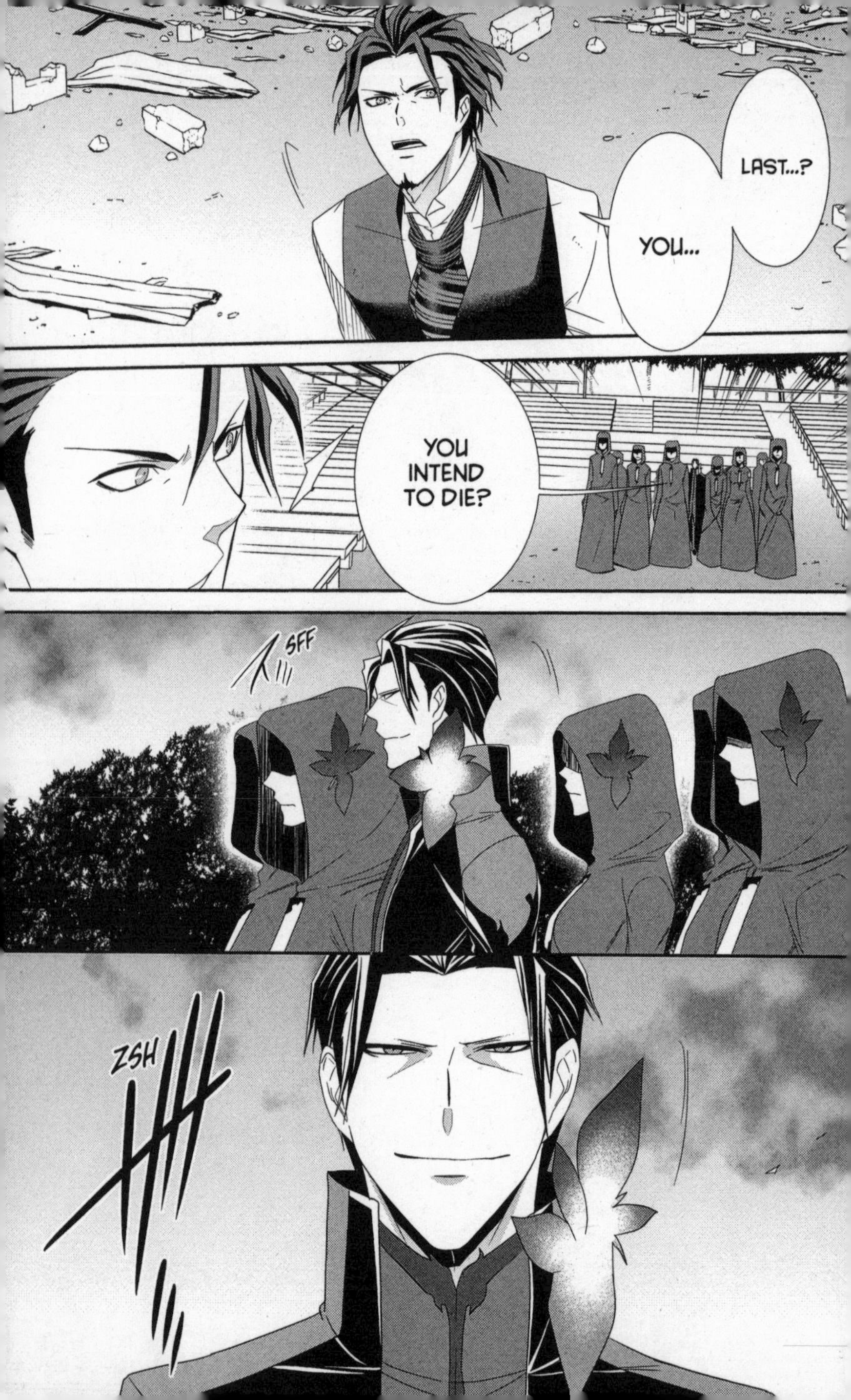
LAST...?
YOU...
YOU INTEND TO DIE?
SFF
ZSH

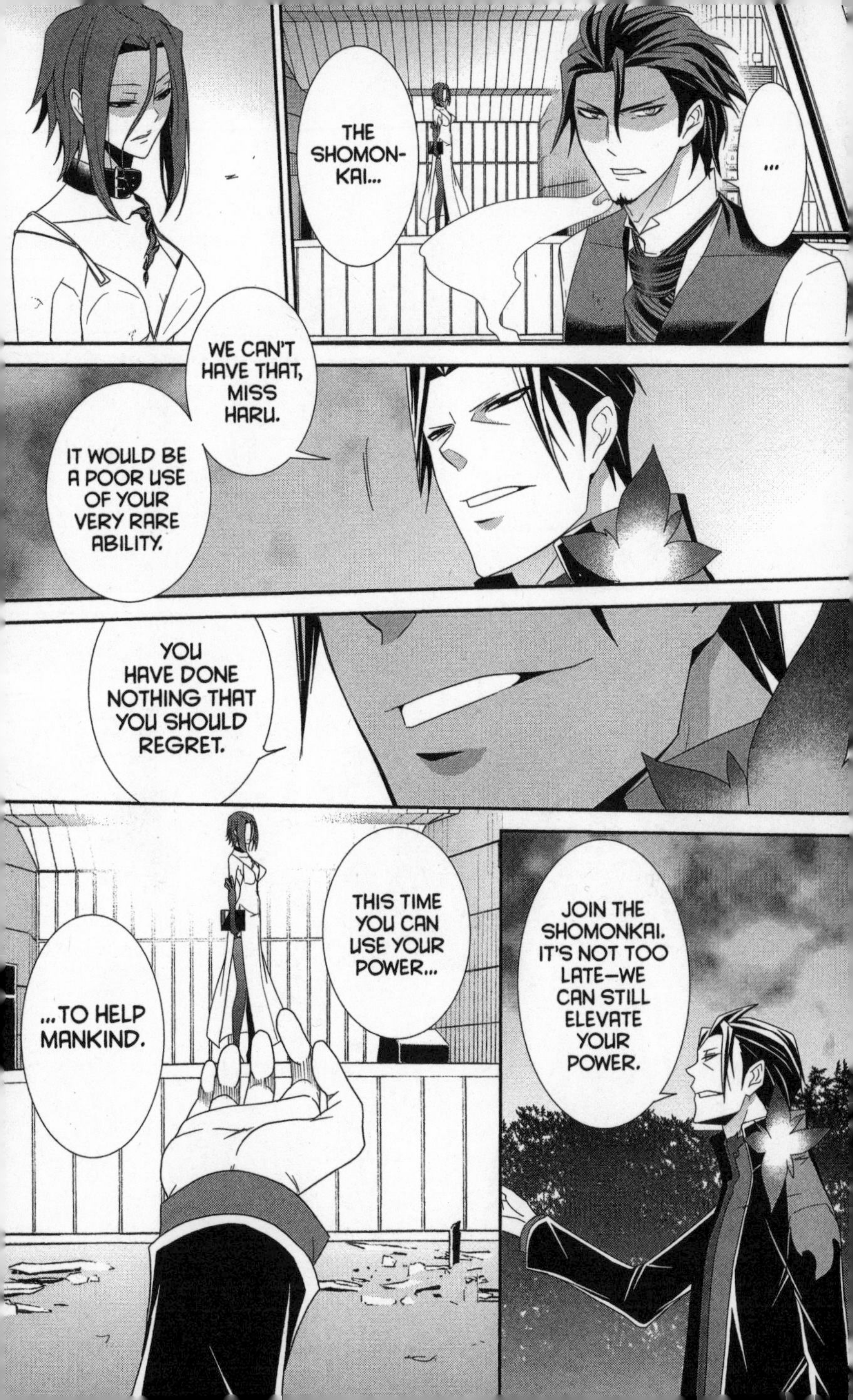
...
THE SHOMON-KAI...
WE CAN'T HAVE THAT, MISS HARU.
IT WOULD BE A POOR USE OF YOUR VERY RARE ABILITY.
YOU HAVE DONE NOTHING THAT YOU SHOULD REGRET.
JOIN THE SHOMONKAI. IT'S NOT TOO LATE—WE CAN STILL ELEVATE YOUR POWER.
THIS TIME YOU CAN USE YOUR POWER...
...TO HELP MANKIND.

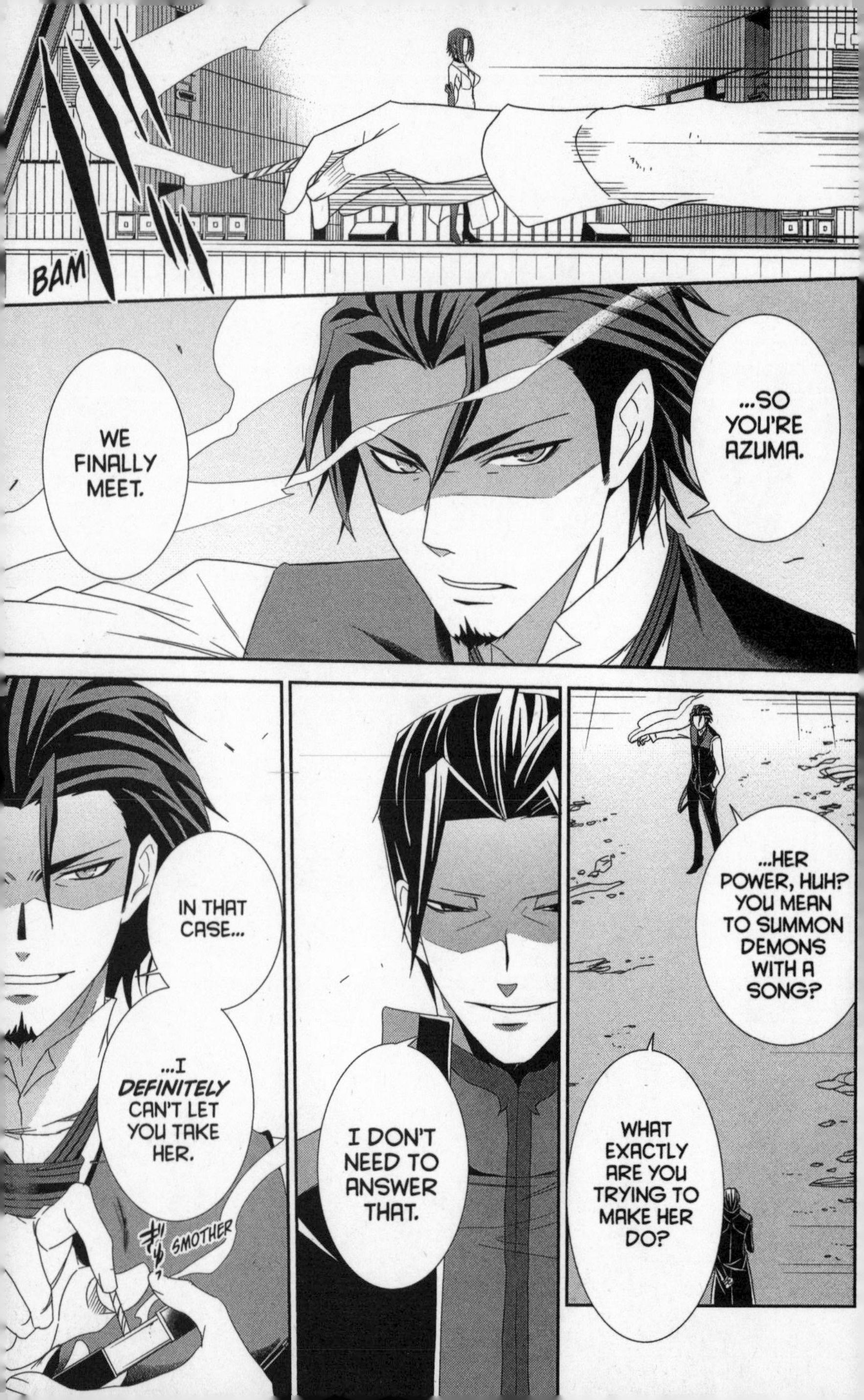
BAM
...SO YOU'RE AZUMA.
WE FINALLY MEET.
...HER POWER, HUH? YOU MEAN TO SUMMON DEMONS WITH A SONG?
WHAT EXACTLY ARE YOU TRYING TO MAKE HER DO?
I DON'T NEED TO ANSWER THAT.
IN THAT CASE...
...I *DEFINITELY* CAN'T LET YOU TAKE HER.
SMOTHER

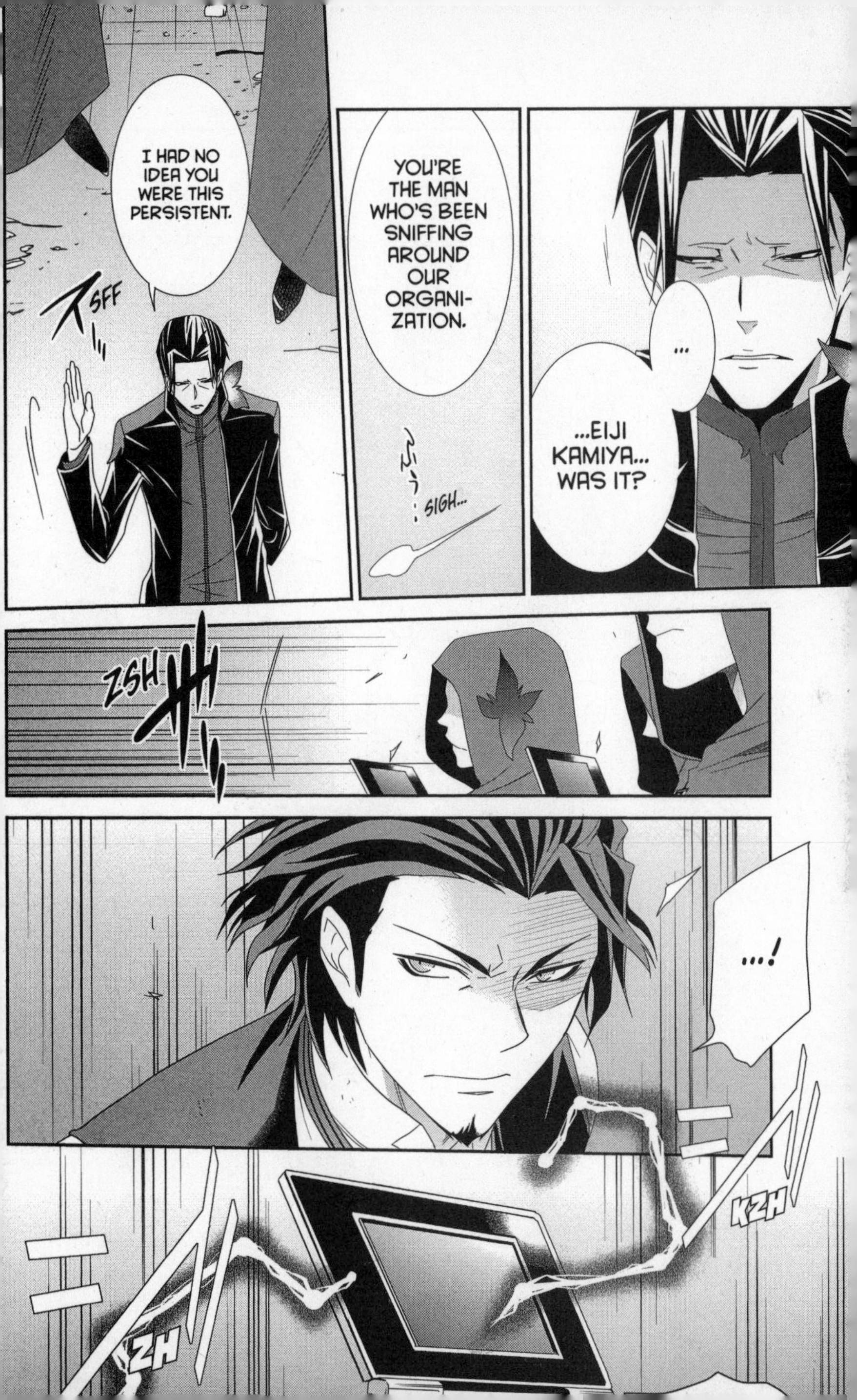
...
...EIJI KAMIYA... WAS IT?
YOU'RE THE MAN WHO'S BEEN SNIFFING AROUND OUR ORGANIZATION.
SIGH...
I HAD NO IDEA YOU WERE THIS PERSISTENT.
SFF
ZSH
...!
KZH
ZH

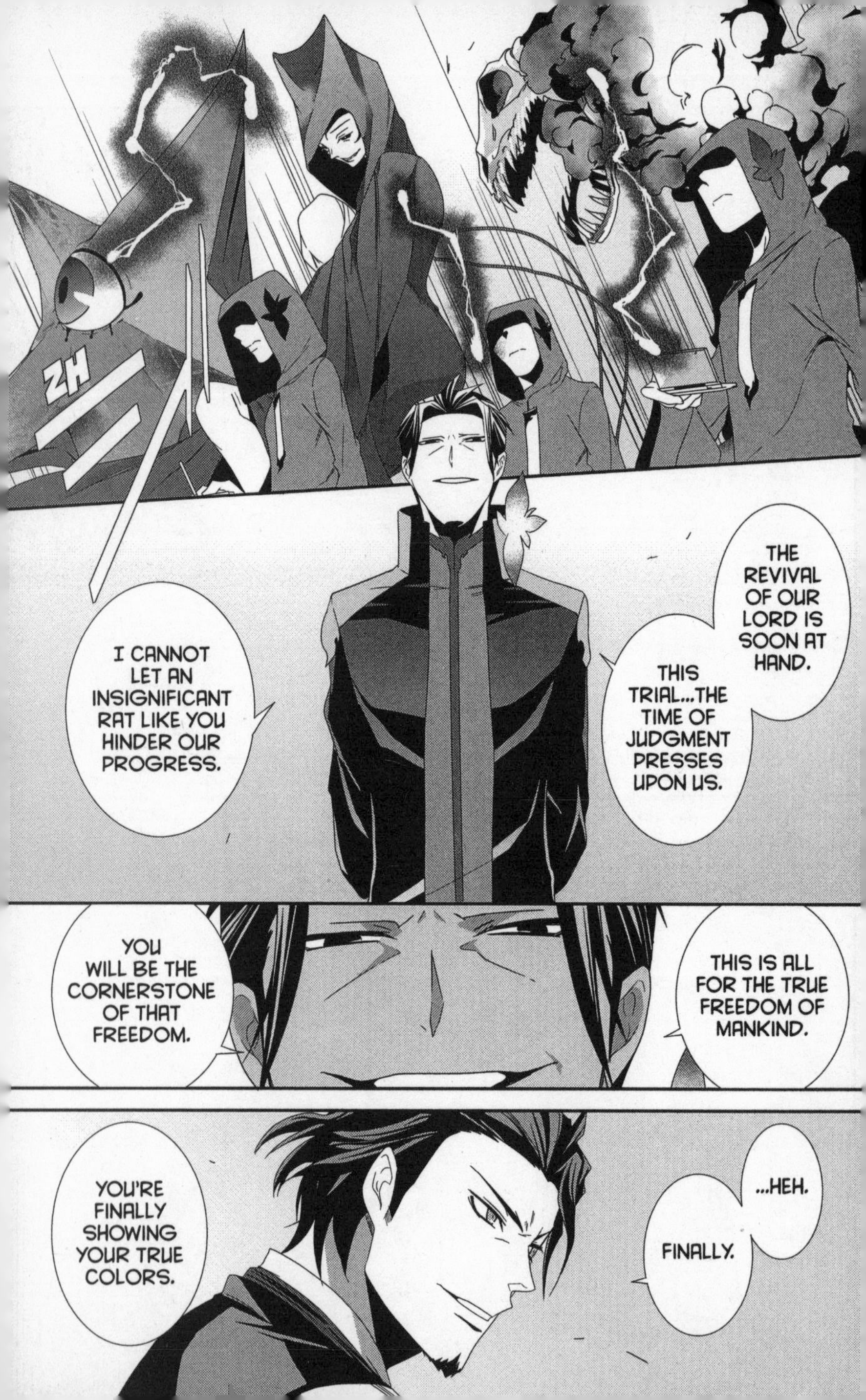
THE REVIVAL OF OUR LORD IS SOON AT HAND.
THIS TRIAL...THE TIME OF JUDGMENT PRESSES UPON US.
I CANNOT LET AN INSIGNIFICANT RAT LIKE YOU HINDER OUR PROGRESS.
THIS IS ALL FOR THE TRUE FREEDOM OF MANKIND.
YOU WILL BE THE CORNERSTONE OF THAT FREEDOM.
...HEH.
FINALLY.
YOU'RE FINALLY SHOWING YOUR TRUE COLORS.

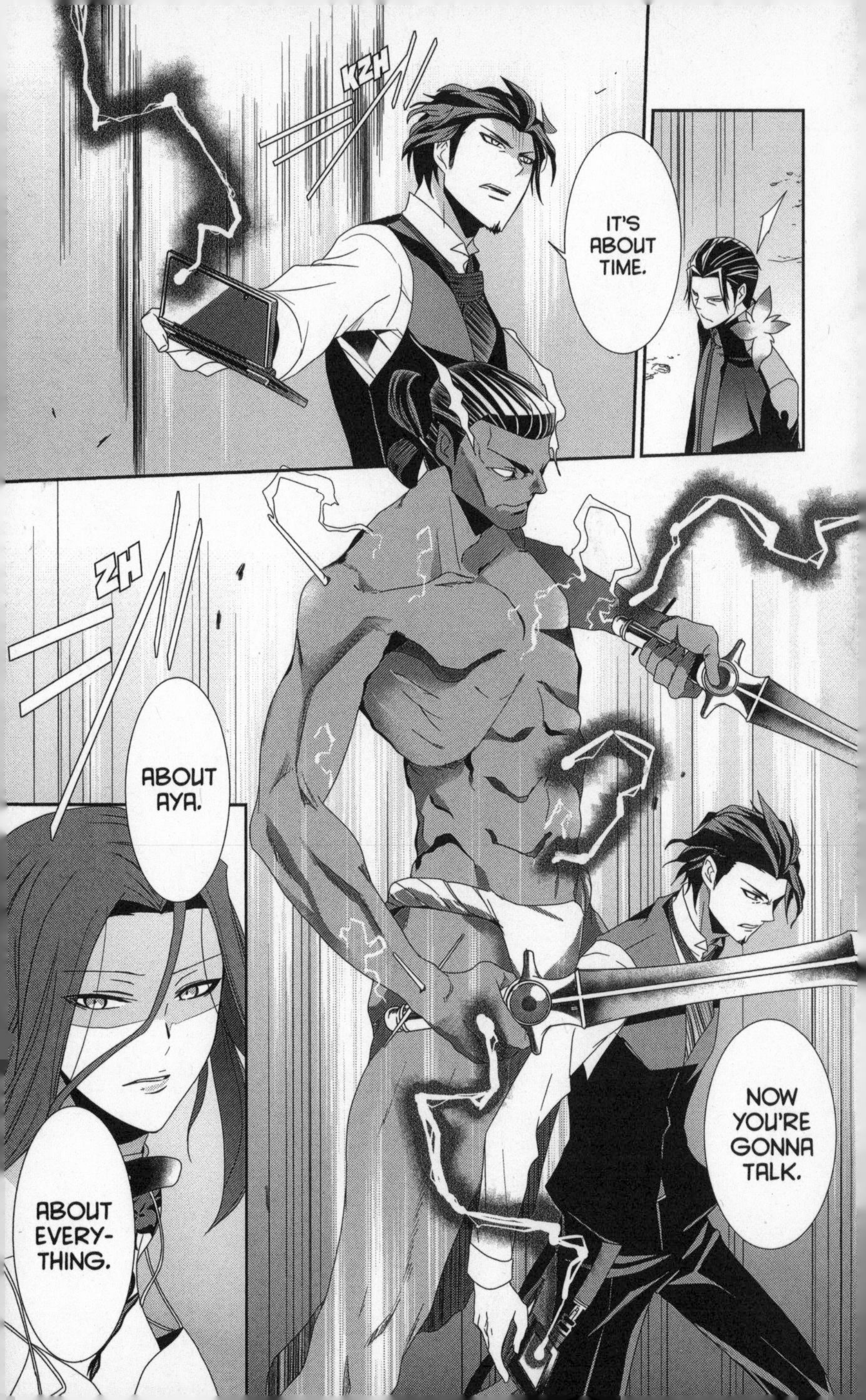
KZH
IT'S ABOUT TIME.
ZH
NOW YOU'RE GONNA TALK.
ABOUT AYA.
ABOUT EVERY-THING.

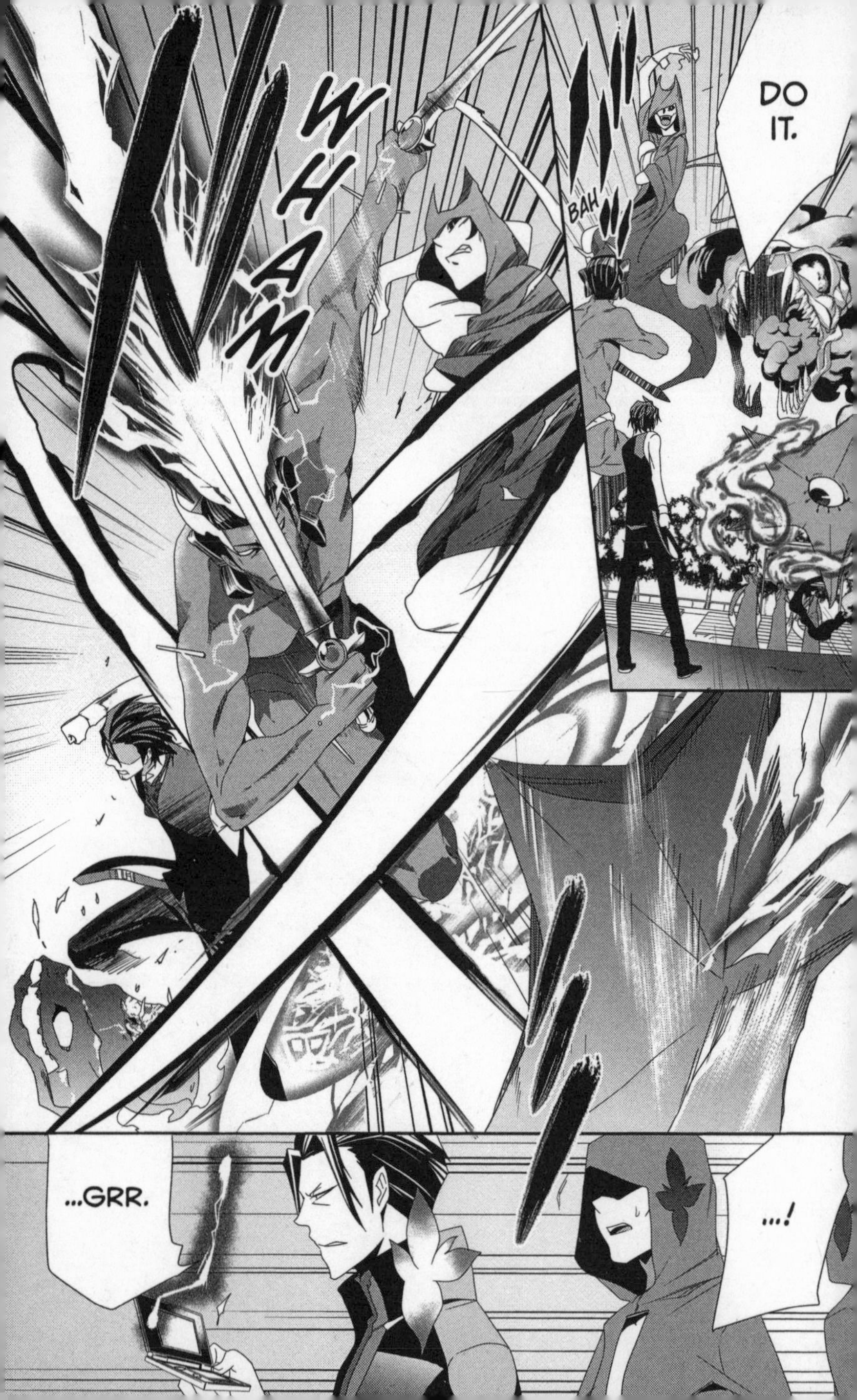
DO IT.
BAH
WHAM
...!
...GRR.

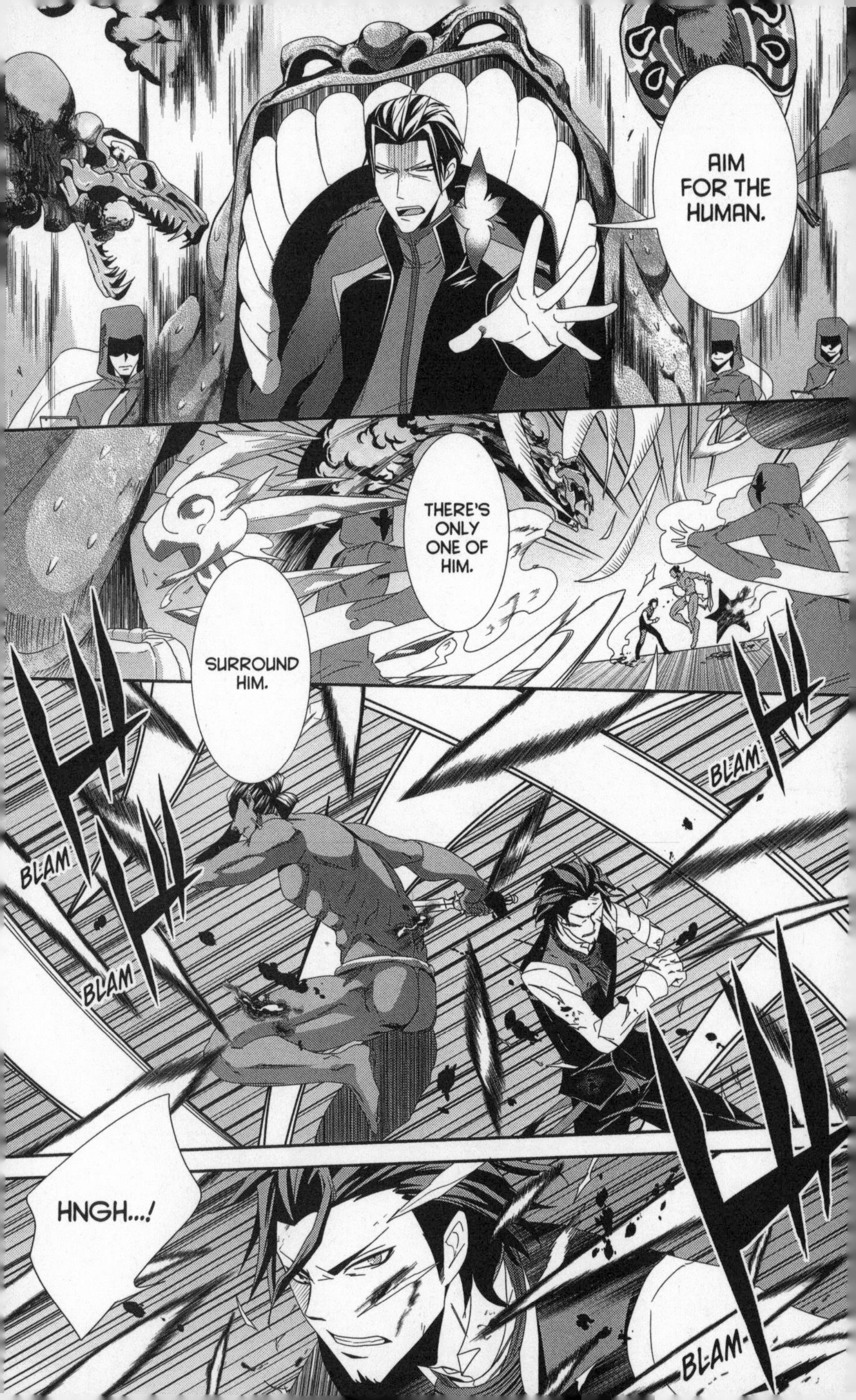
AIM FOR THE HUMAN.
THERE'S ONLY ONE OF HIM.
SURROUND HIM.
BLAM
BLAM
BLAM
HNGH...!
BLAM

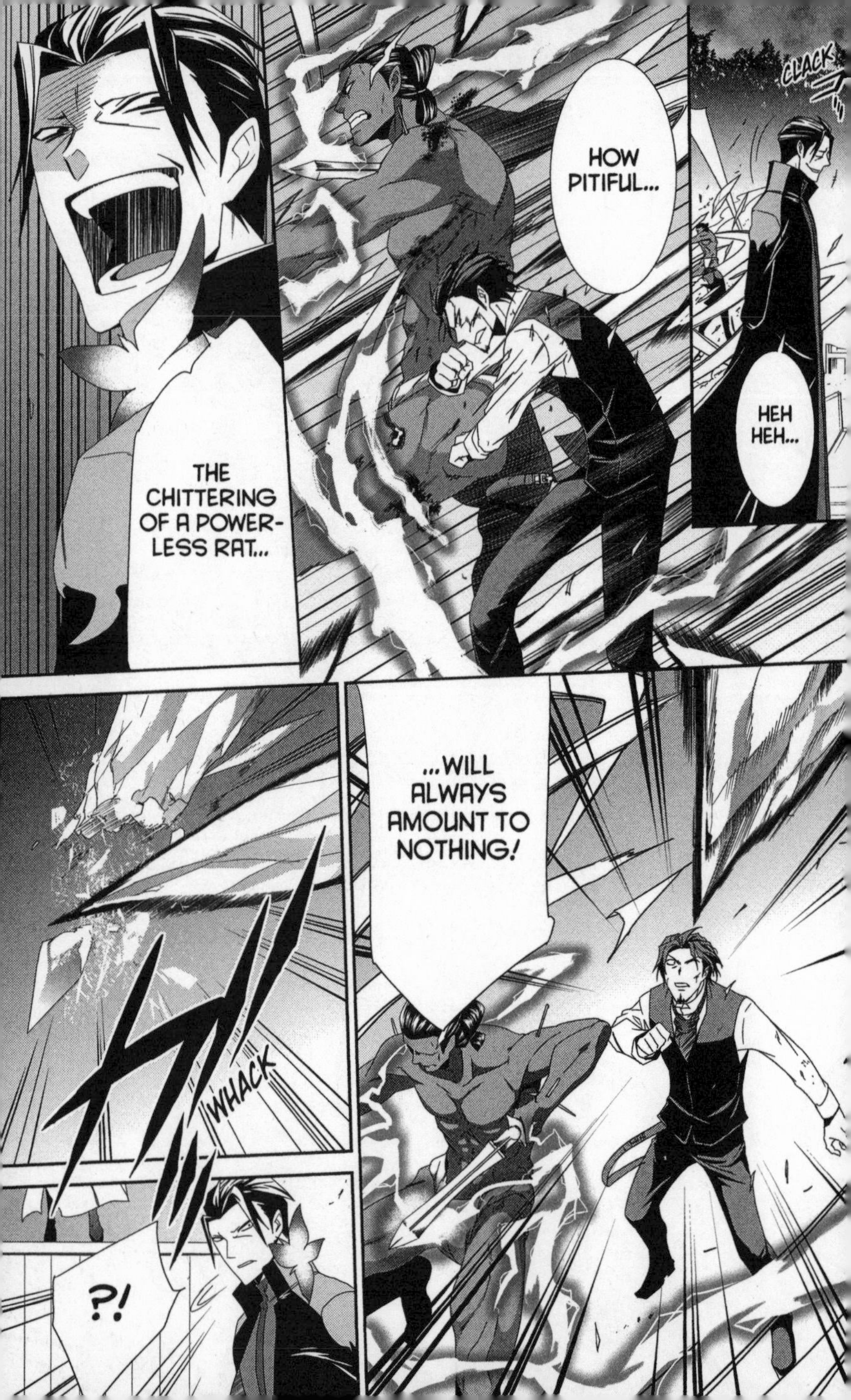

CLACK
HEH HEH...
HOW PITIFUL...
THE CHITTERING OF A POWER-LESS RAT...
...WILL ALWAYS AMOUNT TO NOTHING!
WHACK
?!

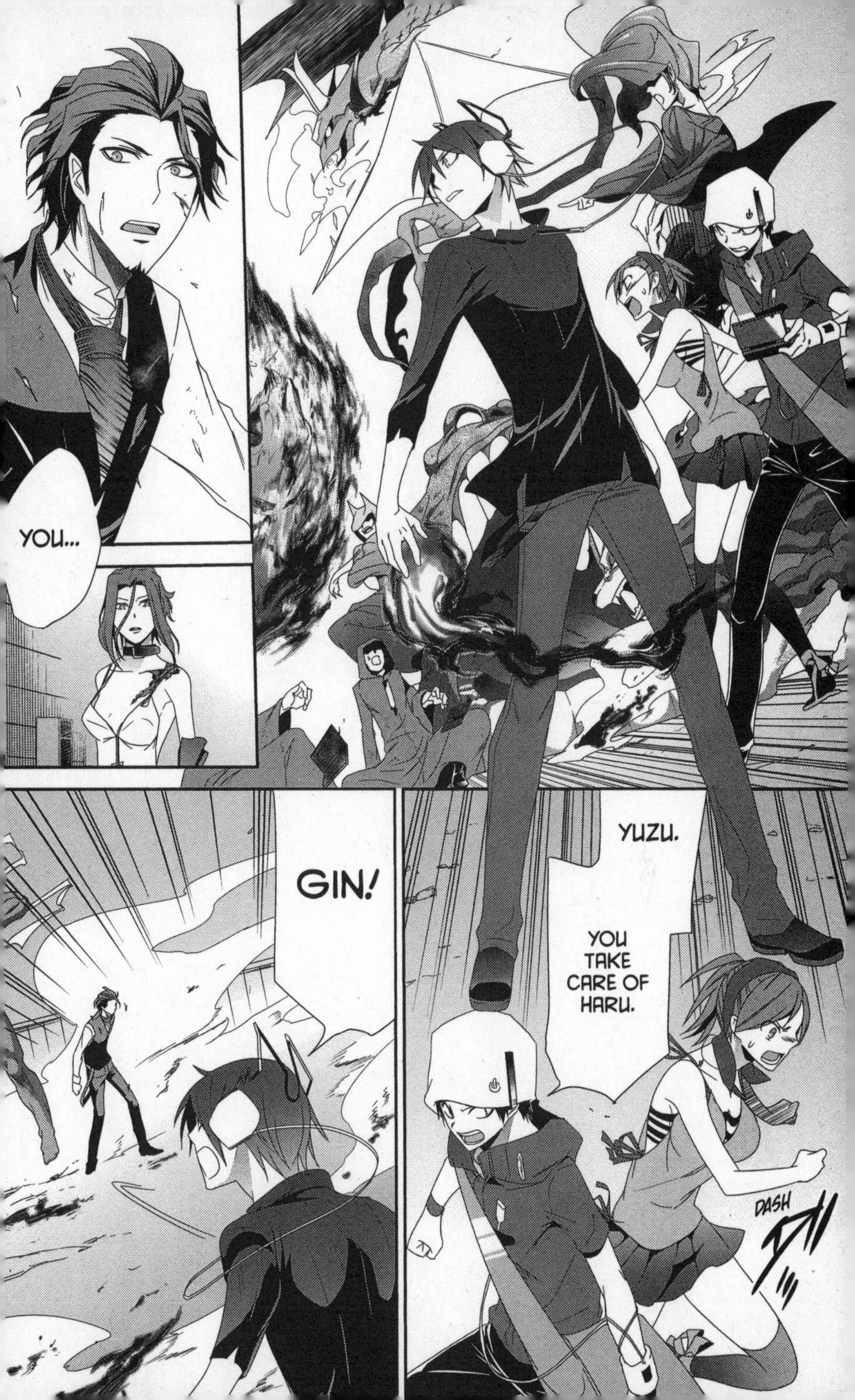
YOU...
YUZU.
YOU TAKE CARE OF HARU.
DASH
GIN!

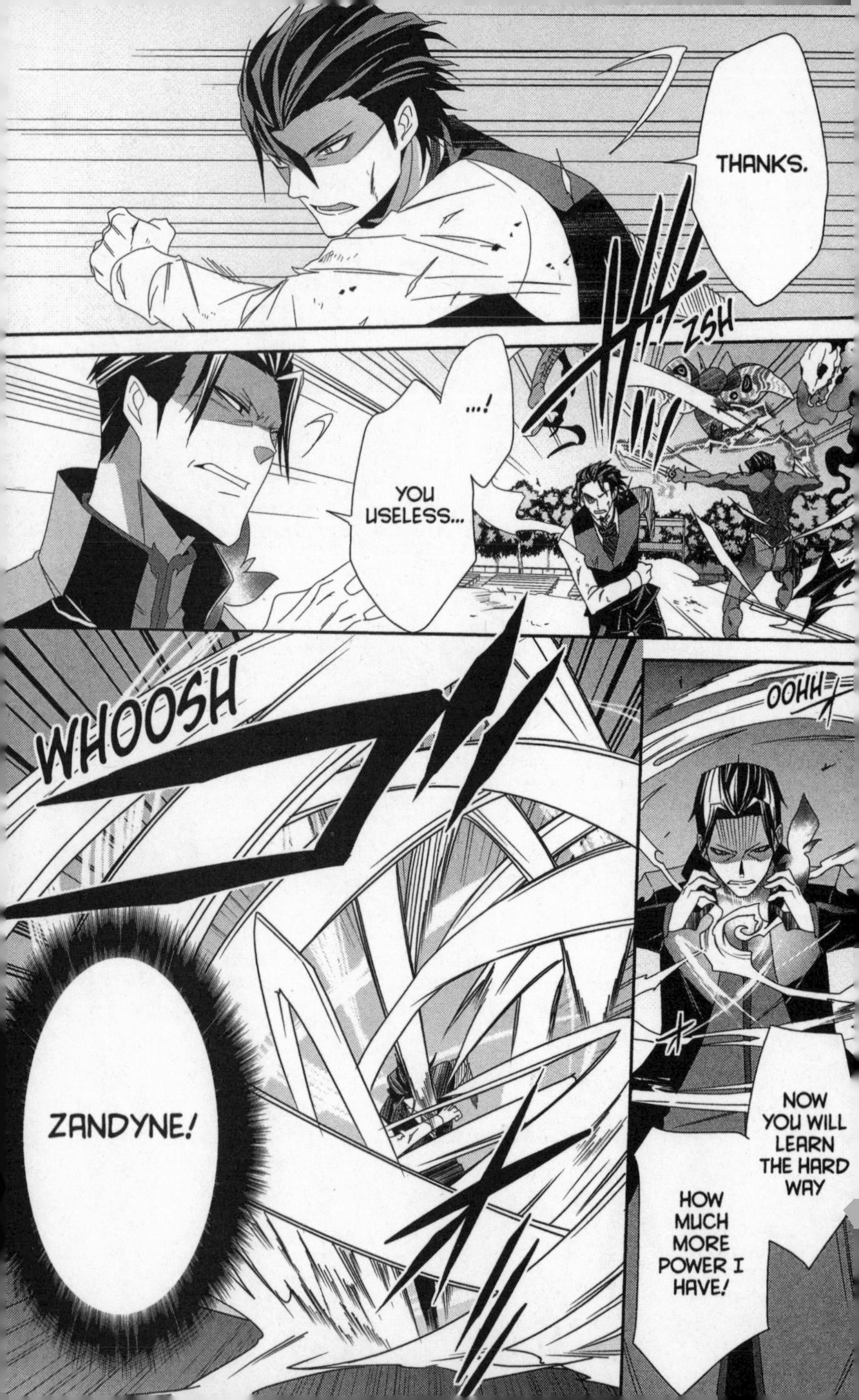
THANKS.
ZSH
...!
YOU USELESS...
OOHH
NOW YOU WILL LEARN THE HARD WAY
HOW MUCH MORE POWER I HAVE!
WHOOSH
ZANDYNE!

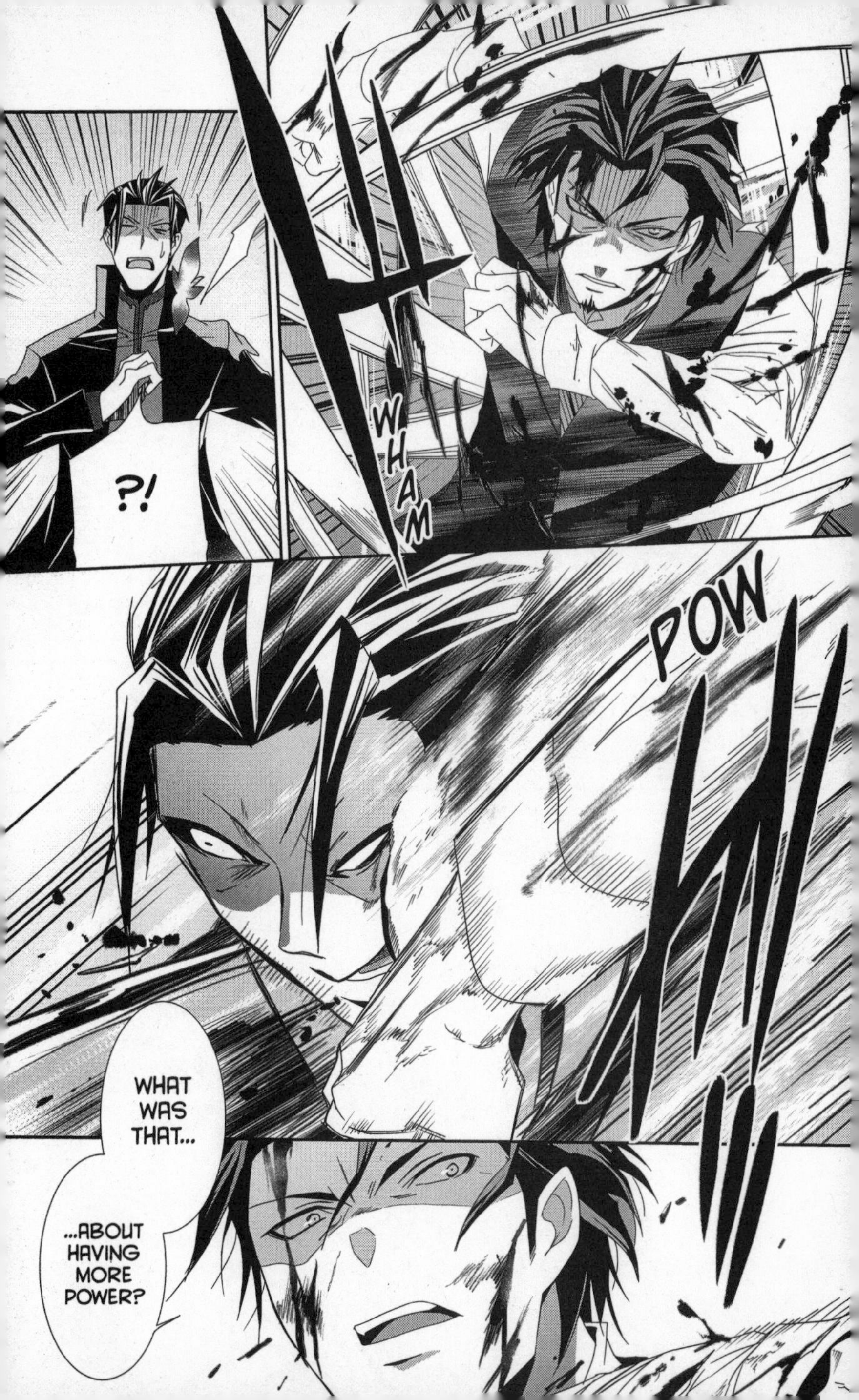
WHAM
?!
POW
WHAT WAS THAT...
...ABOUT HAVING MORE POWER?

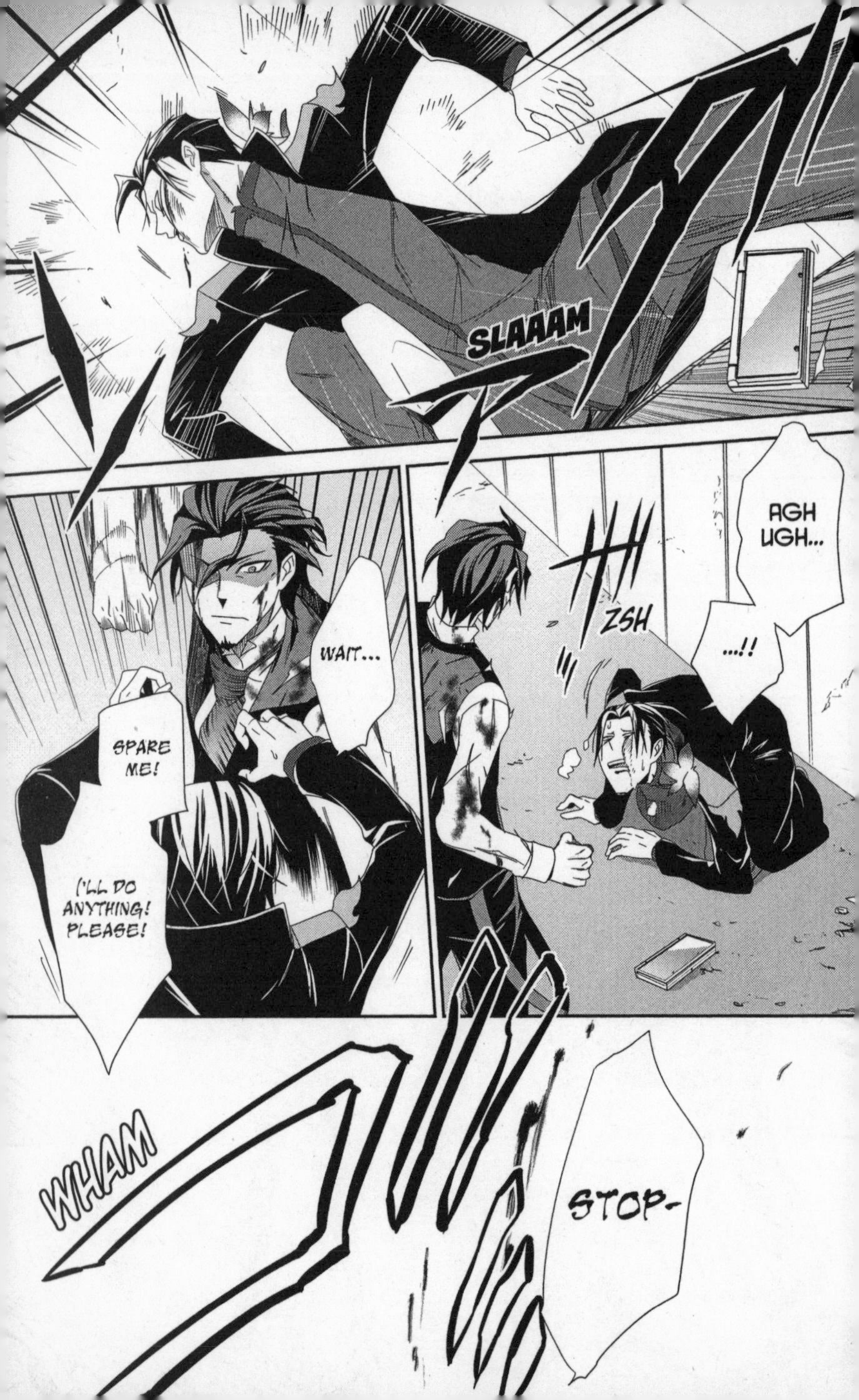
SLAAAM
AGH UGH...
ZSH
...!!
WAIT...
SPARE ME!
I'LL DO ANYTHING! PLEASE!
STOP-
WHAM

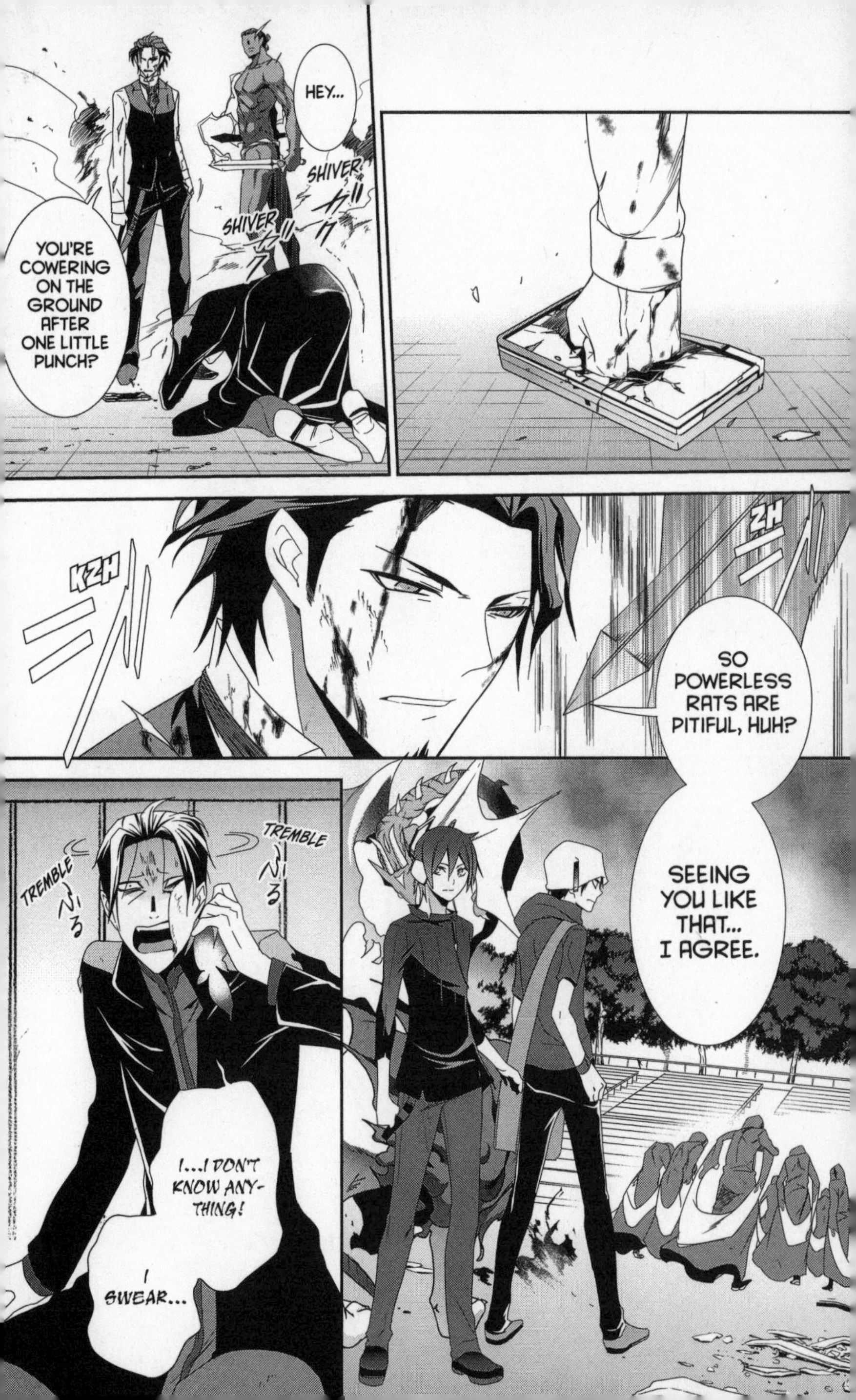
HEY...
SHIVER
SHIVER
YOU'RE COWERING ON THE GROUND AFTER ONE LITTLE PUNCH?
ZH
SO POWERLESS RATS ARE PITIFUL, HUH?
KZH
SEEING YOU LIKE THAT... I AGREE.
TREMBLE
TREMBLE
I...I DON'T KNOW ANYTHING!
I SWEAR...

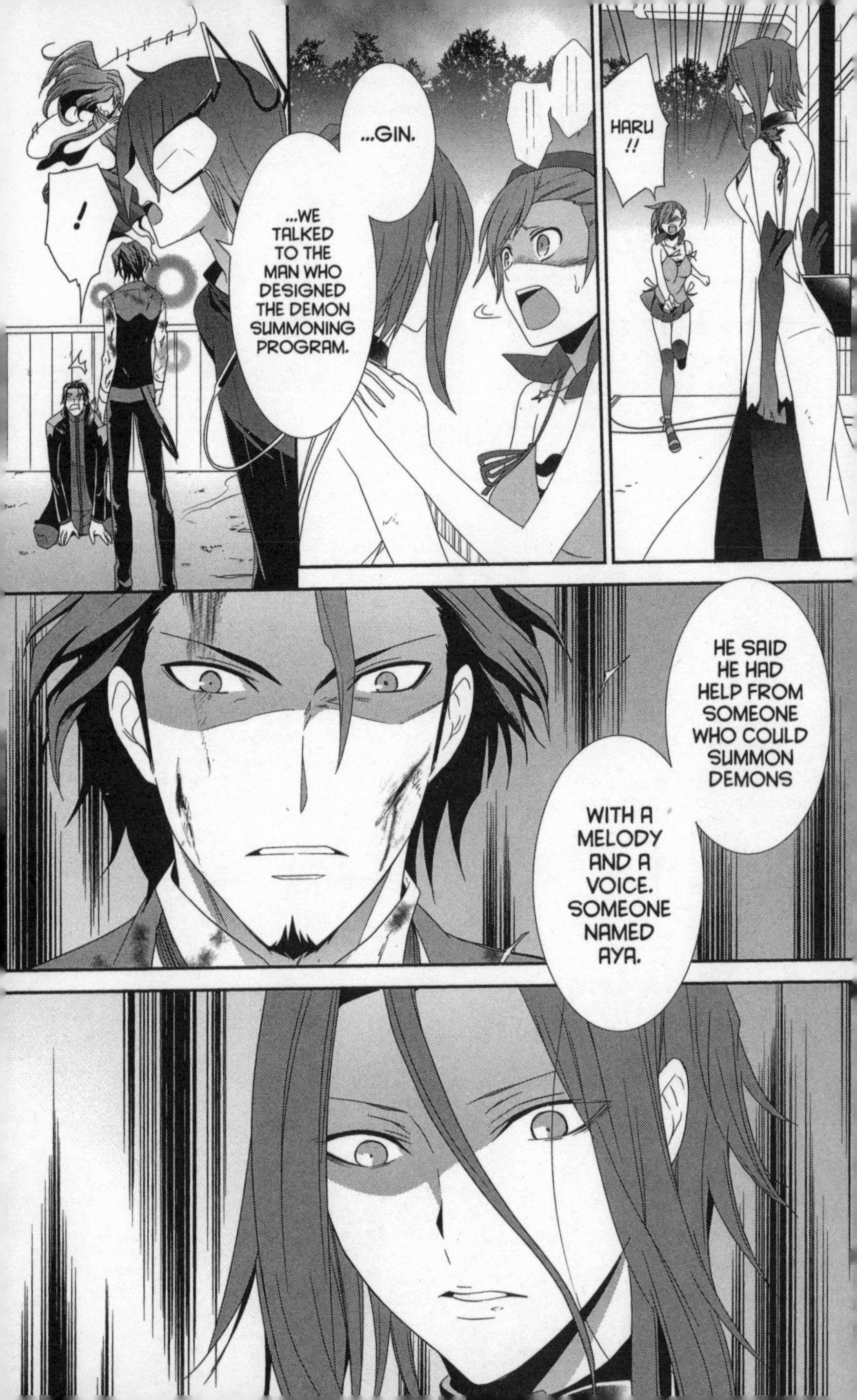
HARU !!
...GIN.
...WE TALKED TO THE MAN WHO DESIGNED THE DEMON SUMMONING PROGRAM.
!
HE SAID HE HAD HELP FROM SOMEONE WHO COULD SUMMON DEMONS
WITH A MELODY AND A VOICE. SOMEONE NAMED AYA.

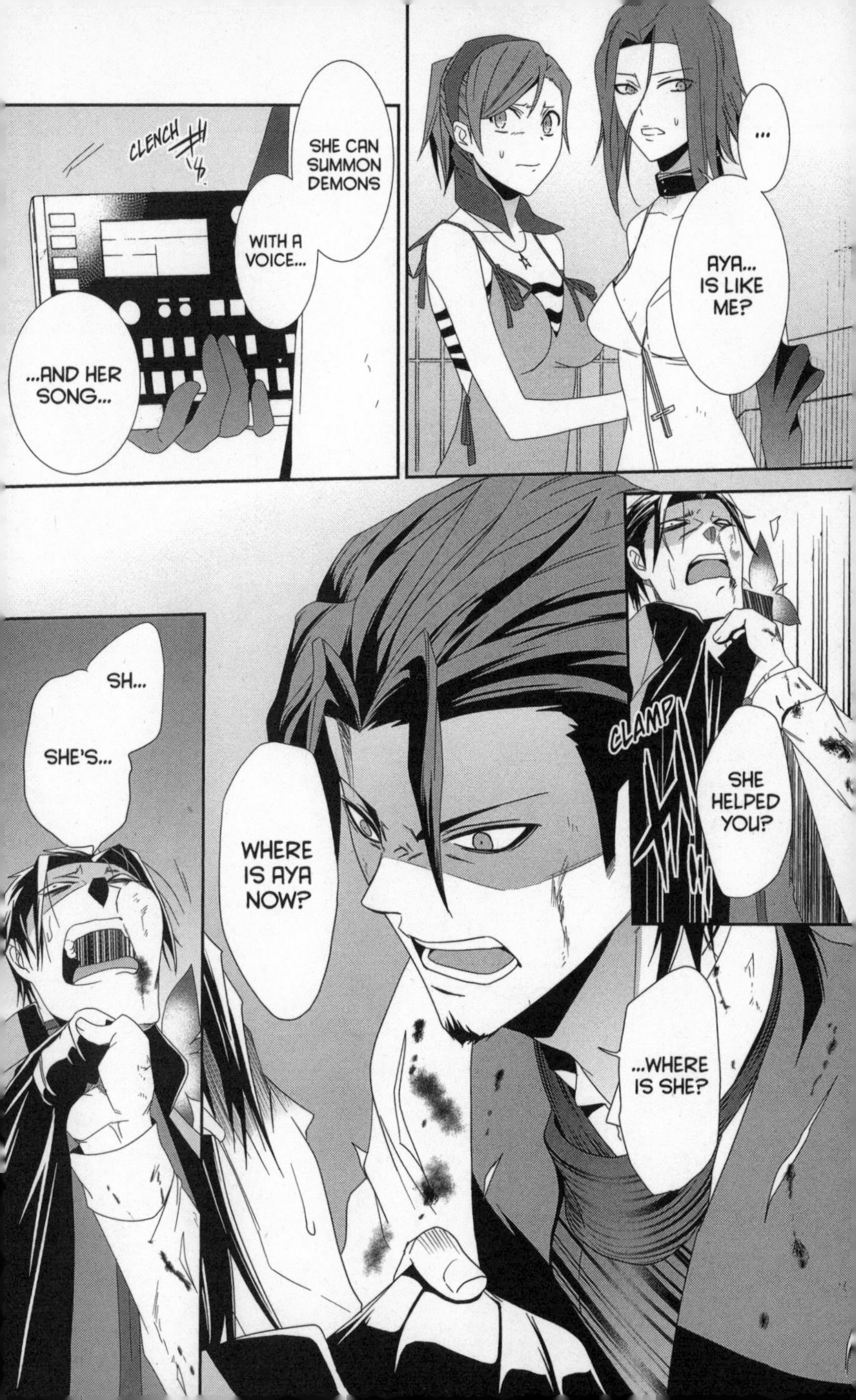
...
AYA... IS LIKE ME?
CLENCH
SHE CAN SUMMON DEMONS
WITH A VOICE...
...AND HER SONG...
CLAMP
SHE HELPED YOU?
...WHERE IS SHE?
WHERE IS AYA NOW?
SH...
SHE'S...

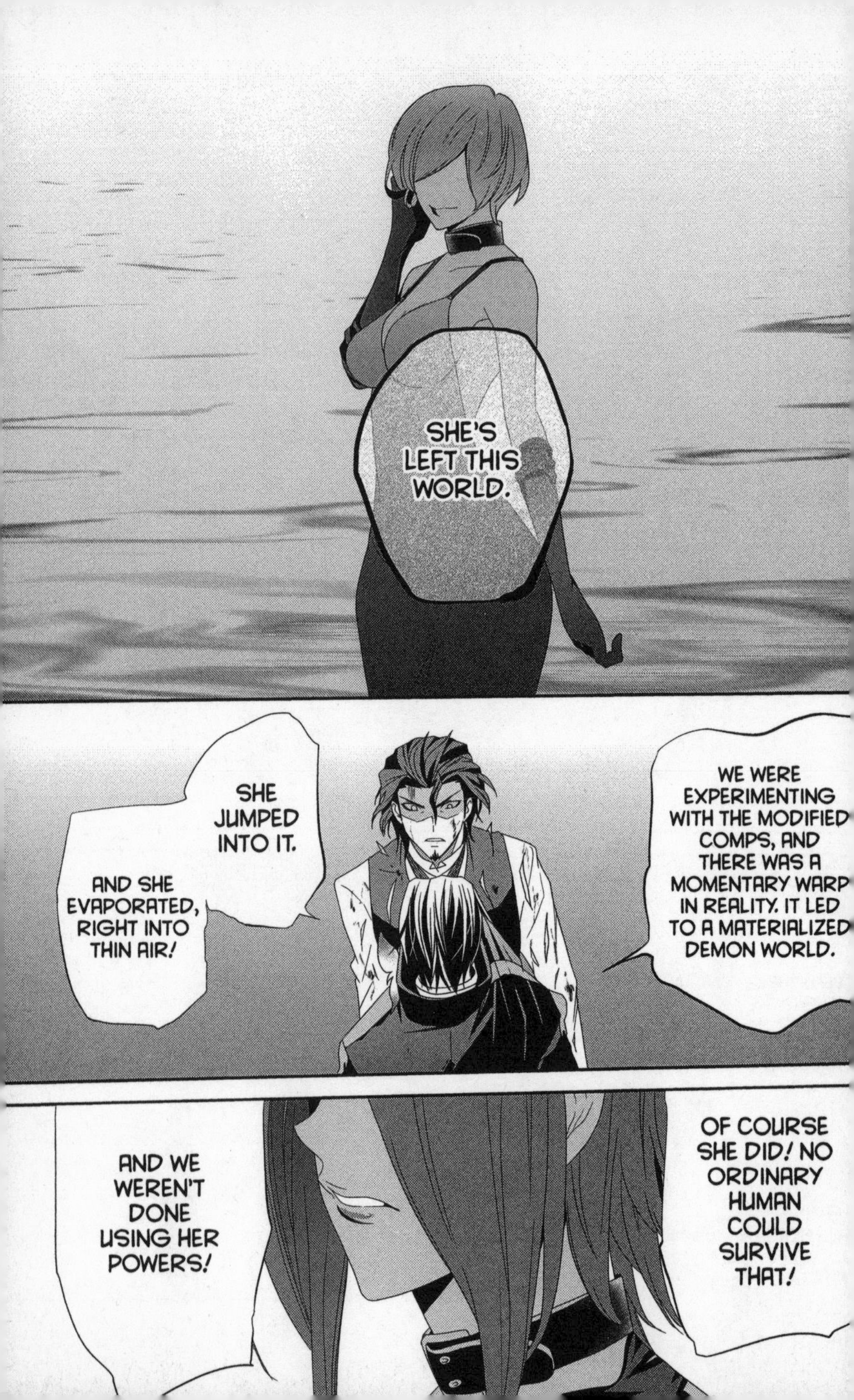
SHE'S LEFT THIS WORLD.
WE WERE EXPERIMENTING WITH THE MODIFIED COMPS, AND THERE WAS A MOMENTARY WARP IN REALITY. IT LED TO A MATERIALIZED DEMON WORLD.
SHE JUMPED INTO IT.
AND SHE EVAPORATED, RIGHT INTO THIN AIR!
OF COURSE SHE DID! NO ORDINARY HUMAN COULD SURVIVE THAT!
AND WE WEREN'T DONE USING HER POWERS!

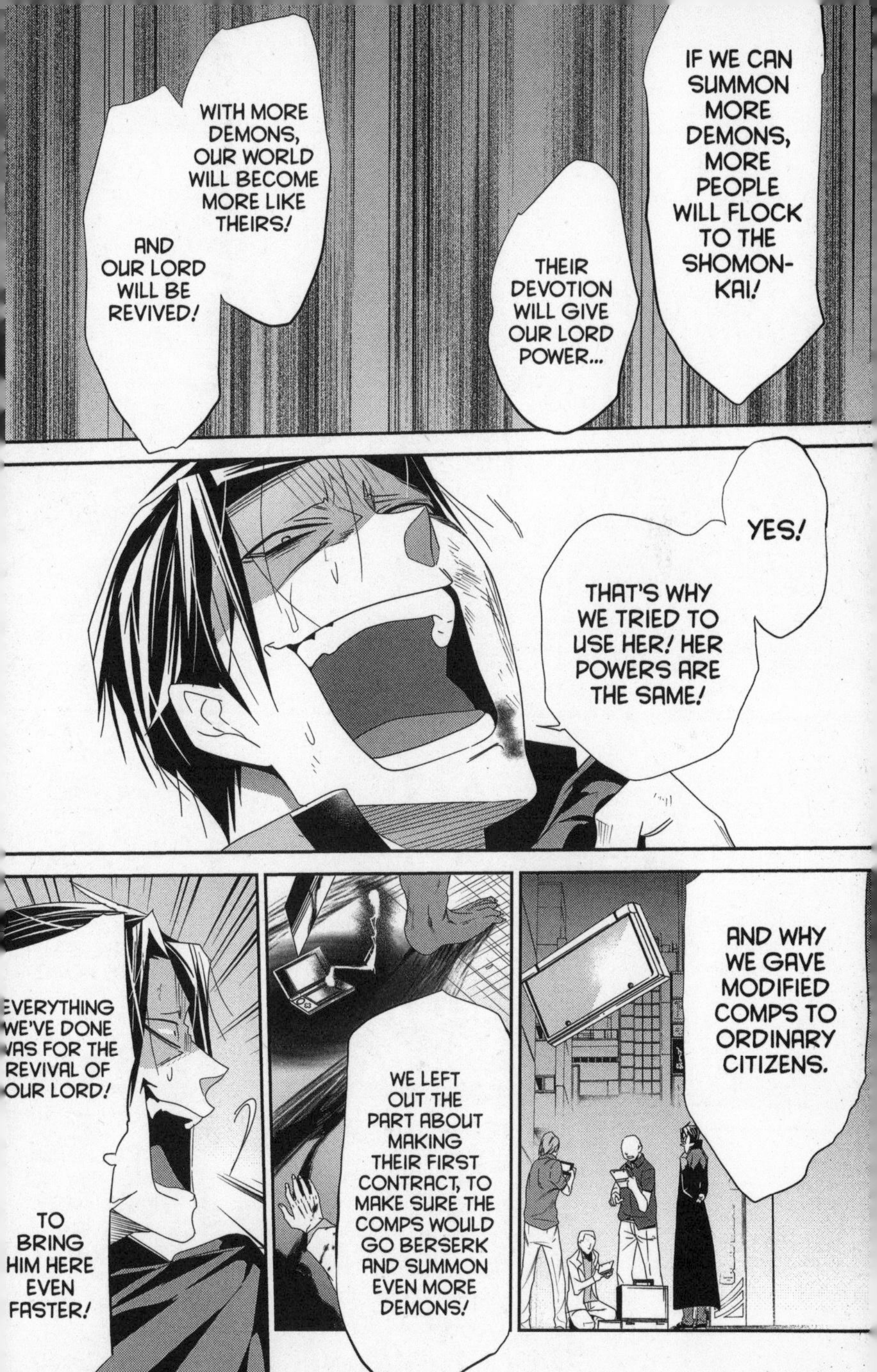
IF WE CAN SUMMON MORE DEMONS, MORE PEOPLE WILL FLOCK TO THE SHOMON-KAI!
THEIR DEVOTION WILL GIVE OUR LORD POWER...
WITH MORE DEMONS, OUR WORLD WILL BECOME MORE LIKE THEIRS!
AND OUR LORD WILL BE REVIVED!
YES!
THAT'S WHY WE TRIED TO USE HER! HER POWERS ARE THE SAME!
AND WHY WE GAVE MODIFIED COMPS TO ORDINARY CITIZENS.
WE LEFT OUT THE PART ABOUT MAKING THEIR FIRST CONTRACT, TO MAKE SURE THE COMPS WOULD GO BERSERK AND SUMMON EVEN MORE DEMONS!
EVERYTHING WE'VE DONE WAS FOR THE REVIVAL OF OUR LORD!
TO BRING HIM HERE EVEN FASTER!

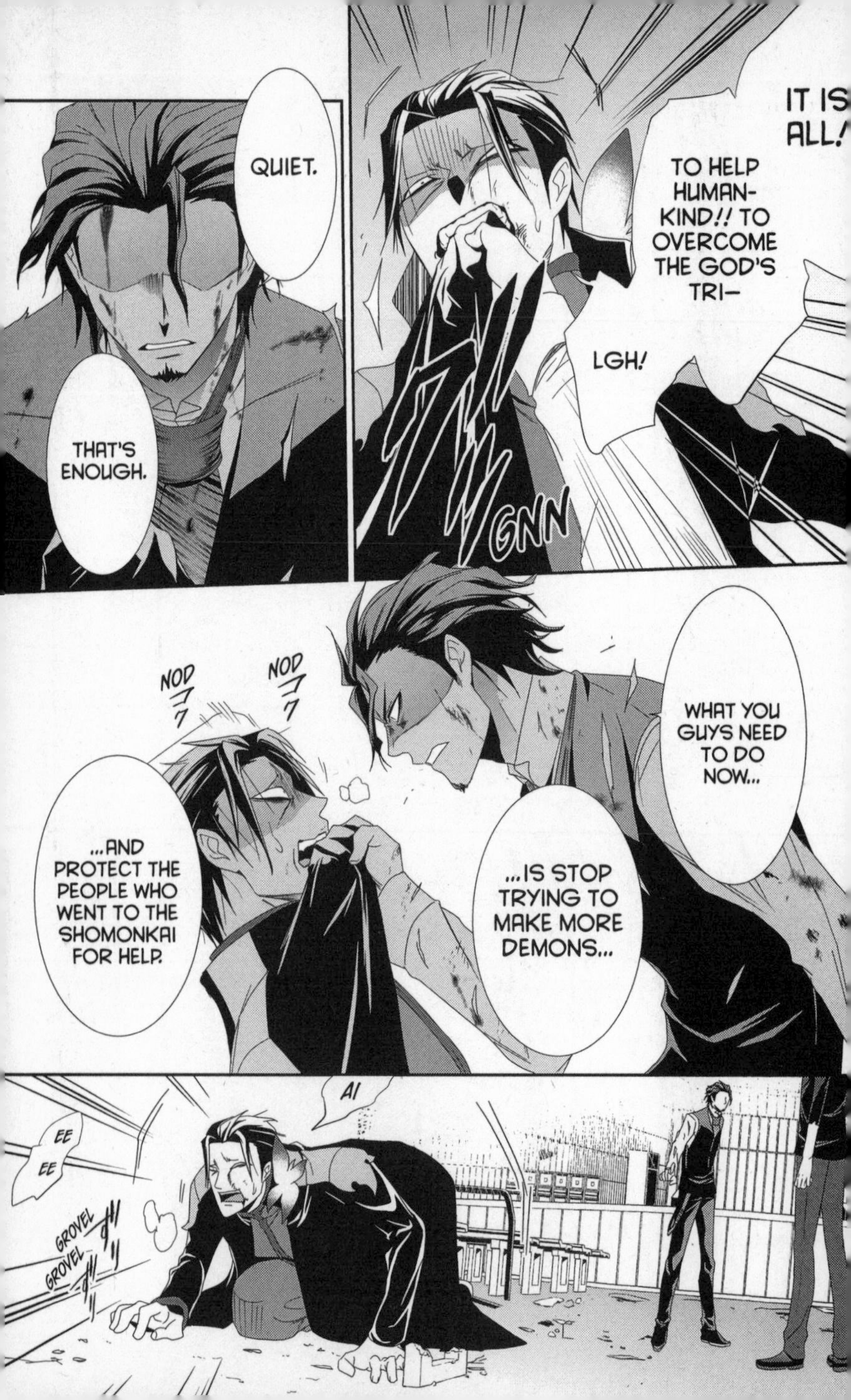

IT IS ALL!
TO HELP HUMAN-KIND!! TO OVERCOME THE GOD'S TRI—
LGH!
GNN
QUIET.
THAT'S ENOUGH.
WHAT YOU GUYS NEED TO DO NOW...
...IS STOP TRYING TO MAKE MORE DEMONS...
NOD
NOD
...AND PROTECT THE PEOPLE WHO WENT TO THE SHOMONKAI FOR HELP.
AI
EE
EE
GROVEL
GROVEL

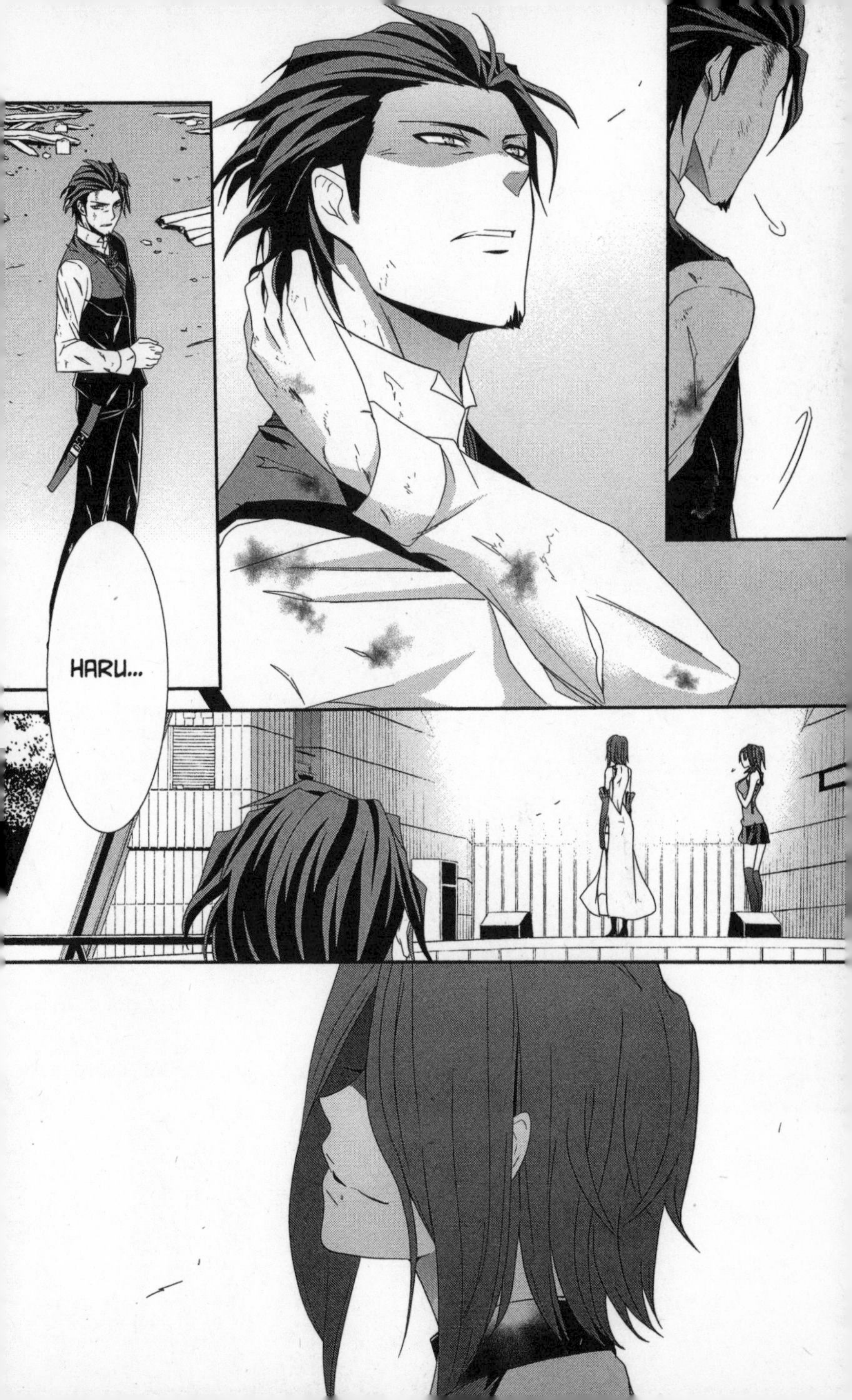
HARU...

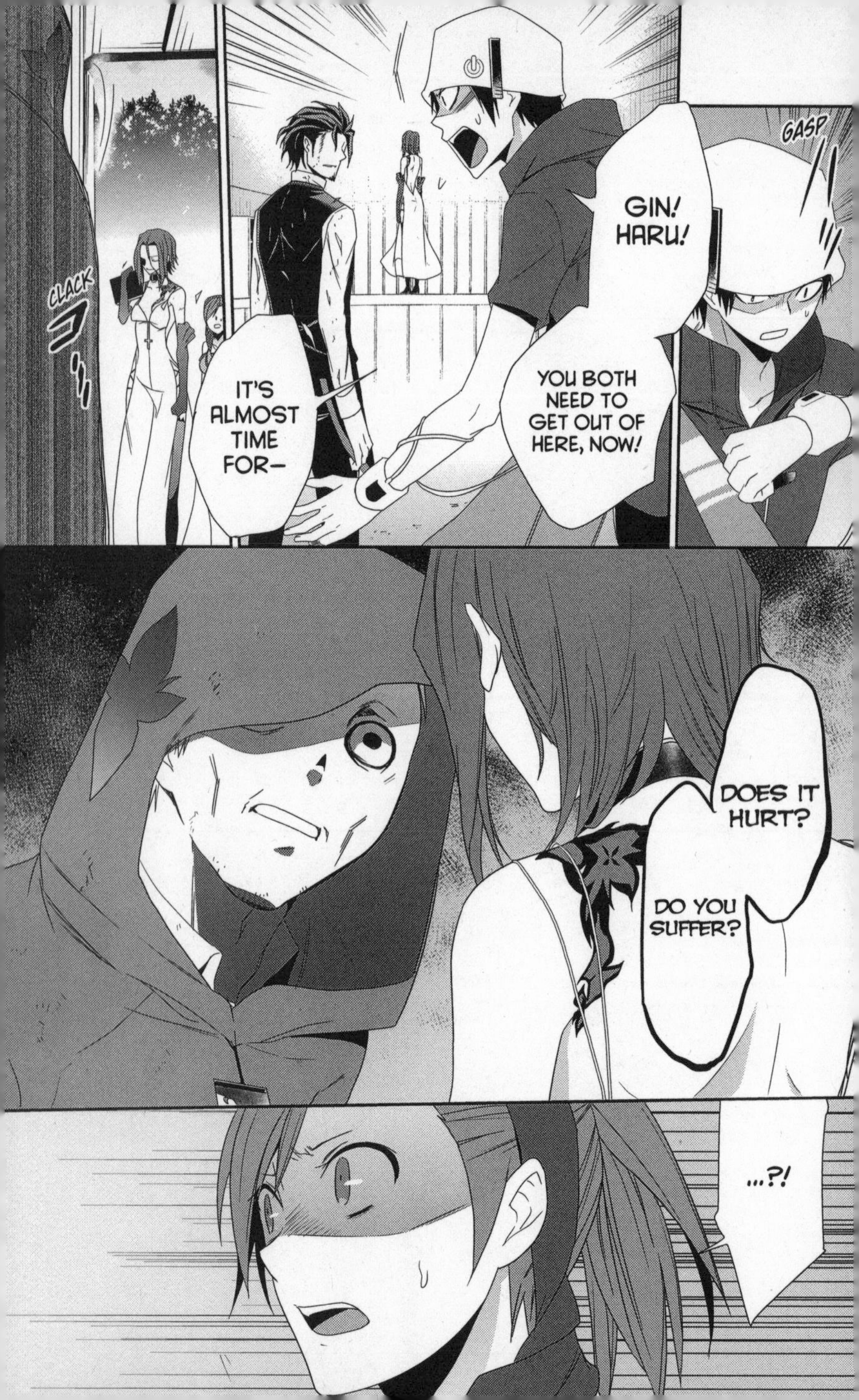
GASP
GIN! HARU!
YOU BOTH NEED TO GET OUT OF HERE, NOW!
IT'S ALMOST TIME FOR—
CLACK
DOES IT HURT?
DO YOU SUFFER?
...?!

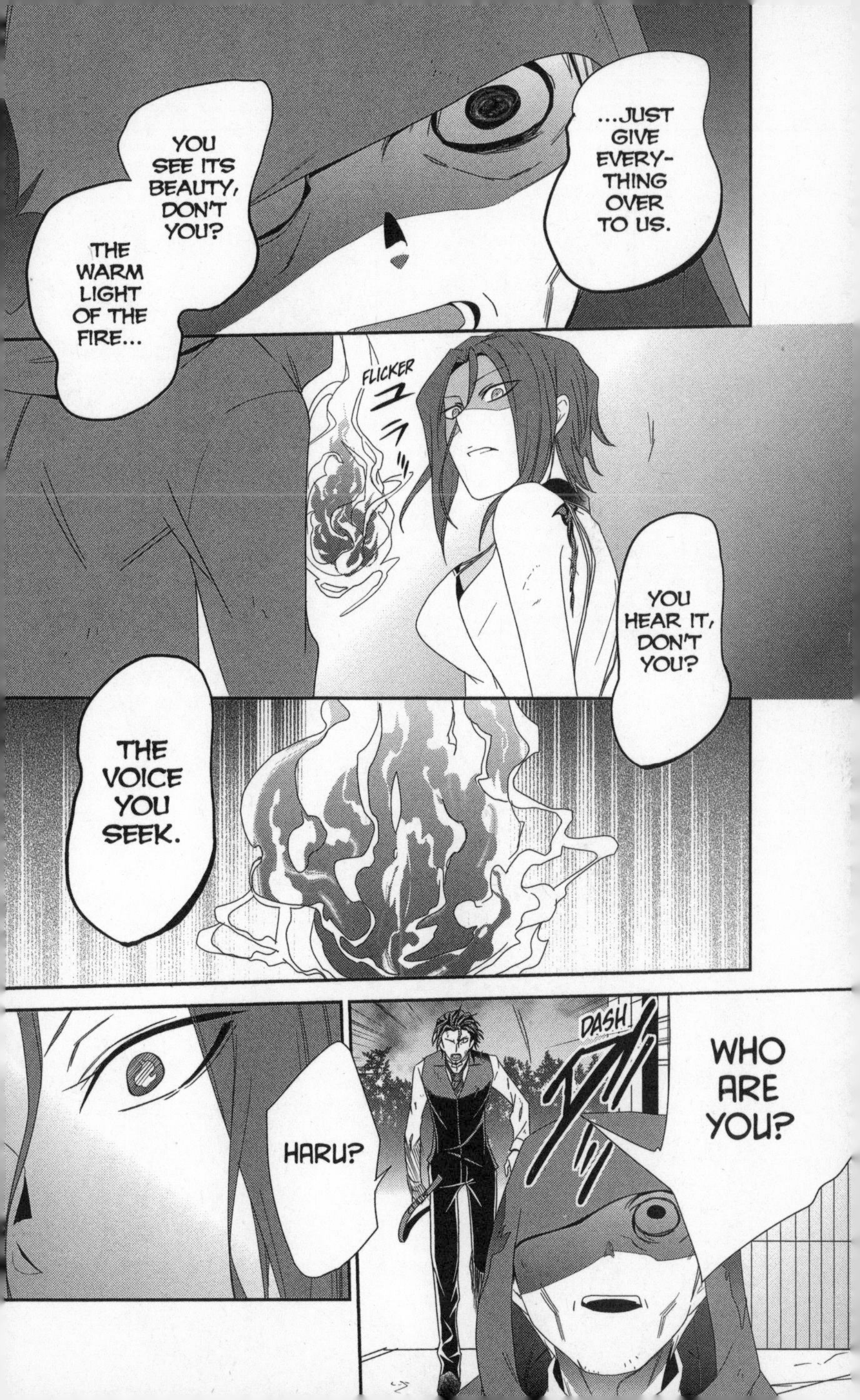
...JUST GIVE EVERY-THING OVER TO US.
YOU SEE ITS BEAUTY, DON'T YOU?
THE WARM LIGHT OF THE FIRE...
FLICKER
YOU HEAR IT, DON'T YOU?
THE VOICE YOU SEEK.
DASH
WHO ARE YOU?
HARU?

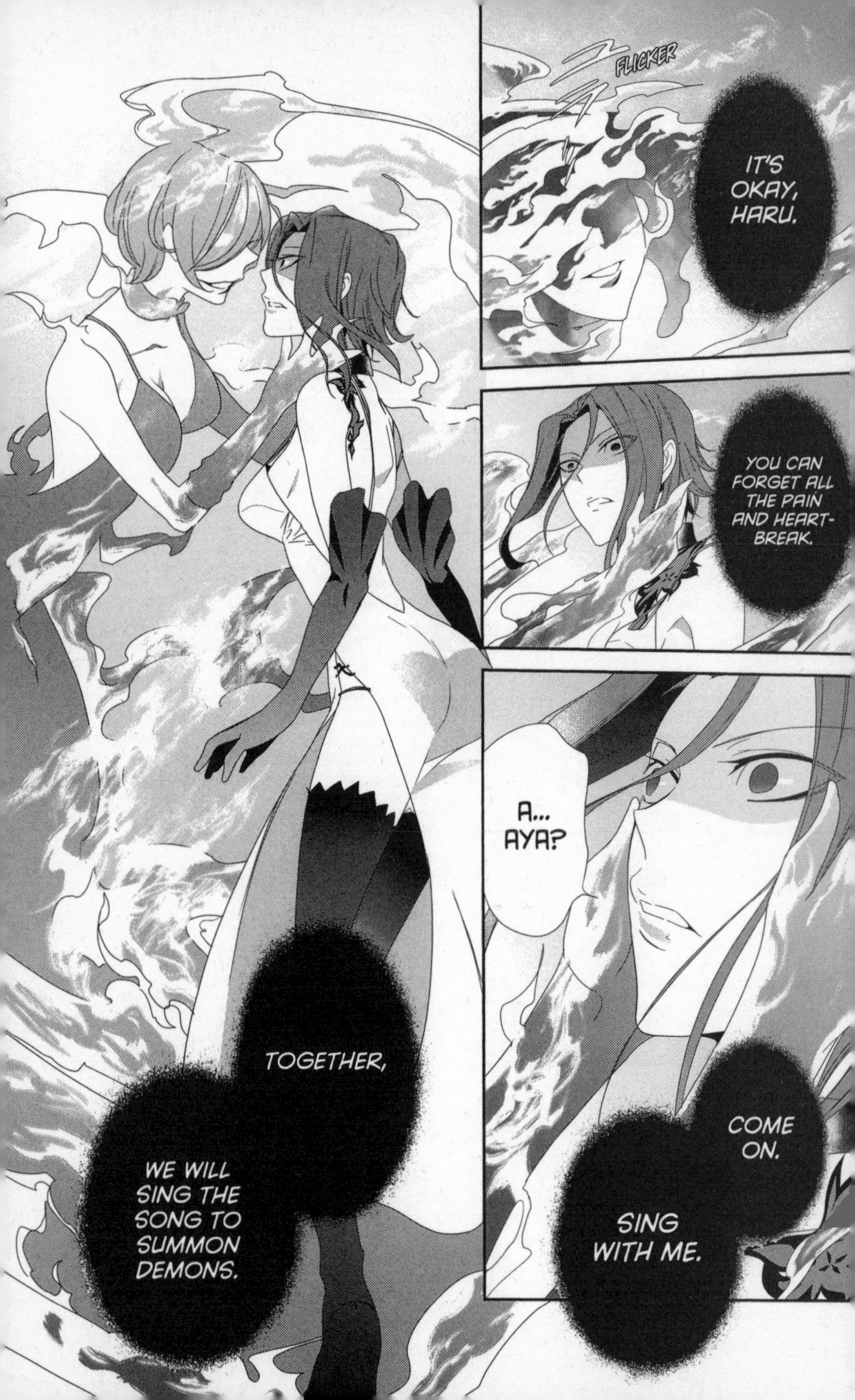
FLICKER
IT'S OKAY, HARU.
YOU CAN FORGET ALL THE PAIN AND HEART-BREAK.
A... AYA?
COME ON.
SING WITH ME.
TOGETHER,
WE WILL SING THE SONG TO SUMMON DEMONS.

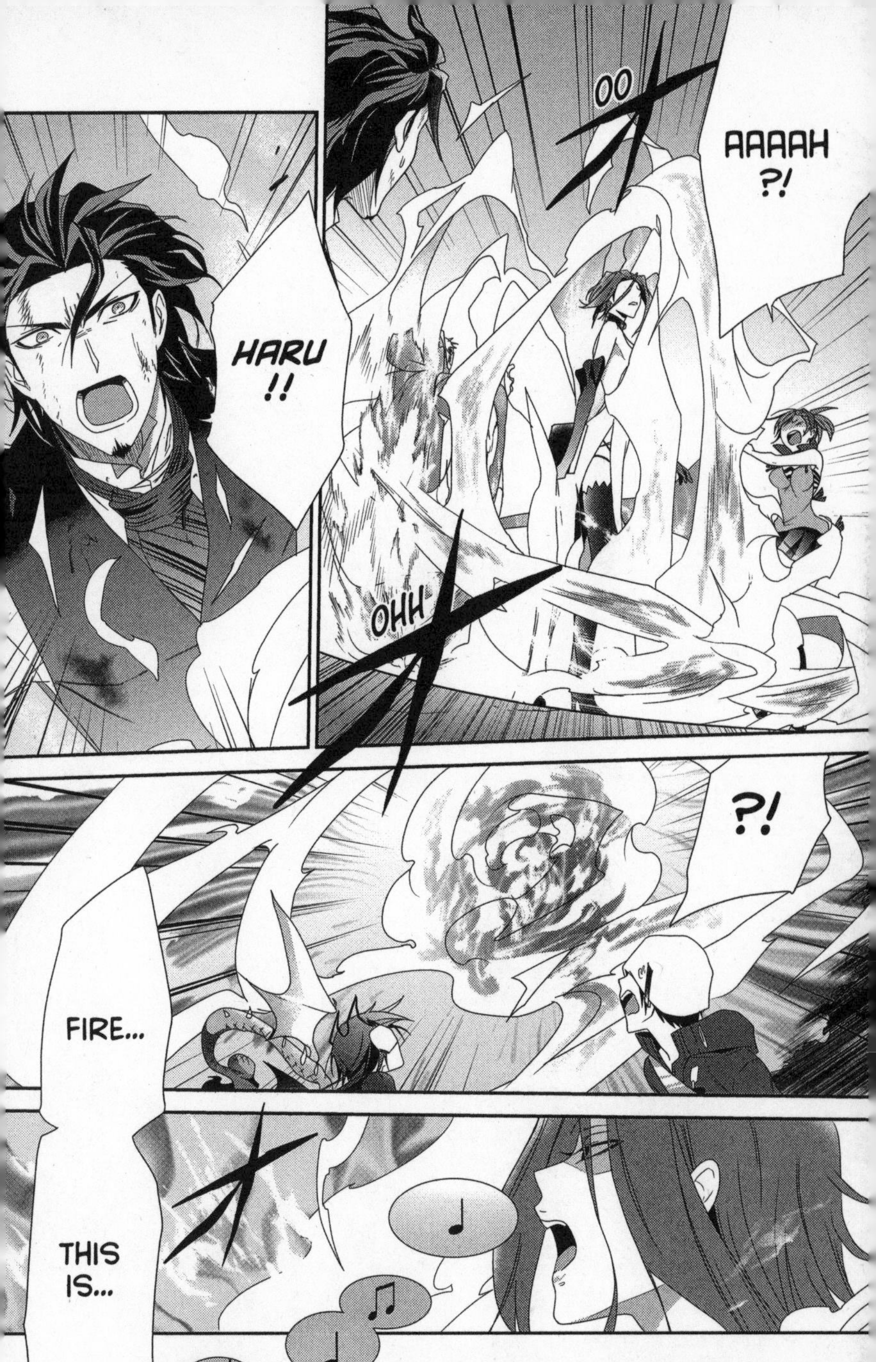
AAAAH ?!
OO
OHH
HARU !!
?!
FIRE...
THIS IS...

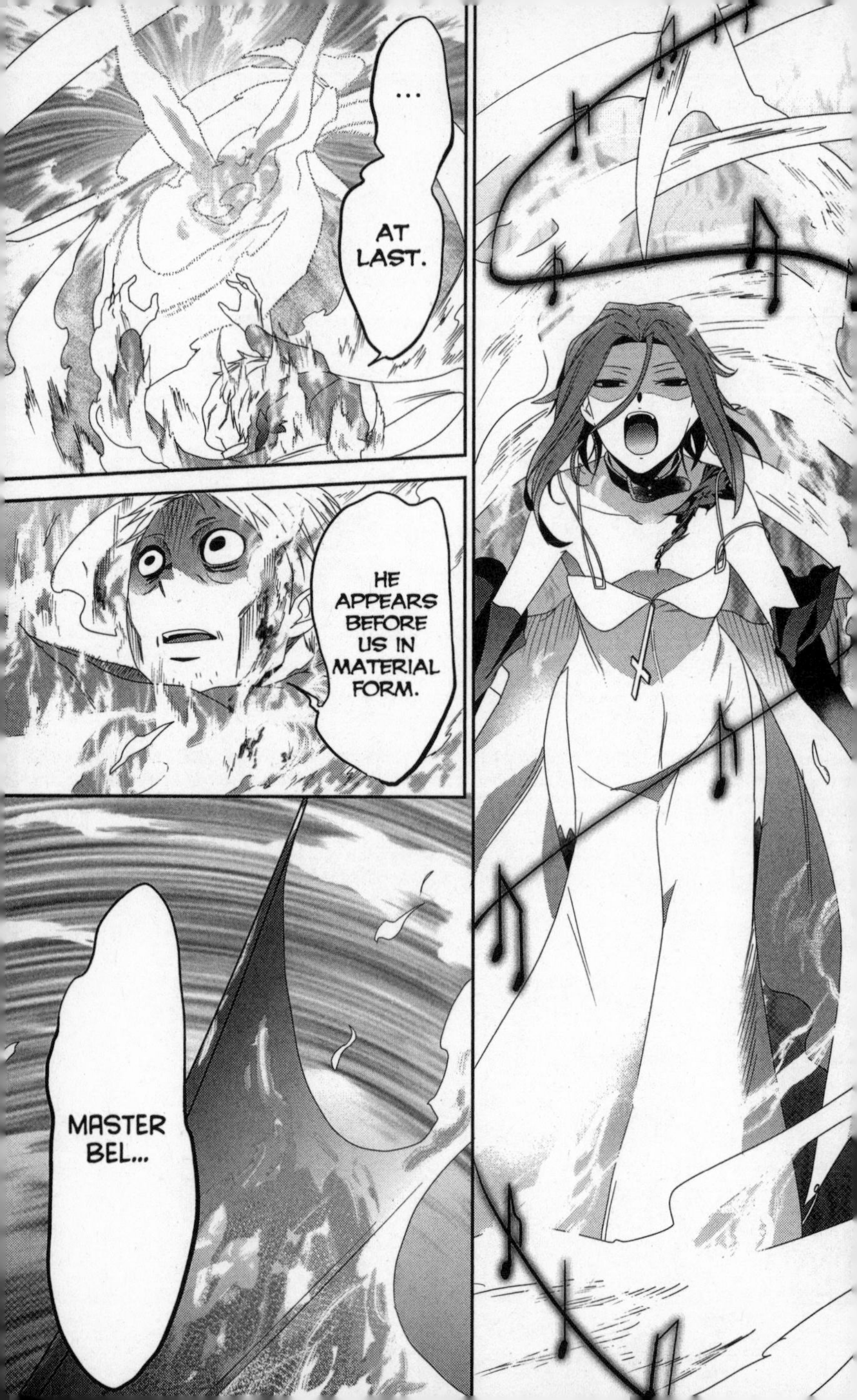

...
AT LAST.
HE APPEARS BEFORE US IN MATERIAL FORM.
MASTER BEL...

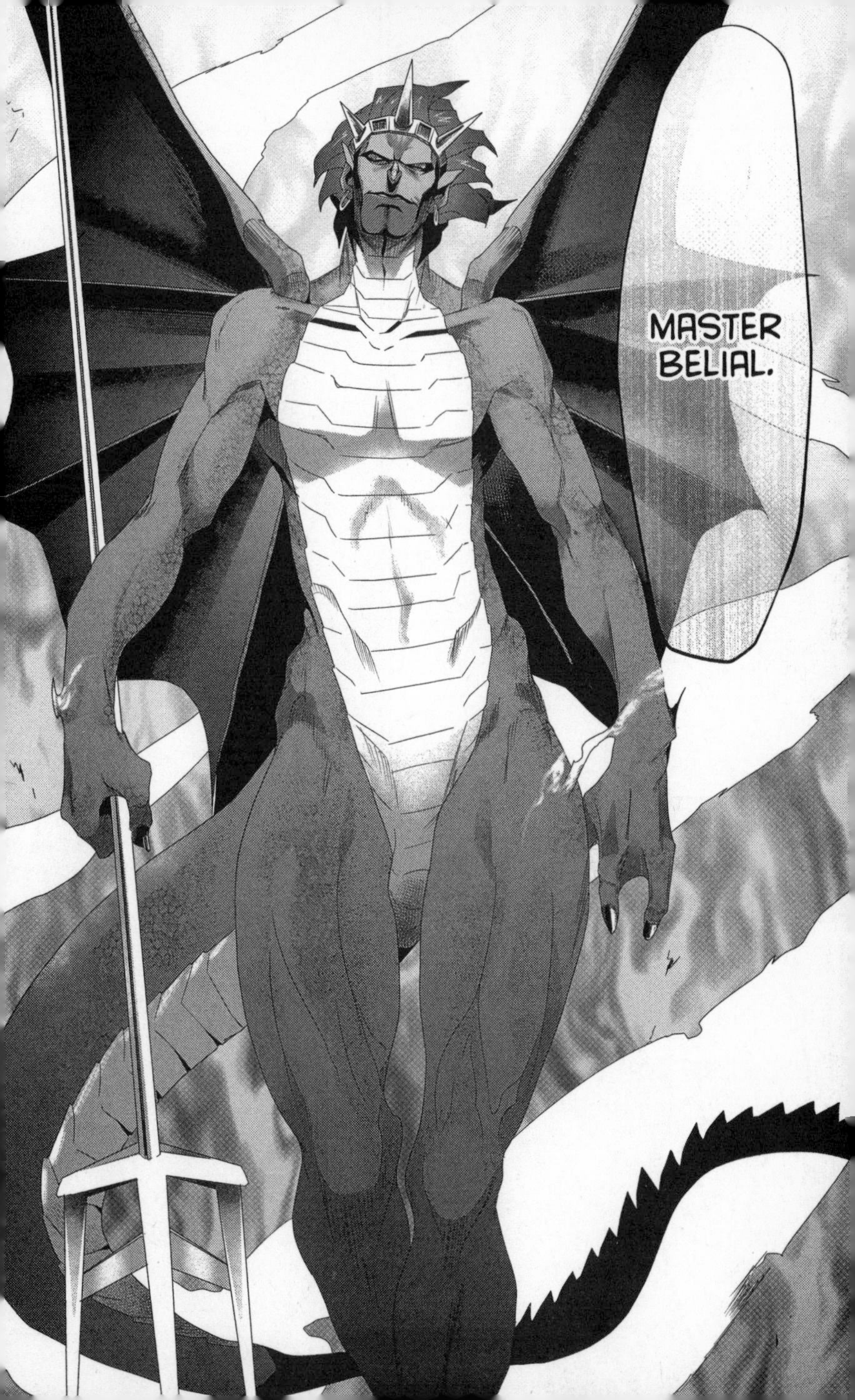
MASTER BELIAL.

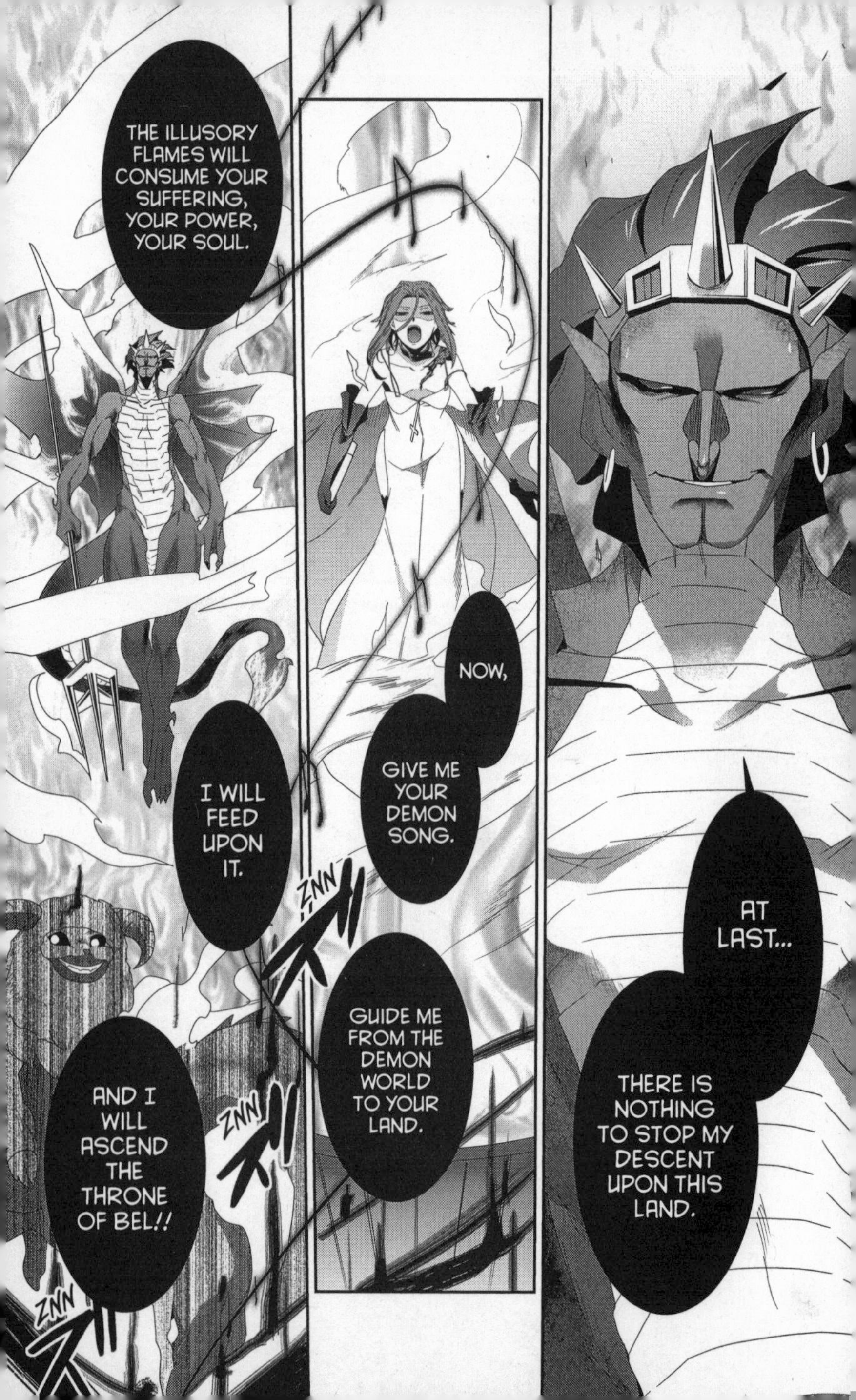
AT LAST...
THERE IS NOTHING TO STOP MY DESCENT UPON THIS LAND.
NOW,
GIVE ME YOUR DEMON SONG.
ZNN
GUIDE ME FROM THE DEMON WORLD TO YOUR LAND.
THE ILLUSORY FLAMES WILL CONSUME YOUR SUFFERING, YOUR POWER, YOUR SOUL.
I WILL FEED UPON IT.
ZNN
AND I WILL ASCEND THE THRONE OF BEL!!
ZNN

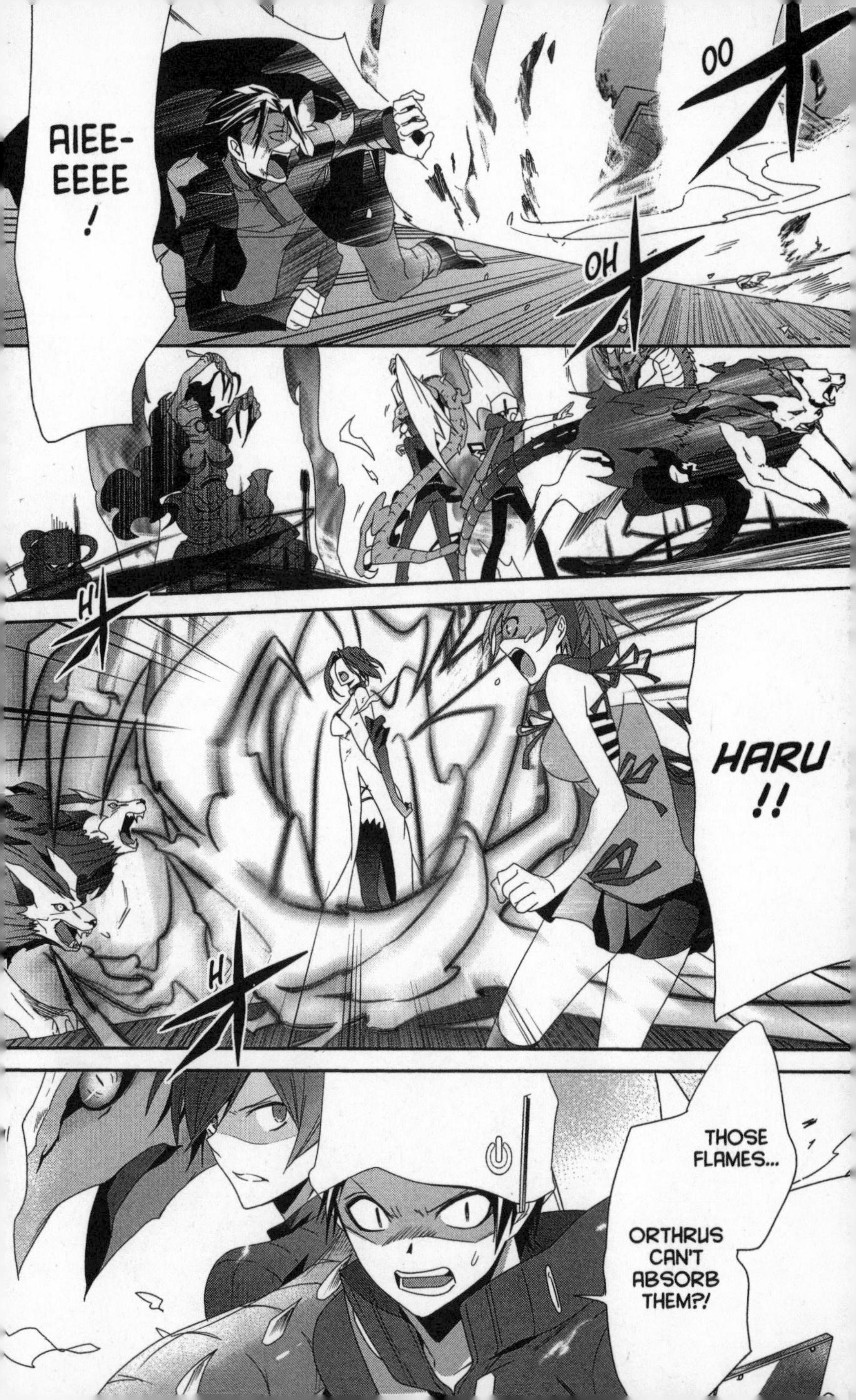

OO
OH
AIEE-EEEE!
HARU!!
H
H
THOSE FLAMES...
ORTHRUS CAN'T ABSORB THEM?!

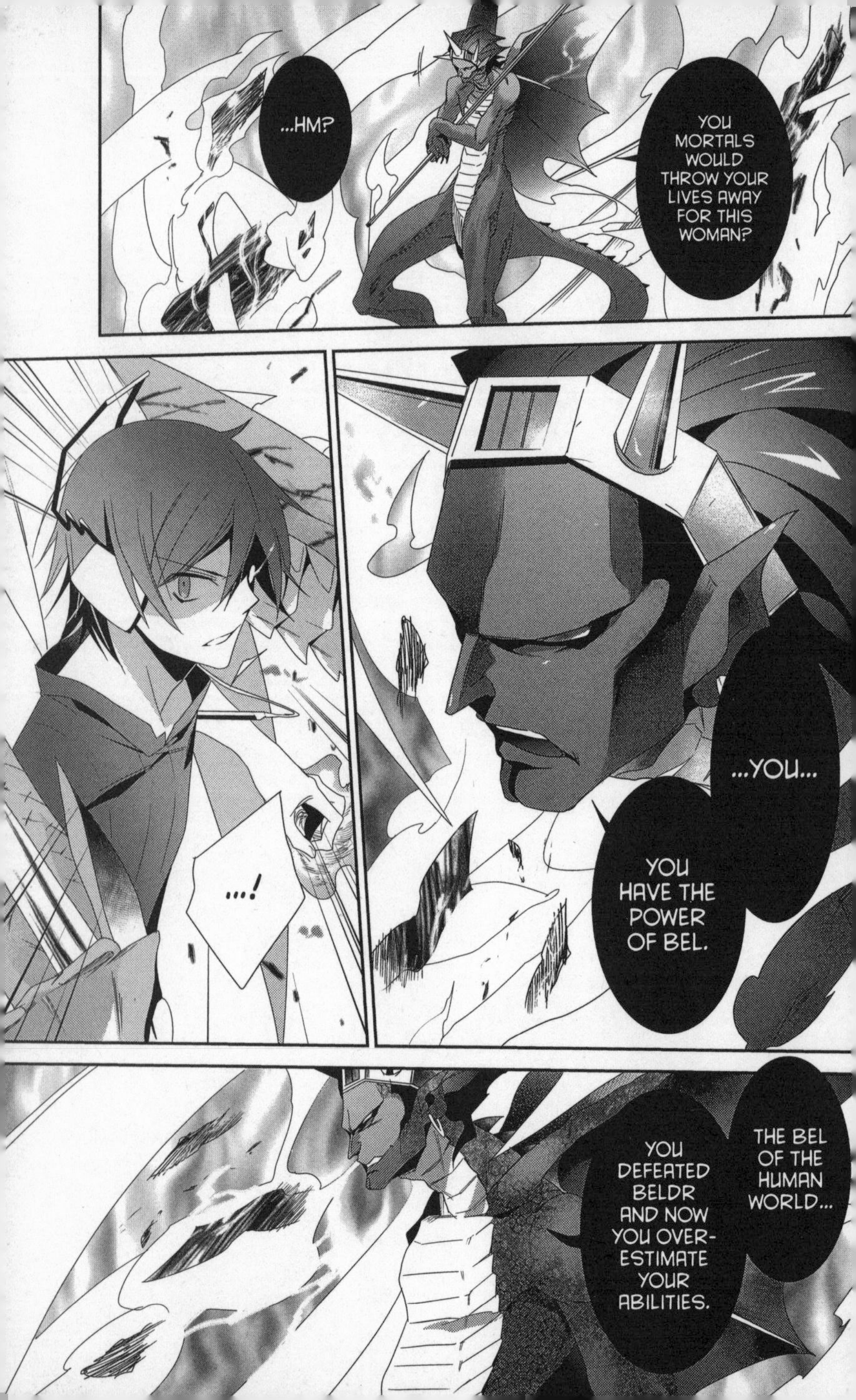
...HM?
YOU MORTALS WOULD THROW YOUR LIVES AWAY FOR THIS WOMAN?
...YOU...
YOU HAVE THE POWER OF BEL.
...!
THE BEL OF THE HUMAN WORLD...
YOU DEFEATED BELDR AND NOW YOU OVER-ESTIMATE YOUR ABILITIES.

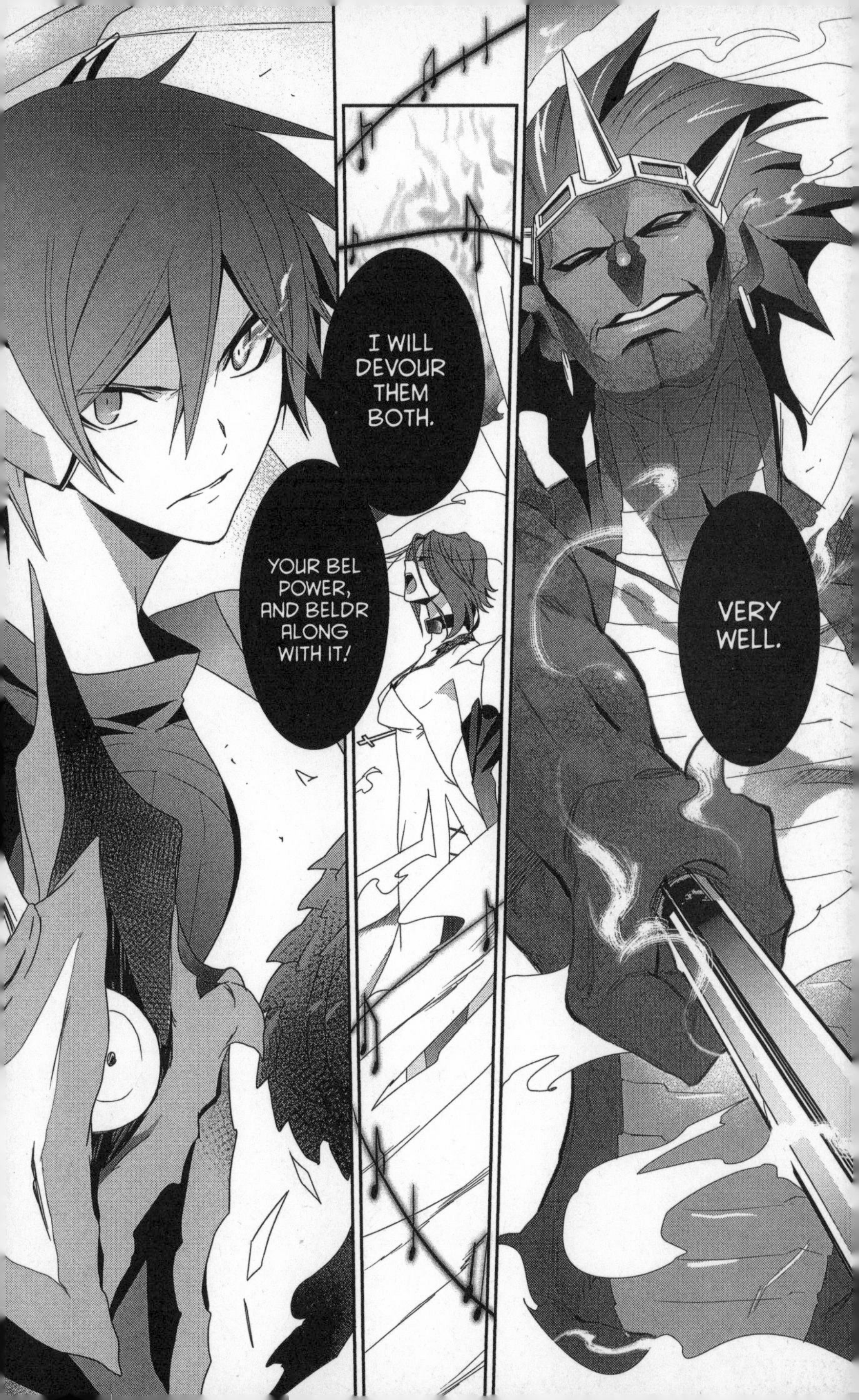
VERY WELL.
I WILL DEVOUR THEM BOTH.
YOUR BEL POWER, AND BELDR ALONG WITH IT!

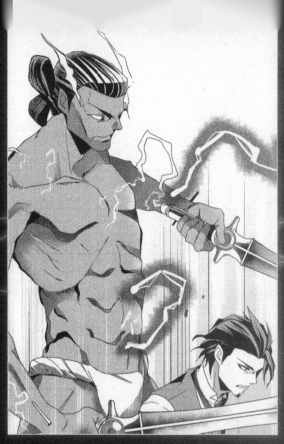

TAKE-MIKAZUCHI

A JAPANESE GOD OF WAR OR THUNDER. HE IS ONE OF THE HEAVENLY DEITIES WHO PLAYED AN ACTIVE ROLE IN THE JAPANESE ABDICATION MYTH. HE WAS BORN FROM THE BLOOD THAT SPATTERED ON THE SWORD IZANAGI USED TO BEHEAD THE FIRE GOD HI-NO-KAGUTSUCHI. HE WAS SENT TO OKUNINUSHI FROM TAKAMAGAHARA TO ORDER HIM TO ABDICATE, BUT BECAUSE OKUNINUSHI'S SECOND SON TAKE-MINAKATA WOULD NOT OBEY HIM, THE TWO HAD A DUEL OF STRENGTH, FROM WHICH TAKE-MIKAZUCHI EMERGED VICTORIOUS.

DEVIL SURVIVOR
デビルサバイバー

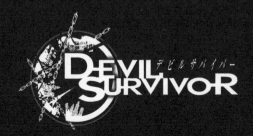

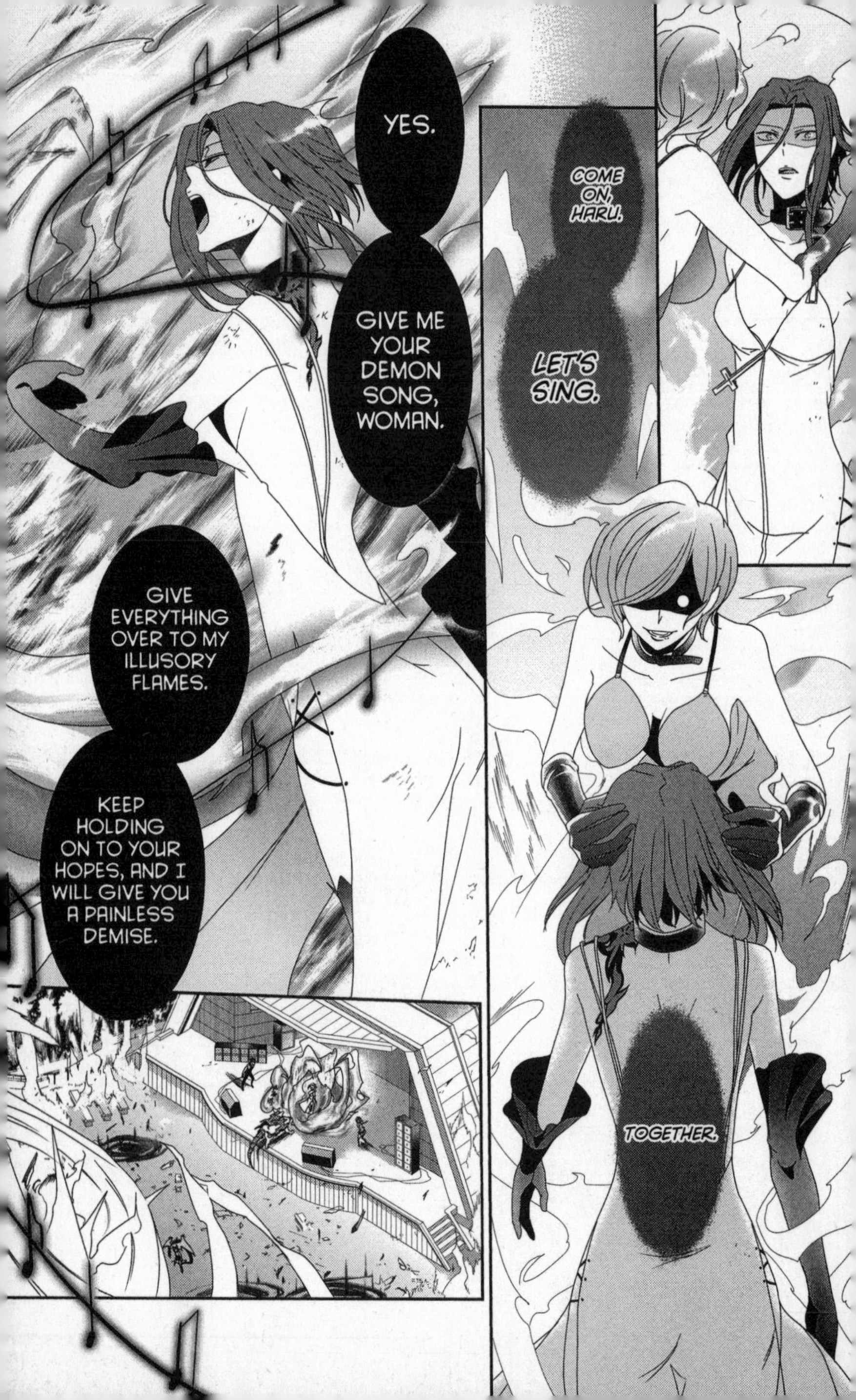
COME ON, HARU.
LET'S SING.
TOGETHER.
YES.
GIVE ME YOUR DEMON SONG, WOMAN.
GIVE EVERYTHING OVER TO MY ILLUSORY FLAMES.
KEEP HOLDING ON TO YOUR HOPES, AND I WILL GIVE YOU A PAINLESS DEMISE.

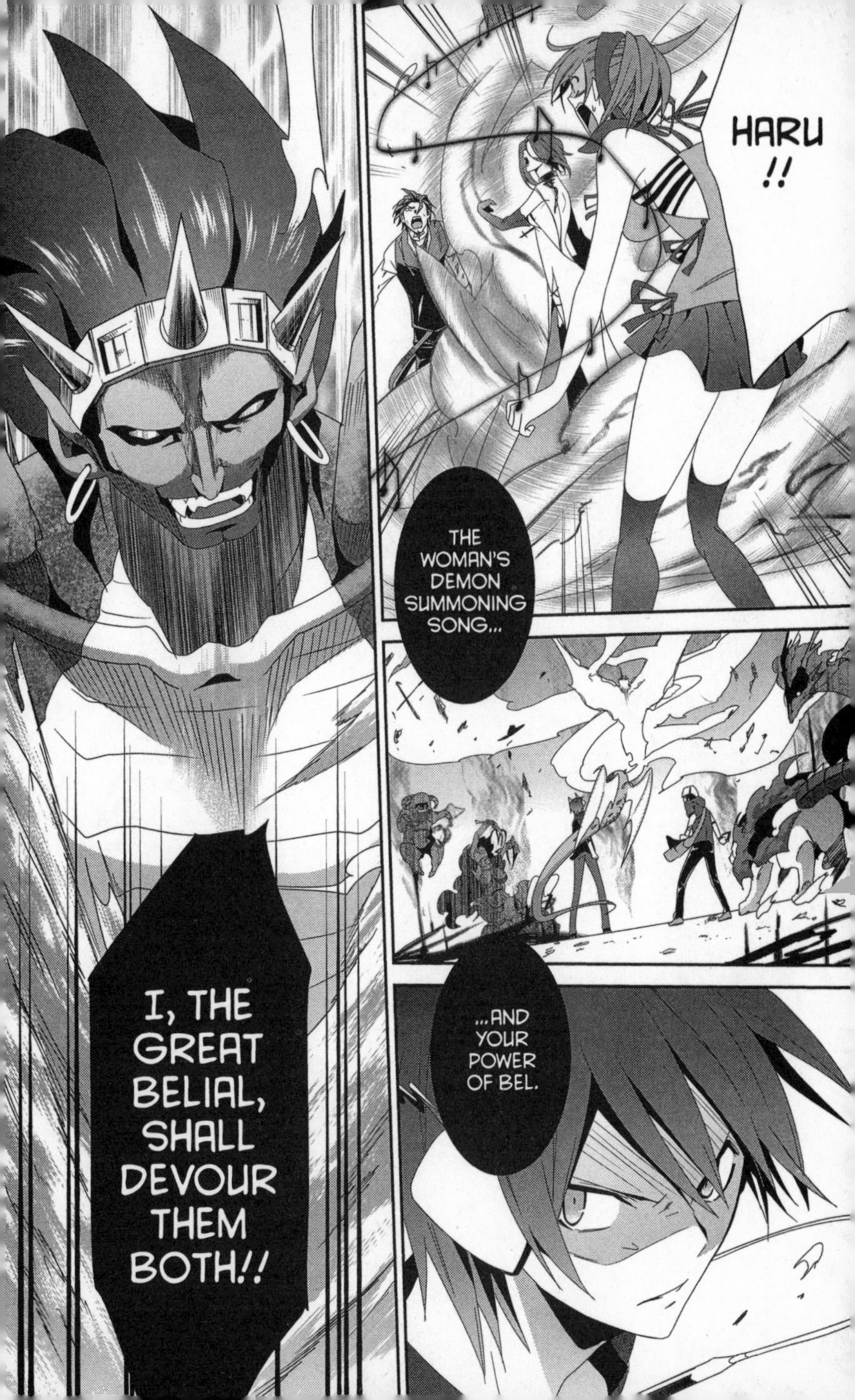
HARU!!
THE WOMAN'S DEMON SUMMONING SONG...
...AND YOUR POWER OF BEL.
I, THE GREAT BELIAL, SHALL DEVOUR THEM BOTH!!

SURVIVAL : 32
THE MELODY OF BANISHMENT

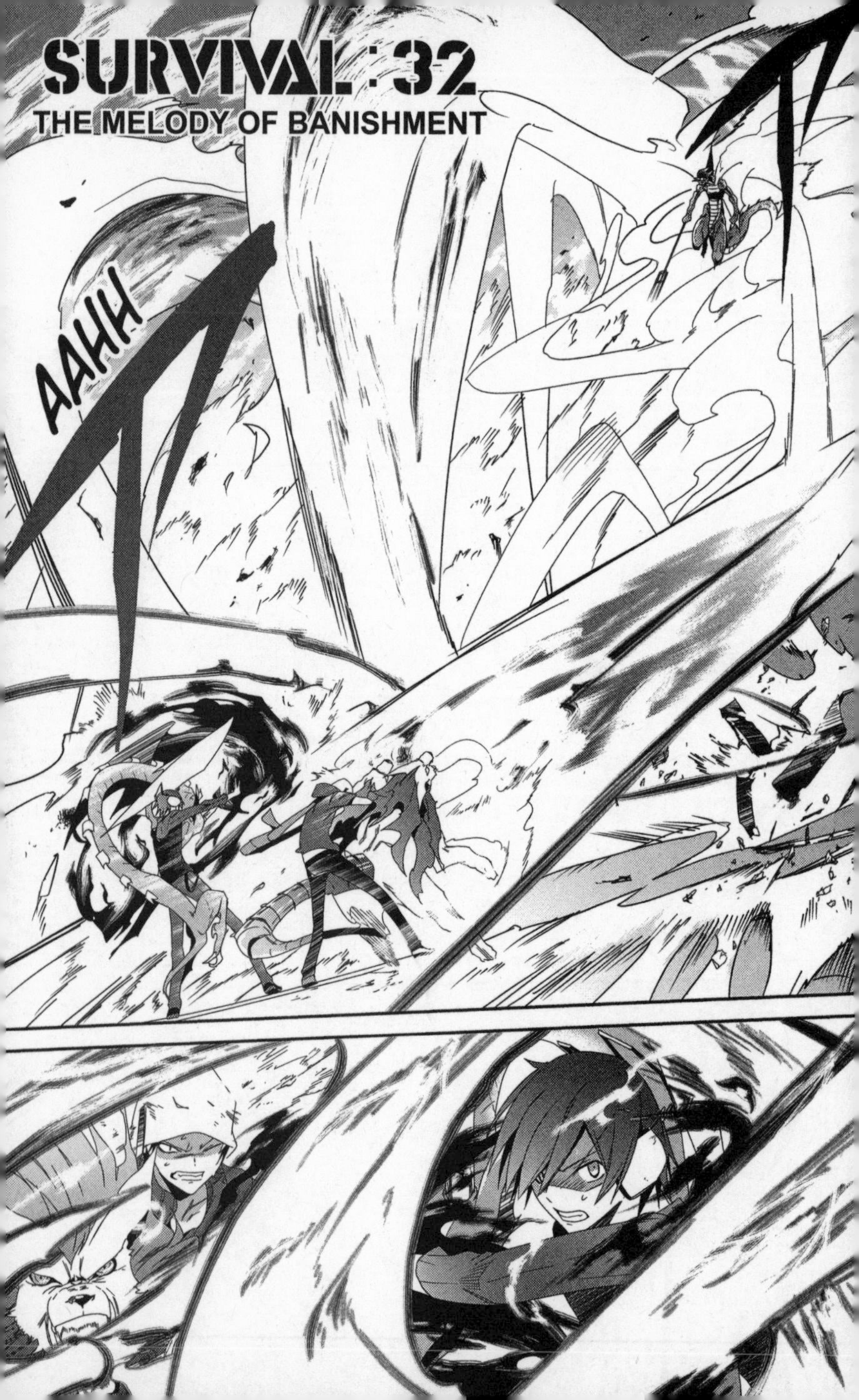
AAHH

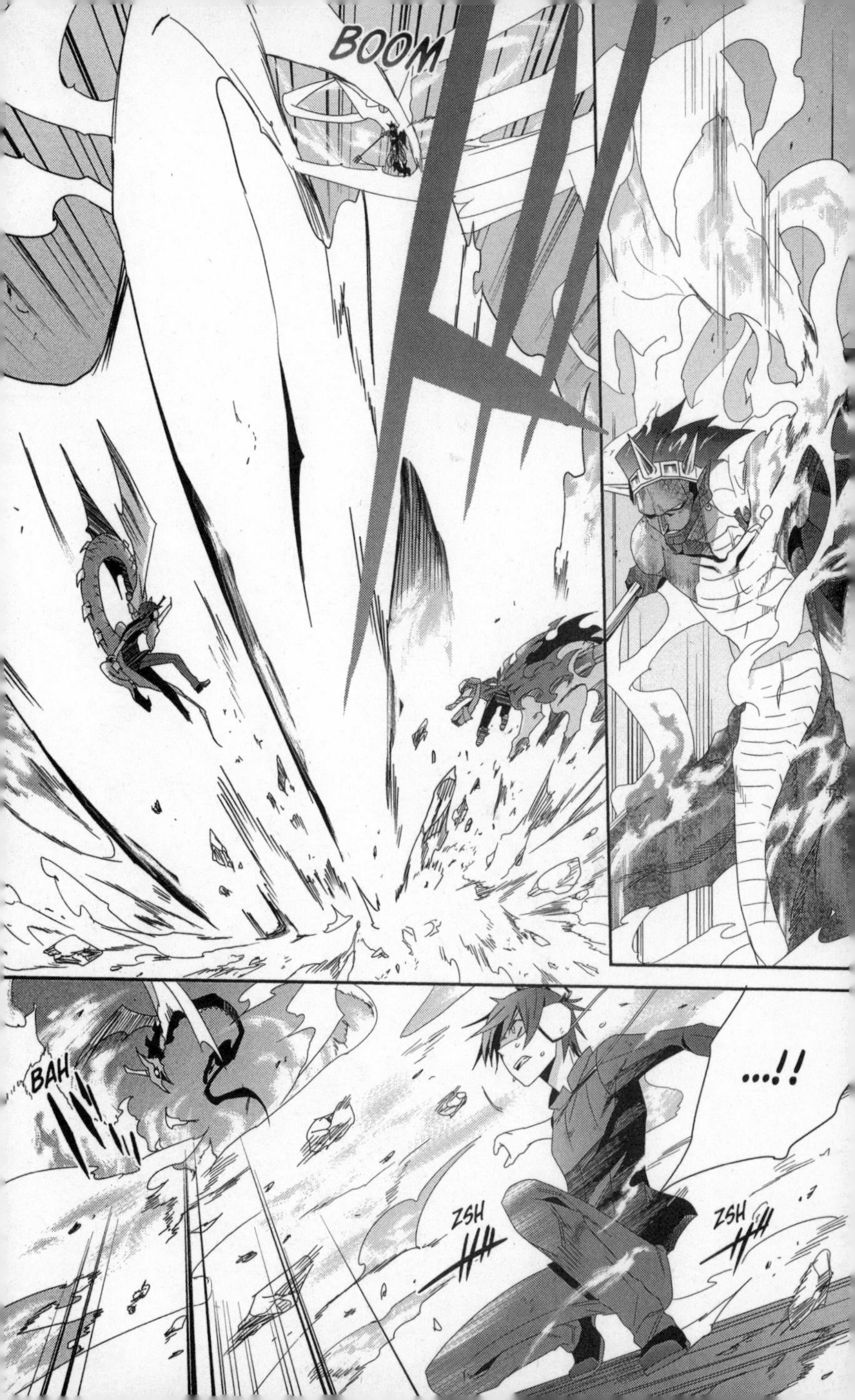
BOOM
...!!
ZSH
ZSH
BAH

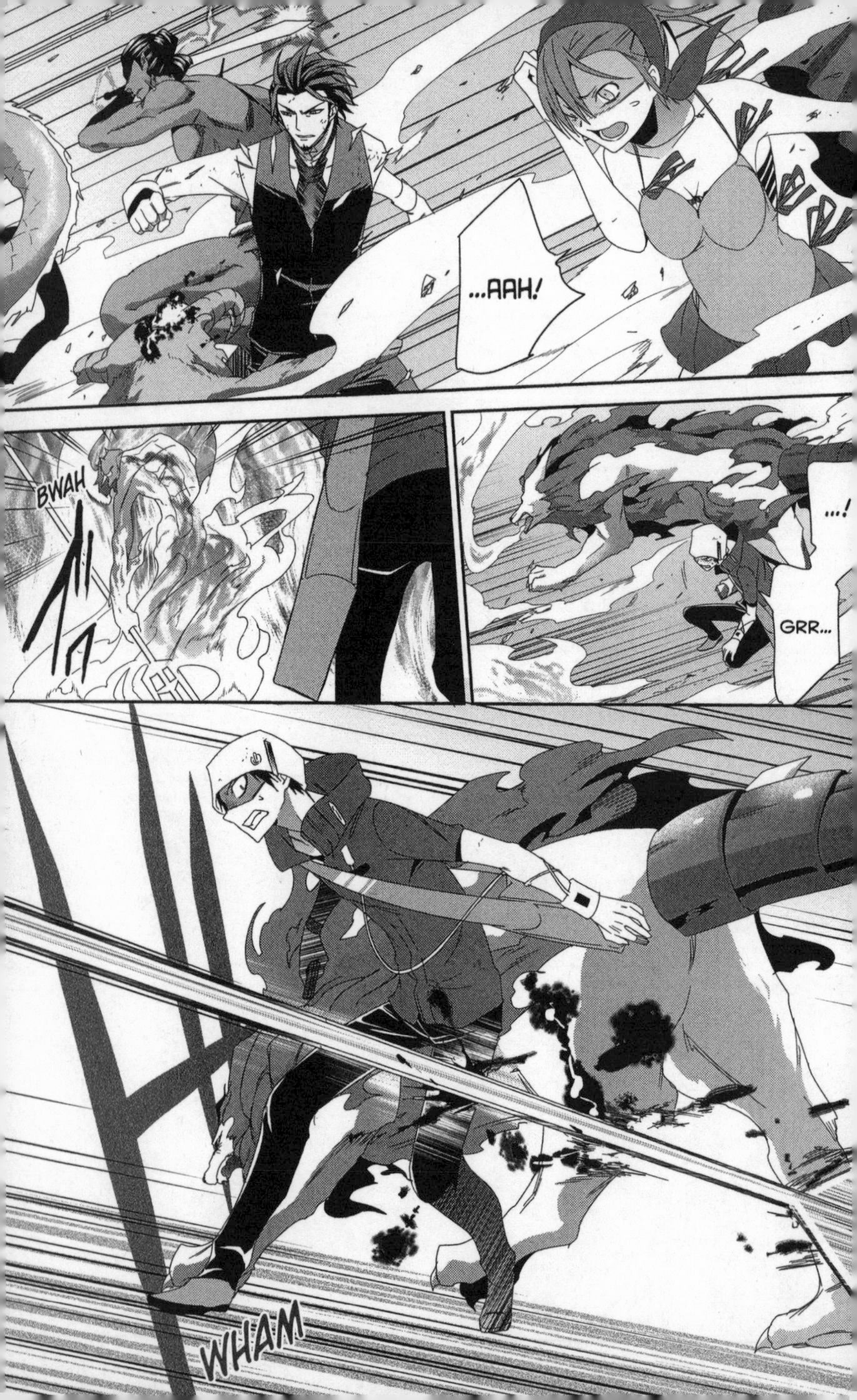
...AAH!
...!
GRR...
BWAH
WHAM

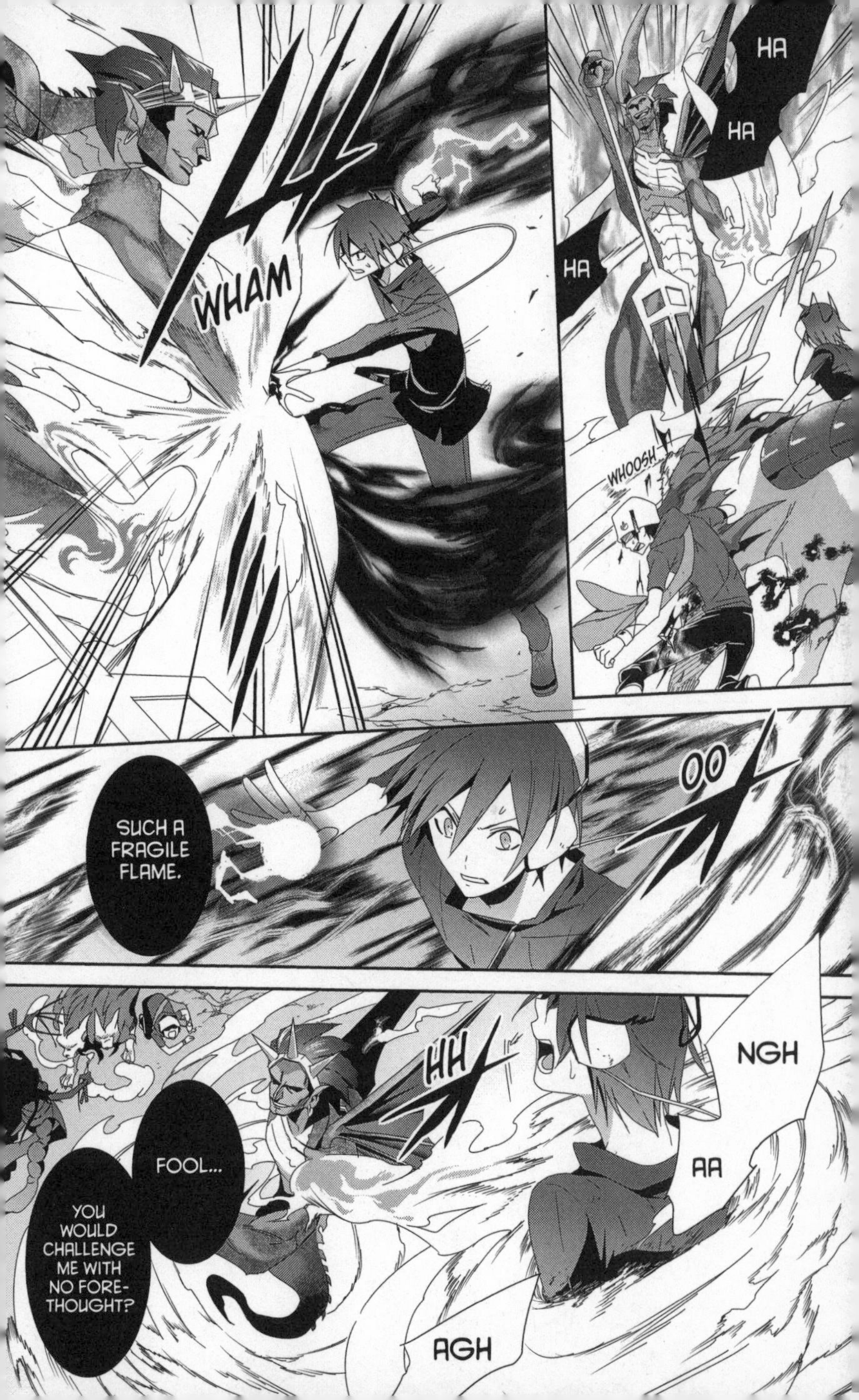
HA
HA
HA
WHOOSH
WHAM
OO
SUCH A FRAGILE FLAME.
NGH
HH
FOOL...
AA
YOU WOULD CHALLENGE ME WITH NO FORE-THOUGHT?
AGH

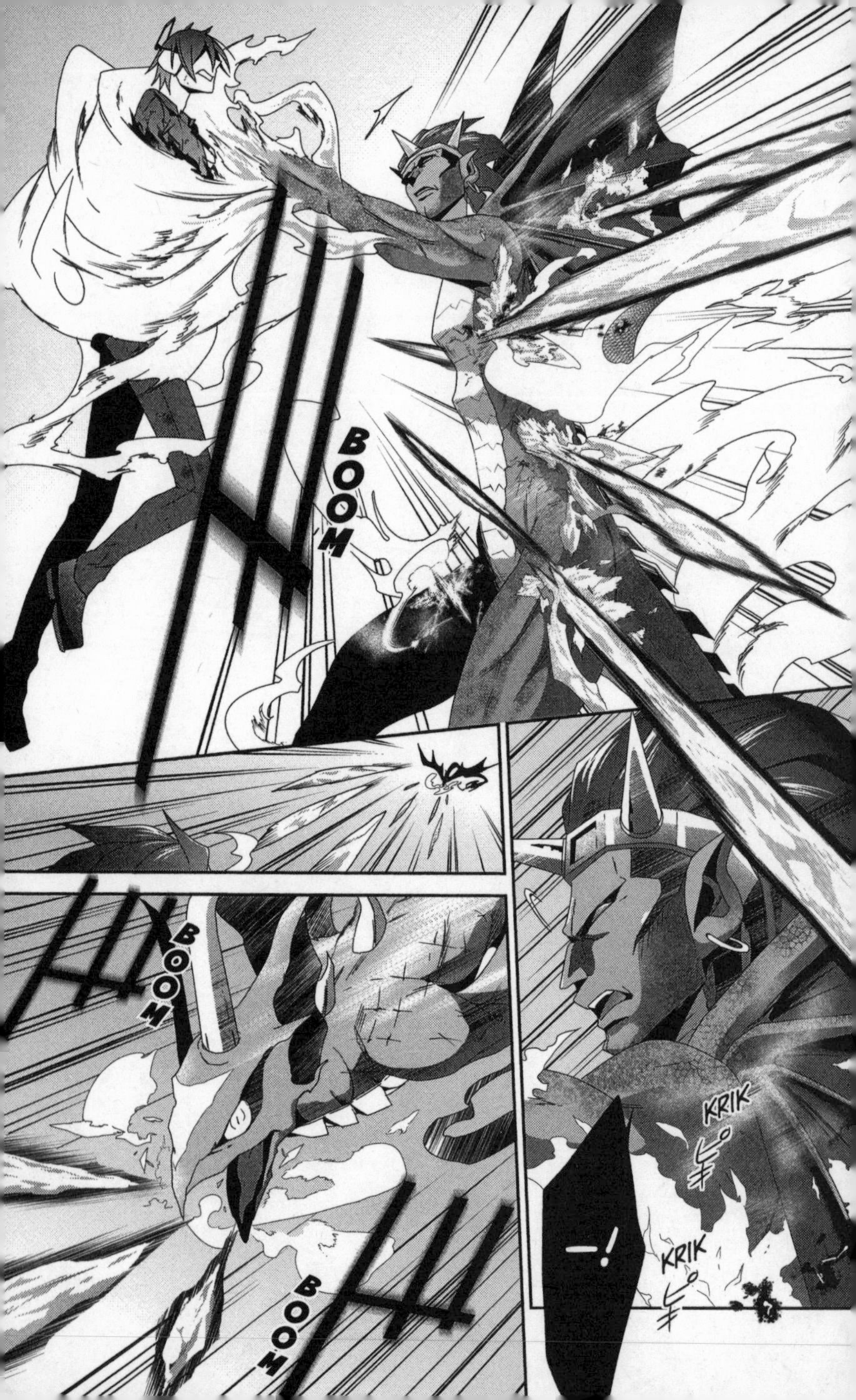
BOOM
BOOM
KRIK
ピキ
KRIK
ピキ
—!
BOOM
BOOM

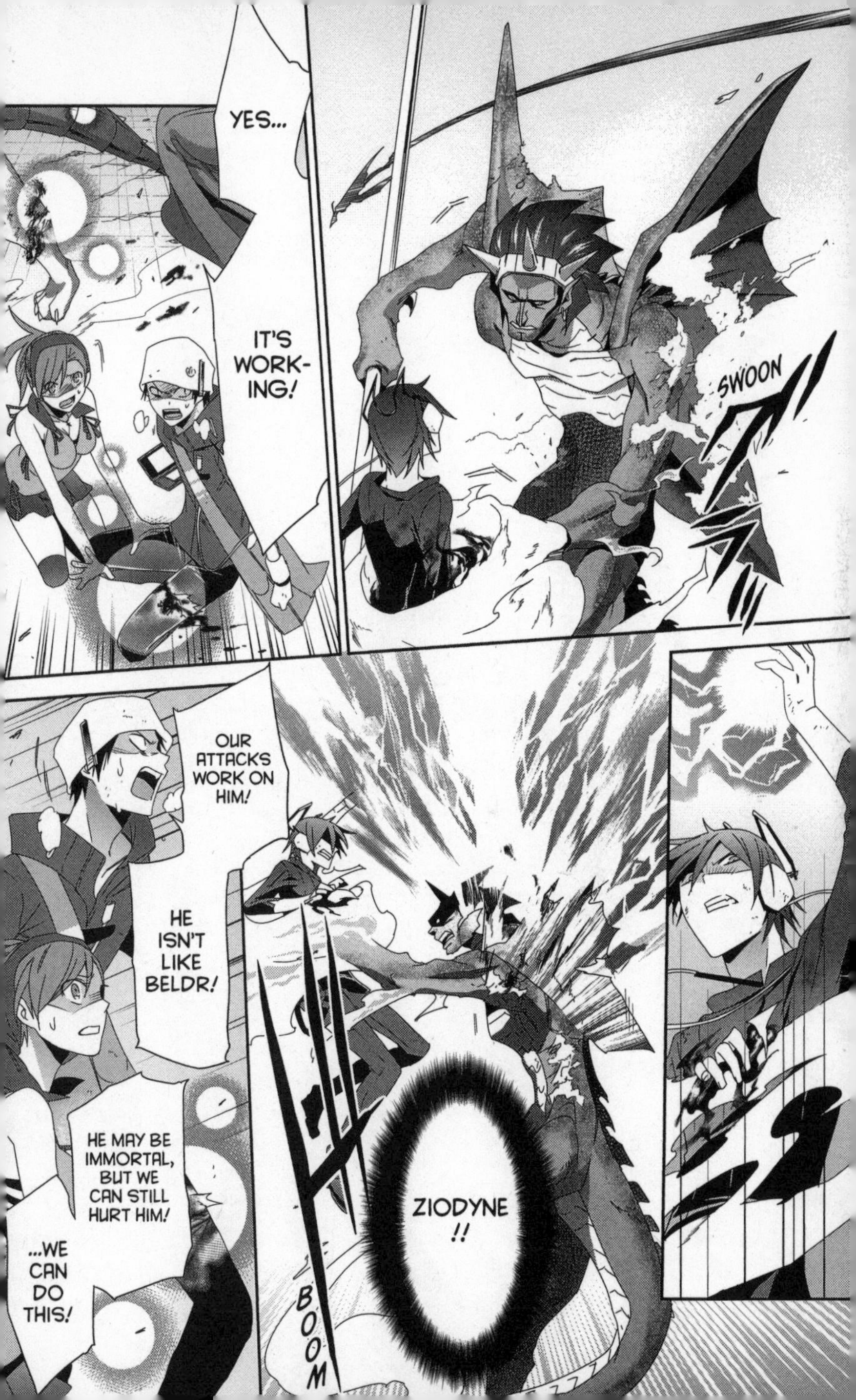
SWOON
YES...
IT'S WORKING!
ZIODYNE!!
BOOM
OUR ATTACKS WORK ON HIM!
HE ISN'T LIKE BELDR!
HE MAY BE IMMORTAL, BUT WE CAN STILL HURT HIM!
...WE CAN DO THIS!

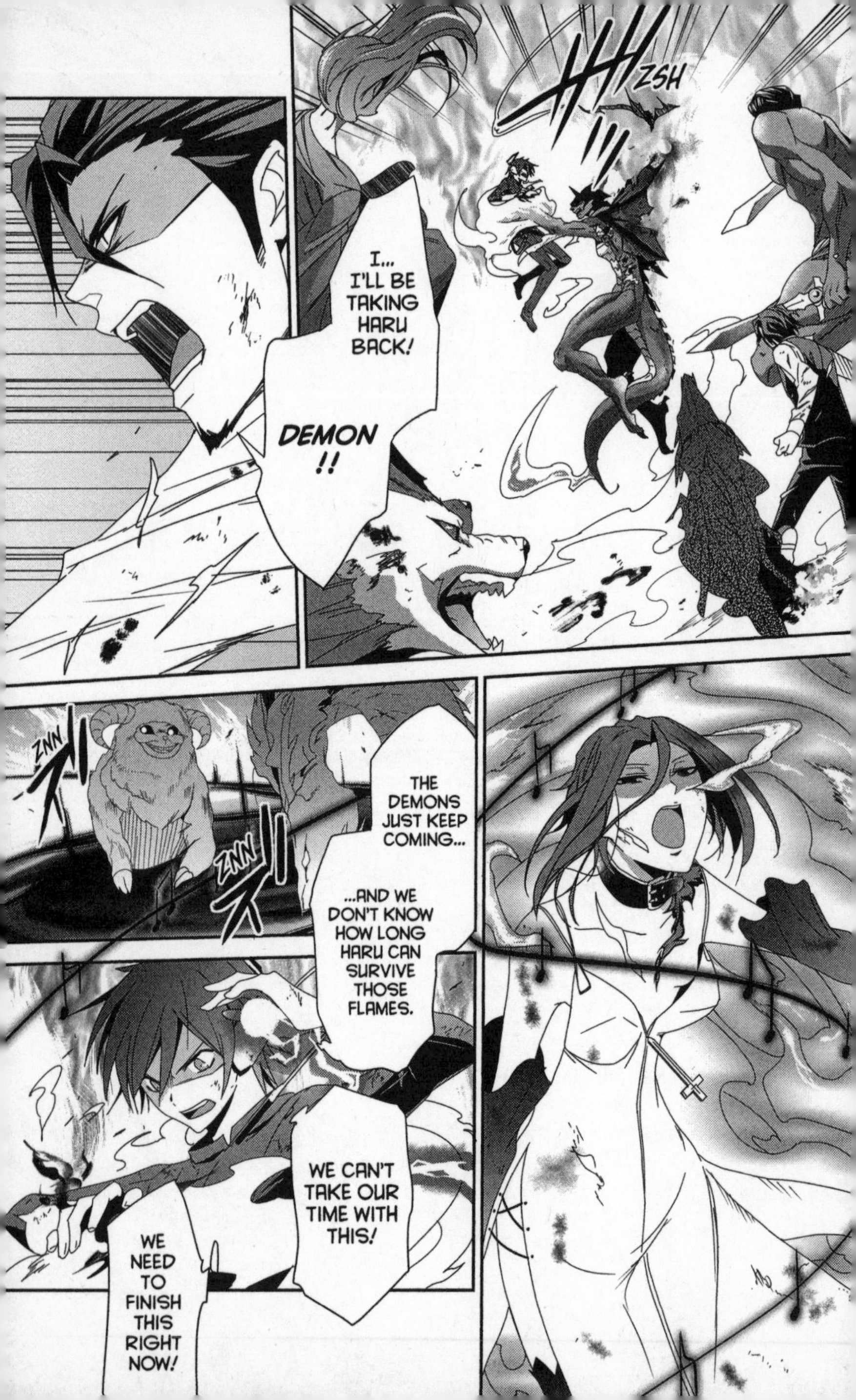
ZSH
I... I'LL BE TAKING HARU BACK!
DEMON!!
ZNN
ZNN
THE DEMONS JUST KEEP COMING...
...AND WE DON'T KNOW HOW LONG HARU CAN SURVIVE THOSE FLAMES.
WE CAN'T TAKE OUR TIME WITH THIS!
WE NEED TO FINISH THIS RIGHT NOW!

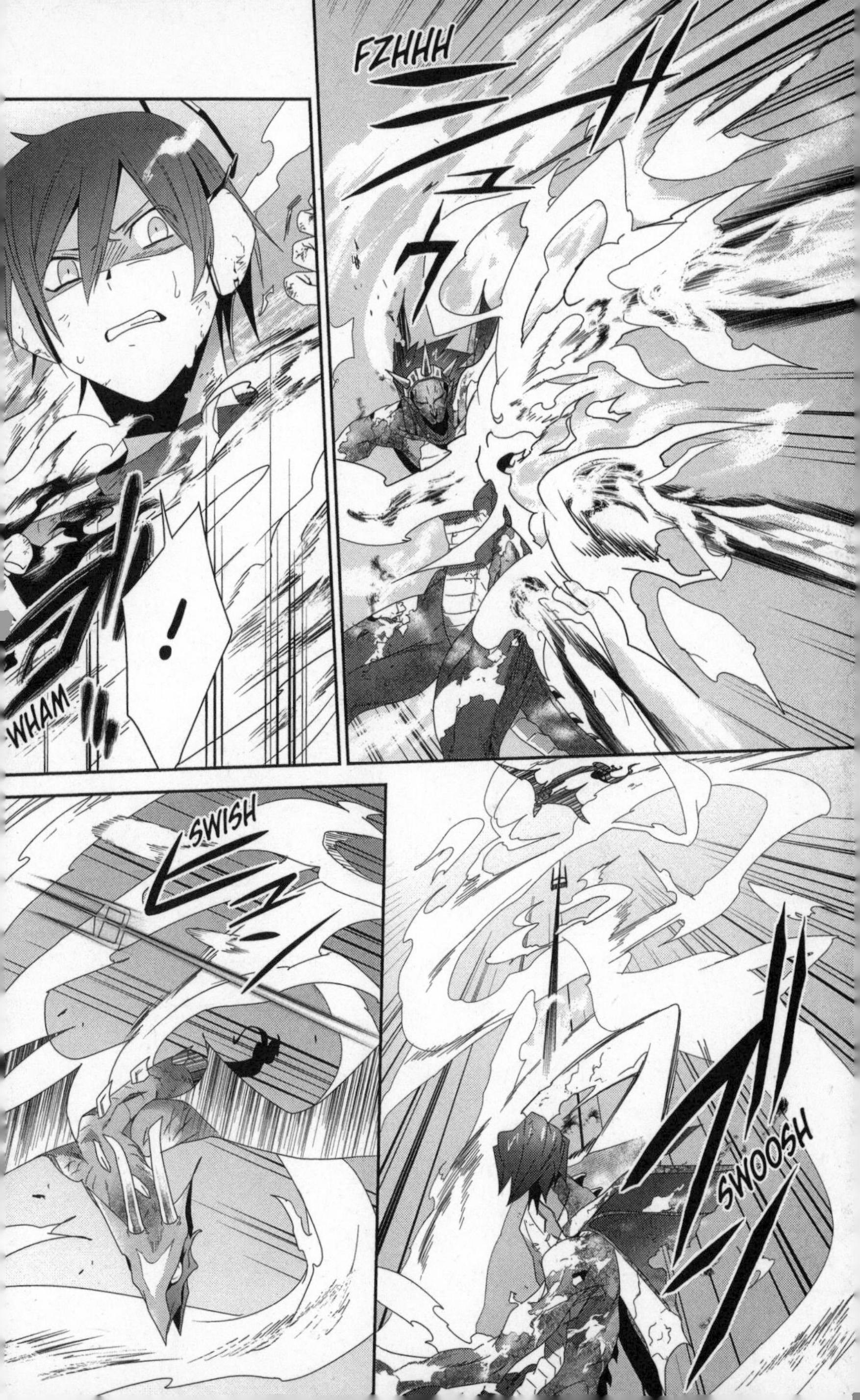
FZHHH
!
WHAM
SWOOSH
SWISH

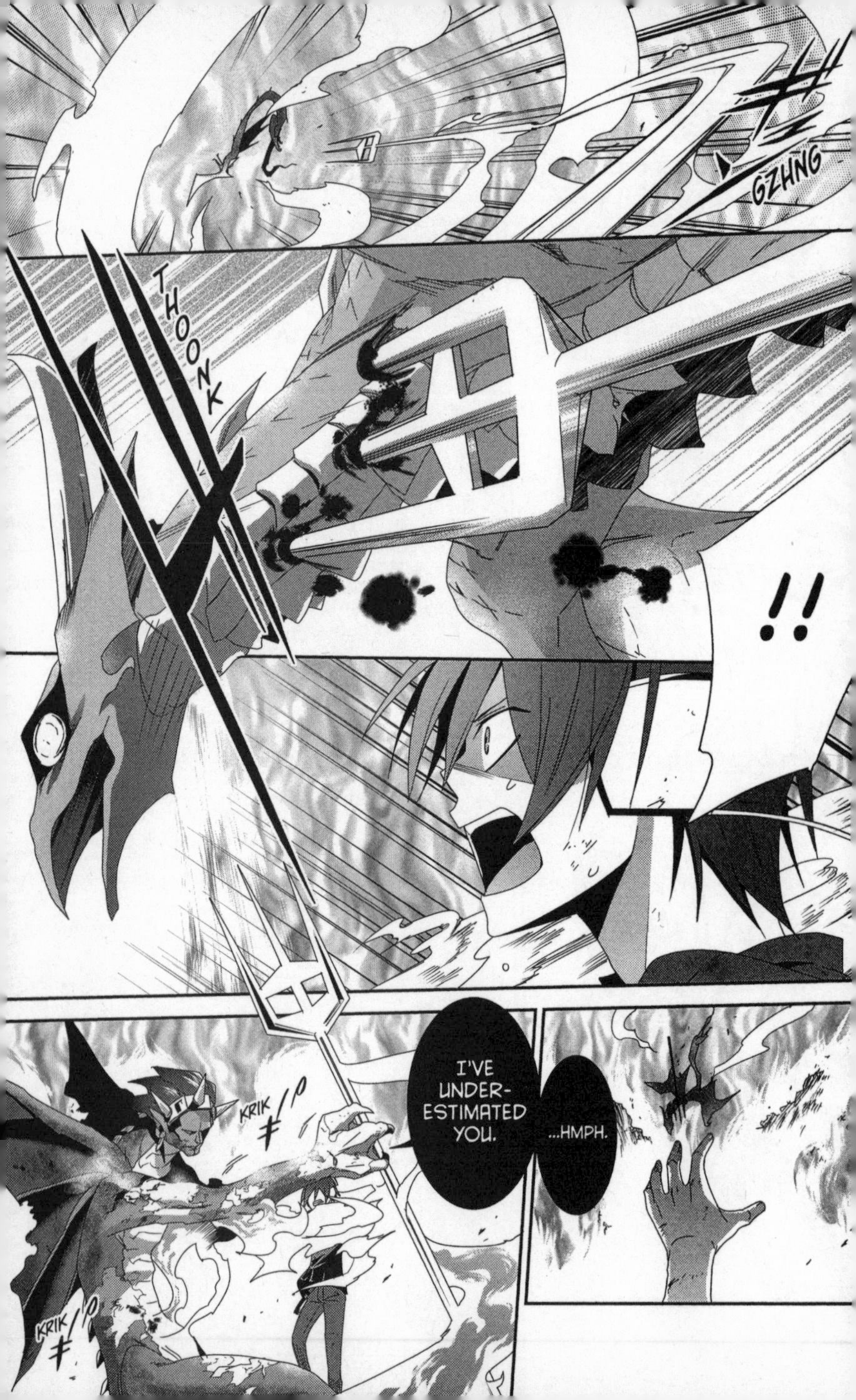
GZHNG
THOONK
!!
...HMPH.
I'VE UNDER-ESTIMATED YOU.
KRIK
KRIK

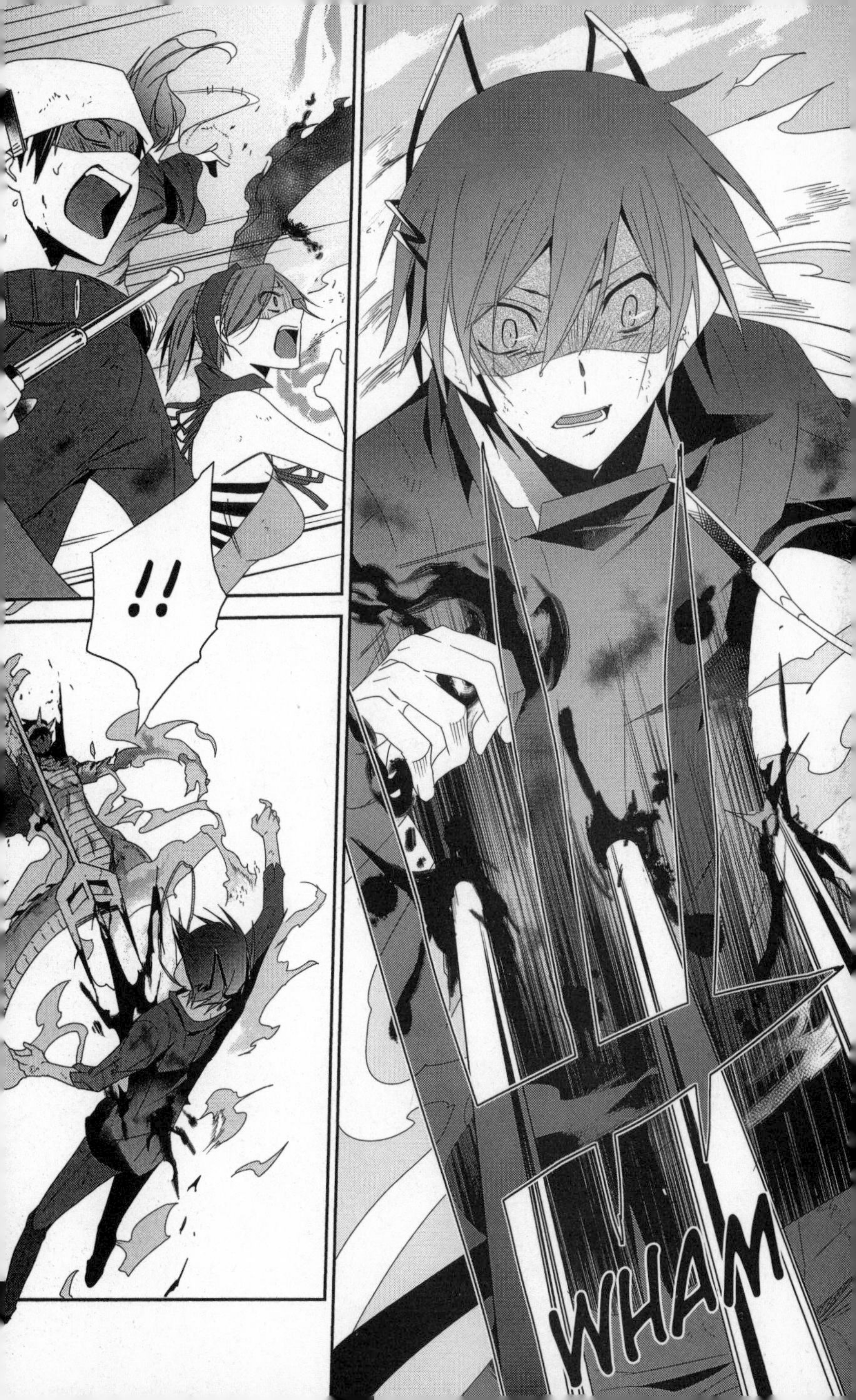
WHAM
!!

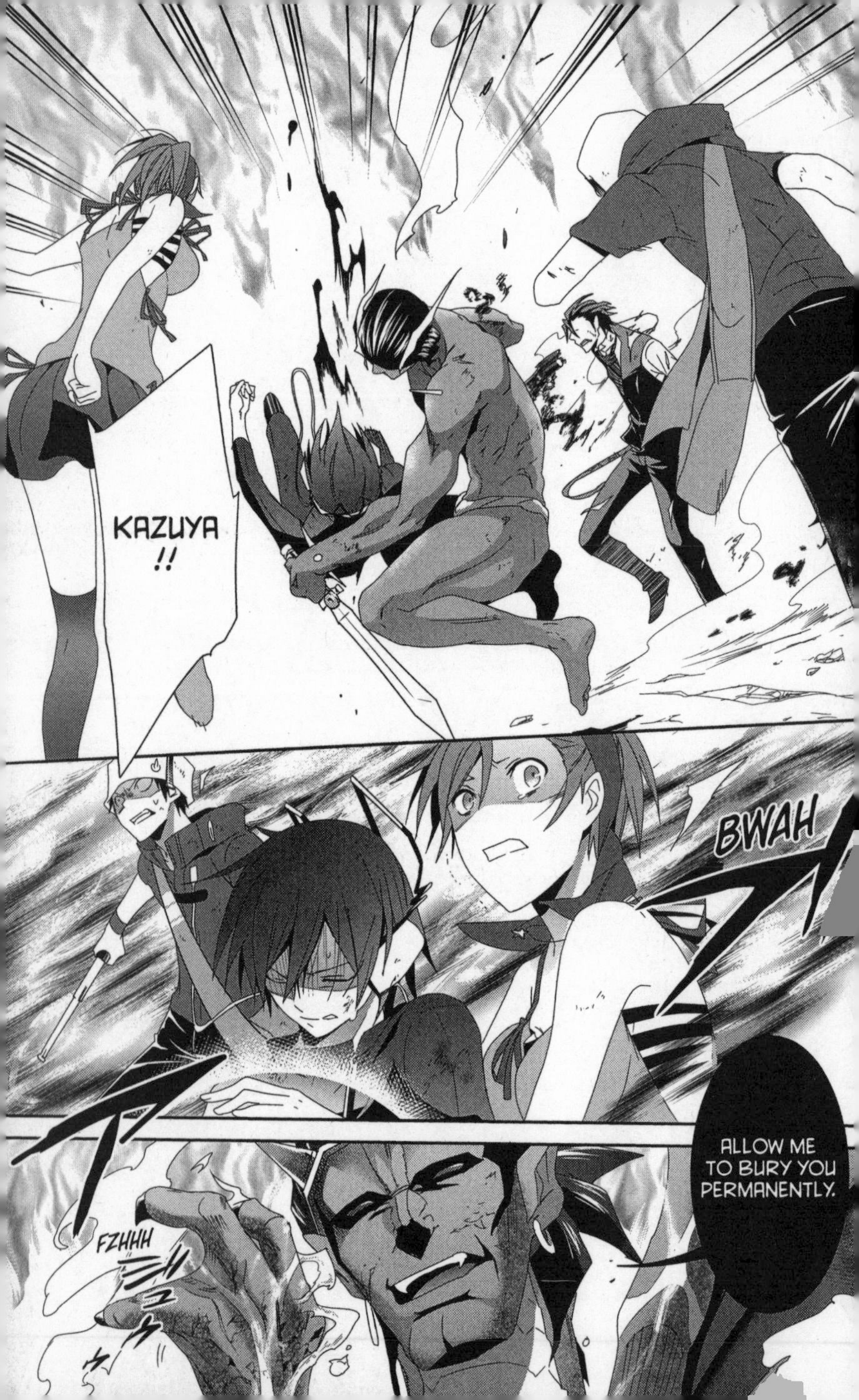
KAZUYA !!
BWAH
ALLOW ME TO BURY YOU PERMANENTLY.
FZHHH

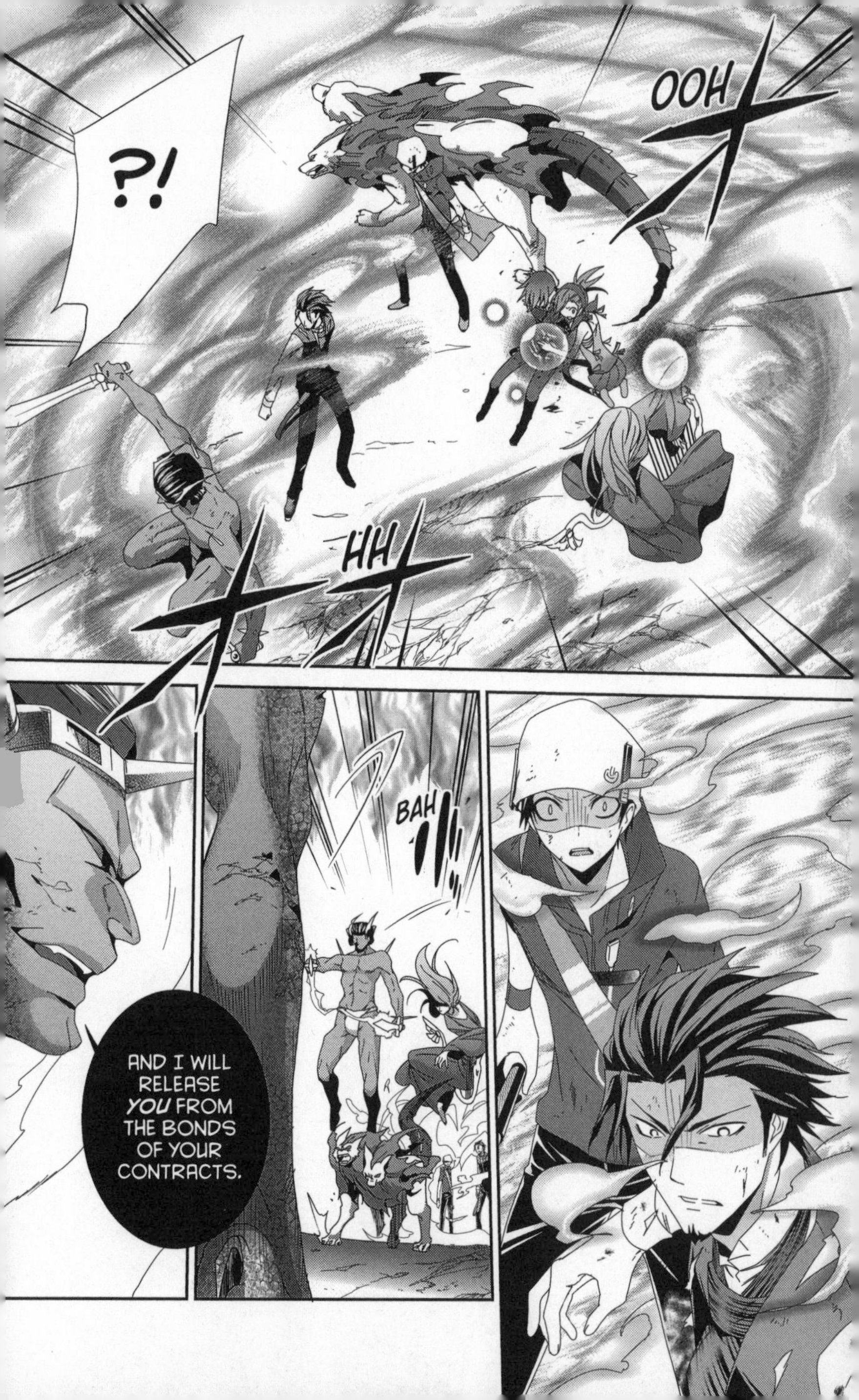
OOH
?!
HH
BAH
AND I WILL RELEASE *YOU* FROM THE BONDS OF YOUR CONTRACTS.

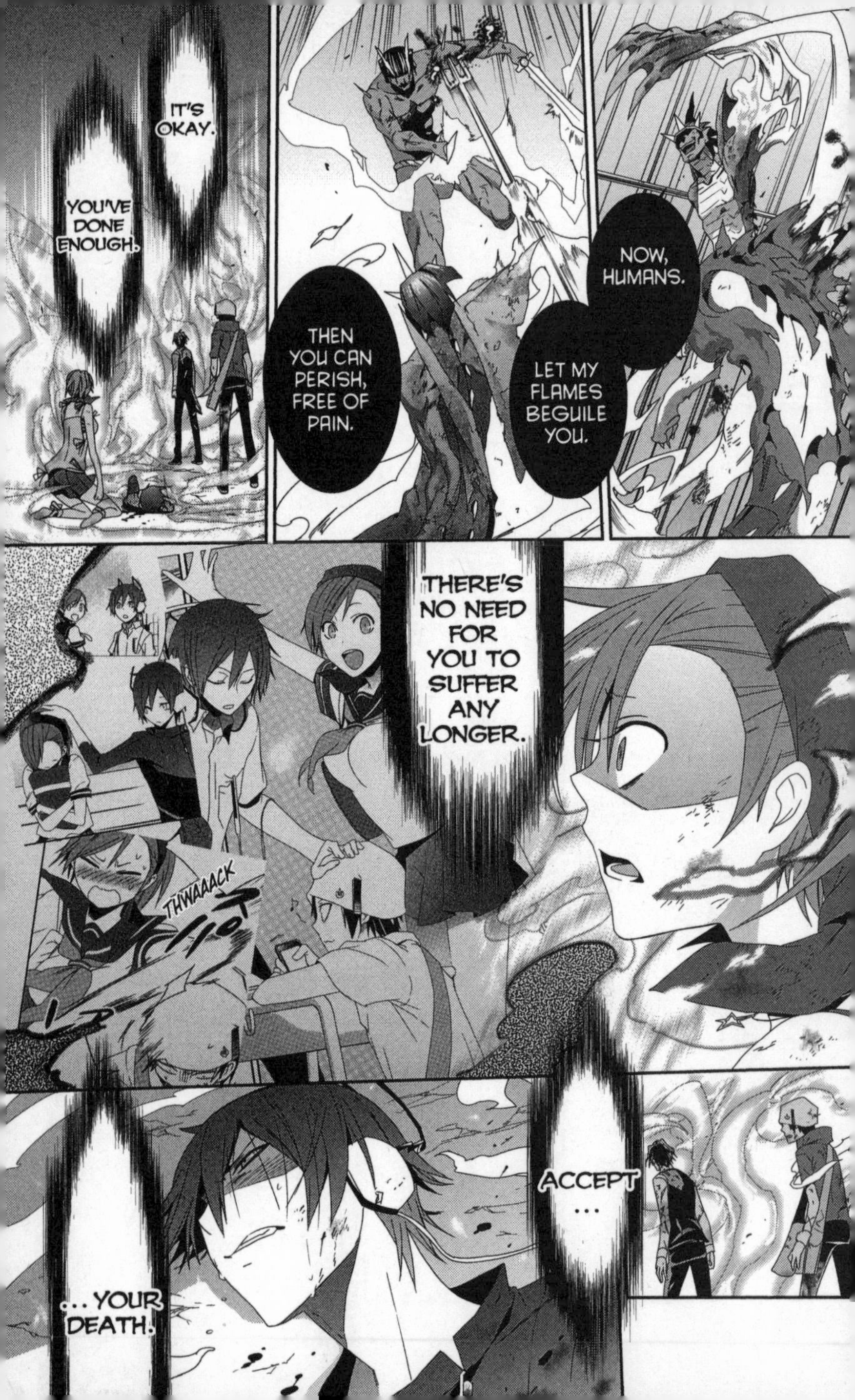
NOW, HUMANS.
LET MY FLAMES BEGUILE YOU.
THEN YOU CAN PERISH, FREE OF PAIN.
IT'S OKAY.
YOU'VE DONE ENOUGH.
THERE'S NO NEED FOR YOU TO SUFFER ANY LONGER.
THWAAACK
ACCEPT ...
... YOUR DEATH.

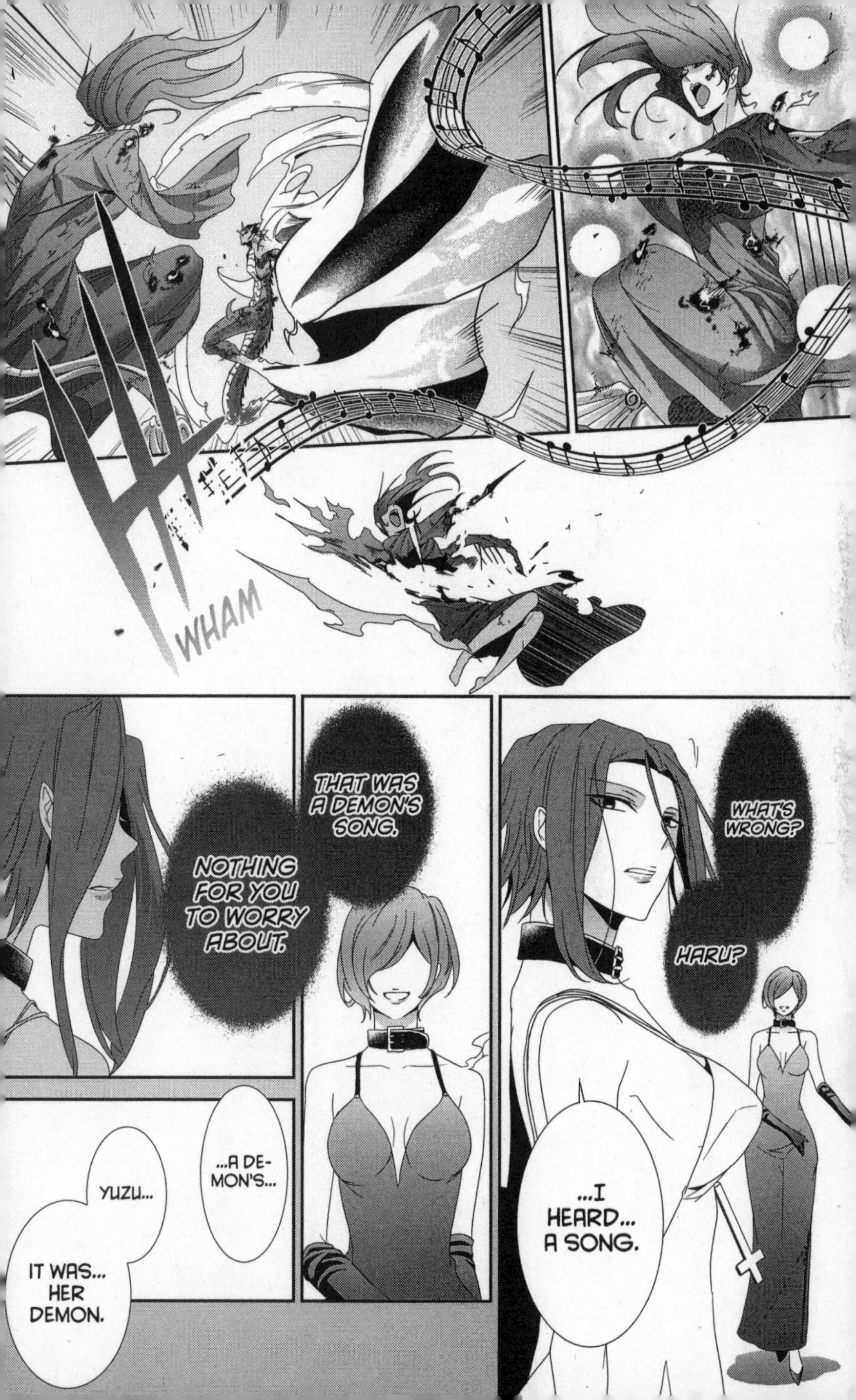
WHAM
WHAT'S WRONG?
HARU?
...I HEARD... A SONG.
THAT WAS A DEMON'S SONG.
NOTHING FOR YOU TO WORRY ABOUT.
...A DE-MON'S...
YUZU...
IT WAS... HER DEMON.

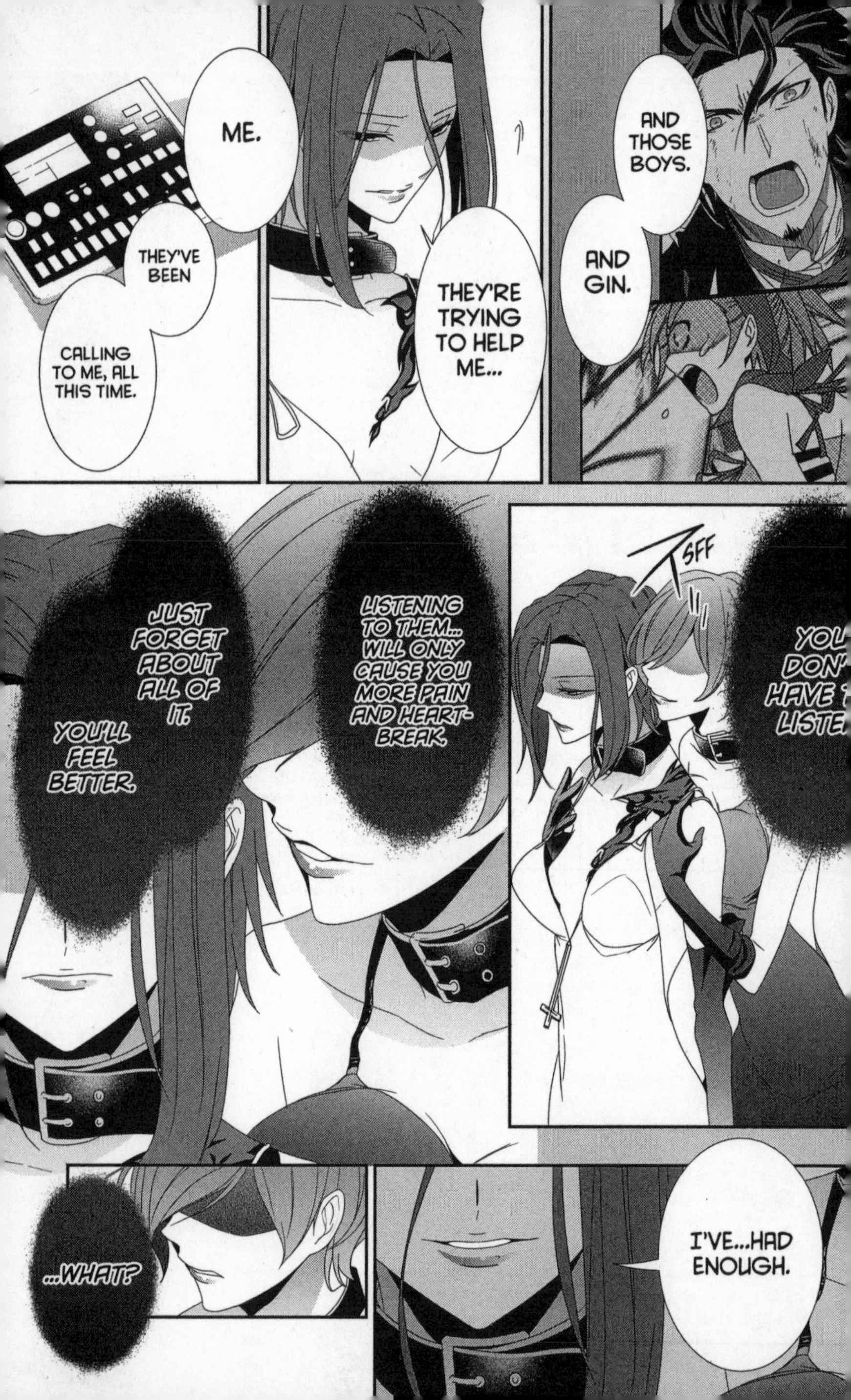
AND THOSE BOYS.
AND GIN.
ME.
THEY'RE TRYING TO HELP ME...
THEY'VE BEEN
CALLING TO ME, ALL THIS TIME.
SFF
YOU DON' HAVE T LISTE
LISTENING TO THEM... WILL ONLY CAUSE YOU MORE PAIN AND HEART-BREAK.
JUST FORGET ABOUT ALL OF IT.
YOU'LL FEEL BETTER.
I'VE...HAD ENOUGH.
...WHAT?

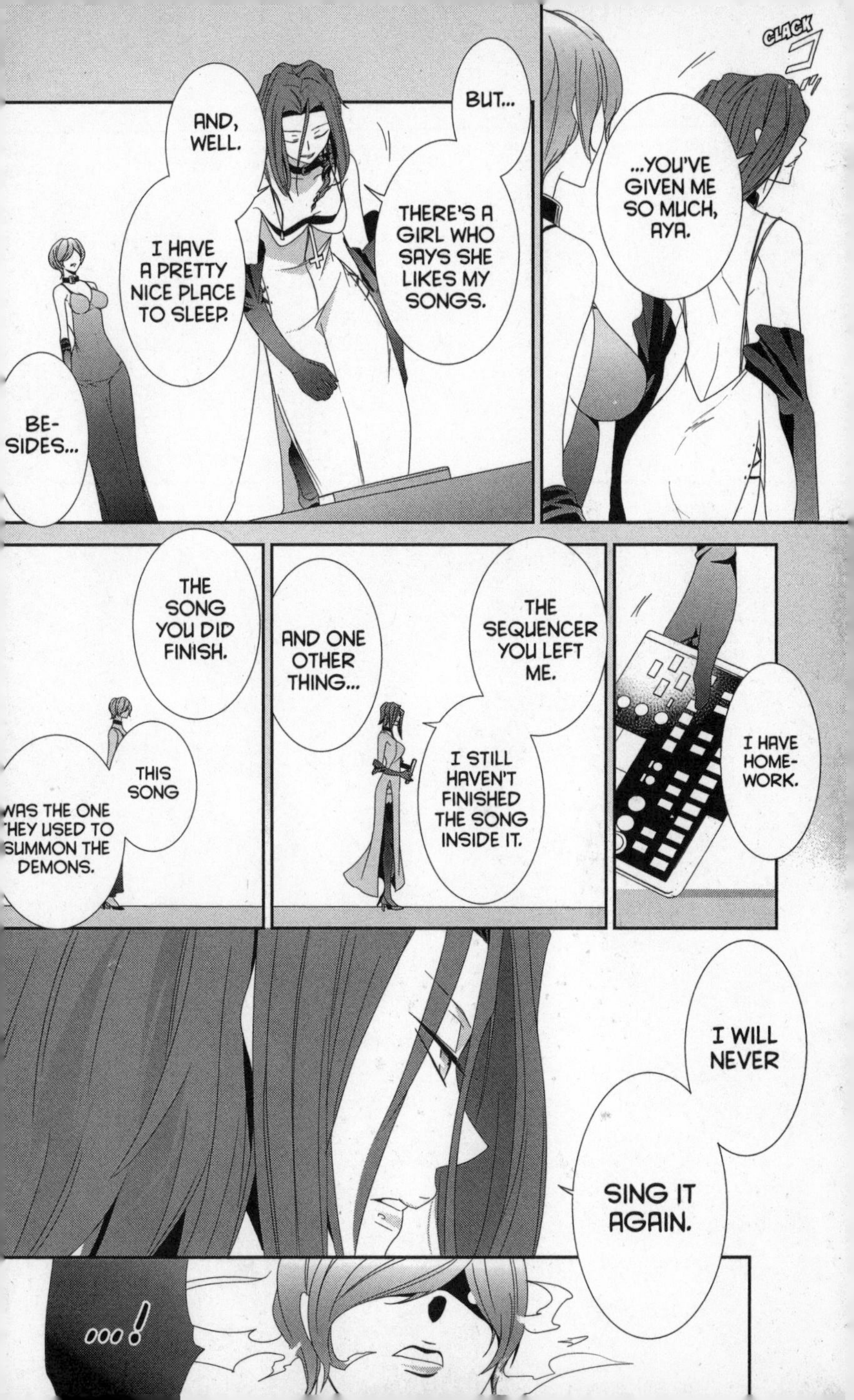
CLACK
...YOU'VE GIVEN ME SO MUCH, AYA.
BUT...
THERE'S A GIRL WHO SAYS SHE LIKES MY SONGS.
AND, WELL.
I HAVE A PRETTY NICE PLACE TO SLEEP.
BE-SIDES...
I HAVE HOMEWORK.
THE SEQUENCER YOU LEFT ME.
I STILL HAVEN'T FINISHED THE SONG INSIDE IT.
AND ONE OTHER THING...
THE SONG YOU DID FINISH.
THIS SONG
WAS THE ONE THEY USED TO SUMMON THE DEMONS.
I WILL NEVER
SING IT AGAIN.
ooo!

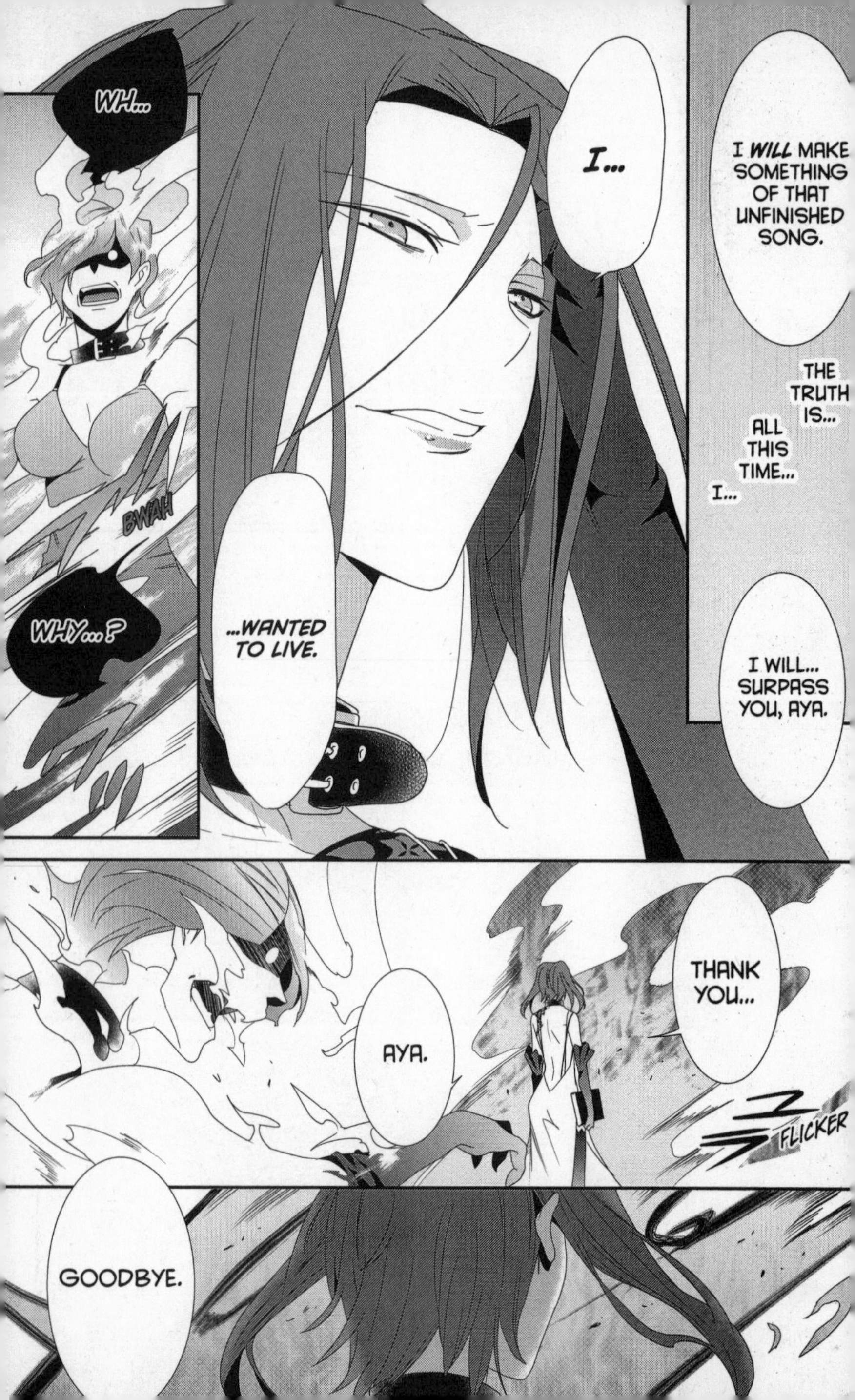

I WILL MAKE SOMETHING OF THAT UNFINISHED SONG.
THE TRUTH IS...
ALL THIS TIME...
I...
I WILL... SURPASS YOU, AYA.
I...
...WANTED TO LIVE.
WH...
BWAH
WHY...?
THANK YOU...
AYA.
FLICKER
GOODBYE.

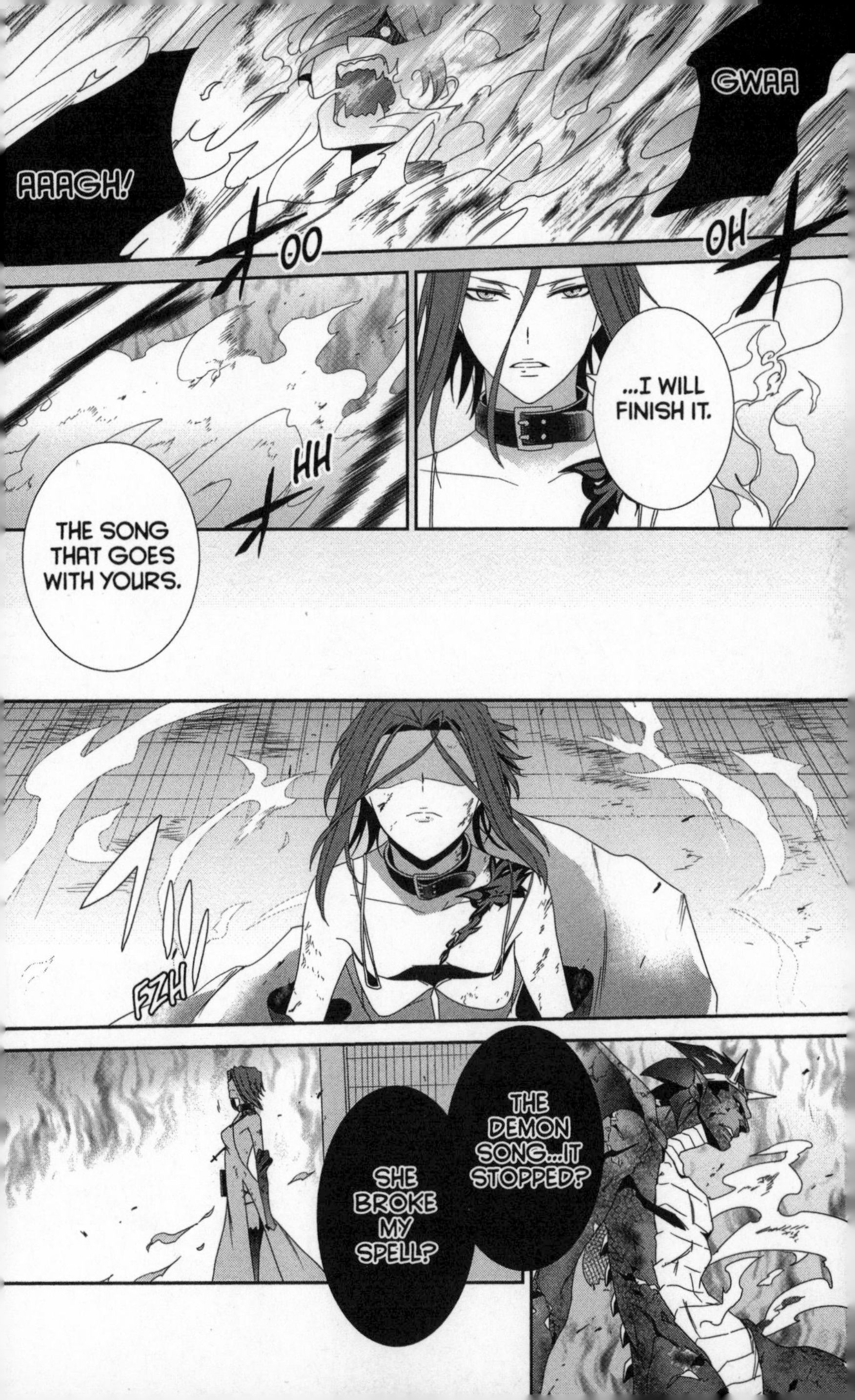
GWAA
AAAGH!
OO
OH
...I WILL FINISH IT.
HH
THE SONG THAT GOES WITH YOURS.
FZH
THE DEMON SONG...IT STOPPED?
SHE BROKE MY SPELL?

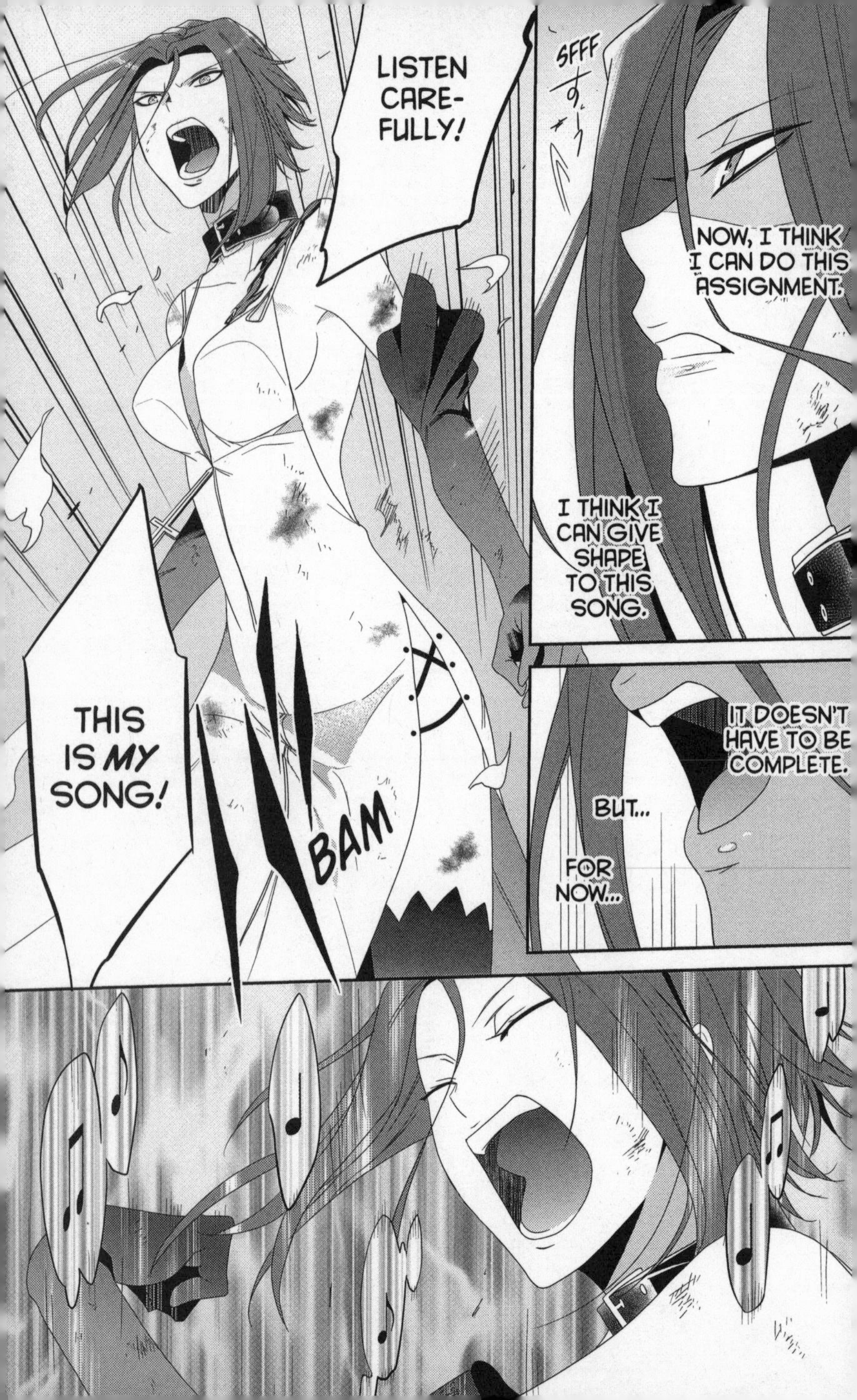

SFFF
NOW, I THINK I CAN DO THIS ASSIGNMENT.
I THINK I CAN GIVE SHAPE TO THIS SONG.
IT DOESN'T HAVE TO BE COMPLETE.
BUT...
FOR NOW...
LISTEN CARE-FULLY!
THIS IS *MY* SONG!
BAM

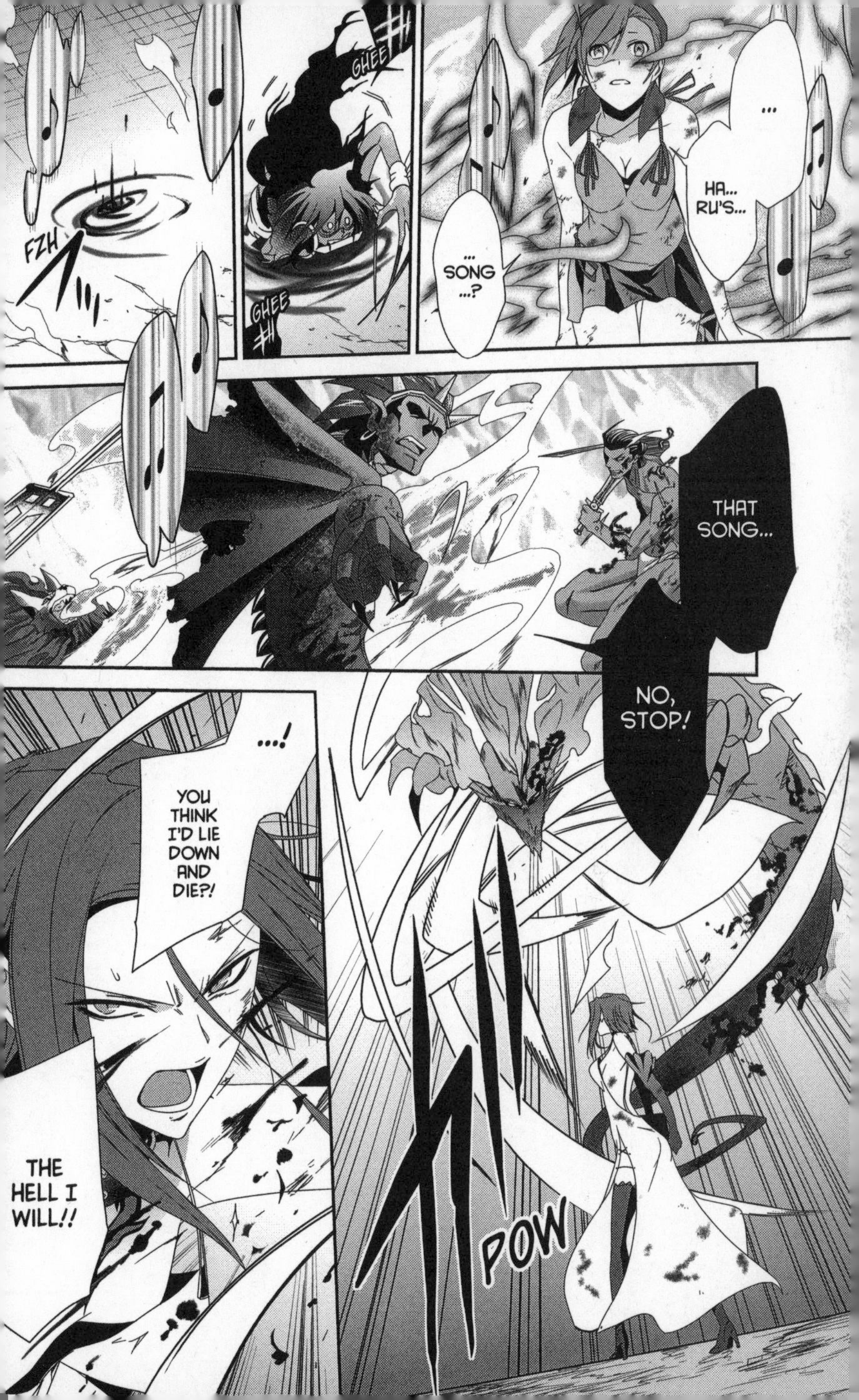
...
HA... RU'S...
... SONG ...?
GHEE
GHEE
FZH
THAT SONG...
NO, STOP!
POW
...!
YOU THINK I'D LIE DOWN AND DIE?!
THE HELL I WILL!!

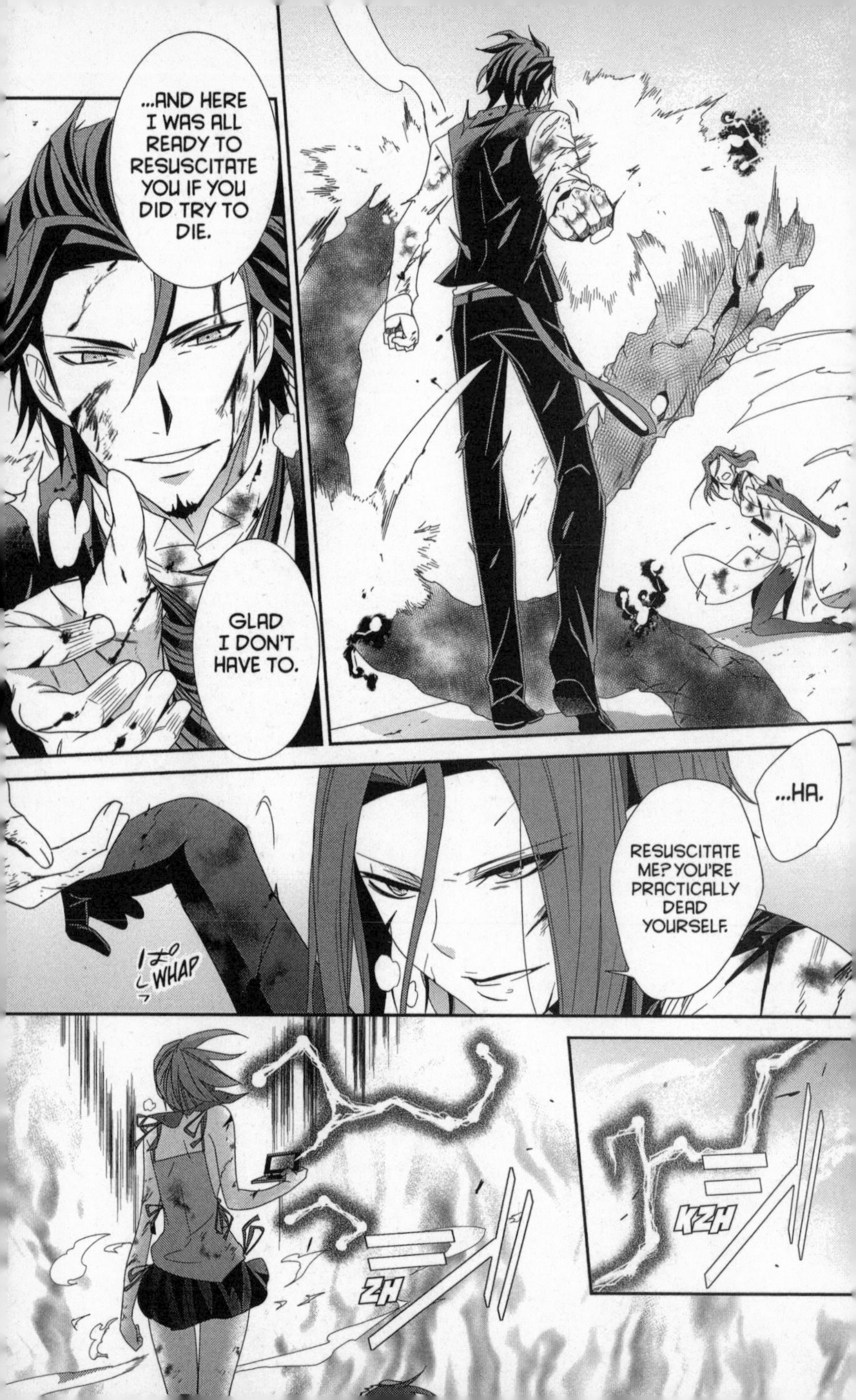
...AND HERE I WAS ALL READY TO RESUSCITATE YOU IF YOU DID TRY TO DIE.
GLAD I DON'T HAVE TO.
...HA.
RESUSCITATE ME? YOU'RE PRACTICALLY DEAD YOURSELF.
WHAP
KZH
ZH

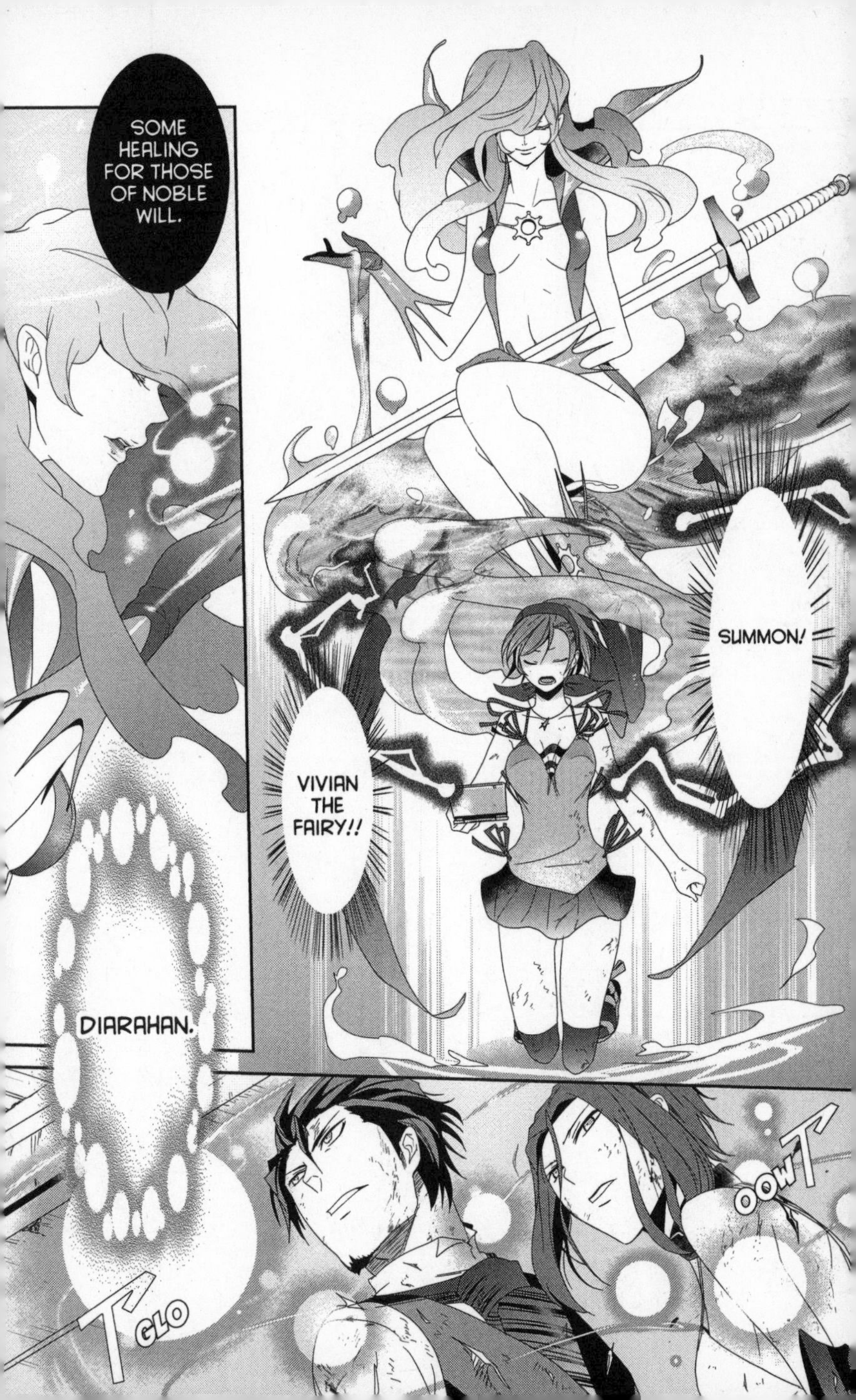
SUMMON!
VIVIAN THE FAIRY!!
SOME HEALING FOR THOSE OF NOBLE WILL.
DIARAHAN.
OOW
GLO

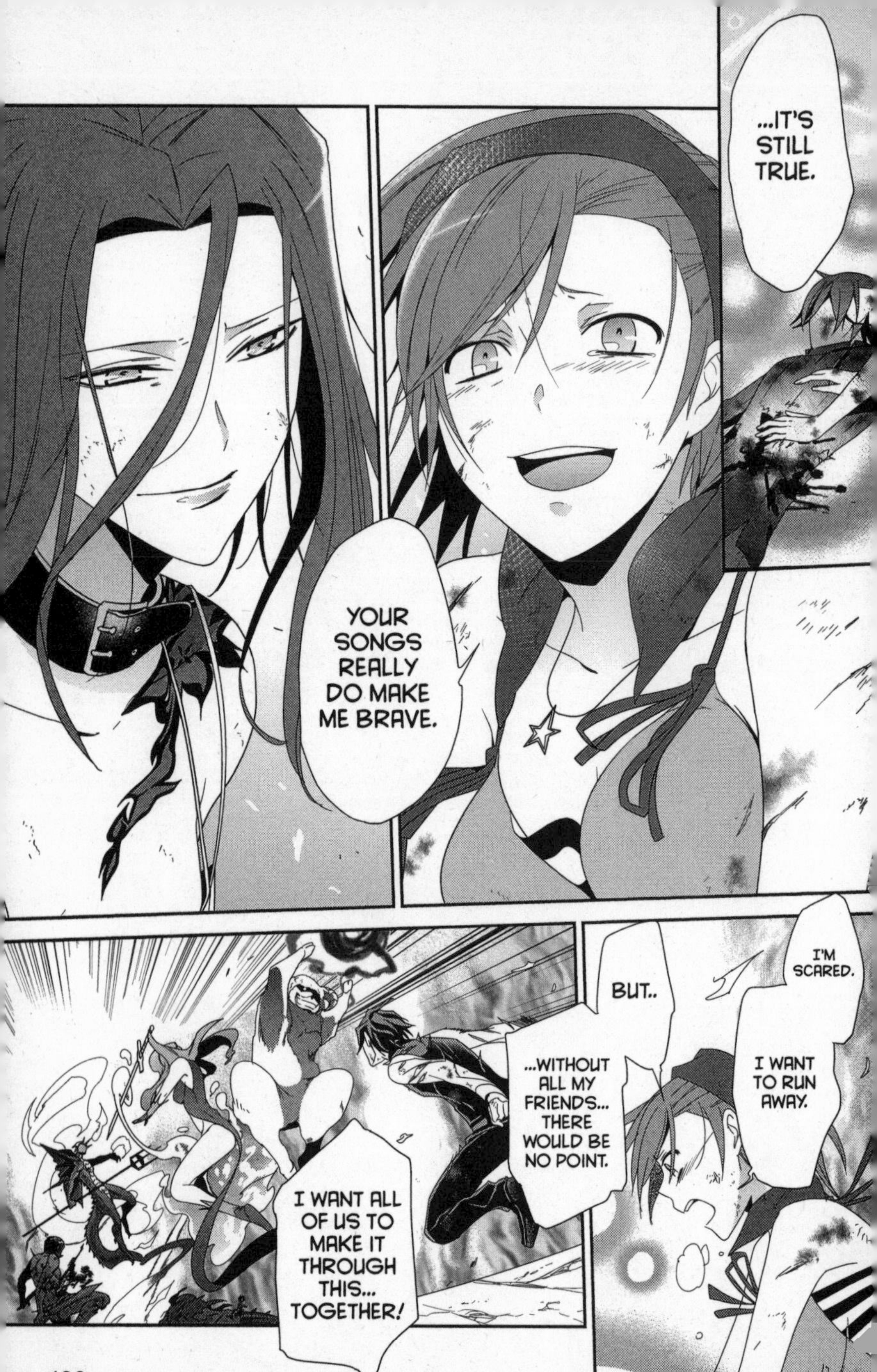
...IT'S STILL TRUE.
YOUR SONGS REALLY DO MAKE ME BRAVE.
I'M SCARED.
I WANT TO RUN AWAY.
BUT..
...WITHOUT ALL MY FRIENDS... THERE WOULD BE NO POINT.
I WANT ALL OF US TO MAKE IT THROUGH THIS... TOGETHER!

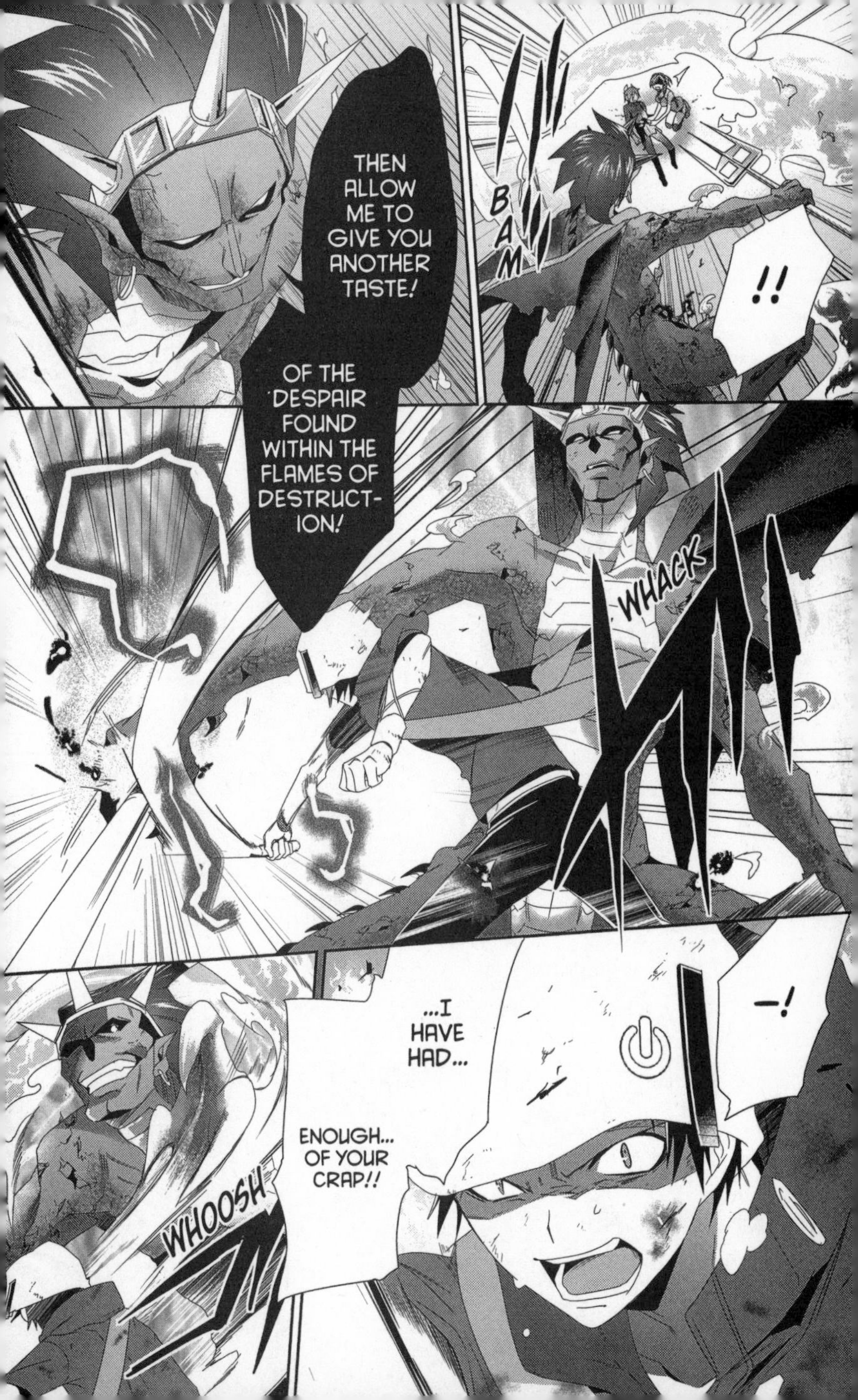
BAM
!!
THEN ALLOW ME TO GIVE YOU ANOTHER TASTE!
OF THE DESPAIR FOUND WITHIN THE FLAMES OF DESTRUCTION!
WHACK
—!
...I HAVE HAD...
ENOUGH... OF YOUR CRAP!!
WHOOSH

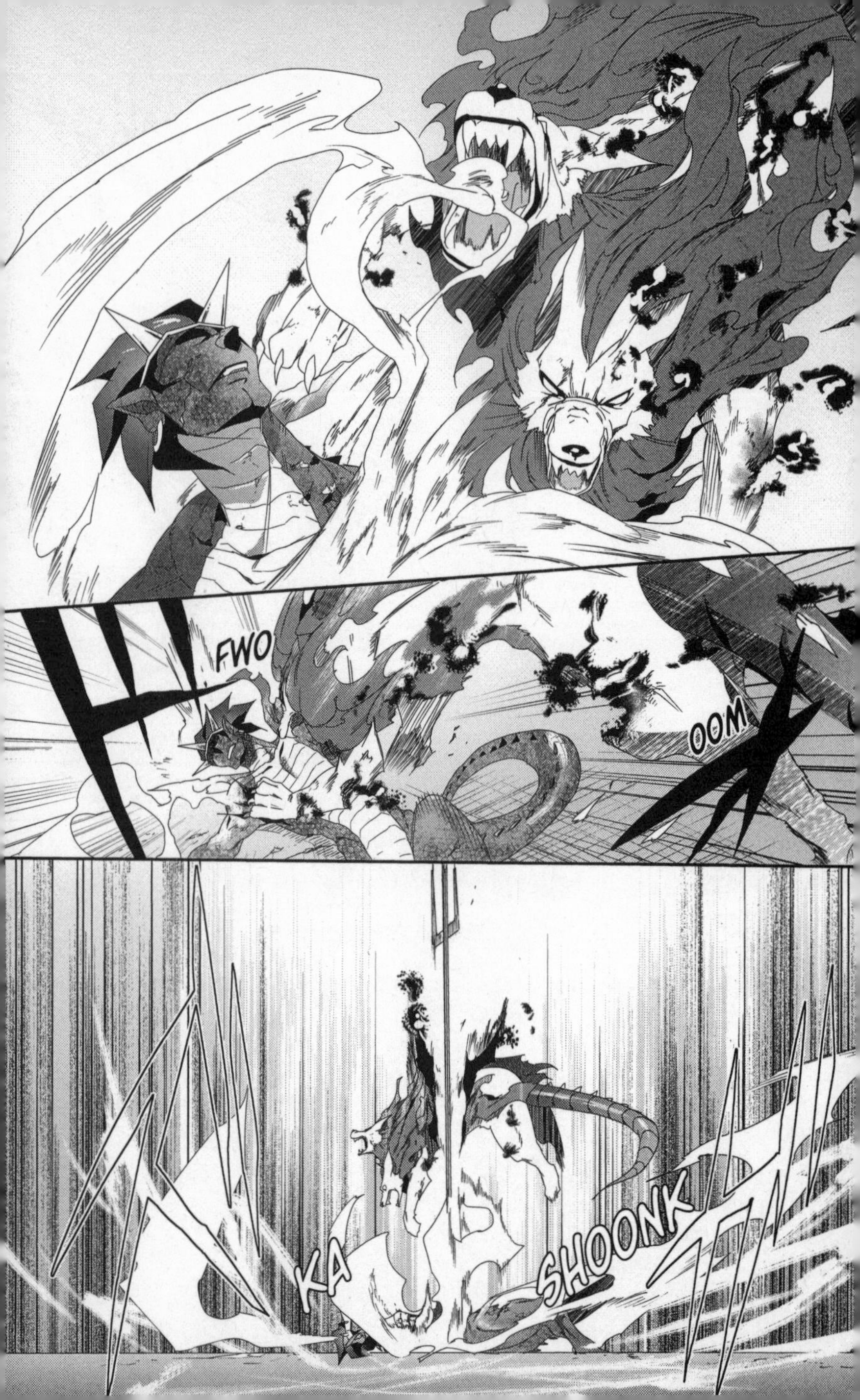
OOM
FWO
SHOONK
KA

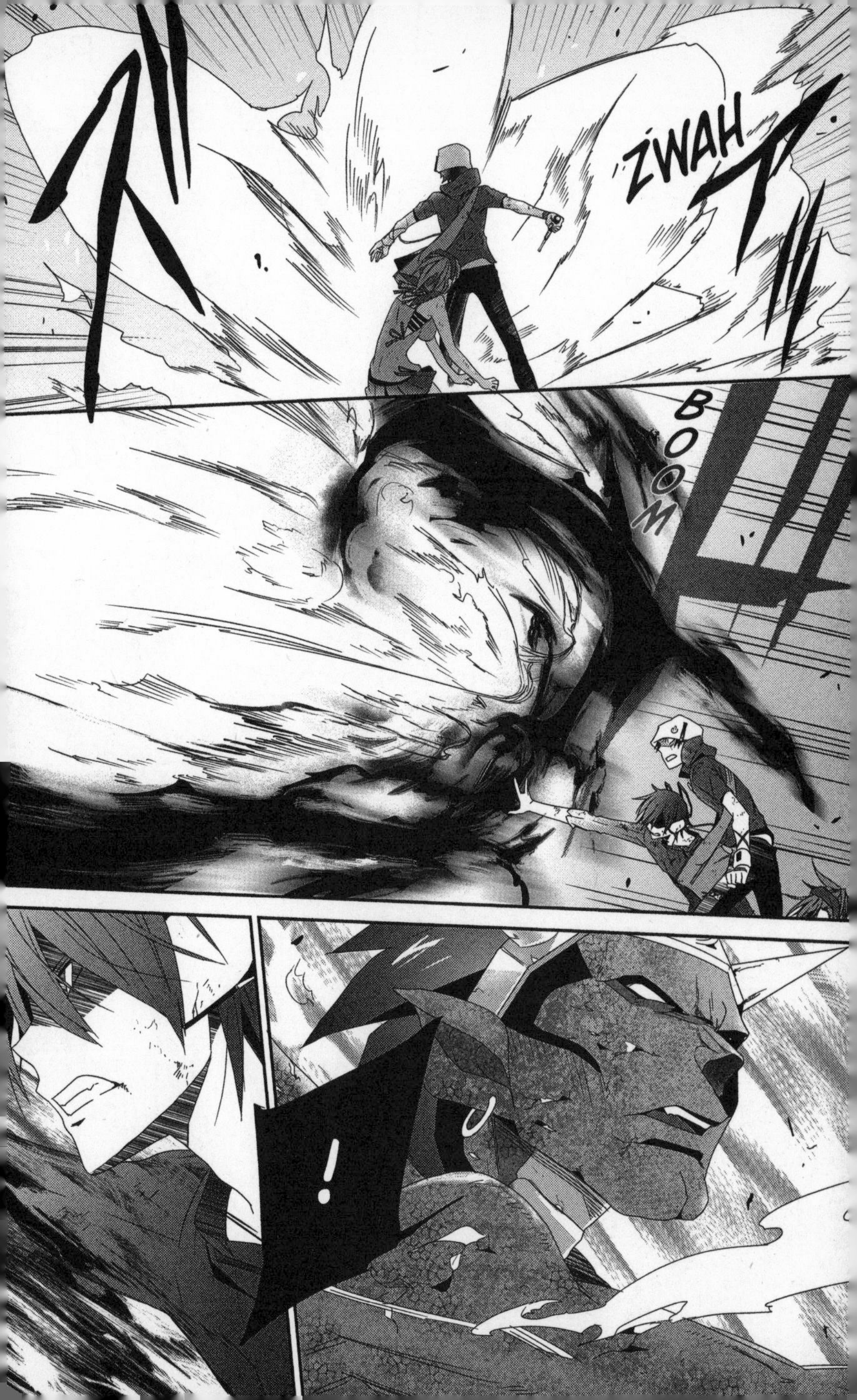
ZWAH
BOOOM
!

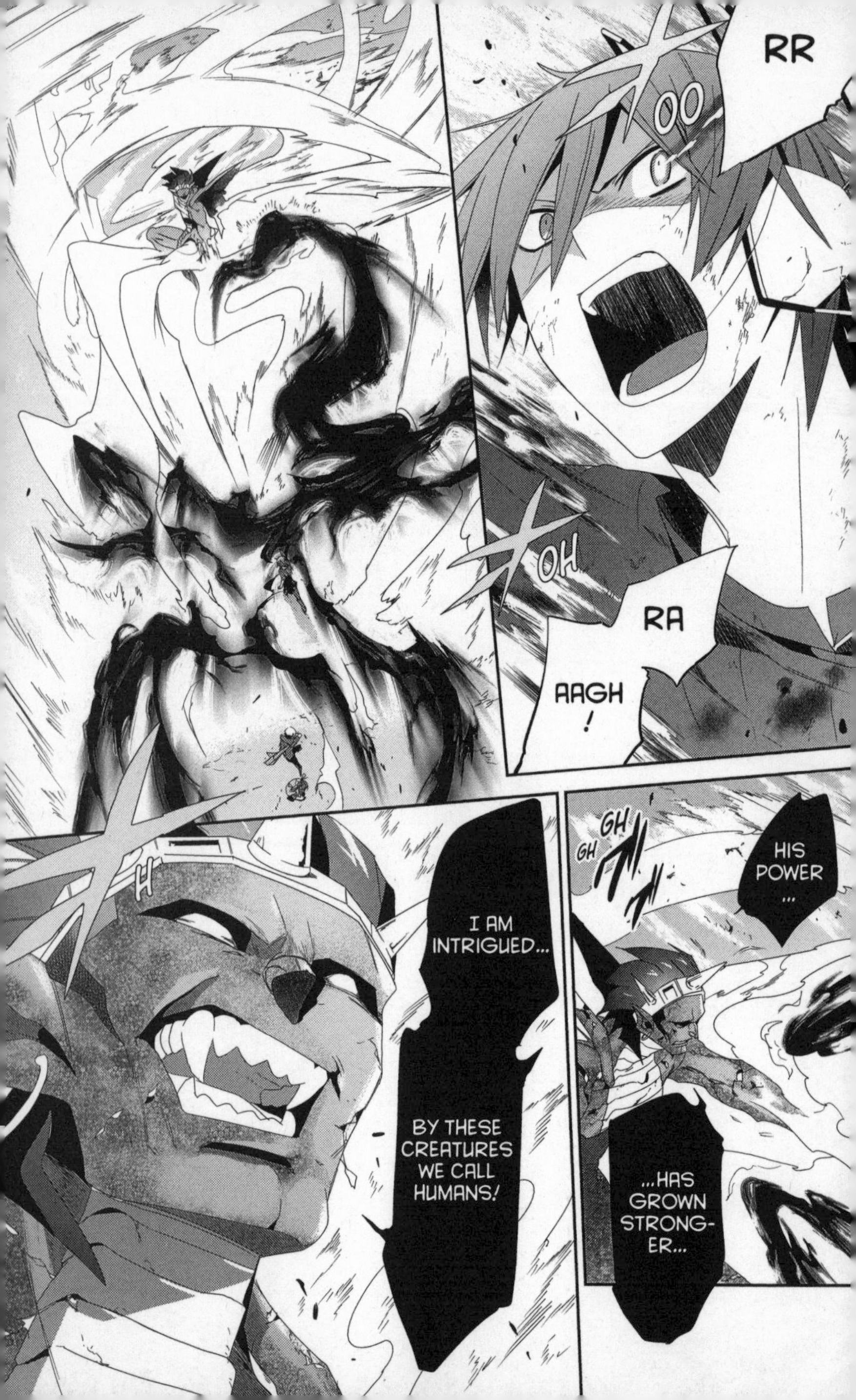

RR
OO
OH
RA
AAGH!
GH
GH
HIS POWER...
...HAS GROWN STRONGER...
H
I AM INTRIGUED...
BY THESE CREATURES WE CALL HUMANS!

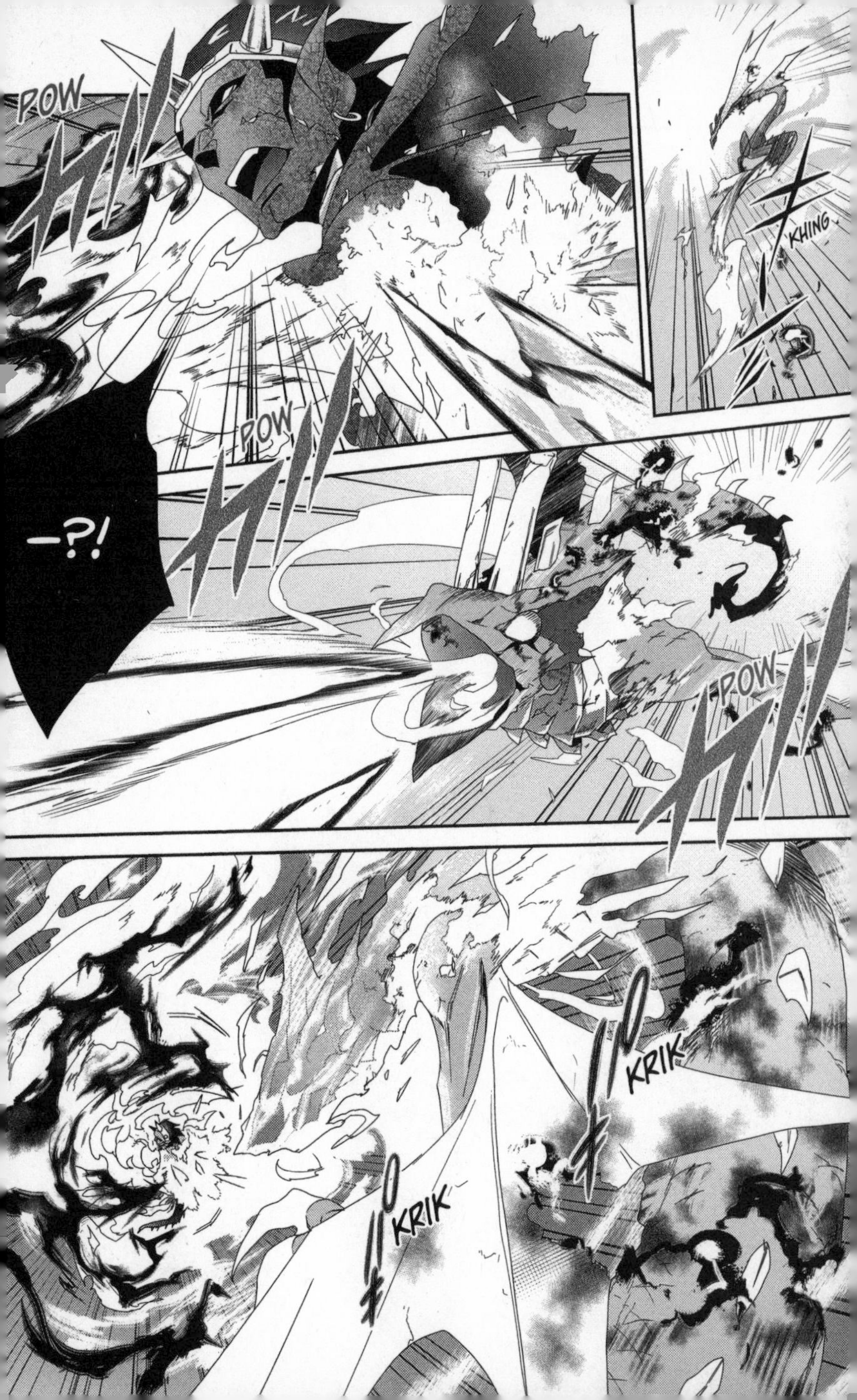
KHING
POW
POW
—?!
POW
KRIK
KRIK

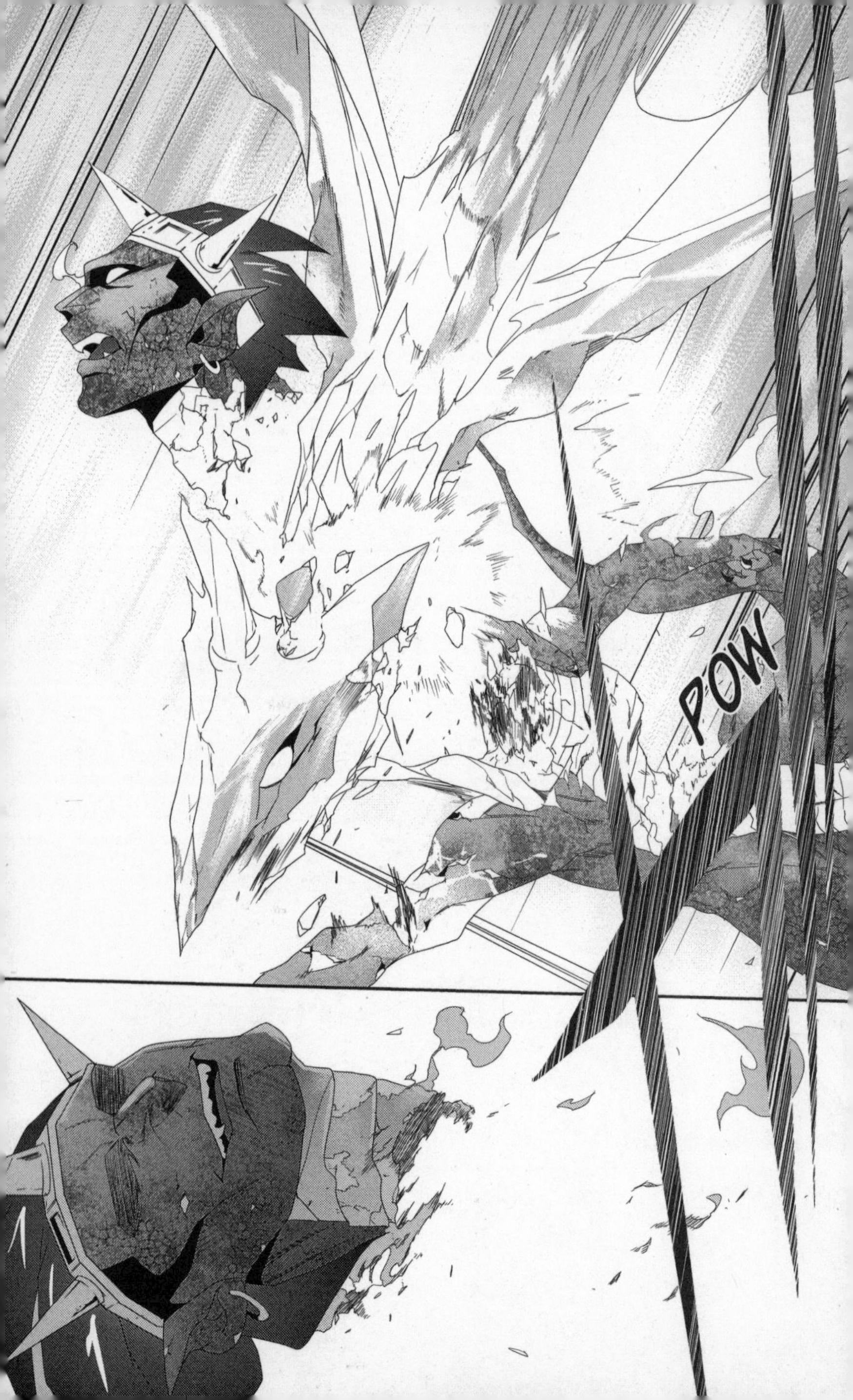
POW

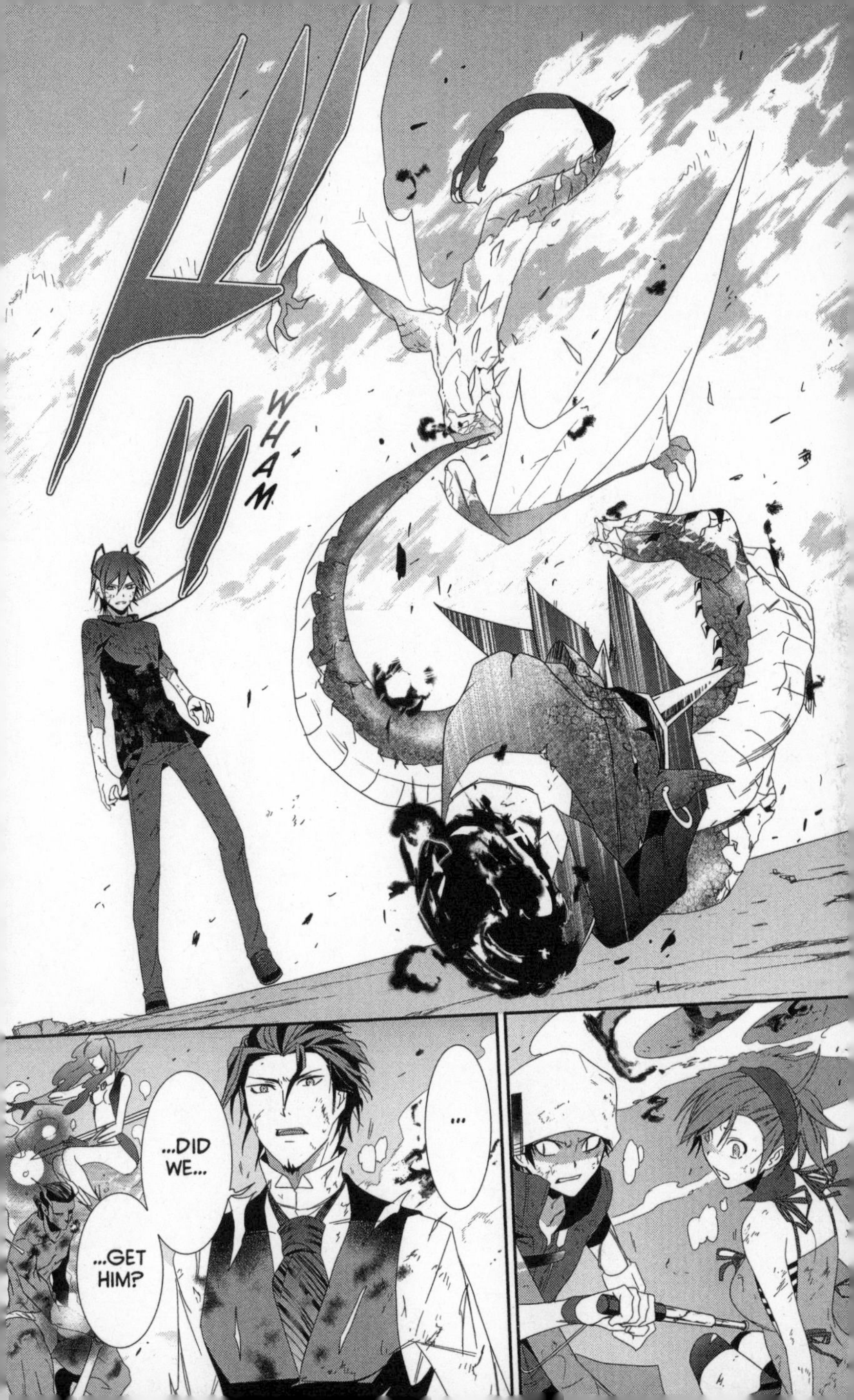
WHAM
...
...DID WE...
...GET HIM?

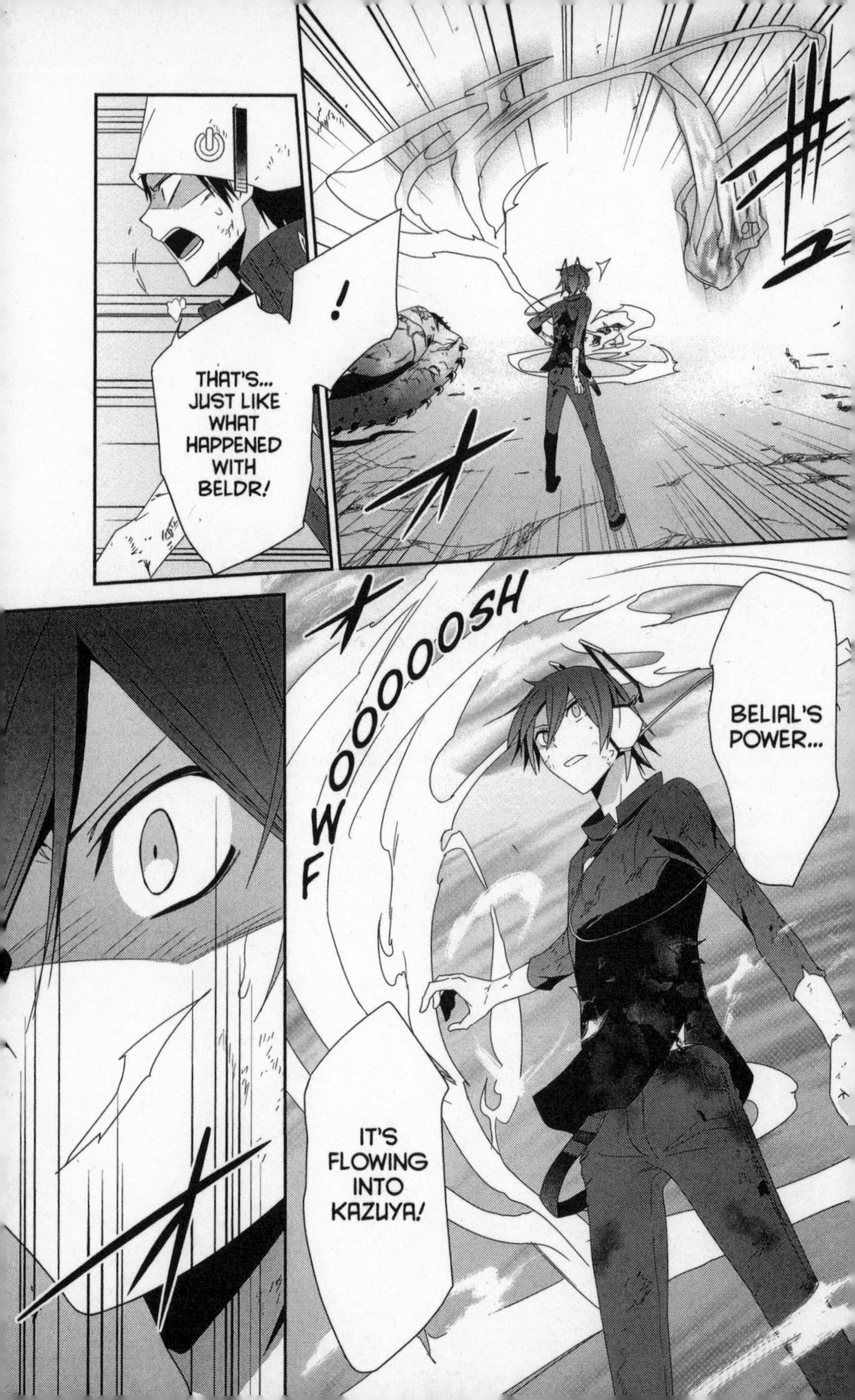
!
THAT'S... JUST LIKE WHAT HAPPENED WITH BELDR!
FWOOOOOOSH
BELIAL'S POWER...
IT'S FLOWING INTO KAZUYA!

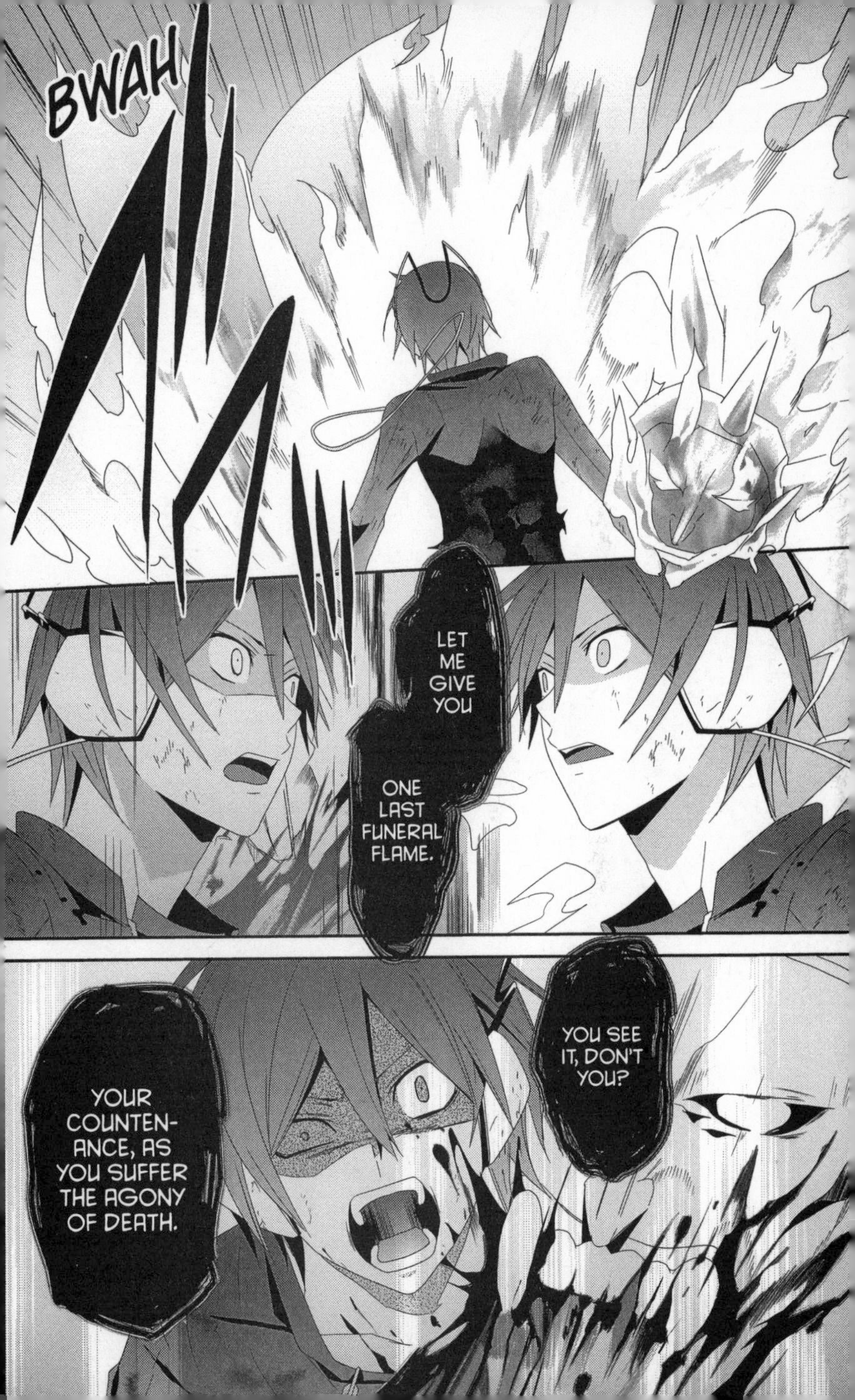
BWAH
LET ME GIVE YOU
ONE LAST FUNERAL FLAME.
YOU SEE IT, DON'T YOU?
YOUR COUNTENANCE, AS YOU SUFFER THE AGONY OF DEATH.

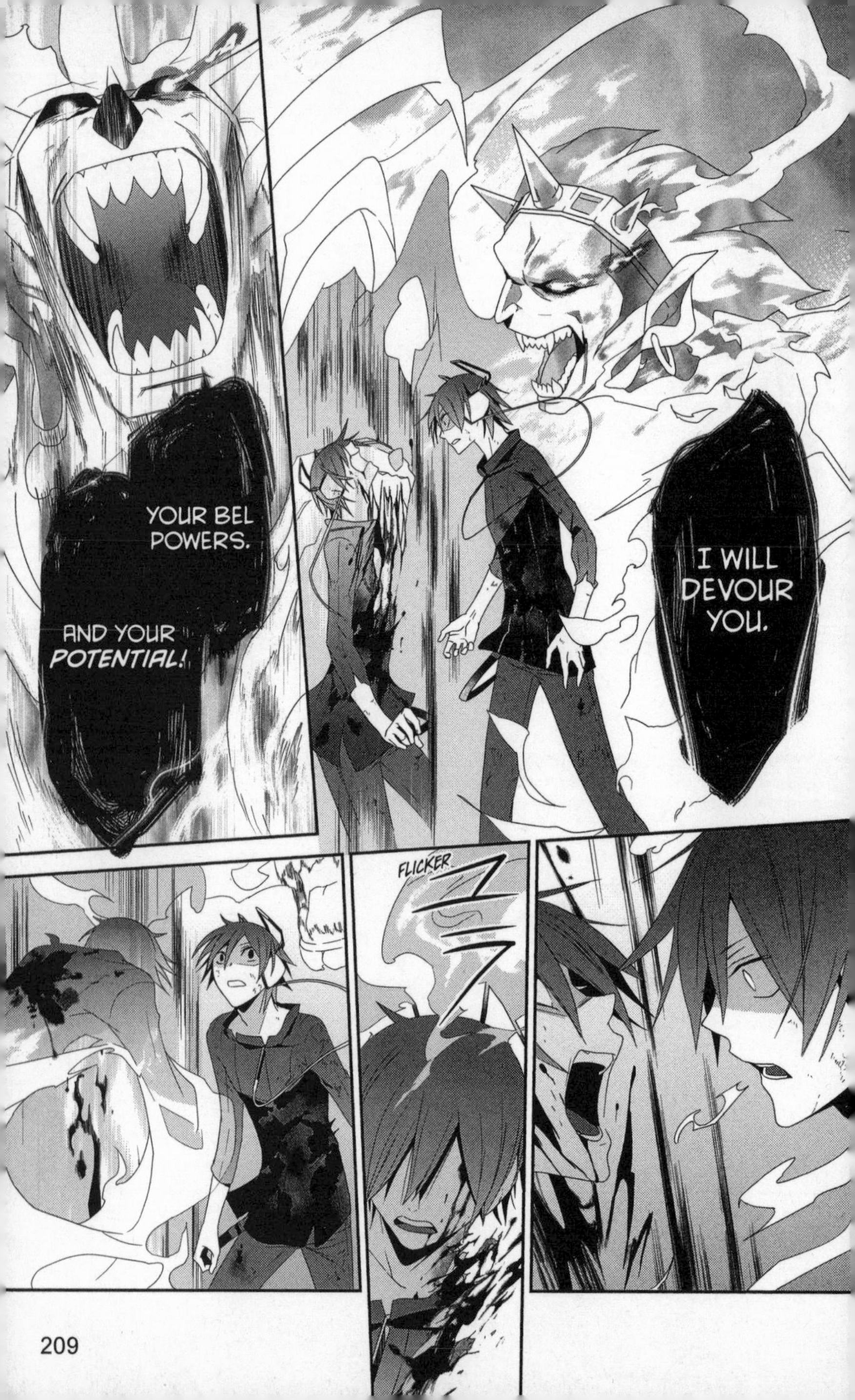
I WILL DEVOUR YOU.
YOUR BEL POWERS.
AND YOUR *POTENTIAL!*
FLICKER

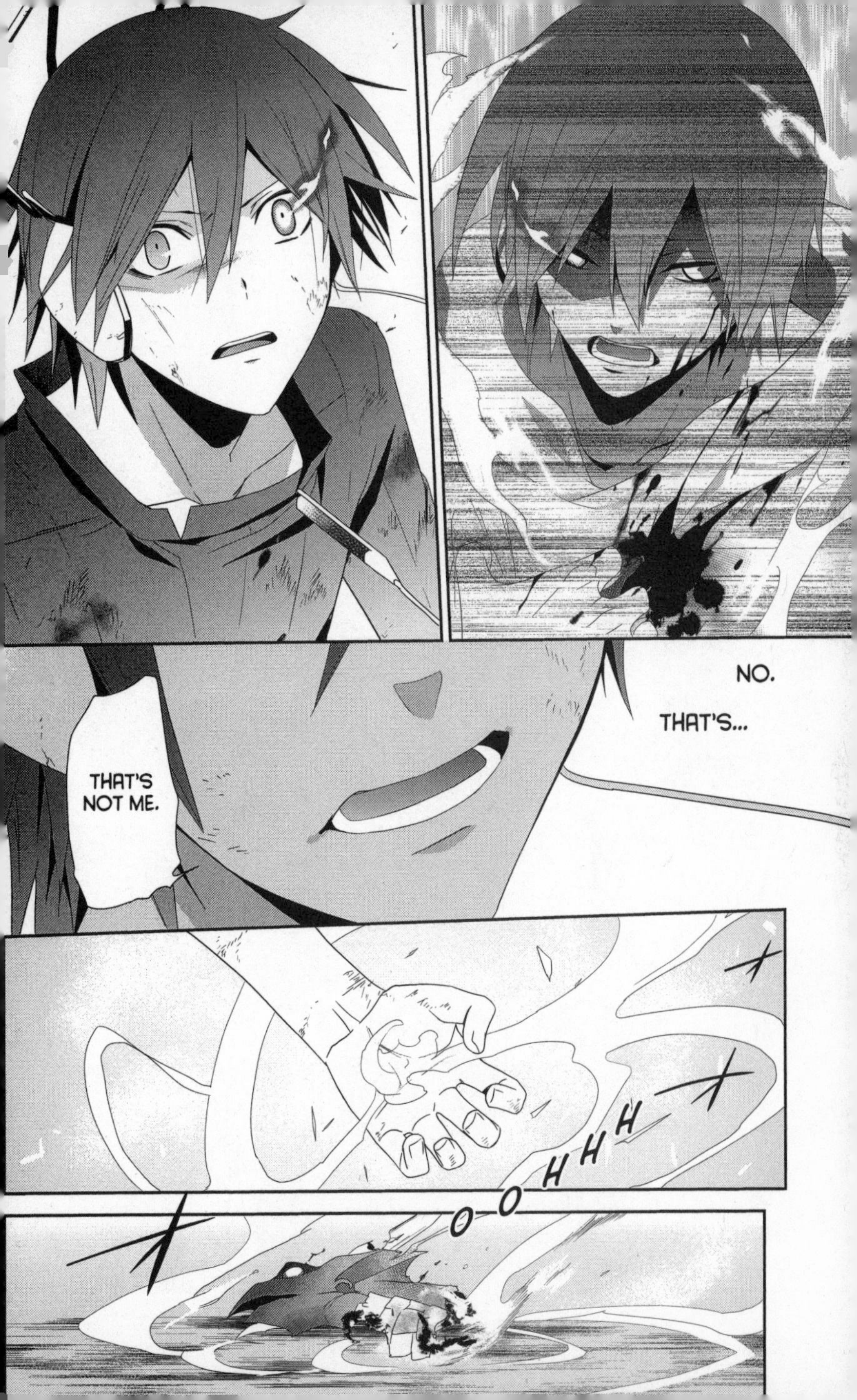
NO.
THAT'S...
THAT'S NOT ME.
OOHHHH

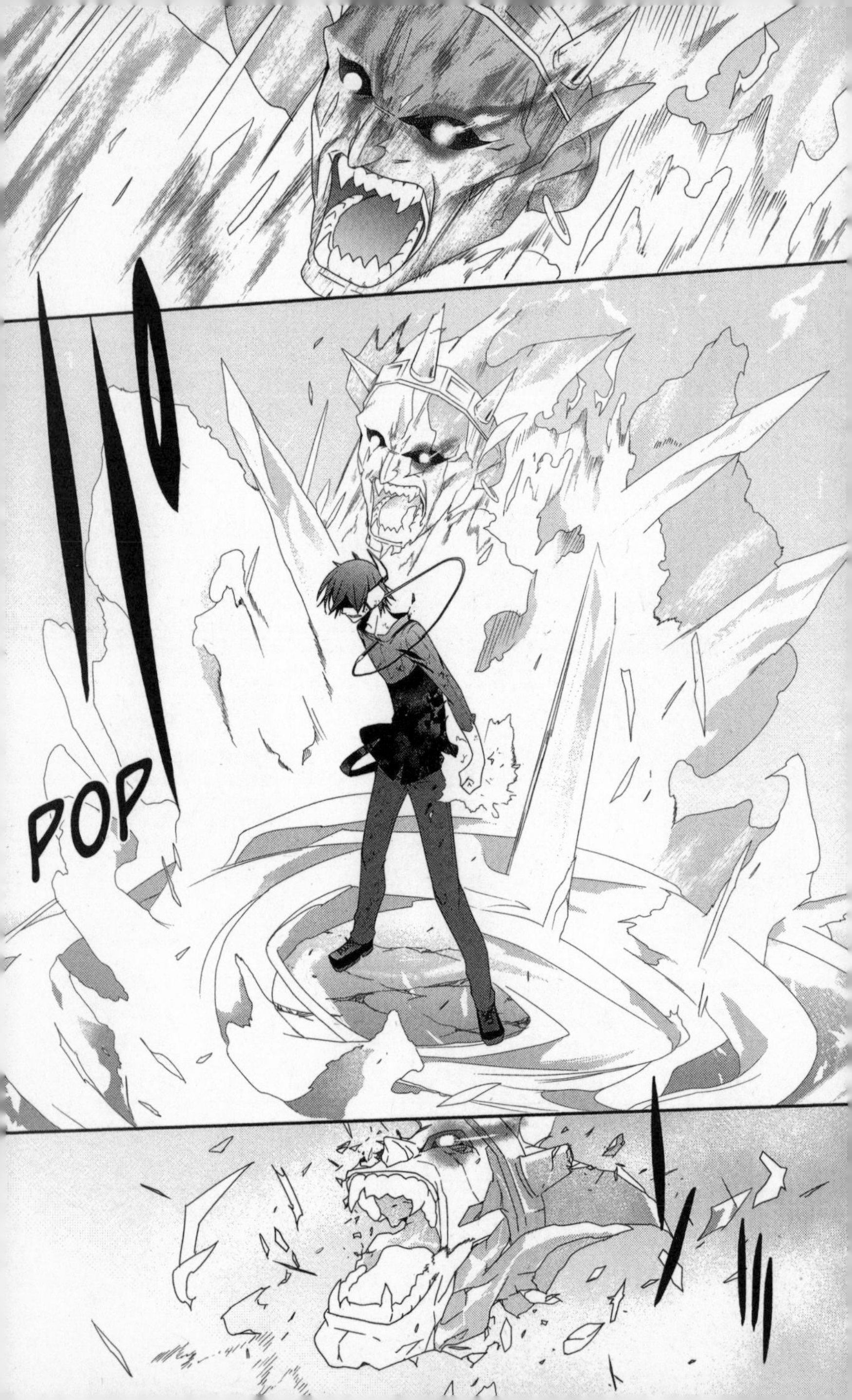
POP

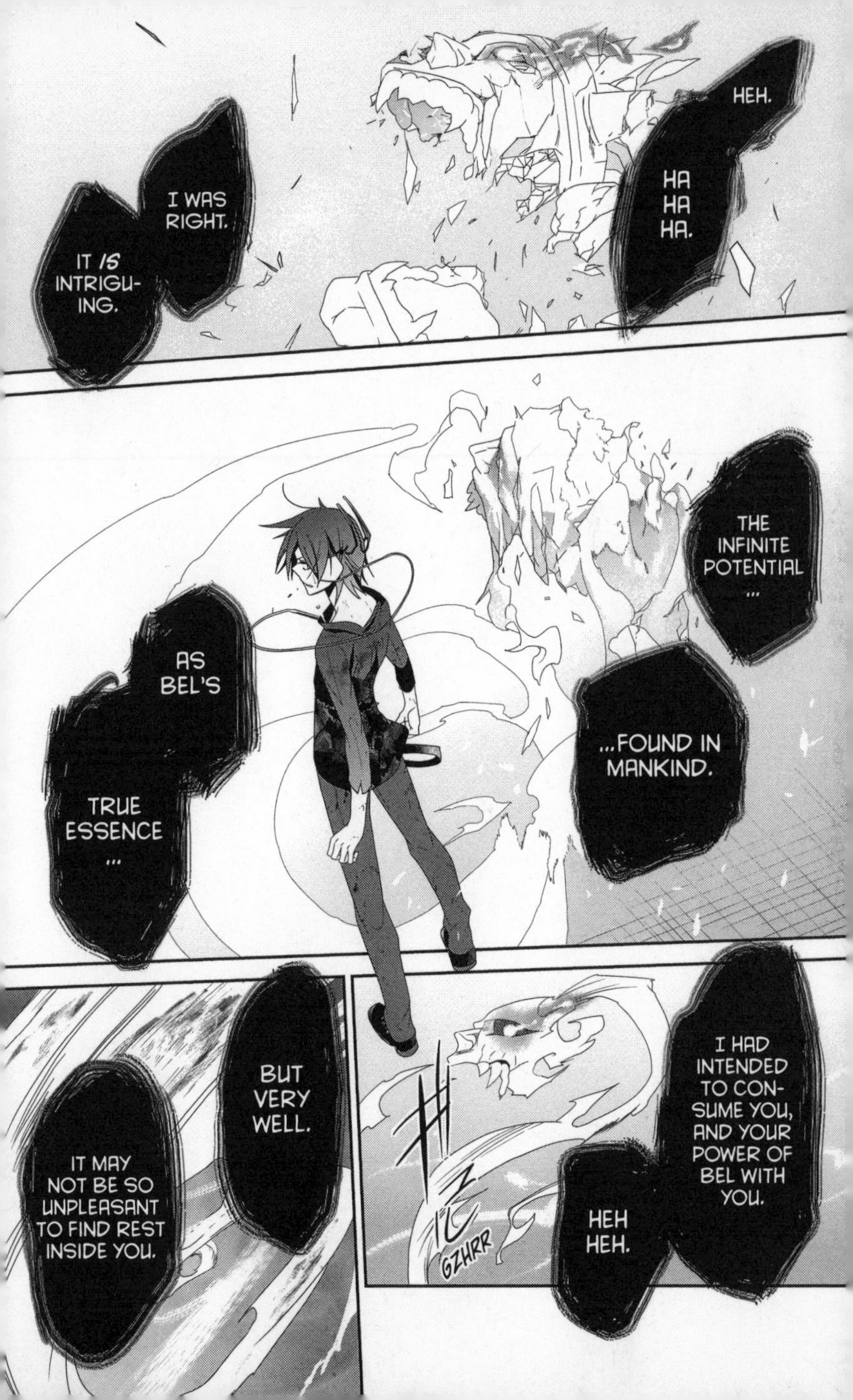
HEH.
HA HA HA.
I WAS RIGHT.
IT IS INTRIGU-ING.
THE INFINITE POTENTIAL ...
...FOUND IN MANKIND.
AS BEL'S TRUE ESSENCE ...
I HAD INTENDED TO CON-SUME YOU, AND YOUR POWER OF BEL WITH YOU.
HEH HEH.
GZHRR
BUT VERY WELL.
IT MAY NOT BE SO UNPLEASANT TO FIND REST INSIDE YOU.

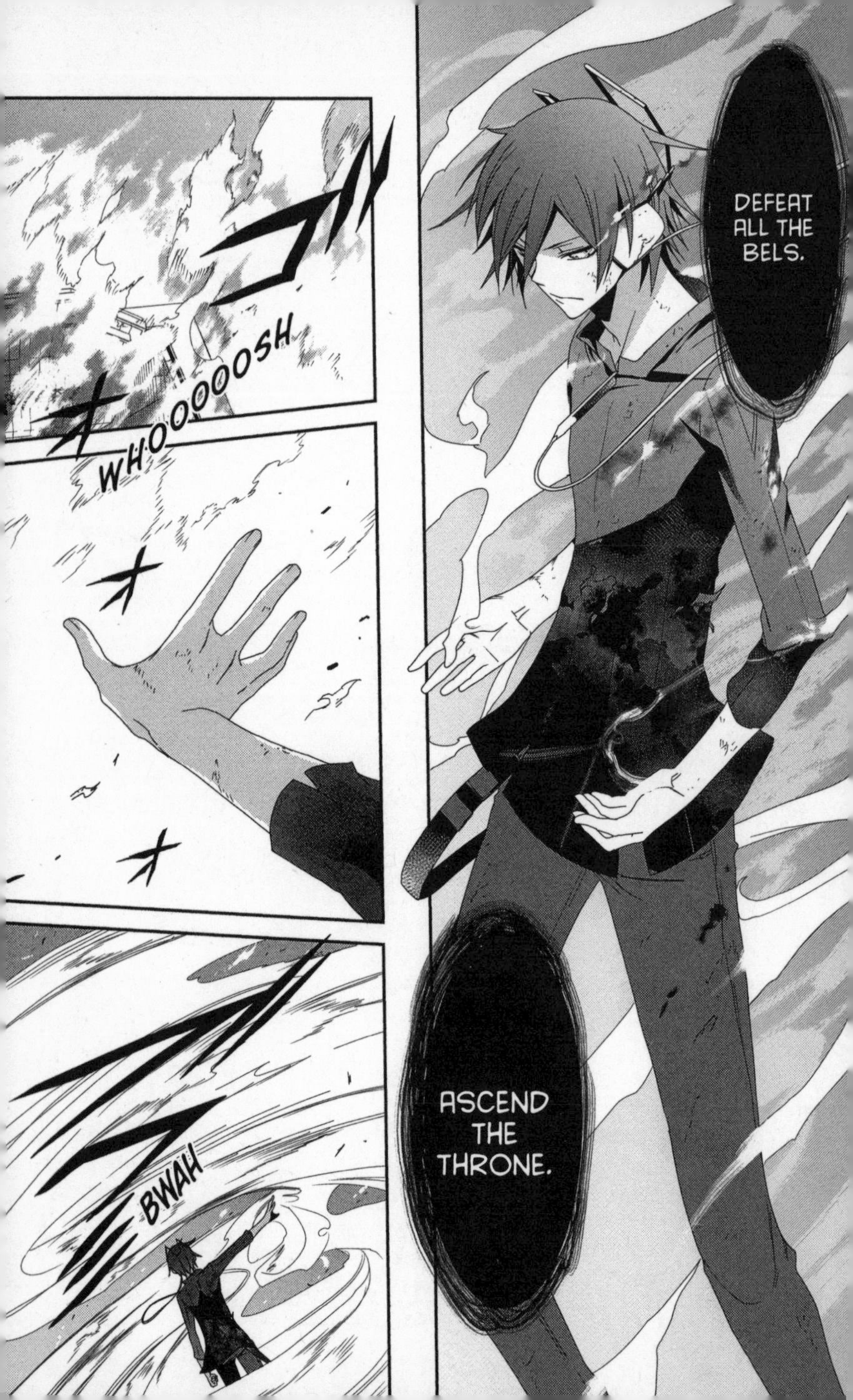
DEFEAT ALL THE BELS.
ASCEND THE THRONE.
WHOOOOOSH
BWAH

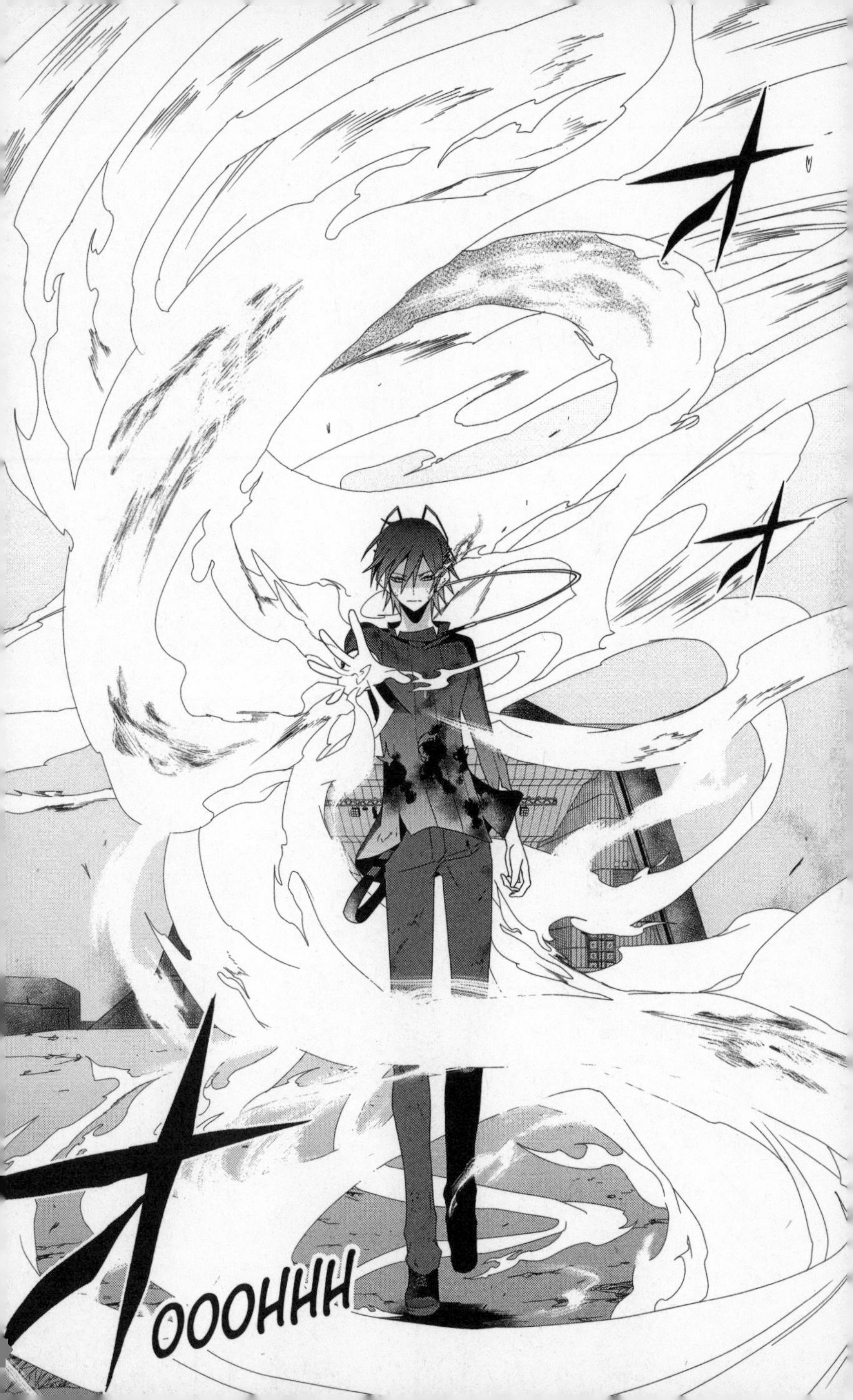
オオオOOOHHH

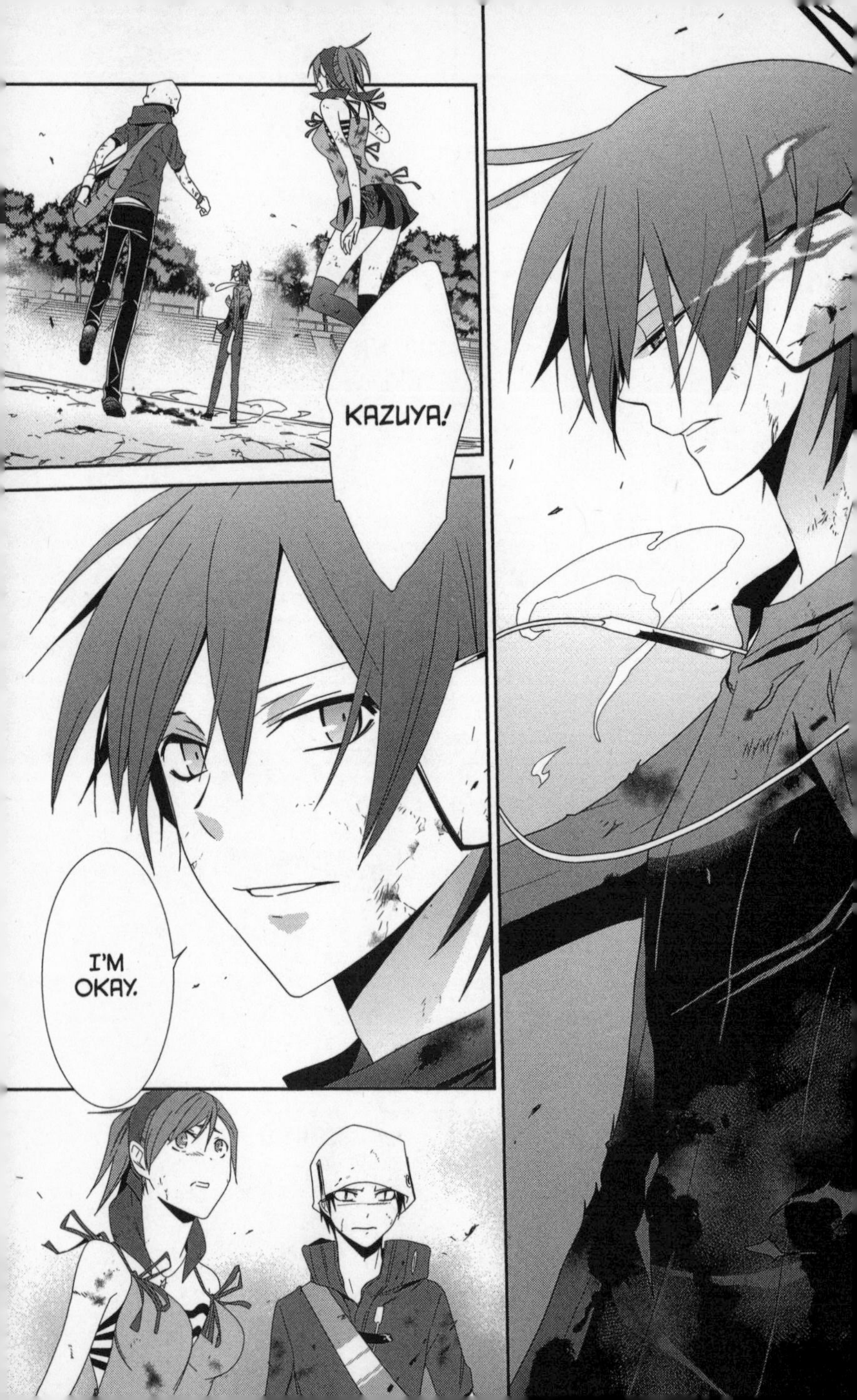
KAZUYA!
I'M OKAY.

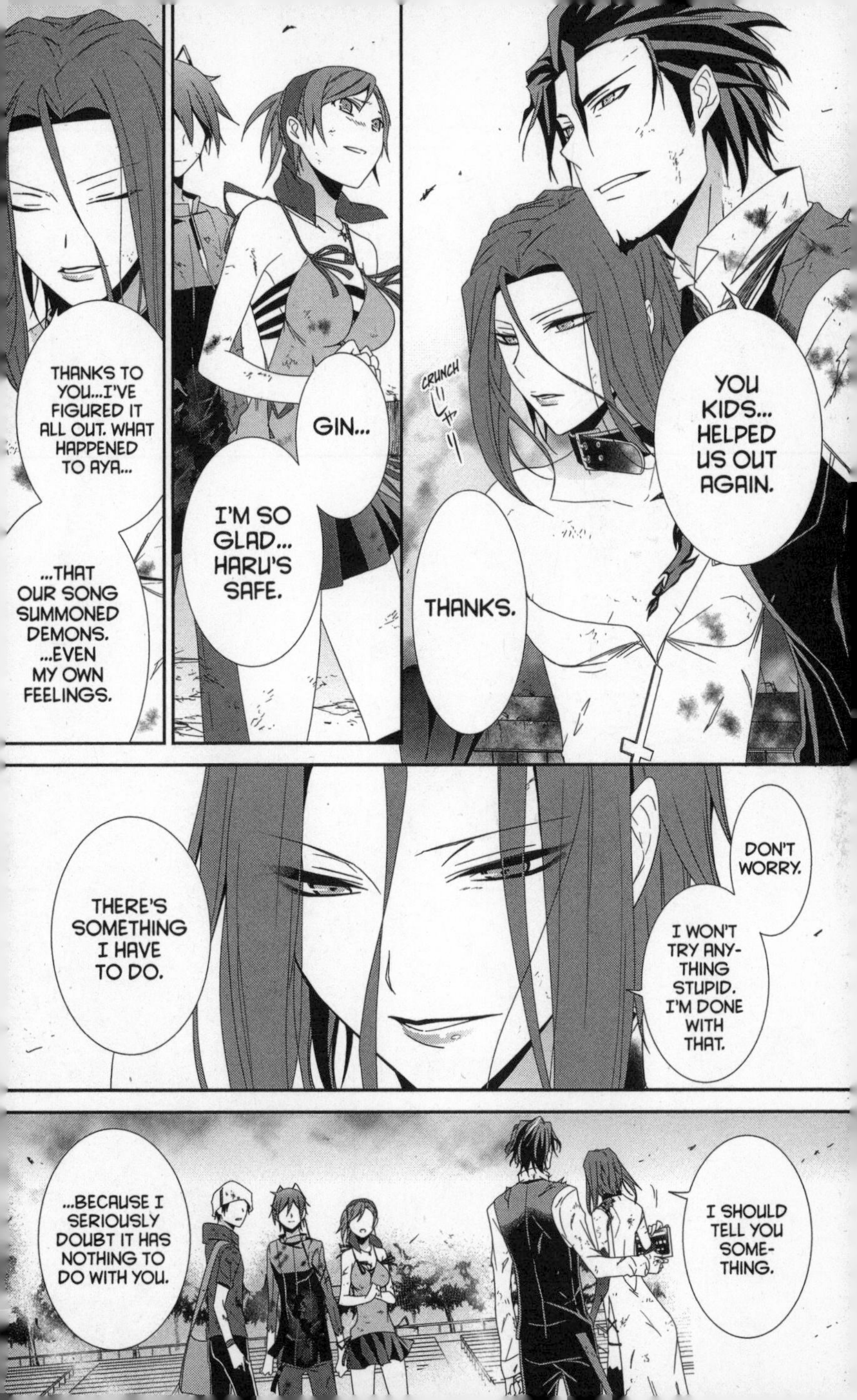
YOU KIDS... HELPED US OUT AGAIN.
CRUNCH
じゃり
THANKS.
GIN...
I'M SO GLAD... HARU'S SAFE.
THANKS TO YOU...I'VE FIGURED IT ALL OUT. WHAT HAPPENED TO AYA...
...THAT OUR SONG SUMMONED DEMONS. ...EVEN MY OWN FEELINGS.
DON'T WORRY.
I WON'T TRY ANY-THING STUPID. I'M DONE WITH THAT.
THERE'S SOMETHING I HAVE TO DO.
I SHOULD TELL YOU SOME-THING.
...BECAUSE I SERIOUSLY DOUBT IT HAS NOTHING TO DO WITH YOU.

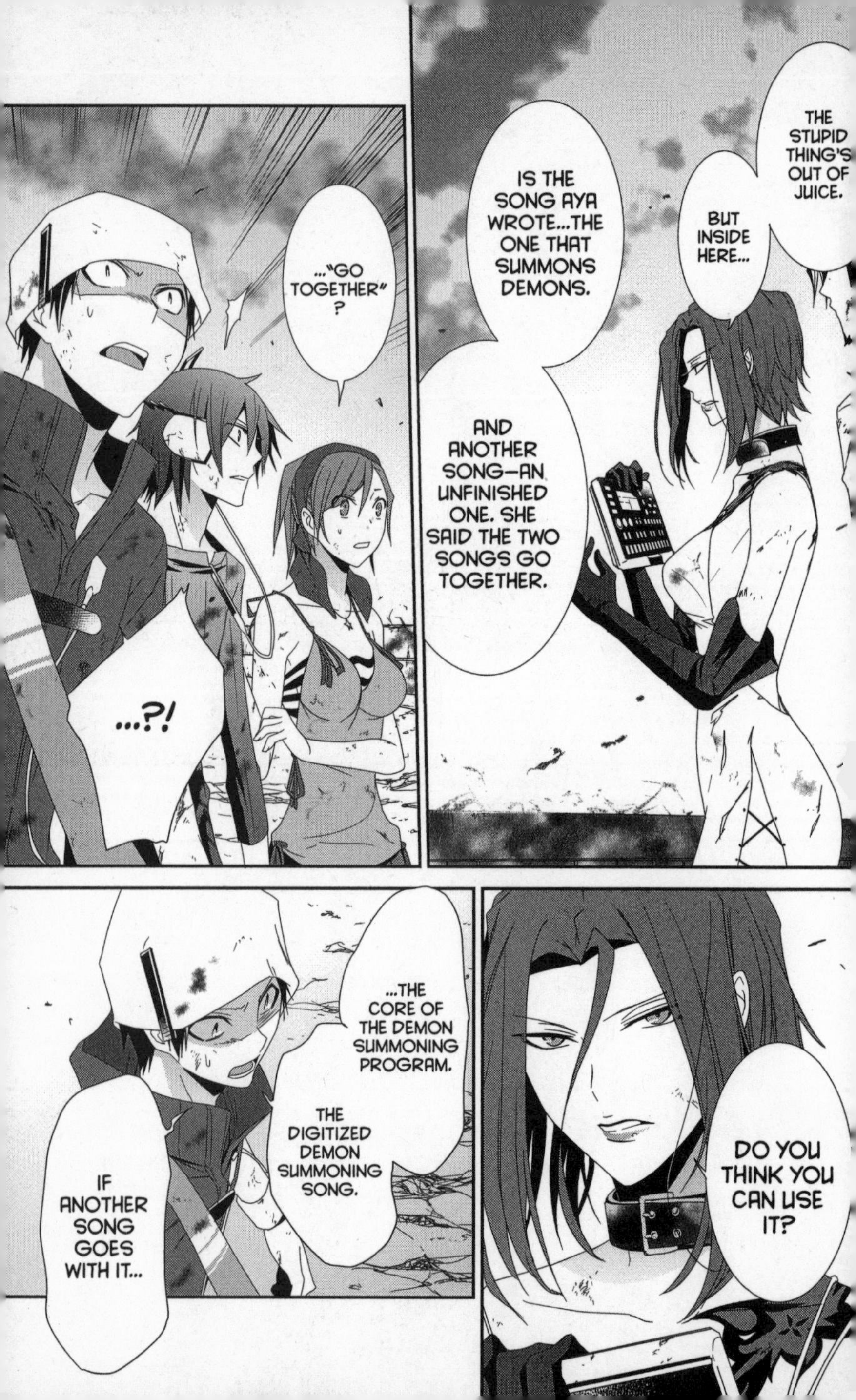
THE STUPID THING'S OUT OF JUICE.
BUT INSIDE HERE...
IS THE SONG AYA WROTE...THE ONE THAT SUMMONS DEMONS.
AND ANOTHER SONG—AN UNFINISHED ONE. SHE SAID THE TWO SONGS GO TOGETHER.
..."GO TOGETHER"?
...?!
DO YOU THINK YOU CAN USE IT?
...THE CORE OF THE DEMON SUMMONING PROGRAM.
THE DIGITIZED DEMON SUMMONING SONG.
IF ANOTHER SONG GOES WITH IT...

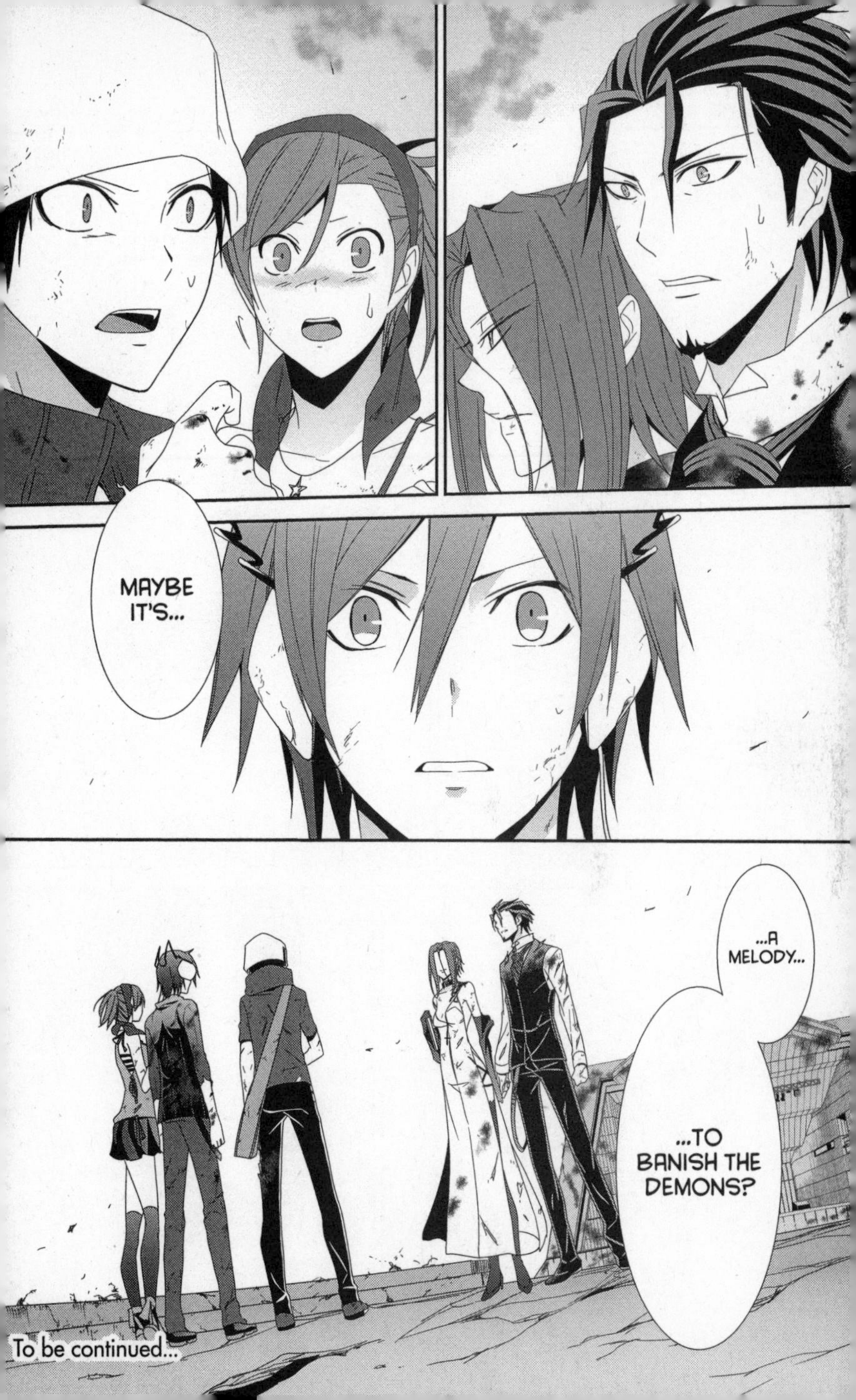
MAYBE IT'S...
...A MELODY...
...TO BANISH THE DEMONS?
To be continued...

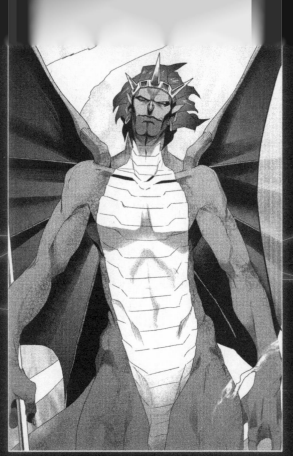

BELIAL

ONE OF THE 72 DEMONS INVOKED BY KING SOLOMON, HE IS A GREAT KING THAT LEADS 50 ARMIES. HE WAS ORIGINALLY A SERAPHIM (A HIGH-RANKING ANGEL), BUT HE WAS DEFEATED IN THE POLITICAL STRIFE IN THE HEAVENS AND CHOSE TO BECOME A FALLEN ANGEL. HE APPEARS IN THE GUISE OF A BEAUTIFUL ANGEL RIDING A CHARIOT OF FIRE, AND BESTOWS HIGH RANKING SOCIAL STATUS UPON HIS SUMMONER, BUT HE IS CRAFTY AND HIS NAME MEANS "WORTHLESS" AND "WICKED." HE LEADS MEN TO THEIR FALL, GUIDED SODOM AND GOMORRAH TO RUIN, AND PROSECUTED JESUS.

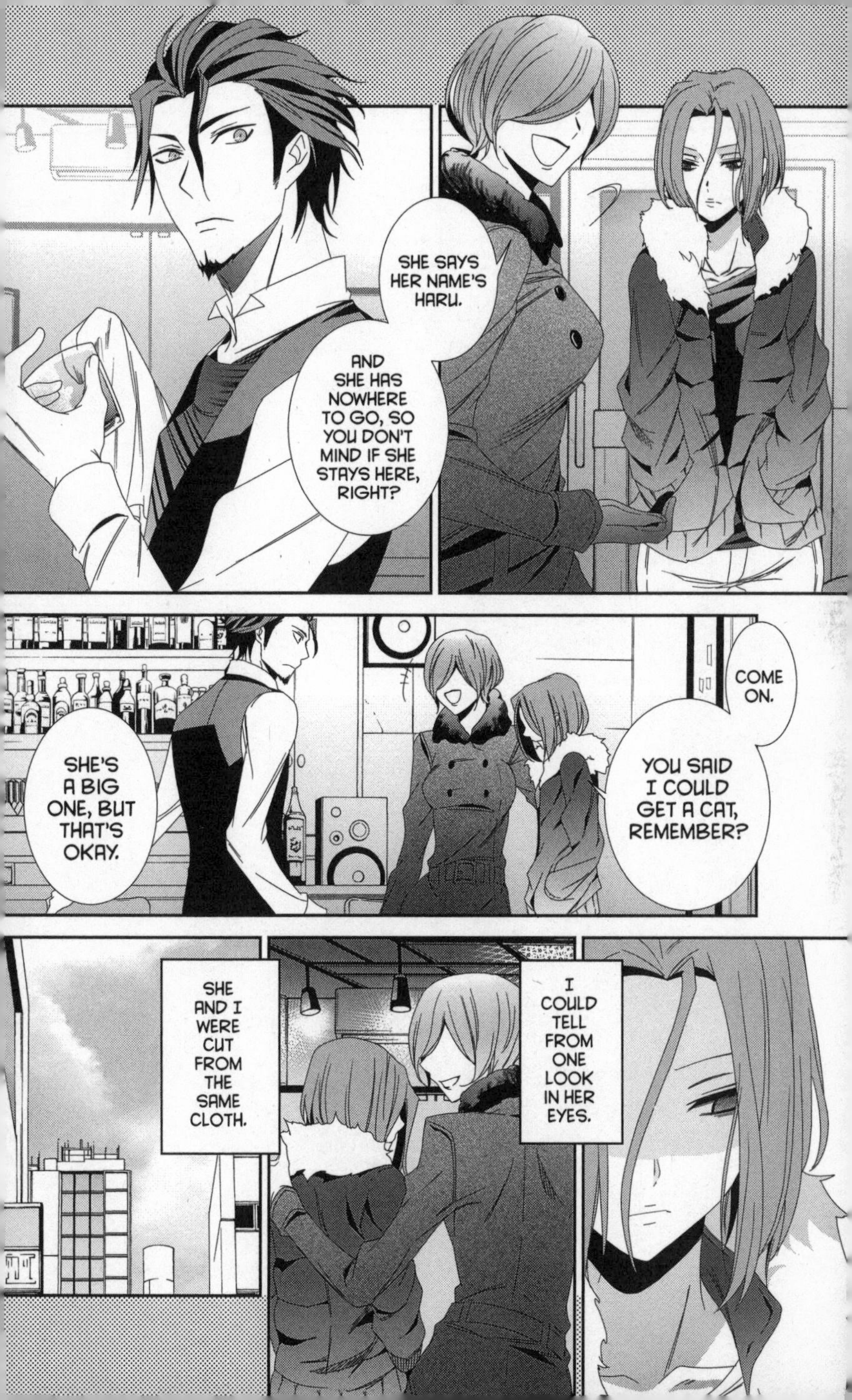
SHE SAYS HER NAME'S HARU.
AND SHE HAS NOWHERE TO GO, SO YOU DON'T MIND IF SHE STAYS HERE, RIGHT?
COME ON.
YOU SAID I COULD GET A CAT, REMEMBER?
SHE'S A BIG ONE, BUT THAT'S OKAY.
I COULD TELL FROM ONE LOOK IN HER EYES.
SHE AND I WERE CUT FROM THE SAME CLOTH.

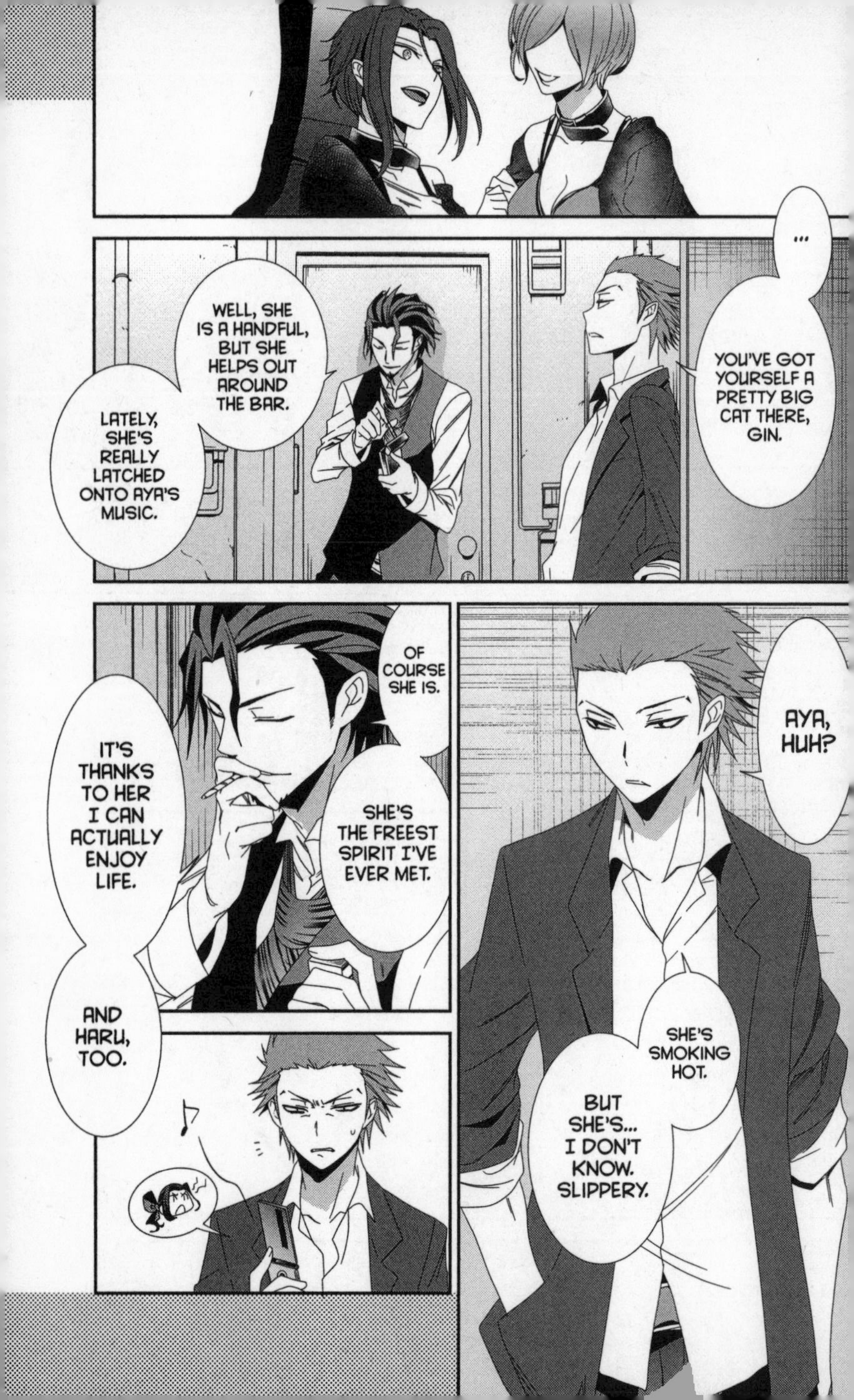
...
YOU'VE GOT YOURSELF A PRETTY BIG CAT THERE, GIN.
WELL, SHE IS A HANDFUL, BUT SHE HELPS OUT AROUND THE BAR.
LATELY, SHE'S REALLY LATCHED ONTO AYA'S MUSIC.
AYA, HUH?
SHE'S SMOKING HOT.
BUT SHE'S... I DON'T KNOW. SLIPPERY.
OF COURSE SHE IS.
SHE'S THE FREEST SPIRIT I'VE EVER MET.
IT'S THANKS TO HER I CAN ACTUALLY ENJOY LIFE.
AND HARU, TOO.

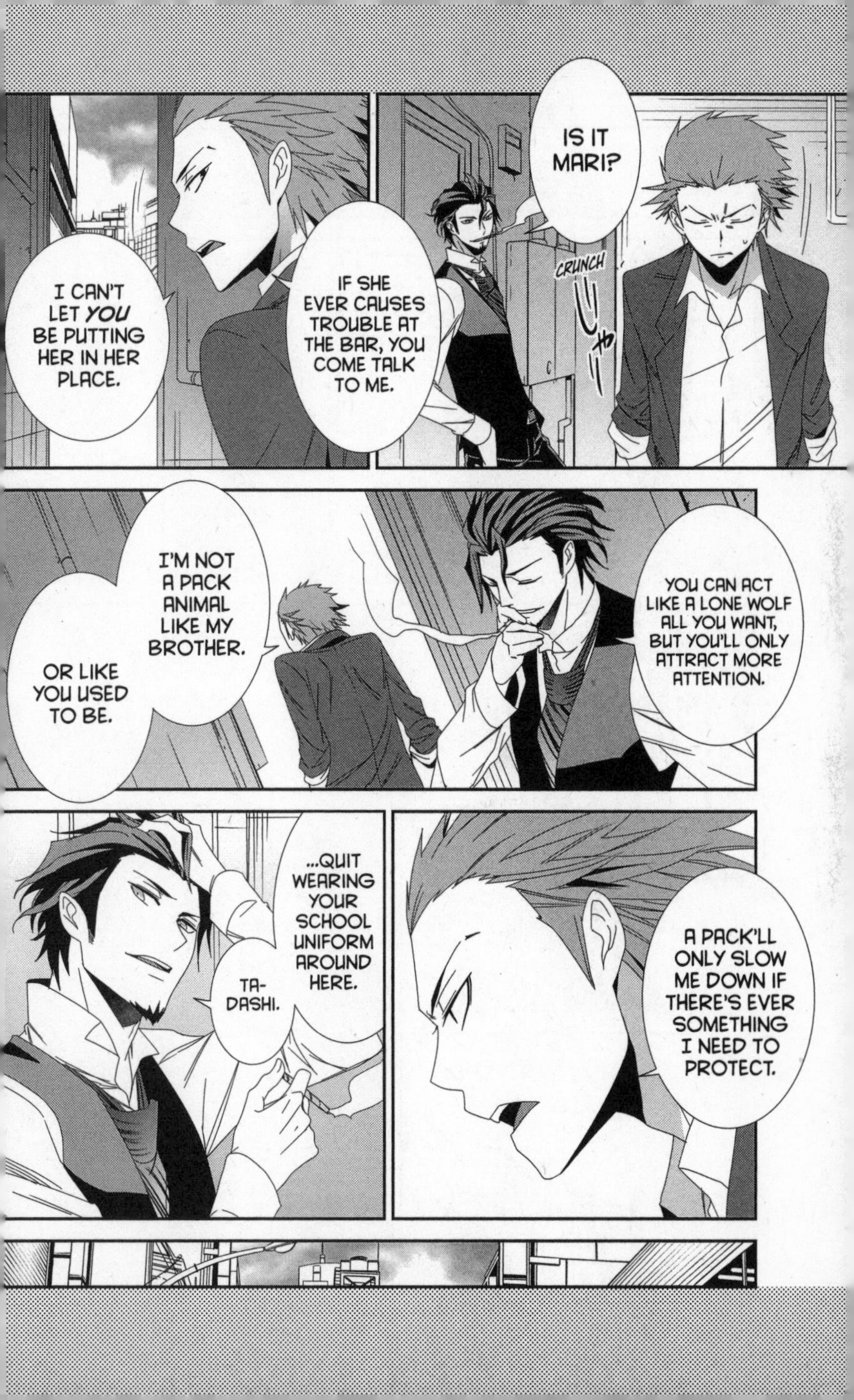
IS IT MARI?
CRUNCH
IF SHE EVER CAUSES TROUBLE AT THE BAR, YOU COME TALK TO ME.
I CAN'T LET *YOU* BE PUTTING HER IN HER PLACE.
YOU CAN ACT LIKE A LONE WOLF ALL YOU WANT, BUT YOU'LL ONLY ATTRACT MORE ATTENTION.
I'M NOT A PACK ANIMAL LIKE MY BROTHER.
OR LIKE YOU USED TO BE.
A PACK'LL ONLY SLOW ME DOWN IF THERE'S EVER SOMETHING I NEED TO PROTECT.
...QUIT WEARING YOUR SCHOOL UNIFORM AROUND HERE.
TA-DASHI.

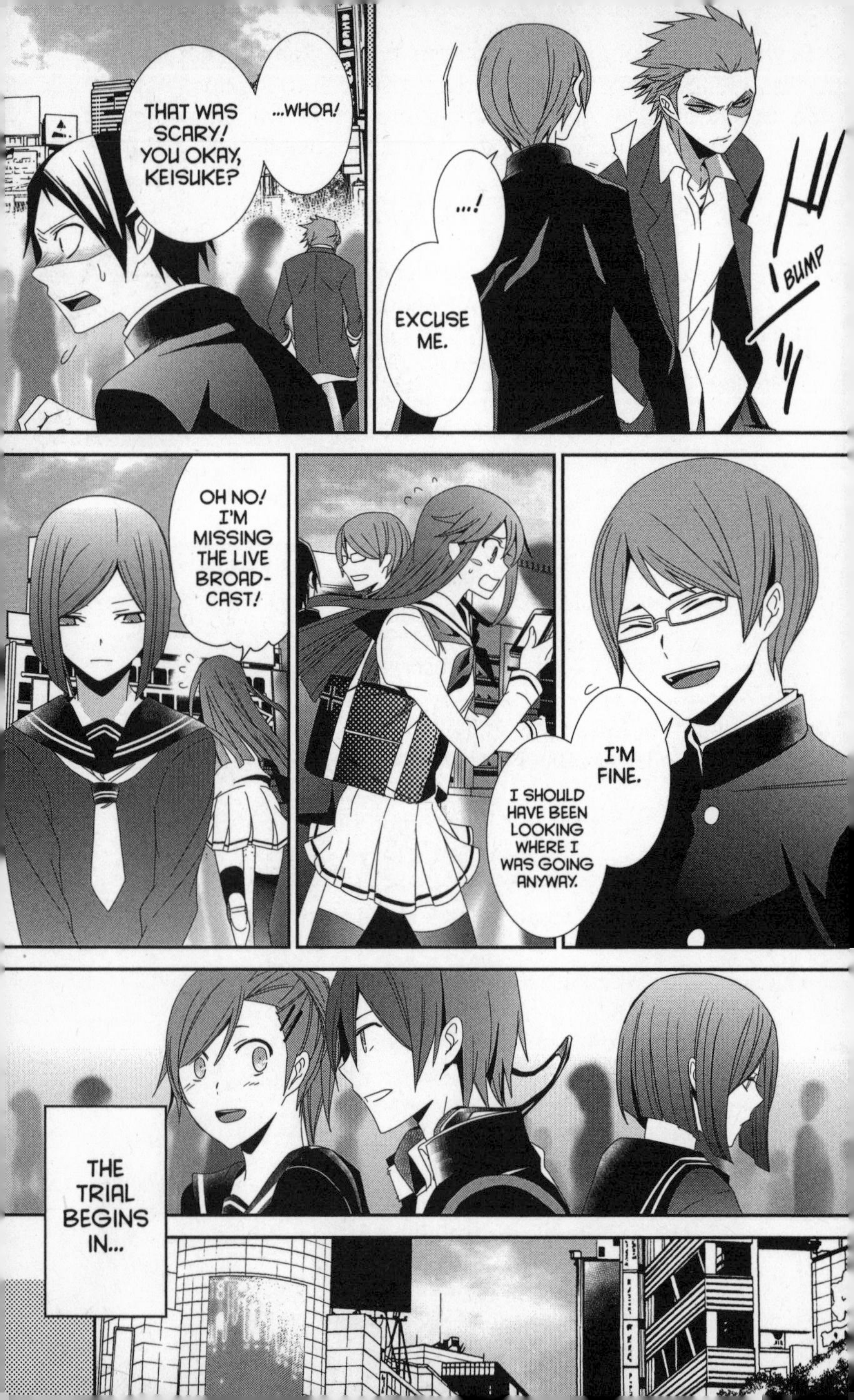
BUMP
...!
EXCUSE ME.
...WHOA!
THAT WAS SCARY! YOU OKAY, KEISUKE?
I'M FINE.
I SHOULD HAVE BEEN LOOKING WHERE I WAS GOING ANYWAY.
OH NO! I'M MISSING THE LIVE BROADCAST!
THE TRIAL BEGINS IN...

A Kodansha Comics Trade Paperback Original.

Devil Survivor volume 6 copyright © 2015
©ATLUS ©SEGA All rights reserved.
©Satoru Matsuba
English translation copyright © 2016
©ATLUS ©SEGA All rights reserved.
©Satoru Matsuba

Published in the United States by Kodansha Comics, an imprint of Kodansha USA Publishing, LLC, New York.

Publication rights for this English edition arranged through Kodansha Ltd., Tokyo.

First published in Japan in 2015 by Kodansha Ltd., Tokyo.

ISBN 978-1-63236-274-2

Printed in the United States of America.

www.kodanshacomics.com

9 8 7 6 5 4 3 2 1

Translation: Alethea Nibley & Athena Nibley
Lettering: Paige Pumphrey
Editing: Lauren Scanlan
Kodansha Comics edition cover design: Phil Balsman